second edition

The PRAYING CHURCH SOURCEBOOK

by Alvin J. Vander Griend
with Edith Bajema

Church Development Resources
Grand Rapids, Michigan

We thank Dr. Alvin J. Vander Griend, director of Houses of Prayer Everywhere (HOPE), Grand Rapids, Michigan, for coordinating the revision of *The Praying Church Sourcebook*. Edith Bajema, a freelance writer from Grand Rapids, Michigan, contributed to several new chapters on strategy.

ISBN 1-56212-258-4

10 9 8 7 6 5 4 3

CONTENTS

stories of praying Christians

resources for praying churches

INTRODUCTION

Why emphasize prayer in the church? Because the church is at the center of God's plan for the world. The church has the utterly important task of helping to build God's kingdom and bring salvation.

However, the church will only be strong in its task if God's power and grace are unleashed within the church. And that power is unleashed only through prayer. As the Heidelberg Catechism states, "God gives his grace and Holy Spirit only to those who pray continually . . ." (Q&A 116).

Some of us might look at the church's prayer habits and despair. But it takes only a minority of members who are strong in prayer to release God's power and grace. Be encouraged when God's "faithful few" in your church have seen the need for prayer and are responding to that vision.

Also, any efforts of one local church are linked to a broader prayer movement within the community and across the nation. God's Spirit is weaving the efforts of individual congregations into a movement of prayer that transcends denominational and geographical boundaries.

The vision behind this broader prayer movement is a burden for revival. People in different countries and communities have begun to pray for spiritual awakening and for the evangelization of the world. The vision, quite simply, is that God's kingdom will continue to come with power and grace, offering salvation and healing to the nations of the world. It is a vision of mission.

Essential to this prayer movement is leadership. We cannot do enough to highlight how important it is for leaders to lead the way in prayer. All those who have been given positions of influence, authority, and oversight in the body of Christ are called to set the example in prayer. They need not be prayer warriors, but they must be willing to set the pace in prayer for the people they lead.

With this objective in mind, *The Praying Church Sourcebook* contains four sections to help leaders stimulate the prayer life of their congregations:

- **Essays on Prayer** examines the biblical principles and teachings undergirding effective prayer.

- **Strategies for Praying Churches** offers dozens of practical ideas for making prayer a more vital part of your church's life.

- **Stories of Praying Christians** provides inspirational anecdotes from many sources that leaders can use in preaching and teaching to interest and encourage people in faithful prayer.

- **Resources for Praying Churches** combines a listing of recommended prayer ministries, resources, and books to inform and challenge your prayer life.

thoughts on the second edition

The church continues to grow in its interest and practice of prayer. In my visits to congregations throughout North America in the past seven years, I have seen a steady increase in the desire of believers to develop strong, effective prayer lives. This greatly encourages me.

In addition, new prayer ministries, resources, newsletters, prayer guides and magazines, and scores of books have been published to nurture the church's prayer life.

This second edition of *The Praying Church Sourcebook* reflects some of the excitement of the prayer movement as it has grown since this book was first published. This edition also provides us an opportunity to include new material on important strategies such as prayerwalking, houses of prayer, solemn assemblies, and preaching on prayer. We have included these and other new chapters in the "Strategies" section of this book.

Much prayer and thought has gone into the development of this book and its revision. May it inspire you, provide concrete suggestions, and lead you and your church into a life of fervent, fruitful prayer. Please let us know what happens in your church as a result!

—*Alvin J. Vander Griend*

ESSAYS *on* PRAYER

INTRODUCTION

This section of *The Praying Church Sourcebook* includes three articles:

- "Keys to a Praying Church"—a simple explanation of how to make prayer a healthy part of your congregation's life and ministry

- "Twice Blessed: Biblical Perspectives on Prayer"—an exploration of prayer as the means by which God blesses both the people prayed for and those who pray

- "Seven Ways Prayer Is Changing the Church in America"—an exciting overview of how God's Spirit is moving through prayer to bring power, victory, and unity to the churches of North America

KEYS TO A PRAYING CHURCH

by Alvin J. Vander Griend

What can your church do to grow strong in prayer? Why should you make prayer a priority in your church's ministry? This chapter will answer these questions. It will also suggest a number of concepts so basic that they may rightly be called "keys" to prayer.

But, first, why all the energy spent on promoting prayer in this past decade?

C. Peter Wagner, prolific church-growth writer and professor at Fuller Theological Seminary, has spent the past several years researching prayer movements in the church. His summary comment: "I sincerely believe that we are now in the beginning stages of the greatest movement of prayer in living memory."

If Wagner is right, we should expect to see earthshaking results in the church. Reformation and renewal have always been rooted in prayer.

J. Edwin Orr, who has made a life-time study of prayer movements in the church, said a few years ago, "There is a greater movement of prayer growing now than ever before in history." His lifelong studies have led him to conclude that "whenever God sets about to do a new thing, he always sets his people praying." Seeing the new movement in prayer, Orr anticipated with excitement a worldwide revival in the church.

The headwaters of this worldwide prayer movement are in Korea. There the church is growing four times faster than the population. If this continues, 50 percent of the Korean population will be Christian by the year 2000. Church observers credit this dramatic growth to prayer, noting that most Korean churches open their doors at 5:00 A.M. every day for prayer. Many Korean Christians regularly pray through the night on Fridays and spend whole weekends at prayer retreat centers. Korean pastors typically spend one-and-a-half to three hours per day in prayer.

Many North American churches are also waking up to the importance of prayer. More than five hundred now have regular 5:00 A.M. prayer meetings. Many have begun around-the-clock prayer vigils. A growing number of churches have made prayer a high priority and have experienced a surprising harvest of blessing.

For some, a new sense of the importance of prayer has come almost spontaneously. For years one large California church held a midweek prayer meeting that was sparsely attended. In recent years, however, numbers have increased to such an extent that the meeting has been moved to the auditorium. Hundreds of interdenominational prayer concerts are attracting thousands around the United States and Canada each year.

This essay will help you answer the question "What can our church do to grow strong in prayer?" The eight "keys" to prayer listed below are basic concepts that are essential if your church is to be a house of prayer.

1. Praying leaders are essential.

Many leaders in the church today are not, by biblical standards, praying leaders. Two thousand pastors who attended a pastors' conference in Dallas, Texas, were surveyed regarding their prayer habits. Ninety-five percent admitted that they spent five minutes or less each day in prayer. Another survey of 572 pastors conducted by Peter Wagner revealed that pastors spend an average of eighteen minutes a day in prayer. The same survey revealed no noticeable difference between leaders' and church members' prayer habits.

The Bible sets high standards for church leaders. Moses, David, Elijah, Daniel, and many other Old Testament leaders were devoted to prayer. The apostle James holds up Elijah, "a man just like us," as an example of powerful praying. He reminds us that Elijah "prayed earnestly that it would not rain, and it did not rain on the land for three and a half years. Again he prayed, and the heavens gave rain" (James 5:17-18). The prophet Samuel regarded it a sin not to pray. He said, "Far be it from me that I should sin against the LORD by failing to pray for you" (1 Samuel 12:23).

Jesus, our Leader of leaders, gave prayer high priority in his ministry—and expected his followers to do the same. He taught them many things about prayer; one parable in particular emphasized that they should "pray and not give up" (Luke 18:1). When his disciples failed to keep watch with Jesus through his hour of sorrow in Gethsemane, he urged them, "Watch and pray so that you will not fall into temptation" (Matthew 26:41). The apostles, overbusied with administrative duties, appointed deacons so that they could devote themselves to the Word of God and to prayer. Paul bathed his life and ministry in prayer and confirmed for all time that powerful and effective ministry comes through powerful and effective praying.

The church's greatest deficiency today is in power—not in programs, strategies, materials, or ideas. And power for ministry can be released only through prayer.

It takes praying leaders to develop praying churches. A stream will not rise higher than its source. Do you expect those following you to be strong in prayer? Then you must set the pace.

Praying leaders are not leaders who only talk of prayer, teach about prayer, encourage people in prayer, or organize prayer efforts. They are first of all men and women who pray. Promoting and teaching about prayer are no substitutes for action.

The church's greatest deficiency today is in power—not in programs, strategies, materials, or ideas. And power for ministry can be released only through prayer. Jesus told his disciples, "Anyone who has faith in me will do what I have been doing. He will do even greater things than these" (John 14:12). This statement no doubt astounded the disciples, until Jesus went on to explain: "I am going to the Father. And I will do whatever you ask in my name, so that the Son may bring glory to the Father. You may ask me for anything in my name, and I will do it" (John 14:12-14). In other words, the disciples would be powerful in ministry because Jesus Christ was on the throne of the universe. His response to their prayers was the key to the "greater things" they would do.

One pastor learned this lesson the hard way. Seeking renewal in his dying church, he spent several years studying at a strong evangelical seminary. Through reading, attending lectures, and brainstorming with other pastors in the same program, he learned all he could about church renewal and church growth. Faithfully he applied all that he was learning to his local church situation. But nothing seemed to work. His church seemed as dead as ever.

Having done his best with all he had learned and seeing no results, he was at the point of giving up. Then one day he walked out of his study into the sanctuary and, feeling led by the Lord, stood at the front of the church in the center aisle. He began to pray for his parishioners one by one. As he did so,

Christ actually meant prayer to be the great power by which his church should do its work.

he moved down the aisle, praying for those who would occupy each pew. Day after day he continued this practice. Soon the renewal he had wanted and worked so hard for began. Before long, worship services were full again, and the church was busy with ministry activities.

This story does not mean to suggest a magic formula for renewal. But it does point out the missing link in spiritual renewal: the power released by the prayers of a praying leader.

2. Give prayer high priority in the church's life and ministry.

Prayer clearly had a high priority in Jesus' life. Luke tells us that "Jesus often withdrew to lonely places and prayed" (Luke 5:16). Mark reports that "very early in the morning, while it was still dark, Jesus got up, left the house and went off to a solitary place, where he prayed" (Mark 1:35). On occasions he even "spent the night praying to God" (Luke 6:12).

The New Testament church gave prayer that same high priority. When their leaders were threatened by the Sanhedrin, they "raised their voices together in prayer to God"—and after they had prayed, "the place where they were meeting was shaken" (Acts 4:24, 31). When Peter was in prison and scheduled to die, "the church was earnestly praying to God for him" (Acts 12:5) throughout the night. It is not possible to explain the power and effectiveness of the New Testament church without reference to prayer.

O. Hallesby contends that "prayer is the most important work in the kingdom of God. It is a labor for which there is no substitute in the kingdom of God" (*Prayer*, p. 68). Believing, persistent prayer is the first step required for victory against Satan's influence. "We can do more than pray after we have prayed," says A. J. Gordon, "but we cannot do more than pray until we have prayed."

Of course, prayer has its place in every church and in every church member's life. The question is "How important a place?" We open and close our meetings with prayer. We offer congregational prayers and remember the sick and suffering. We usually offer mealtime prayers as well. But we need to look honestly at how much priority we give to prayer.

Martin Luther once described his struggle with the place of prayer in his life: "In a typical day I am charged with the pastorate of three congregations. I teach regularly at the seminary. I have students living in my house. I am writing three books. Countless people write to me. When I start each day, therefore, I make it a point to spend an hour in prayer with God. But, if I have a particularly busy day and am more rushed than usual, I make it a point to spend two hours with God before I start the day." That's one way of giving prayer priority.

3. **Correct thinking about prayer is important.**

Powerful, faithful, and effective prayer must be built on a correct mind-set about prayer. If we understand how prayer fits into God's rule of our lives, we are more likely to give prayer its rightful place.

Where does prayer fit in with our relationship to God? To what extent does God need our prayers to work out his plan for this world? If our prayers are weak, will they hinder the outcome God has planned? If all things are predestined in accord with God's will, won't they happen whether or not I pray? If God is sovereign, all-wise, and loving, does he not make his decisions in accord with his character and thus have no need for our prayers? If he needs our prayers, does that mean his plans are insufficient? How we answer these questions has much to do with how we pray.

Scripture instructs us on the place of prayer in God's rule. James 4:2 teaches us that we do not have because we do not ask. God is ready to give believers the very things they most need in order to live for him. However, this readiness on God's part does not settle the question. Believers will have these things only if they ask. In the parable of the friend who calls at midnight, Jesus urges persistent prayer as the way to receive blessing from God (Luke 11:5-9). Those who pray halfheartedly, lacking in persistence, will not receive what they might have received had they prayed more faithfully.

James also teaches us that the prayer of a righteous person "is powerful and effective" (James 5:16). Intercessory prayer has a powerful effect in our world. It makes a difference in the lives of those we pray for. It effects change. Conversely, lack of prayer leaves things unchanged.

One extraordinary passage is Ezekiel 22:30-31. The context reveals that Israel had sinned greatly against the Lord and deserved to be punished (vv. 1-29). But God, wanting to show mercy, says, "I looked for a man among them who would build up the wall and stand before me in the gap on behalf of the land so I would not have to destroy it, but I found none. So I will pour out my wrath on them and consume them with fiery anger." This passage leaves no

Ministry without prayer becomes work in the power of the flesh. Prayer without ministry is complacent Christianity.

doubt that if God had found a faithful and powerful intercessor—one like Moses, Samuel, or Elijah—the land would have been spared. Not finding such an intercessor, God poured out his wrath.

All of these passages make it clear that God has sovereignly determined to move in response to our prayers. God rules the world through the prayers of his people. This elevates our prayers to a position of highest significance in God's way of working, so much so that we are coworkers with God in what is accomplished in this world.

The great South African Reformed theologian Andrew Murray wrote his book *The Ministry of Intercession* to enforce two truths:

> that Christ actually meant prayer to be the great power by which his church should do its work, and that the neglect of prayer is the great reason the church has not greater power over the masses in Christian and in heathen countries.

and

> that we have far too little conception of the place that intercession . . . ought to have in the church and the Christian life. In intercession our king upon the throne finds his highest glory; in it we shall find our highest glory too. Through it he continues his saving work, we can do nothing without it; through it alone we can do all work and nothing avails without it. . . . The power of the church truly to bless rests on intercession—asking and receiving heavenly gifts to carry to men.

John Wesley had the same idea when he said, "God does nothing but in answer to prayer."

God waits to be asked not because he is powerless but because of the way he has chosen to exercise his will. We are not pawns on a giant chessboard. We are involved. Only a cold, hard, mechanistic view of God's sovereignty and predestination assumes that God discounts our prayer and simply moves in accord with a predetermined, once-and-for-all plan. This is not a biblical view of God; it more resembles a fatalistic, Islamic view of sovereignty, which the Bible repudiates.

The church that clearly understands that outcomes in history do depend on our prayers will not presume upon God's goodness. Rather, it will be inclined to bathe every aspect of life and ministry in powerful and effective praying.

4. **Clear communication of needs and answers to prayer is vital.**

A simple way to increase the amount of effective prayer within a congregation is to effectively communicate prayer needs and answers.

Almost all congregations communicate prayer needs. Bulletins carry announcements of the sick, injured, those who have lost loved ones, and other major prayer needs—including the need to give thanks or to rejoice when things have gone well. Needs that are not included in the bulletin are sometimes announced in other ways.

There are many needs, however, that are too personal to put in the church bulletin or to announce from the pulpit. To do so would cause undue embarrassment to the person and might contribute to gossip. These more personal needs, however, can be addressed by other members of the congregation. Prayer chains, for example, can handle information that is more personal or confidential than those that are publicly announced, especially if the chain is of limited scope. Prayer cells and prayer teams often handle very personal needs in a delicate and confidential way. The point is that an effort should be made to communicate all kinds of needs, including things like unemployment, mental illness, marital conflict, concern over wayward children, and problems like alcoholism, drug addiction, moral lapses, or sexually-related diseases. These needs can be shared with smaller groups in such a way that the person sharing them gains prayer support and yet is protected from gossip.

In addition to communicating a broad array of needs, church leaders should be careful to communicate prayer answers as well. It's not surprising that people grow weary of prayer when all they ever see are lists of prayer needs and announcements that call them to prayer. If we expect our prayers to make a difference, it's important to watch for the answers and to report these to all who have been asked to pray. Communicating requests without answers dampens the faith of those who are praying. If the "prayers" don't hear of God's answers, they have no opportunity to praise the Lord for having heard their prayers.

5. **Prayer should be linked to ministry.**

It's possible for believers to use prayer for selfish reasons. The prayers of self-centered persons will focus on personal health and well-being, personal success and fulfillment, financial prosperity, ease, pleasure, God's blessing on their personal projects, personal happiness, and so on. Such prayers are not always wrong. We should seek God's blessing for ourselves in every area of life. But if our primary focus is on getting more for ourselves, we are misusing prayer.

It's possible for a congregation's prayer to be self-centered also. Were God to summarize the content of many congregational prayers, they might sound like this: "God bless our church. Bless our pastor. Help him to preach good sermons. Give us a strong youth program. Care for our sick and sorrowing. Give all of us generous hearts so that we may meet our budget," and so on.

Such prayers have their place in the church. The Scriptures encourage us to ask so that we may receive. The problem is with the focus—a self-centered desire to obtain God's blessing, rather than a selfless offering of ourselves to God for his service and an acknowledgment of our need for his strength to accomplish his will.

God has called us to pray not only so that we may obtain a blessing but also so that we may be a blessing. The focus of our prayer should be the petition, "Your kingdom come." In the last days of his ministry, Jesus repeatedly emphasized the importance of prayer (Matthew 7:7-8; 18:19; 21:22; John 14:12-14; 15:7, 16; 16:23-24). He was concerned that his disciples realize they could build the church *only* if strengthened by his hand.

A church strong in prayer will know how to link prayer and ministry. It will pray not only for its own needs but also for the needs of its community and for its efforts to reach the unsaved. The church will pray not only for the comfort of the distressed but also for the too-comfortable, that they may be distressed at their complacency. It will pray for generous giving—but also for conversion growth. It will pray for ministries to church members, but it will pray just as urgently for the church's outreach efforts. It will pray faithfully for its own wayward members, but it will also pray persistently for friends, neighbors, work associates, and others who are running away from God. It will pray for power to do the works of God, wisdom to serve its community, and grace to touch this world for Christ.

One congregation linked prayer to ministry by praying for one particular street in its neighborhood. They did not know the names of the residents; they simply prayed faithfully for all the households represented on that street. Within a few weeks they noticed that people from three homes on that street had begun to attend church. Before long, one family was ready to consider joining. The church credited these results to prayer.

It is in private prayer that we most easily get in touch with our spiritual selves.

Another church linked prayer to ministry by praying for a list of sixty unchurched friends, relatives, and neighbors of its members. After the church had prayed for several months, almost half of the people on this prospect list had come to Christ. Most of them associated with the church that was praying for them.

Ministry without prayer becomes work in the power of the flesh. Prayer without ministry is complacent Christianity. The two belong together.

6. **Make times, ways, and places for people to pray together.**

When invited to pray with a group or participate in a prayer vigil, some people respond, "I can pray just as well by myself at home!" This is partly true—but also partly false. Those with weak and sporadic prayer discipline might be encouraged, strengthened, and challenged by praying with a group.

Why can praying with a group be valuable? There are several reasons.

First, it encourages consistency in prayer. We are more consistent about those things in our lives that are built into a regular schedule. Once we've committed ourselves to a group and a time, we tend to work other things around that commitment and keep with it even if we don't always feel like it.

Second, praying with others expands our prayer life. As we listen to others pray, we learn from them things that will strengthen our own prayer lives. They are aware of needs and answers that we would have forgotten. They have ways of saying things that we never would have thought of. We pray with them through their prayers. The Holy Spirit works differently in each one, using first one and then another to lift and lead the whole group.

Third, praying together strengthens our faith. If we only pray privately, we don't know who else is praying or what they are praying for. How can we agree in prayer? Jesus said, "I tell you that if two of you on earth agree about anything you ask for, it will be done for you by my Father in heaven. For where two or three come together in my name, there am I with them" (Matthew 18:19-20). Jesus' power is evident in unified prayer.

Fourth, mutual praying makes the large task of prayer more manageable. None of us can carry the whole prayer burden of a congregation. But when the broader task is broken down into smaller responsibilities, the impossible challenge is met by the group. Being with others who are praying, and knowing that others are picking up other responsibilities of the overall task, is encouraging to those who are doing their part.

The most obvious time and place for people to pray together is the worship service. A one-hour worship service often contains five to ten minutes of prayer. Usually the leader chooses the content and verbalizes the prayer. Those gathered are invited to pray with the leader. Church meetings or ministry efforts also provide the chance for people to pray together. Family mealtime prayers give families one of the most regular and helpful ways to pray together. However, the church wishing to stimulate prayer can provide several additional ways for people to be together in prayer.

Prayer meetings, prayer cells, and prayer teams provide an excellent way for people to share together in prayer. It's best if leaders do not dominate the prayer time but, rather, create an atmosphere in which everyone present feels free to share and to pray. It's helpful also to record prayer needs and answers so that people can remember these in their private prayers.

Commitments to pray for others in prayer partnerships, prayer triplets, or prayer support groups make our prayers for others intentional and specific. Usually the commitment to pray is reciprocal; each person shares their joys and concerns for the others to remember.

Prayer support teams link a number of persons who agree to pray for a person or cause. Members in some congregations commit themselves to pray for the pastor, who in turn regularly informs them of his concerns and needs. Prayer support teams of three or more may commit to pray for a particular individual, for an important cause, or for a person in a challenging ministry.

7. **Encourage personal devotions.**

Private prayer is an indispensable part of every Christian's life. It is the high-est activity in which any soul can engage. In prayer we are able to have personal communion with the almighty God, in whom we live and move and have our being.

The Bible elevates personal prayer. Private prayer was important to Abraham (Genesis 19:27), Moses (Exodus 17:8-13), David (Psalm 5:3; 27:4, 7-9), and Daniel (6:1-10).

Jesus advised his disciples not to pray in the synagogue or at street corners in order to be seen by people but instead to go into their own homes and shut the door and pray to the Father in secret (Matthew 6:5-6). Jesus himself often withdrew to private places to be alone with his Father and to restore his spirit. Paul was praying alone when he had his "third-heaven" experi-ence (2 Corinthians 12:1-4). Peter was praying alone on the housetop in Joppa when servants of Cornelius came (Acts 10:9-23). John was deep in personal meditation on the isle of Patmos when Jesus appeared to him in a vision (Revelation 1:10).

God has chosen prayer as the key by which his church does its work. Through prayer we impact the world for God.

It is in private prayer that we most eas-ily get in touch with our spiritual selves. When we are alone with God, there is no one else to impress. We don't have to meet anyone else's expectations. In personal prayer we dare to look into our heart of hearts to discern those most private problems and issues we need to place before the Lord.

To say that prayer is important does not mean that it is easy. Many believ-ers have experienced serious obstacles and hindrances to their personal devotions. Some struggle with knowing what to say. Others wrestle with wandering thoughts, and still others fight the nagging doubt that God does not hear or that he is not concerned. Perhaps the most difficult of all is our lack of desire to pray.

The church needs to encourage people in personal prayer. Emphasizing the need for private devotions in sermons, church education classes, retreats, young people's groups, new members' classes, and children's schooling will help make personal prayer a standard for the Christian community. Leaders, of course, must be the first to make a wholehearted commitment to this standard.

> **If family worship is neglected, other attempts at prayer are like sprinkling the foliage of a plant with water while leaving the roots dry.**

Any course on prayer should include a segment on personal devotions that answers these questions: What are personal devotions? Why have personal devotions? When? How often? What are some different approaches? Standard catechism courses for new-members classes might also include a couple of hours on this important discipline.

The church can also help by providing resources for personal devotions.

8. Encourage family devotions.

Family devotions should be part of every Christian family's experience. As the basic unit of society, the family provides the most natural group of persons to pray with and for each other. Deuteronomy 6:6-9 reminds us that the primary responsibility for spiritual training belongs to the parents:

> *These commandments that I give you today are to be upon your hearts. Impress them on your children. Talk about them when you sit at home and when you walk along the road, when you lie down, and when you get up. Tie them as symbols on your hands and bind them on your foreheads. Write them on the door frames of your houses and on your gates.*

Family devotions provide an excellent time and place for parents to do what this passage requires.

One of the greatest forms of support for a church's ministry is praying families. Piterim Sorokin, a Harvard sociologist, called attention to statistics that show that while "two out of every five marriages end in divorce . . . for those families who have prayer and Bible study there is only one divorce in 1,015 marriages" (quoted in Elva Anson's *How to Keep the Family that Prays Together from Falling Apart*, Moody Press, 1976, p. 9). Family worship is basic to other kinds of worship. If family worship is neglected, other attempts at prayer are like sprinkling the foliage of a plant with water while leaving the roots dry.

Family worship usually includes such things as Bible reading, Scripture memory, reading of devotional materials, music, and prayer. Its value lies not only in the ideas transmitted but also in the quality family time—spirited conversation and loving and caring for one another through prayer.

Some ways churches can encourage family devotions:

Teach a course on family devotions. We can no longer assume that family devotions will be carried on from one generation to another. In too many cases the link has been broken, so that children growing up in Christian families no longer understand the value and the practical aspects of family devotions. A congregation could help its members significantly by offering a course that presents the importance of family devotions, gives creative methods, suggests resources, and includes testimonies of those whose lives have been blessed through family devotions. Newly married couples and those who are new to the congregation especially should be invited. Such a course should be repeated yearly.

Reinforce the value of family devotions. References in sermons will reach the whole congregation. The theme of family worship can be introduced into couples' clubs, societies, youth groups, parent classes, and premarital counseling by means of special speakers or special topics. Every-member or every-family visitation can also pick up on this theme. Consider coordinating preaching with family devotions by announcing texts or series of messages in advance so that they can also be used in family devotions.

Provide members of the congregation with resources. Some churches make available for their members resources like the Back to God Hour's *Today: The Family Altar, Daily Manna,* or something similar. Denominational prayer guides may also be included for use in family prayers. The church library should carry a wide range of helpful devotional guides, children's Bible-story books, and Bible helps that can be periodically displayed in the church narthex. Also consider giving new members specific guidelines and resources to use if they are not familiar with family devotions.

Hold up family devotions as your church's expectation of its members. Challenge all leaders to have regular family devotion times. Reinforce this in pastor's classes for new members who are joining the church.

conclusion

This essay has provided a wide spectrum of insights to think about and practical suggestions to implement in your church. We hope that you understand that God has chosen prayer as the key by which his church does its work. Through prayer we impact the world for God.

May your church be all that Christ means it to be. As you daily consider and apply these concepts, may your church grow strong in prayer, so that you experience the release of God's power for dynamic ministry.

TWICE BLESSED: BIBLICAL PERSPECTIVES ON PRAYER

by Eugene Rubingh

As Shakespeare said of mercy, so we may say of prayer: it is twice blessed. It opens the windows of heaven as God rains his blessings upon those for whom we pray, and it blesses those who pray. Prayer calls for bold, faith-full requests by those and for those whose lives are spent in serving God. We are heralds of the king of kings, invested with explicit promises of answered prayer.

Christians engage in prayer for two reasons: first, because it is a biblical imperative, mandated clearly, forcibly, and repeatedly throughout the Bible. Second, because we have a natural and felt need for it in the depths of our being. In a moment of agony and desperate need, even the agnostic has the sense to cry out, "God, save me!"

There are, in the Scriptures and the church's history, wonderful accounts of the blessing of answered prayer—answered better than we dare dream. We hear of such things in our own culture and today especially from our brothers and sisters in Christ in the Third World. Often these answers to prayer are far different from the requests of those who prayed. The answers are often broader in scope, far more incisive and to the point, and from a completely different perspective.

There is in Romans 8 an explanation for this phenomenon: "The Spirit helps us in our weakness. We do not know what we ought to pray for, but the Spirit himself intercedes for us with groans that words cannot express" (v. 26). So, right at the start, let's accept and affirm the fact of tangibly, visibly, and miraculously answered prayer. We know it; we have seen it even if sometimes we have not experienced it as we could. The front line for answered prayer is not just in places of missionary expansion in the Third World but also in every office, kitchen, store, and workplace around us. You and I stand in the thick of Satan's efforts to resist the coming kingdom. This is the real arena, and prayer is part of our war material.

The second part of the blessing comes to the one who is praying. Here I mean the person's growing fellowship with God, the increasing ability to throw open one's life to God's far better leading, the peace of committing the crisis into his hands. A particular blessing for those who put prayer at the center of their evangelism is the discipline of unselfishness, of searching for power and blessing in the lives of others rather than in one's own life. The horizons of prayer expand when we pray for missions.

Let's chart the biblical perspective on prayer. As we do so, we will understand why God's power and blessing are sometimes missed in today's church. As we peel back the layers of misunderstanding placed on us by our culture and society, we will recapture the Bible's teaching on the meaning and enormous potential of prayer.

the reality of the conflict

Not only did Jesus teach us what to pray (Matthew 6:9-13), but he also modeled such aspects as intensity, allotted time, locations, and content. Reflection on those characteristics shows how near at hand and immediate is the presence of the enemy and the conflict with the kingdom of darkness. Not only was this true for Jesus, but a sense of the immediacy of the battle with evil also pulsates throughout the New Testament. When the struggle is right at hand, one's sense of personal involvement is greatly heightened.

In effect, that sense of the immediacy of the spiritual world is what our culture questions. We have scientific explanations for the growth of crops, for epidemics of sickness, and even for the fortunes of war. The miracle of conception and birth is antiseptically and dispassionately described for us in terms devoid of transcendence. We have supposedly "outgrown" that primitive idea of sacredness and awe, while banishing God to Sunday morning. In turn, angels and the demonic get little consideration in our secularized society.

In such an atmosphere it is possible that believers begin to miss the presence of the supernatural and fail to anticipate the attention of God. Prayer life can be battered by the attitudes of modern life. If that happens, it is a Christian's duty and joy to rediscover the presence of the Holy Spirit.

In this venture we can learn from our brothers and sisters in Christ around the world. The gospel light is dawning after centuries of darkness, and Satan's bondage is being challenged. He is on the counterattack! Let no academic theory dispute that. Demon possession is virulent. Disorder and evil appear in frightening ways. There is constant awareness of the immediacy of the conflict between God and the evil one.

This reality is present everywhere, even if our eyes and ears and spirits are

The gospel light is dawning after centuries of darkness, and Satan's bondage is being challenged.

not sensitive to it. Our secularized society is much poorer for having exorcised the unseen. As Christians, we must bravely say and live by what we know!

In this context of living at the heart of a spiritual battle against principalities and powers, prayer gains its full stature. The authority provided by Christ must be unleashed.

the important power line

Our society is also one that delights in action and organization. We have mission boards and evangelism committees that get the machinery humming. The factors that contribute to that humming include the recruitment of people, funding, and administration. Every task is carefully described with an appropriate time frame and budget. But how carefully is it bathed in prayer?

In a sense, prayer should not be tightly orchestrated. It should not be robbed of its free-flowing potential or confined, prescribed, or pigeon-holed. But a greater danger is that our most potent power line is unrecognized, rendering the rest lifeless. Hence every evangelism program and strategy should be specifically enveloped in prayer. The dimension of prayer work should be carefully included as an essential part of every evangelism project. Then we will evidence what we confess: that the power comes from God.

Recognizing that evangelism is God's program before it is our program is particularly important today. This is an age of "finding God within," which often reduces prayer to a "divine expression" of our own potential. This insidious New Age teaching rejects the sovereign God of the Scriptures and seeks instead to create God in our image. The power of God is wholly absent from such concepts, for they flow from humanity's age-old flaw of pride.

not convincing God

Understanding completely the nature of prayer is beyond us. A whole series of mind-boggling questions arise as we attempt to describe it. But let us say what it is not, and so get to its heart—that core which is so much more than asking God for things.

Prayer is not the art of convincing God. It is not getting him to do something he's reluctant to do. It is not deity manipulation. Consider Jephthah, who wished a victory so fiercely that he prayed a vow that if Israel won he would sacrifice as a burnt offering the first thing that came out of his house to meet him (Judges 11:30). His army was victorious, but as he came home, who should run out to meet him? His only daughter. Jephthah's prayer stands as a classic teaching of how not to petition. God's answer is never a forced response. It is purely a gift of grace.

Yet if God's purposes and plans are already good, why petition him at all? The answer is because he commands it. Psalm 50:15 says, "Call upon me in the day of trouble; I will deliver you, and you will honor me." God has

Every task is carefully described with an appropriate time frame and budget. But how carefully is it bathed in prayer?

sovereignly chosen to move and act through his people, using their complexities and hopes to reach the coming of his kingdom, and listening to his people as they journey along the way.

John Calvin summarizes it succinctly: "God's command and promise is our motive for prayer." Prayer is obedience. We may rebel against obedience, but in submission to God we claim a victory over our childish pride. It's a lifelong hammering at our will as God chisels us into shape in the school of prayer.

not the art of asking

We're not yet at the core of prayer when we say it is not the means to change God's mind; prayer is not even the art of asking God for things. _Prayer is offering yourself to God._ Make prayer the time to give yourself this day as a gift to God. Prayer then becomes the opening up of yourself for the Lord to take control, to possess you. Then your energy and God's energy flow together. You seek for God's will in your prayer, and in doing so you marvelously find your path fulfilled, your purposes achieved, and your desires responded to.

This perspective on prayer transforms everything. Prayer then is not switched on by our crises and needs, but it is the daily gift of ourselves to God. It becomes the expression of our intimacy with God. We confess and listen and hear. It is a wonderful way to accept God's love. In the process he hears about our needs and dreams.

The Old Testament sacrifices represented gifts to God—the gift of an animal's blood in place of mine. In Christ's sacrifice those old sacrifices are forever finished, but I like to think that the church father Tertullian was right when he said prayer in the New Testament takes the place of sacrifice in the Old. In the concept of prayer as gift we become God's instruments for his use.

prayer and power

In John 14-16, Christ says prayer can have limitless results. Think of the verses in James that tell us about healing as the answer to prayer, and about Elijah, who prayed for rain and was answered (James 5:15-18).

Does God need the reinforcement of our prayer to wage war with Satan? And if all is predestined and laid out, does prayer have the power to alter that decree? These are thorny issues to confront in our understanding of prayer.

Why should we pray for the salvation of Nigeria or Chicago? Do such prayers add a dimension of power to God's salvation force, which would be somehow less if we did not pray? Or is it perhaps that God was not giving Chicago the attention that we might crave for it, and that our prayers might simply direct his loving gaze there? Neither of these possibilities is absurd! They are sincere questions that have been asked, and both contain hints of the biblical perspective.

Let us not for a moment belittle the power of the enemy. Jesus took that powerful enemy very seriously. In fact, his face is turned toward Satan in the gospel record as much as it is turned toward the Father. The struggle is very real, even though we know the final outcome.

It is in this context that God mandates our involvement with him in the conflict of the kingdoms. In the struggle, he says prayer is effective. Through prayer God empowers his people toward achieving his purpose in bringing in his kingdom. Therefore, we should pray with passion for Chicago and Nigeria, and for the defeat of the enemy.

Finally, what of those who wonder if prayer can change what God has willed to come to pass? Do we not worship a God whose plans are immutable, who says, "I the LORD do not change" (Malachi 3:6)? This is also the God who says in the very next verse, "Return to me, and I will return to you" (v. 7). Clearly God does turn and return in response to his people.

It is true that God's nature and decrees are perfect and not subject to change. What is difficult for us to understand is that God lives in an eternal present. It was not in some remote past that he shaped events, but everything for him is now. Thus he takes into account every prayer ever offered and is forever involved with us in charting the course of history. He is the sovereign God who stoops to hear and love. Unfettered by time, he decrees and answers in his eternal present. Such thoughts tax our capacities, and we simply obey his mandate and bow in prayer.

prayer and mission

Prayer, like mercy, is twice blessed, for it blesses also the one who prays. That blessing is felt in the assurance of being at the center of God's will as we give ourselves to him each day anew. While the psychic benefits are not the reason for prayer, let's claim these benefits too! Prayer is good therapy; it cleanses and purifies.

He takes into account every prayer ever offered and is forever involved with us in charting the course of history.

In this *Praying Church Sourcebook*, the focus is on prayer. And prayer launches us into mission. In prayer we open ourselves up to God and give ourselves to him. God does not just leave us kneeling there! His energy now impels us to move out into his world and to radiate his presence.

As we receive God in prayer, he takes over. As Jacques Ellul has said,

"Prayer is God's grace in the extreme." Prayer is Immanuel, "God with us." Prayer equips us for mission and enables us to boldly recommend Jesus. In our very powerlessness we find power from God. In our obvious weakness we receive strength. In our despair we find hope.

prayer and hope

As Christians, we do not expect much progress at the hands of the powerful and the rich. But we are the people of hope, for we desire the future, when we shall see Jesus. It is in prayer that we articulate our despair with the present and our anticipation of the coming kingdom. Prayer throws us upon the promises of God. We have nothing else.

Here is the hope of our prayer: the kingdom of the enemy will fall, and all its false pride will be exposed. Killing and blasphemy will pollute the earth no more, and death will die. No more insults hurled at Jesus, no more defacing of our Father's world. Instead, we will be driven to say and to show that our God reigns!

Already now we march to a different drummer, and in our mind's eye we see another kingdom rising. It is time for Amen, time to spend ourselves for the King.

Eugene Rubingh has been involved in world missions for more than thirty years. Currently he is a vice president of International Bible Society, Inc., overseeing its worldwide Bible distribution program.

essays

27

TWICE BLESSED: BIBLICAL PERSPECTIVES ON PRAYER

SEVEN WAYS PRAYER IS CHANGING THE CHURCH IN AMERICA

by John Quam

1. PEOPLE—Prayer is calling people to a supernatural worldview.

A kind of pragmatic secularism has crept into the American church. While people continue to maintain a belief in a supernatural God, they have planned and directed their lives and ministries in ways that appear to short-circuit that belief. Even less time and energy are given to strategies to overcome the supernatural influence of evil through the work of Satan and his demons. While Christians in many other countries experience daily the implications of these supernatural realities, American Christians seem to be overly fascinated with new facilities, programs, and materials. But there seems to be a change on the horizon. Evidence of this is seen in the popularity of all sorts of books about prayer, spirituality, angels, and spiritual warfare. Prayer puts us in contact with our supernatural God and brings his resources into play to impact the circumstances and realities that surround us.

In a message delivered at the ACMC National Conference in 1988, John Piper addressed the issues of what prayer is for and what kind of God we approach when we come to him in prayer. In one illustration Piper referred to his own church elders, who prayed over a girl the day before her surgery. When the doctors examined her, the tumor they were to remove was gone. Piper said that his elders were ecstatic at the news, not because they had great faith, but because of the discovery of their great, supernatural God. Prayer is a channel between our personal, physical world and the supernatural realities that surround us. The more we pray, the more our horizons expand and the more we come to expect from a supernatural, miracle-working God.

2. PASTORS—Prayer is helping pastors understand their role in the church.

In Acts 6 we read that the early church leaders found themselves in a dilemma. All kinds of disputes and difficulties were arising that required their attention. Particularly, there was a dispute between the Grecian and Aramaic widows concerning the equitable distribution of the church's resources. The apostles' involvement with administrative responsibilities was becoming detrimental to the spiritual health of the church—a change was needed. In response to this need, gifted individuals were appointed to assume responsibility over these administrative tasks so that the spiritual leaders of the church might give themselves to two things: prayer and the ministry of the Word.

From my seminary experience in the 1960s and in following the work and role of pastors throughout the seventies and eighties, I've discovered that the American church is reliving the experiences of the early church in Jerusalem. Administrative tasks and congregational expectations are overwhelming pastors to the degree that many, if not most, pastors have little time for study of the Word and prayer (the average time spent in prayer by pastors across the United States, as pointed out in "Keys to a Praying Church," is about eighteen minutes a day).

As suggested in the first point above, prayer represents our supernatural worldview. When we short-circuit prayer, we give our lives and ministry a secularistic or humanistic framework within which to work.

Living the Christian life requires supernatural, spiritual power. Without prayer this power is not at work in us as individuals or in the church as a whole. Fortunately, some changes are on the scene. Groups of pastors are beginning to gather in cities around the country. They are beginning to reassess their role in the church and the power that is at work within them. They are beginning to insist on more time for prayer in the ministry of the Word and to delegate other responsi-

bilities to gifted people in their congregations. It is a small beginning, and prayer is the key to an accelerated and growing understanding of this important principle.

3. **PROGRAM—A growing number of congregations are making prayer a high priority.**

As I visit churches around our country, I am often disappointed to find that collective prayer is not mentioned anywhere as one of the key activities for the church's ministry. Even large, well-known churches have no time for the congregation to gather for concerted, united prayer on behalf of its people and mission. On the other hand, aerobics is often mentioned as a regular activity. Sometimes two or three well-attended exercise-oriented groups are active each week. Something is desperately wrong with our churches when the people will flock to physical activities, such as aerobics, softball, basketball, or bowling, but very few show any interest at all in the spiritual activity of corporate prayer. We should not be surprised, then, when our well-attended, prosperous-looking evangelical churches are besieged by problems of divorce, family breakdown, and immoral and ethical crises on all sides.

In community-wide and city-wide prayer rallies across the country, churches are coming together to unite in prayer for spiritual awakening and world evangelization.

Fortunately, some pastors and congregations have recognized the problem and are making drastic changes. They are bringing prayer back into the centrality of the life of the church. Churches are having weeks of prayer to start out the year. They are dedicating time to concerted, united prayer.

Churches are asking families and individuals for commitments. One church has a number of prayer groups that meet at 5:30 in the morning, and another group meeting at 5:00 A.M.

"Does God exist to help fulfill our plans, or do we exist to help fulfill the plans of God?"

You have to be faithful at the 5:30 prayer groups before you are invited to participate in the 5:00 prayer group. Another church has three hundred people who come regularly to pray. All day there are people praying for the life and ministry of the church. Other churches have designated a room where people gather for prayer during the worship services on Sunday morning. They pray for the power of God's Holy Spirit to be evident through the program and the preaching of the Word. They pray that Christians will be built up in the Word and that non-Christians will be converted. Other churches have large groups that gather and pray in depth for the missionaries and mission outreach of their congregation and for unreached peoples around the world. The percentage of these kinds of churches is small but is growing. Prayer is changing the program of the church.

4. **PURPOSE—Prayer is giving focus to the mission of the church.**

In the address mentioned earlier, Piper summarizes some of his thoughts with this simple statement: "If you do not believe that life is war, you will not know what prayer is for." Unfortunately, many people in our congregations have no working idea of the warfare or purpose of the church. For many people, the first words heard after becoming Christians are "God loves you and has a wonderful plan for your life." Without further explanation of the right kind, this can be very misleading. A person might easily confuse the wonderfulness of God's plan with his own personal desires and expectations. It's a short step from there to believing that God and the church exist to meet our needs and make us happy. This is far from biblical Christianity, but is very close to the way that many evangelical Christians practice their Christianity. The question is: "Does God exist to help fulfill our plans, or do we exist to help fulfill the plans of God?"

Prayer helps us focus on the true mission of the church. When the early church gathered for prayer, they went out and spoke the Word boldly, even though it brought persecution and difficulty for them personally. Prayer helped them focus on their mission. Jesus looked on the world as a great harvest field, ready to be reaped. He urged those who were following to pray that the Lord of the harvest would send out laborers, people who would give themselves to this important work. For this reason, the Concerts of Prayer movement focuses on spiritual awakening and world evangelization.

It is important that we first get a new glimpse of who Christ is, then be thrust out into the mission he calls us to. He warns us, however, to wait until we have been clothed with power from on high. The church does this waiting in prayer. Prayer launches us out into our mission. It helps us focus on our purpose. When we pray for personal needs and concerns for loved ones and relatives, it is in order that we might be able to work effectively for the accomplishing of his mission for us and for the church. Our prayers echo back to God his own concerns. Our purpose is to serve God and his cause.

5. POWER—Prayer gives us power for witness.

There is a difference between doing right things and doing things right. We are commissioned as Christ's witnesses, but what does it mean to be an effective witness? In Luke 24:45-49 we have an important Great Commission passage. First, Jesus opens his disciples' minds to understand the Scriptures. Second, he commissions them to preach in his name to all nations. Third, he tells them to wait for power. Effective witness is dependent on the power of God's Spirit. In Acts 1:8 Luke continues the same theme. Jesus promises them the power of the Holy Spirit to be his witnesses from Jerusalem to the ends of the earth. How did they wait? Acts 1:14 gives us the answer: They met together "constantly in prayer." There is a direct relationship between prayer and the power of the Holy Spirit.

The book of Acts records the rapid growth of the early church in spite of a hostile environment. That growth was related to the power of their witness, and that witness was preceded by consistent, persistent prayer. (See Acts 2:42; 4:31; 12:5, 12.) No amount of training, materials, programs, technology, or the like can substitute for the concerted prayers of God's people.

Charles H. Spurgeon was once asked the secret of the success of his ministry. He took that person into the basement of the church and said, "When I am in the pulpit preaching, three hundred people are down here praying." Whether preaching or sharing our faith in the streets, the "secret" is the same: the prayers of God's people.

6. PROGNOSIS—Prayer changes the prognosis for the future.

In *Kingdoms in Conflict*, Charles Colson describes a poignant scene of the dying moments in the life of Winston Churchill. This great man—who led the way in the struggle for freedom during World War II—surveyed the world before him and said, "There is no hope." Many young people who are questioned about the future express deep apprehensions and fear of the powerful forces at play in the world today. It is this apprehension that often drives them to an existential, get-it-now, approach to life.

Jeremiah 29:10-14 describes God's long-range plan for the people of Israel. Even though the situation looked bleak at the time, God wanted his people to be a people of hope. When they stopped trusting themselves and truly began seeking God in prayer, hope would rekindle in them, and through that hope God would restore them to their inheritance. There is a powerful connection between prayer and hope. Through prayer we recognize the promises of God and place our trust in them. Prayer engenders hope, and hope places in us the ability to receive God's promises.

The application of this principle is wide and varied. James 5:13-18 instructs us in how we ought to pray even over physical illness. Although this passage does not teach that no one should ever be sick or that all sickness will be healed, it does say that we should look first to God for help and that there is reason to hope for his healing. This hope, however, does not supplant our ultimate hope in eternity with him—free from pain and death.

Ultimately, the hope in our prayers has to do with the accomplishment of God's purposes. John 16:24 instructs us to ask for things in Jesus' name, and we will have the joy of receiving them. We often think this means we must end our prayers with "in Jesus' name." That is not the meaning of this verse. It means that when we ask for the things Jesus would want, then we will have them. It is the same as praying according to his will. This truth is reinforced in James 4:2-3. The closer we are to the Lord and the more we perceive his purposes, the greater our hope in answered prayer.

7. PARTNERSHIP—**Prayer is uniting congregations as they move from polarization to partnership.**

One of the most destructive realities of the North American church is its divisiveness. As churches compete with one another for the attention of the surrounding community and dispute with each other over traditions and biblical interpretations, they contradict one of the central themes of Christ's prayer for the church—that we might be one, even as he and the Father are one (John 17:20-23). In another place he expresses his desire that we might be known as his followers by the way that we love one another (John 13:34-35). This is, in fact, the very thing that the world searches for in the church. The absence of this love is probably the greatest obstacle to people who would take seriously the claims of Christ. Once again, however, positive changes are taking place through prayer. In community-wide and city-wide prayer rallies across the country,

When we short-circuit prayer, we give our lives and ministry a secularistic or humanistic framework within which to work.

churches are coming together to unite in prayer for spiritual awakening and world evangelization. These concerts of prayer represent a dramatic step toward partnership and away from the polarization that has existed in the North American church.

In 1988 more than two hundred churches united in a Concert of Prayer at the Minneapolis Metrodome. That is just one of many examples of people gathering to pray. Local prayer-movement steering committees are active in at least forty to fifty different communities around the United States for the purpose of uniting congregations in concerted prayer. Together they are celebrating their common convictions in the lordship of Christ and in the mission of his church, while setting aside their differing interpretations in specific aspects of the practice of the church. In some places, even the secular media have reported these new signs of unity in the evangelical body of Christ. Prayer—united, concerted prayer—is a means of expressing our partnership in the greater causes of the kingdom of God.

victory in prayer

The following principles will help us gain victory in prayer:

- *Prayer is spiritual warfare.* Because of this fact we can be sure of two things. First, we will experience opposition to our desire to pray. Forces will seek to keep us from actually getting to prayer. All kinds of unexpected events or interruptions will appear. We will feel that there is no time for prayer, even though we have clearly made it a high priority. And, if we do pray, we will be distracted or tempted to pray for the wrong things. These are the effects of the spiritual forces that hate prayer and are the most threatened by the power of prayer. Second, we can know that if we do pray, we have the potential of unleashing the power of God for the binding of Satan and the releasing or freeing of his possessions. This is the secret of evangelism as well as the release from depression, oppression, and demon possession. It is through prayer that the kingdom of God advances against the kingdom of Satan.

- *Prayer involves persistence*. Luke 18:1-8 tells us the story of the persistent widow. Her persistence demonstrated her conviction that the judge could fulfill her request if he wanted to, so she continued asking until he did. Jesus says that God will not ignore his children who call to him day and night. However, he warns that a time may come when the Son of Man cannot find faith on the earth. This faith is represented in the willingness of people to call out to him day and night with the conviction that only he can fulfill their need. Our persistence demonstrates our faith. It is for this reason that not all of our prayers are answered immediately.

- *Finally, prayer is both public and private*. When Jesus condemned the public prayer of the Pharisee, it was because his praying was a show for others. He was a hypocrite. Public gatherings of the church need to demonstrate their relationship to God in prayer just as individuals do. The early church was characterized by constantly meeting together in prayer. If prayer is not clearly visible in all aspects of our corporate church life, new believers will falsely be led to believe that prayer is not a necessary component of church life. How tragic! Yet this appears to be exactly what has happened to the North American church.

John Quam is former executive director of Concerts of Prayer, International.

Used by permission of John Quam and Concerts of Prayer, International.

STRATEGIES *for*
PRAYING
CHURCHES

INTRODUCTION

Why do we need strategies to get our churches moving in prayer? Because whenever people become involved in a common activity, some kind of organization is required. This also holds true for prayer. Organization won't ensure that your efforts will be a live and vital part of the church's life, of course. Only God's Spirit can do that. But good organization will channel people's energy and enthusiasm into prayer activities that have proved beneficial to many different churches.

The following chapters will suggest ways in which other churches have successfully organized their prayer activities and ministries. As you read through this section, remember that the effectiveness of any strategy depends largely on the people assigned to organize and direct it. You will need to identify those persons in your congregation who have gifts in prayer, leadership, and organization.

Remember, too, that a strategy that works in one church may not necessarily work in another. Choose your strategies carefully, tailoring them to the situation in your local church.

Do not try to implement all of the following strategies at once—it's impossible! Nor are all of these ideas expected to be used in a single congregation. Your church will probably be able to use only a few of these. So read them carefully to decide what might work best for you.

Here are some suggestions to keep in mind as you implement some of the strategies in this section:

- Begin your efforts by appointing a prayer coordinator. Don't assume that members who are currently responsible for the congregation's spiritual development should be in charge. They already carry a heavy responsibility; don't add to it. Instead, find a person (or team of two persons) with the spiritual gift of organization and a heart for prayer. Give them some resources for doing ministry, a mandate, and someone to be accountable to. Be sure to let them know the limits of their responsibility and authority. Then give them this *Sourcebook* and set them to work!

- Designate a different person to lead each prayer ministry that you develop. Working with more than one strategy is too much for one person to do. And don't expect your coordinator to develop every ministry. The coordinator's job is to locate gifted people who will lead each ministry and to act as a resource person for those individuals.

- Develop one new prayer ministry at a time. Go on to your second and third efforts only after the first has been well received and established. Also, be sure that the new ministries you're considering will meet the different needs of various people. Overlap your prayer ministries as little as possible.

- Your church may already be using some of these ideas. If so, use this material to review, upgrade, and improve what you're already doing.

- Begin with the prayer ministries that are most natural to your situation. Consider the type of people who make up your congregation, for example. What do they feel comfortable with? What do you think they can achieve? You should lead them in strategies that (1) will give them what is needed and (2) are likely to succeed. For example, the success of the senior intercessors strategy will probably depend on the number of seniors in your congregation.

- Some strategies are more important than others. For example, praying leaders are essential (see page 13, "Keys to a Praying Church"). A pastor's prayer support group (see chapter 20 in this section) is another vital strategy, since the pastor is key to the church's spiritual development. Also, establishing a church prayer support group (see chapter 16) adds strength and support to all the church's ministries. Its efforts will touch the very heart of the church.

1

THE PRAYER COORDINATOR

Why do we include a section devoted solely to a prayer coordinator? The coordinator is an essential element for a praying church. He or she is the person who will help integrate prayer into the total life of the church. As you read the following chapters and the many ideas and suggestions they give for the praying church, the need for a prayer coordinator will become self-evident.

Paul Billheimer writes in *Destined for the Throne*, "Any church without a well-organized and systematic prayer program is simply operating a religious treadmill." This statement could be a fairly accurate description of your church. In any case, it does underscore the value of organizing, coordinating, and intentionally encouraging prayer activities in the local church.

A renewed interest in and commitment to prayer may develop slowly in your church. But as it does, you will see an increasing need for a system in which to share ideas and resources on prayer, to gather and distribute prayer requests, to organize prayer groups, to recruit leaders and "pray-ers," to inform your congregation of the opportunities in prayer that are available, and so on.

Is a prayer coordinator necessary? Yes—though it may take some effort to convince your congregation of this. The ministry of prayer is often taken for granted: "Oh sure, we pray. We open our meetings with prayer, include a congregational prayer in the worship, encourage family prayer at home." But a ministry of prayer is much more than that. Faithful, committed, daily prayer is the lifeblood of the church's ministries. Churches should be willing to invest the same kind of organizational effort into their prayer life that they put into youth ministries, education, evangelism, worship, and more.

You don't have to hire someone from outside, however. A number of people in your congregation are gifted for this strategic position. But if these people are already too busy or too committed to take on the position alone, you might want to recruit them as a team. Whichever persons you choose, make sure that they wholeheartedly accept this responsibility with a sense of calling from God.

qualifications

The person(s) appointed to this position should possess the following qualities:

- a strong personal prayer life
- spiritual maturity
- gifts to organize, encourage, and give leadership in prayer (the gifts of

administration, communication, leadership)

- a good reputation in the congregation and the confident approval of church leaders

- enough time to attend key prayer events in the church and the community

mandate of the prayer coordinator/team

One of the first things on the coordinator's agenda will be to identify those people in the congregation who have the gift of intercession and to ask for their support in this new venture of prayer.

Gathering a wide array of resources in prayer (books, videos, audiotapes, prayer guides, bulletin inserts, workshops, and so on) is another initial task. The coordinator should become familiar with these resources and consider how they might fit into the church's existing worship, education, small group fellowships, and more.

Next, the coordinator should research and evaluate the church's current prayer ministries, beginning with questions like these:

- What prayer materials are now available to the congregation?

- What training and educational opportunities in prayer are now in place? Are they effective?

- Are there active prayer groups within the church?

- What systems in the church encourage intercessory prayer (for example, prayer chains, prayer phone lines, prayer vigils, prayer partners, and so on)?

- Does our church hold regular prayer services or especially emphasize prayer for missions, community concerns, denominational prayer needs, and so on?

- Do we give our church members the opportunity to offer prayers during the worship service, council meetings, committee meetings, and so on?

- Does our church participate in cooperative prayer efforts with other churches?

Answering these and other questions will give the coordinator or team a feel for the strengths and weaknesses of their church's prayer life and some ideas on where to begin.

The coordinator should also look for areas that need prayer within the congregation. For example, are the pastor and other key leaders being strongly supported in prayer? How much support through prayer is given to members in ministries like church school, youth programs, activities for children, outreach programs, and evangelism? Are elderly and shut-in members being challenged to develop prayer ministries? Do members have a place to which they can bring prayer needs in times of crisis or major decision? Making a list of all the areas for potential prayer needs will help determine what kinds of prayer ministries are most needed in your church.

> **"Any church without a well-organized and systematic prayer program is simply operating a religious treadmill."**

Having gathered information and asked key questions, the coordinator needs to develop and put into place a plan to involve more people in prayer. (This should always be done in consultation with the pastor and other leaders of the church.) Here are several principles to keep in mind:

1. **Begin with simple strategies, then move into harder, more complex ways of involving people in prayer.** For example, it's relatively easy to secure and use resources such as prayer-bulletin inserts, inspirational books on prayer, videos, and so on. Adding a prayer course to the church's education curriculum might be less challenging than starting a weekly prayer meeting. Scheduling more sermons on prayer means some commitment on the part of the pastor but requires no structural changes in the church's worship. Forming people into prayer triplets might be easier than establishing larger prayer groups.

   > One of the first things on the coordinator's agenda will be to identify those people in the congregation who have the gift of intercession and to ask for their support in this new venture of prayer.

2. **Start your work among leaders in the congregation.** Once the council members and leaders of various ministries are convinced that the church's prayer life should be nurtured and challenged, your task will be much easier.

   You might start by involving the church's council and committees in longer, more focused times of prayer. One church, for example, simply decided to give all those who participated in any church meetings a chance to share and pray. They found that members were eager to share their struggles and concerns and were willing to be prayed for and to pray for others. The extended prayer time set a different tone for the church's meetings and filled a void in the church's fellowship life.

   Don't try to immediately change your church's worship. It takes more support to change the worship than to achieve a narrowly defined prayer effort. After you've "converted" more of the leadership to new ways of praying, you'll find changes in the worship more easily accepted by the congregation.

3. **If possible, upgrade prayer activities or systems that are already in place.** For example, your church may have a prayer chain that is not working as well as it might. Use the suggestions in chapter 10 to improve its effectiveness and usefulness.

4. **Begin changes where they are most natural and where you expect the greatest receptivity.** Though you may be enthusiastic about innovative and creative ways to pray as a church, remember that every congregation is at a different stage in its prayer life. Some ideas will be more acceptable than others to the members of your church. This *Sourcebook* offers a wide range of ideas and methods; it won't be possible to implement all of them in your setting.

5. **Develop one idea at a time.** Don't overwhelm people with change, with new ideas, with new ways of doing things. (People tend to resist change. Introducing too many innovations will probably trigger negative reactions.) A couple of new opportunities for prayer each year may be enough. (It's also a more realistic approach, given the busyness of most people's schedules.)

6. **Work with other church committees to help infuse more prayer into their areas of responsibility.** For example, encourage your evangelism committee to make their prospect list a matter of focused, concentrated prayer with the help of small groups, prayer cells, prayer partners, and so on. Inform them of the possibilities of canvassing the community through prayer (see

chapter 30). Mention the idea of a school of prayer to your education committee and provide the committee with resources, organizational hints, and ideas for content (see chapter 4). When working with the mission-emphasis committee, you might suggest ways in which the congregation can pray for its missionaries (see chapters 7, 14, and 18).

The next step is to involve others in leadership roles and to coordinate their efforts. The prayer coordinator should appoint a team or person to direct each new prayer ministry developed in the church. For example, the church will need one person to prepare and distribute a monthly prayer guide, one person to set up the prayer triplet structure, one to organize (and possibly lead) a prayer workshop and/or a course on prayer, one to oversee the prayer cells within the congregation, and so on.

In addition to overseeing and coordinating the work of these leaders, the coordinator should bring them together for prayer as often as possible, encouraging them, offering support, and suggesting improvements or new ideas.

The coordinator should also develop an information network to keep everyone informed of prayer concerns, to receive prayer requests, to share ideas and resources, to encourage the "pray-ers," to pass on information about training, to remind people of prayer opportunities, and so on. This could be done through a biweekly newsletter, a weekly handout, or brief meetings at convenient times. The information network should be integrated into the other information systems of the church, such as the bulletin, newsletters, announcements, and handouts.

The prayer coordinator (or team) will work closely with the pastor and staff, who will pray for them, guide their vision, and plan with them. It's important that the prayer coordinator report to the council on the different steps the church has taken to nurture and deepen its commitment to prayer.

Finally, the prayer coordinator should encourage prayer involvement beyond the local church. This means informing church members of needs in the community, in the nation, and throughout the world. For this the coordinator will want to appoint someone to receive prayer requests from outside the church and communicate them to praying members. Organizing a concert of prayer that focuses on spiritual awakening and world evangelization is also an effective way of focusing the church's prayers outward (see chapter 21).

As you will see from this *Sourcebook*, the possibilities for prayer in your church are many. A prayer coordinator will be an invaluable asset to an already overworked pastor, to a council that's probably had its fill of meetings, and to the gifted intercessors in your church who wish to see more happen in the area of prayer.

You will probably also find that appointing a prayer coordinator makes the ministry of prayer in your church more visible and more intentional than it was before. Allow yourself and your church to take prayer as seriously as you take education, worship, outreach, and fellowship. The resulting outpouring of prayer will enrich all of your ministries with God's vision and power.

2
PRAYING LEADERS

A pastor began a new charge in a large, conservative church. He noted that prayer in the council meetings had become routine, almost mechanical. His predecessor had traditionally opened with Scripture reading and a short prayer and had asked an elder to close with prayer at the end. The rest of the meeting was "business as usual."

The new pastor noticed that the monthly elders' meeting had the same flavor. In fact, the elders' discussion of problems within the church family often took on a tone of gossip rather than pastoral care.

When the pastor considered how to bring his council into a more effective prayer life, he knew that change would have to be introduced gradually. He began with the opening-prayer time in council meetings. After the Scripture reading, he assigned each council member a specific concern to pray for: a hospitalized child, a man who had lost his job, a couple filing for divorce.

If the pastor needed more items, he moved to broader denominational concerns: missionaries supported by the church, prayer items from the various church agencies, and so on. Then, if requests were still needed, he included world concerns: earthquake victims, nations at war, and so on. After these requests, there was a time of silence in which council members could offer additional concerns or simply meditate. Then the pastor closed with a prayer.

As a result, the council prayer time stretched from five minutes to fifteen or twenty. Though at first reluctant, the council members soon came to appreciate and enjoy this time. One elder said to the pastor, "When this started, I was very uncomfortable with it. But as the year progressed, I grew to like it more and more. It really added to the whole tone of the meeting. I hope you do this with the next council as well."

The pastor found that the tone of the elders' meetings also changed when the elders began to stop and pray for each of the family concerns mentioned. The gossip lessened as they began to see the church's problems as part of a spiritual war in which they played a vital role—with prayer as their most effective weapon.

leadership is a spiritual task

Praying leaders see their leadership as primarily spiritual: helping others to grow more and more in the knowledge and love of God. For this they set aside regular times of prayer, individually and as a group. They live under the banner of the leaders of the early church who gave "attention to prayer and the ministry of the word" (Acts 6:4).

How vital is prayer to spiritual leadership? We need only look at the powerful role prayer played in the lives and ministries of Jesus and Paul to find the answer. Jesus taught his followers that prayer was his vital link with the Father. He often withdrew to solitary places to pray, often when he was struggling with great weariness or tough decisions. He taught his disciples to pray—through his parables, his example, and his teaching. He often reminded his followers that prayer was an essential gift from God; he assured them that God would certainly hear and answer prayers spoken in his name—that is, in line with God's will.

Paul's letters are interwoven with his prayers for the early church and with his pleas that church members pray for his ministry. He knew where the true power was, and he constantly urged the young churches to lay hold of God's power through prayer. The book of Acts records the marvelous—and often unexpected— answers that came in response to the apostles' prayers.

the value of praying leaders

Prayer is the primary way in which leaders accomplish their tasks. In prayer they admit that things happen on God's initiative, that the work is primarily his, not ours. Since this idea goes against our society's preference for independence and self-reliance, church leaders who are serious about prayer are a strong testimony that God's kingdom is not of this world. Their effectiveness depends on prayer.

A congregation will follow the example of its praying leaders. Leaders strongly committed to prayer will convey more to their congregation about the power and reality of prayer than sermons, articles, or special speakers will. Regular and devoted prayer is one very specific way to carry out the elders' and deacons' mandate to "set an example of godliness" for the congregation.

Your leaders' prayers are also a ministry of caring that communicates love and concern to the people they shepherd. What can be more affirming than to hear, "I think of you regularly in my prayers. What can I pray about for you?" People respond warmly to this concern.

Praying leaders see their leadership as primarily spiritual: helping others to grow more and more in the knowledge and love of God.

A high priority on prayer also benefits the church leadership itself. It gives leaders the opportunity to bear each other's burdens and to find encouragement and support in the struggles of leadership. The pastor needs to hear the council members praying for him; and they need to hear his prayers for them.

Commitment to pray for each other brings protection from Satan's attack. In a vital, growing church, the leaders are often the devil's first target. Prayer will keep your leaders aware of the reality of spiritual warfare. It reminds them of who protects them and against whom they are fighting. Prayer is the most powerful weapon God has given us against the evil one.

Will an emphasis on prayer make for longer council meetings? Not necessarily. Some councils are committed to spending one-third of their meeting time in prayer. They have found that an hour of prayer at the beginning of the meeting actually shortens the overall meeting time—by bringing a greater spirit of unity, by emphasizing spiritual priorities, and by opening people's hearts to the Spirit's guidance.

practical ideas

Faced with these examples and the compelling blessings that God has promised in response to believing prayer, how can the leaders of the church not make prayer a vital part of their ministry? Below are some ways to bring the freshness and power of prayer to your church's life—through praying leaders.

Obviously you can't change your leaders' prayer habits and patterns immediately. Your enthusiasm for prayer power in church ministry may put off some who are not used to change. Be prepared to move slowly at first.

A good place to start may be with the prayer time in the church council or the elders' meeting. There are many ways to help the church council get out of the routine and into the power of prayer. Schedule a definite time slot during your council meetings—longer than simply the perfunctory opening or closing prayer time. Encourage council members to pray about the church's concerns—financial, ministry, family, or whatever—as they are brought up in the meeting. Ask council members to bring their family or personal requests in prayer—and keep track of the answers God gives.

An hour of prayer at the beginning of the meeting actually shortens the overall meeting time—by bringing a greater spirit of unity, by emphasizing spiritual priorities, and by opening people's hearts to the Spirit's guidance.

If your council members are not used to praying for each other, you might try the following idea as described by the woman who introduced it to her church council:

I had served as a deacon on our church's council for a number of years, and before my term was up, I told the council I wanted to leave them with a gift. Before the council meeting got under way, I placed members into groups of three. I asked them to share with each other what was the hardest thing about being an elder or deacon. After the sharing, they were to pray for each other, based on what they had talked about. At the end of the prayer time, people were crying, holding hands, hugging each other.

At the next meeting, I asked everyone to divide again into the same groups of three. This time the sharing question was "When did the word 'God' first have meaning for you?" After that, they prayed for each other in small groups again.

At the third meeting, the sharing question was "What comes between you and the Lord?" After the time of sharing and prayer, one of the most conservative members of the council came up to me and said, "Ann, that was wonderful!"

During our last meeting, it was obvious from the conversations that council members had been praying for each other during the weeks between meetings. I asked the groups of three to use a list of descriptive words to express how they felt about each other. They spent about forty-five minutes on this exercise—and the meeting still ended on time!

Another way to encourage more prayer among your church leaders is to schedule a weekend retreat on prayer and leadership for all church leaders. Invite not only your council members but also the leaders in your ministries of music, church education (including all teachers), neighborhood Bible studies, outreach ministries, worship planning, and so on. Plan to take at least one full day to focus on the subject of prayer and leadership.

You may want to ask participants to read Bill Hybels's book *Too Busy Not to Pray*, or R. C. Sproul's book *Effective Prayer*. Set aside time to discuss what you've learned from your reading. Pray together about what the Spirit may be urging you to do as a result of your reading and discussion.

Perhaps the most important thing you can do is help your council members see their God-given role as the church's spiritual leaders. Most council meetings are so bogged down with business details that members easily lose sight of the larger spiritual ministry of the church—of which prayer is a vital part. Elders and deacons alike are called to be people of prayer. Note that the early church leaders took steps to cut down the administrative load in order to pray (Acts 6:4)!

Prayer and spiritual renewal go hand in hand. And this begins with the congregation's leaders. A vital prayer life in your church leadership is one of the most important indications of your congregation's spiritual health.

3

PRAYER IN THE WORSHIP SERVICE

Prayer and worship belong together. From the beginning call to worship to the benediction, prayer is a vital part of the dialogue between God and his people in worship.

Prayer is the most direct way to acknowledge that God is present in worship. We speak directly to God and listen for his voice in response. It heightens our awareness that he is there, ready to act in our lives. Psalms and hymns are also forms of prayer as we sing praise to the glory of God.

Prayer in worship builds deeper community by allowing individuals to express their needs in the midst of community. When the gathered group hears of one member's pain or need, the others are touched and turn toward that person with compassion, help, and prayer. Sharing God's answers to prayer in the service encourages everyone with evidence that God is working powerfully among them.

Below are nine ways to make prayer a more vital part of your worship service. Some of them will fit your situation; others may need to be adapted for use by your congregation.

ways to pray

1. **Plan a brief, fifteen- to thirty-minute prayer meeting before the worship service.** The group at this meeting will ask specifically for the Spirit's presence and work in the pastor's message and leadership and among the people as they worship, serve, fellowship, and welcome guests.

The group may include elders, but others should also be encouraged to participate—especially those with the gift of intercession. Perhaps you would find it helpful to set up a rotation of members (inviting ten different families each month, or having individuals sign up for every third or fourth week). This prevents participants from feeling as though they must be present every Sunday—a big commitment for most church members.

2. **Divide the common elements of prayer (adoration, confession, thanksgiving, supplication, surrender) into smaller segments, spread throughout the service.** Many churches do this with separate prayers for confession and supplication. Consider also having a separate prayer time for adoration, during which the leader or members of the congregation offer their own prayers of praise or passages from Scripture. You may even encourage people to offer familiar songs of praise during this time. This time of praise and adoration can

become one of the most meaningful parts of the worship service.

The prayer of thanksgiving can also stand alone. It can be offered in response to a time in which people share answers to prayer, or it can be the pastor's creation. The prayer of dedication could come after the sermon, allowing people to respond in obedience to the Word of God just spoken.

Not only will this approach make people more aware of the different elements of prayer, but it will also help them connect prayer to the liturgical flow of the worship service, from the call to worship to the benediction. Also, people are more likely to sustain their concentration throughout shorter, separate periods of prayer. Rare is the person who doesn't find his or her mind wandering during the long, catch-all congregational prayer!

3. **Share members' joys, concerns, and answers to prayer just prior to congregational prayer.** The content of the congregational prayer should relate to the items people have shared. Some churches make this sharing a regular part of their morning or evening service; others schedule it once or twice a month.

The sharing time does not have to be verbal; members can record their requests and answers to prayer on cards and hand them to the person leading the congregational prayer. This approach may be most practical in a large church. However, having people stand and speak about their concerns and joys is another way members can become actively involved in the service; it also encourages a closer sense of community and intimacy. Whatever approach you use, be sure to emphasize answers to prayer

as well as requests. Nothing is more encouraging than hearing how God has responded to prayer.

This sharing time prior to prayer helps guarantee that the congregational prayer will relate to specific congregational needs rather than focusing on broad generalities. And if members share their requests personally, the congregation hears the concern from the primary source, not indirectly through the pastor.

Perhaps the greatest benefit of this sharing time is the element of spontaneity and intimacy that it brings to the worship service. The sharing time allows us to see directly into people's lives and to bring their needs immediately to God, rather than remaining insulated from the feelings and thoughts of those worshiping around us. Those who bring a great burden of grief or guilt can lay it at the altar of prayer and then freely join in worship. Worship will begin to touch members at a personal, emotional, and experiential level rather than remaining primarily intellectual.

4. **Ask different people to participate in leading prayer.** The deacons can give the offertory prayer, the elders can pray for the pastor and for the church's needs, the leaders of various ministries can lead in prayer for their ministry, and so on. A caution here: the pastor may want to oversee the writing and the preparation of such prayers initially,

> **Prayer is the most direct way to acknowledge that God is present in worship. We speak directly to God and listen for his voice in response.**

especially if members are not used to praying aloud in the service. Encourage careful preparation on the part of those who participate.

Using designated people to offer prayers during the service will bring fresh new prayers and new insights. This practice also gives more visibility and credibility to those who are in leadership. Hearing the elders lead in prayer for specific congregational concerns, for example, enables church members to see them more clearly as spiritual leaders alongside the pastor.

A helpful resource is the pamphlet *So You've Been Asked To . . . Lead in Prayer* (CRC Publications, 1996). Call 1-800-333-8300 for more information.

5. **Encourage members' spontaneous participation in prayer.** As mentioned above, this could include a time of praise and worship as well as prayers of confession, thanksgiving, or petition. Some prayers of confession, for example, can be introduced by a leader who names a specific area of prayer ("We ask forgiveness now for our personal sins . . . for the sins of our city and nation . . . for the sins of the world") and asks members to offer short spontaneous prayers appropriate to each topic. This approach works best with small churches, but it's not impossible in a large church. Just be sure that those who pray can be clearly heard.

Spontaneous participation in prayer gives members a chance to pray about things that are important to them. It allows members to see and hear each other worshiping, praising, and submitting to God in prayer. As a result, such prayer is a bond that will create and sustain a vital sense of community in your church. This kind of prayer is patterned after the worship style of the early church, to which Paul wrote, "When you come together, everyone has a hymn, or a word of instruction, a revelation, a tongue or an interpreta-

tion. All of these must be done for the strengthening of the church" (1 Corinthians 14:26). Allow your prayer times to strengthen your life together.

6. **Regularly encourage all members to pray silently and intensely while the pastor is preaching.** Their prayers are to focus on the pastor, on all those hearing the Word preached, and especially on guests and the unsaved who may be present. Such support can be electrifying to the pastor:

> *In nearly all congregations where we plead for every listener to pray hard, we feel a strange, strong, delightful response from all parts of the room. Always, when congregations pray with great earnestness and unanimity, we feel lifted almost as though an invisible arm held us up; our hearts burn, tears lie close, and ideas come fresh and far better than any written address. Commonplace truth becomes incandescent and burns like liquid metal. A congregation is three-fourths of a sermon! Pastors around the world in ever-increasing numbers are testifying that their preaching has been transformed by asking people to lean forward and pray.*
>
> —Frank Laubach, *Prayer: The Mightiest Force in the World*, p. 45

Not only is the pastor supported and freed to minister in the Spirit's power, but the whole congregation also is more open to the Spirit's work through the Word. Such prayer keeps members finely tuned to the spiritual reality that takes place in worship and through the preaching of the Word. It releases the Spirit's power to work in response to the Word, and it heightens members' awareness of the needs and presence of guests.

Remember, however, that a one-time request for such prayer is not going to do the job. If people are to develop this prayer habit, they will need to be reminded frequently—if not weekly—to do so. Don't depend on one or two bulletin announcements.

7. **Ask everyone present to pray aloud at the same time, focusing on a specific request or area of prayer (adoration, thanksgiving, and so on).** This idea may sound a bit odd at first, but many churches have found it to be a powerful and moving part of their prayer life. Rev. Paul Cho, pastor of the world's largest church—Yoido Full Gospel Central Church of Seoul, Korea—writes,

> One of the most important ministries of the Full Gospel Central Church is the prayer in unison we have during every service. We always open our services with everyone present praying together at the same time. We may pray for the salvation and protection of our nation. . . . We also pray for our leaders together. . . . We pray in unison for the thousands of requests that come to us from America, Japan, and the rest of the world. . . .
>
> When we pray together, we pray with determination and assurance. When I hear my people praying, it sounds like the forceful roar of a mighty waterfall. We know God must hear the sincerity of our prayer because we are praying in unison and unity!
>
> —*Prayer: Key to Revival*, pp. 101-102

After initial feelings of discomfort with this kind of praying, your congregation may find it to be an invaluable and uplifting experience. Hearing others pray aloud around us encourages our own participation in prayer; the reality and power of communal prayer sinks in as we hear our voices joining with others in petition, adoration, and thanksgiving. There is a dynamic here that is entirely missing from our usual ways of praying together. Everyone is focused at once; everyone participates in verbal prayers, which hold their attention more easily than mental prayers.

If members worry about the distraction caused by the multitude of voices, remind them that God doesn't find it disconcerting in the least. Hearing many prayers at one time has never seemed to be a problem for God.

8. **Make a prayer altar call a regular part of your service.** Invite people to come forward for prayer—whatever their needs. Though some may need to meet Christ and experience his salvation, many of your members may also need prayer for personal crises,

Using designated people to offer prayers during the service will bring fresh new prayers and new insights.

bad habits, friends or family members in trouble, guidance in difficult decisions, or physical or emotional healing. As you encourage people to come forward, stress the power of prayer in such situations. Whether you do this during the service or at the end, be sure to have a team of people ready to pray for the needs of those who come.

Some churches set aside a prayer room for this purpose. Christ Community Christian Reformed Church in Nanaimo, British Columbia, is one. When Christ Community was planning its new building, it designed a "power room" right off of the sanctuary. The pastor lets people know the room is available for their use. During the congregational prayer in the worship service, the pastor reminds people that the prayer room is available for those whose requests are too personal to share in public. At the end of the sermon, he offers a brief prayer of invitation and again reminds people that they can use the prayer room to make their commitment to God. People challenged by the sermon are also invited to "pray through" the challenge after the service.

> **"When I hear my people praying, it sounds like the forceful roar of a mighty waterfall."**

Teams of two are always available at these times to pray with those who wish it. Composed of volunteers from the church, these teams work with a set of guidelines that help them understand their role as "pray-ers." Guidelines include such commonsense advice as referring troubled people to a trained counselor, getting a clear statement of the person's need, praying for a short period of time, following up after prayer, and so on.

Who uses this room? Community people as well as church members. Christ Community has drawn many unchurched guests from the town of Nanaimo, making the prayer room an important part of community outreach. "Unchurched people expect the church to pray for them," says the pastor. "They are often much more open than traditional Christians are to the church's prayer. This is a ministry that touches a felt need among the unchurched."

If you do not have space for a separate prayer room, you can set aside a quiet corner of the sanctuary for prayer. The council room or the minister's study can also double as a prayer room. If you call people forward for prayer as part of the worship service, you will probably use the space available at the front or back of the sanctuary.

To the congregation that believes in the place and power of prayer, the prayer altar call can become an essential part of the worship service. It offers those with special needs the opportunity to be prayed for; it allows those who are gifted in prayer to use their gift; and it involves the church in an intense, personal ministry to its members and community. When you see the Lord respond in answer to this prayer ministry, your worship will deepen in its awareness of a God who is present and who hears his people when they pray.

9. **Ask the congregation to respond in prayer immediately following the sermon.** This combines the teaching of the Word with prayer, bringing the spoken message to the hearts of those who have listened.

You might do this by asking people to pray for five to ten minutes in small groups, responding to the sermon in three different ways:

- **adoration**—praising God for all they have learned about him through the sermon

- **awakening**—asking God to make the church more alive in response to the Word that was preached, so that they may know the fullness of Christ's life in them

- **advancing**—praying for the local and worldwide implications of the message they've heard, especially as it relates to the mission of Christ

If the congregation is small enough, you may simply want to open this time of prayer to anyone who wishes to pray. Or, if the congregation isn't comfortable praying aloud, allow for a time of silent prayer and reflection, using the specific guidelines above.

4
THE SCHOOL OF PRAYER

School implies learning, and a school of prayer means just that—a group of people gathered for solid teaching on prayer. Along with the teaching, a school of prayer will give people the opportunity to practice what they've learned. They'll go beyond simply taking in information; they will practice the principles of prayer as a group and experience God's answers together.

what form could a school of prayer take?

A school of prayer adapts easily to many structures. Before you settle on a particular format, look at what your church is doing now. Are there existing classes or structures to which you can add a course of teaching on prayer? Where does such teaching already take place?

You can bring a school of prayer to your church's life in a wide variety of ways. The most obvious, perhaps, is a standard **six- or eight-week course for adults.** The group can use a textbook that provides material for reflection, discussion questions, and practical exercises. Or the leader may want to gather his or her own materials or distill teaching from a good seminar on prayer.

A **weekend retreat** is ideal for a concentrated look at prayer. It's an excellent setting for motivating, challenging, and inspiring people—away from the pressures and distractions of everyday life. If members wish to, they can continue their journeys into prayer as a group in the following weeks and months.

Cell groups (home fellowship groups, small group Bible studies, discipleship groups, and so on) are natural structures for weekly or bimonthly studies on prayer. Such groups often feel comfortable enough to pray together and share personal needs, and they can easily set aside six to eight meetings for a study on prayer. In cell groups there will probably be no leader giving a presentation; rather, the study material will provide all the teaching information necessary. The group will discuss and work through the study guide together. If your church has a number of cell groups, encourage them to work on a study of prayer simultaneously.

You can also integrate a school of prayer into a **pastor's class or new members' class.** Devoting one or two sessions to teaching on prayer (as well as making prayer a significant part of the class time together) is invaluable for deepening spirituality and developing fellowship in the members you want to assimilate into the church's life.

Another form the school of prayer can take is a **preaching series** that focuses on prayer. Such a series should include specific exercises that members can do during the week—exercises on listening to God, on praise, on confession, and so on. If possible, be sure to leave time in your church service for personal sharing on what's happened as a result of this teaching and the exercises.

Another way to involve church members in a school or prayer is to incorporate it into your church's **discipling relationships.** If your congregation has adopted a discipling system in which mature believers meet regularly with new Christians or people who are younger in the faith, by all means encourage them to use some of the school of prayer materials listed in the Resources section of this chapter.

Other options: Set up a midweek course for adults; ask the men's or women's society to devote a series of meetings to teaching and practicing prayer; involve your youth group in a good study of prayer, aimed at the needs and questions of teenagers. Remember: It's important to have good resources available for such studies.

what will a school of prayer do for your church?

Presenting members with a concentrated, deliberate study of prayer will accomplish many goals. First, it will give people a chance to evaluate their prayer lives. Are they frustrated with the lack of discipline in their prayer life? Are they confused about what they can ask in prayer? Do traditional forms of prayer not work for them? Do their prayers seem to bounce off the ceiling?

A school of prayer will help people deal with these questions. It will give members a chance to analyze their own problems with prayer. Solid teaching enables them to rethink the purpose and theology of prayer. And praying with other group members allows them to experience in prayer a power and encouragement they perhaps had not known. For some people, the school of prayer will ignite their prayer lives.

A school of prayer can acquaint your members with the basic disciplines of prayer: journaling, personal retreats, meditation, using the Bible in prayer, listening to God, and so on. Members will be able to encourage each other in daily discipline as they talk about their own weaknesses, share disciplines that work for them, and pray for each other's growth in prayer.

School **implies learning, and a school of prayer means just that—a group of people gathered for solid teaching on prayer.**

A concentrated group study on prayer can nurture church fellowship as well. Your people will discover the excitement of learning from each other. Members will come to see that they aren't alone in their problems and guilt, that others struggle with the same issues and can offer help.

The school of prayer can have a "ripple effect" in your congregation's spirituality, spreading out to all members. How? By teaching parents and church leaders how to pray more effectively. Parents will in turn pass this on to their children in family devotions; elders and deacons will model a deeper, more fervent prayer life to the congregation. The power of example speaks louder than a dozen books or lectures.

Finally, a school of prayer can have a profound impact on your church's spiritual life. Prayer is central to any believer's relationship with God. If a class on prayer can break people free of their feeling stuck when they're in prayer, it will bring new vitality and power to their entire spiritual lives—and to the life of your church.

organization

A school of prayer need not consume large amounts of energy and time. You probably have all that it takes already! As mentioned above, look at where you can plug a school of prayer into existing structures—home cell groups, youth groups, retreats, young couples groups, and so on. Use your imagination to find ways to fit solid teaching on prayer into your church's life. You probably already have good teachers and willing students; all you may need are good materials.

Keep your training times and methods varied. If you limit the school of prayer to one time slot and one format, you'll reach only one slice of the congregation. People's lifestyles fall into different patterns. Some will not be able to attend a retreat or day-long workshop; others are too busy with work and family to consider a weekly evening session that lasts six to eight weeks. But you can catch most of them by offering a variety of formats and times—and by constantly reinforcing the importance of prayer for everyone.

If you limit the school of prayer to one time slot and one format, you'll reach only one slice of the congregation.

resources

Your pastor may already have gathered enough material on the subject of prayer to teach the class. In some cases this may be ideal, since the course can be tailored to the church's needs in the area of prayer ministry.

However, several excellent courses on prayer are available:

- *Space for God: Study and Practice of Spirituality and Prayer* by Don Postema (CRC Publications, 1983, 1997) will guide group members to a greater awareness of God in their lives. Postema uses devotional readings from a wide selection of writers to stimulate faith, discussion, and prayer. The book also leads participants through a schedule of exercises that involve them in prayer and reflection each day. Call 1-800-333-8300 for more information.

- *The Living Workbook of Prayer* by Maxie Dunnam (The Upper Room, 1974) provides daily meditations and exercises for six weeks of adventure in prayer. Designed to be shared and discussed with a small group of believers, the course emphasizes the importance of finding creative, practical ways to make prayer a living part of one's life. (Four optional lessons are included at the end of the study.)

- *Discover Prayer* (Church Development Resources, 1986)—designed for the Coffee Break Bible study program, this eight-lesson study looks at a variety of Bible passages on prayer and helps participants ask questions and seek answers directly from the passages studied. Guides for leaders and participants are available. Call 1-800-333-8300 for more information.

- *More Than Words* by Leonard J. Vander Zee (CRC Publications, 1996) is a course that focuses on praying rather than prayer, including Bible studies and practical exercises. The six sessions encourage participants to try various forms of prayer to enrich their own prayer lives. (This course for adults is a revision of the youth course *Can I Call After Midnight?*) Call 1-800-333-8300 for more information.

leadership training

Who in your church has a healthy, disciplined prayer life? Look to these prayer warriors for leadership in the school of prayer. The person who leads these sessions must be able to teach from his or her own experience. This qualification is perhaps the most crucial. The power of example and personal testimony is far more effective than the ability to speak well in public.

You might automatically look to your pastor or to an elder or deacon for such leadership. However, don't overlook the church member who may not be active in other ministries but whose life is a vivid example of the power of prayer.

Consider a team leadership approach as well. If one person finds the work of preparing a retreat or series of classes overwhelming, look for one or two others to work with that person as a team. Combining efforts and sharing leadership make the load manageable. In addition, team leadership provides mutual support for each leader and allows each one to do what he or she is best at—teaching, organizing, leading the discussion, and so on.

do's and don'ts for the school of prayer

Do give plenty of opportunity in class for prayer; give assignments in the practice of prayer.

Do offer a variety of times and formats.

Do include some kind of "prayer schooling" every year for your congregation.

Do encourage positive growth in prayer and honest sharing of struggle and weakness.

Do encourage individuality in prayer, and help people to avoid styles of prayer that don't work for them.

Do repeat courses to get other church members involved.

Do encourage reading on prayer for those who don't attend the courses.

Do use stories of how God has answered prayer, and invite people to tell their own stories.

Do give lots of opportunity for feedback and discussion.

Don't teach only content.

Don't put the school of prayer into only one time slot and format.

Don't view the school of prayer as a one-time experience.

Don't put a guilt trip on participants.

Don't enforce one style of prayer.

5

TEACHING CHILDREN TO PRAY

Jesus,

I feel very near to you.

I feel like you are beside me all the time.

Please be with me on Thursday. I am running in a three-mile race then. I will need all the speed in the world. If you are not busy with other things, maybe you could be at the starting line, the finish line, and everywhere in between.

Frankie (age 11)

Dear God,

I love you. I just want to let you know ahead of time that I'd like to be there with you in heaven.

Love always,

Sarah (age 8)

Dear God,

What do you do with families that don't have much faith?

There's a family on the next block like that. I don't want to get them in trouble. I don't want to say who.

See you in church,

Alexis (age 9)

—From *Dear God* by David Heller (Doubleday, 1987)

We may smile at these prayers, but we will probably also be touched by their simplicity, trust, and direct honesty, for these are the qualities that children bring to prayer, along with a depth of intimacy with God that may surprise many adults.

Children have an intuitive awareness of God, and they are quick to respond to God with trust, awe, and love. Their prayer lives are genuine. The seeds of faith sprout and bear fruit in young children. Churches and families need to nurture, not stunt, children's capacity for prayer. This chapter will look at how children pray and at how we can nourish and encourage their budding awareness of a God who hears and answers their prayers.

about children

Perhaps the first thing adults need to be reminded of is the importance that God has bestowed on children. They are models of the kingdom. Three of the gospel writers record an incident that tells us much about how God values young children:

At that time the disciples came to Jesus and asked, "Who is the greatest in the kingdom of heaven?"

He called a little child and had him stand among them. And he said: "I tell you the truth, unless you change and become like little children, you will never enter the kingdom of heaven. Therefore, whoever humbles himself like this child is the greatest in the kingdom of heaven.

"And whoever welcomes a little child like this in my name welcomes me." . . .

"See that you do not look down on one of these little ones. For I tell you that their angels in heaven always see the face of my Father in heaven."
—Matthew 18:1-5, 10

When his disciples tried to prevent parents from bringing their children to Jesus, he reprimanded them indignantly: "Let the little children come to me, and do not hinder them, for the kingdom of heaven belongs to such as these" (Matthew 19:14).

Jesus made clear that children are very important to God. God has given them a central place in his kingdom and in his heart. They serve as role models for adults, reminding us of the simplicity and honesty with which God asks us to enter his kingdom.

So as we think of ways to improve the prayer life of our churches and families, let's not forget children. Why? First, children's prayers are "real" prayers—not just practice or learning for later. When children pray aloud, adults must not assume the role of monitor, supervisor, or instructor. They must realize that the child is leading everyone present in prayer.

Adults should both listen to and pray with the children, as they would with any other adult. As one adult writes from her own experience with children, "Expect that God will inspire you and guide you in learning to pray with them, and that their prayers will have great

power and will be answered in many ways."

Adults should also ask children to pray for them, not just expect that children should bring their needs to the adults for prayer. Asking children to pray for adults' needs is often best introduced in the context of family prayers, where most family members are used to praying aloud.

Children are also able to pray uncluttered prayers, with freedom of emotional response to God's presence. Their joy is so vivid, their compassion so empathetic, their hope so ardent, their anxious questions so full of honest fear, that they model for us the personal expression of real prayer.

When adults attempt to teach children to pray, therefore, they should not ask the children to repeat stilted prayers, full of clichés and spoken in solemn tones. Rather, they should encourage the children to keep doing what they do naturally: retain a simple, conversational approach to prayer.

guidelines to remember

Help children understand that prayer is a process of developing a deep love relationship with God. Like other person-to-person relationships, prayer grows and is nurtured with time and practice. Our relationship to God thrives on praise, thanks, confession, and asking—elements of any good relationship. Prayer is an expression of our yearning for an intimate friendship with God.

Encourage children to use prayer as a way to experience the love of their kind and forgiving Father. The home is often

Children have an intuitive awareness of God, and they are quick to respond to God with trust, awe, and love. Their prayer lives are genuine. The seeds of faith sprout and bear fruit in young children.

the primary place where children learn to pray in this way. That's why the child's relationship to his or her own parents is such a vital one. Here they learn the meaning of dependence, trust, and unconditional love—all essential to prayer.

As you work with young children, **relate to God in an unaffected way.** Many adults have slipped into habits of artificial language and formal, pietistic expressions. Learn again to use normal vocabularies and tones of voice during prayer. Encourage brief, one-sentence prayers. Be simple and straightforward with God.

> **Children need to feel confident that their prayers will not be laughed at.**

Learn to listen to God, to wait in silence for God to speak to you. Help your children to become comfortable with silence in prayer. Teach them to listen to the still, small voice within them. Use brief periods of silence to help them become centered and quiet as they meet God. Encourage them to talk about the things they have learned from the prompting of God's Spirit.

Teach children the value of praying together, and help them to find their voices. Start with short sentence prayers ("popcorn prayers"), in which children can offer their own thoughts and concerns on a certain topic (praise for God's greatness, healing for someone who's sick, requests for their family members, thanks for things they enjoy in nature, and so on). Whether in the classroom, the congregation, or the family, work to foster an atmosphere of trust and acceptance in group prayer. Children need to feel confident that their prayers will not be laughed at by others.

Many children and adults have a rich inner spiritual life, and praying with others is a way to articulate that inner life, to share with others the thoughts and insights that God has given us as individ-uals. We do well to include children in this sharing and to listen respectfully to their prayers. "From the lips of children and infants you have ordained praise," the psalmist observes in Psalm 8:2. God often chooses children to reveal wisdom that adults have overlooked.

As children experience acceptance from God and from each other, they will pray more freely for others in the group, becoming attuned to each other's joys and struggles. They will learn honest sharing with God and with each other. Such prayer teaches them the meaning of Christian community.

Encourage children to talk to God about everything on their hearts. Their successes, failures, fears, experiences with rejection, plans for summer vacation, anticipation of good things coming up—these are the stuff of which prayer is made. Help them to know that prayer is not just a way to ask for things that they need. It's a way to help us live closer to God in good times and bad. Prayer helps us face the darkness in our lives as well as the light, our woundedness as well as our healing. It is not an escape from life; it is the way we touch life itself. (You may find the children teaching you in this area, rather than vice versa!)

Remember that children learn by doing. Yes, children do learn some things from our words, but they learn far more from our actions and attitudes. We may tell them that God hears and welcomes their prayers, but what do they learn when all that we ask of them during group prayer is to sit still and not bother the adults? Unfortunately, we often teach children plainly by our attitudes and practice that "real" prayer is something reserved for grown-ups.

It is true that children learn in part by observing adults, but children learn primarily by doing—by seeing, touching, tasting, feeling, hearing. It's important to give them the experience of prayer. For example, gather together in a darkened room with one lit candle. The candle is passed from person to person. The person holding the candle may say a prayer or simply hold the candle in silence and then give it to another person. The rest of the group listens in stillness, participating in each spoken prayer or listening reverently to the silence of the one holding the candle.

This kind of experience (using light/dark imagery in prayer) also taps into the child's rich capacity for imagery and symbolism. The images of light, water, seeds, harvest, rocks, thorns, bread, wine, leaven, salt, colors, fruit, leaves, roots, soil, shepherds, and sheep also help us understand inner spiritual realities. Though children don't have the adult's capacity to make all the logical, rational connections, their imaginations take flight with these images and symbols. They find such spiritual symbols very satisfying, especially in the realm of prayer. It gives them a language with which to express the mystery of life in God.

Children also learn by observing. Adult models are very important. Children should hear adults praying for them. They will catch an adult's enthusiasm for prayer and will be keen observers of the priority that adults give to prayer. Adults should share their own spiritual discoveries in prayer with children. Parents or teachers might keep daily records of their prayers, along with the children, to discuss the insights they've gained and the experiences they've had with God through prayer. Children will see prayer as one of the most vital activities of their lives if the adults around them communicate their own enthusiasm and encouragement.

Adults can help children develop good prayer habits. Some of these are the simple basics: closing eyes, folding hands, kneeling, lifting hands, and so on. Though the importance of these physical actions has been questioned, they are use-

ful in teaching children the meaning of prayer. By closing our eyes, for example, we offer God our complete attention, undistracted by anything that might catch our attention visually. Folding hands not only keeps little hands out of mischief but also communicates for adults as well that we come to God unable to accomplish these things on our own. Our folded hands are a sign of our dependence on God's power and our waiting for his timing. Kneeling is a symbol of humility and adoration; lifted hands have communicated praise and thanksgiving down through the centuries. (But emphasize that God hears us pray any time and anywhere, regardless of whether our hands are folded or our eyes closed.)

Other good prayer habits are internal. The most important, perhaps, is that of learning to give our undivided attention to the person who is praying aloud. We can teach our children not only to listen but also to actively pray along with that other person.

> **Folding hands not only keeps little hands out of mischief but also communicates for adults as well that we come to God unable to accomplish these things on our own. Our folded hands are a sign of our dependence on God's power and our waiting for his timing.**

times, places, and ways to include children

Worship services are one of the most important settings in which we can nurture the child's capacity for prayer. In encouraging children to participate, however, we must remember one thing: the goal of worship is not a flawless pageant, impressively performed. If this is our goal, children have no place in worship. They can be unpredictable and disruptive. But if our goal in worship is to praise, glorify, and adore our God, children will occupy a strategic place. The whole family of God gathers to bring a gift or song or prayer to share in worship.

How might we put this theory into practice? Here are just a few suggestions from *A Family Affair: Worshiping God with Our Children* (CRC Publications, 1990, 1994).

- After the children have learned the meaning of the time of confession and assurance of pardon, you might occasionally ask them (along with the rest of the congregation) to keep a list during the coming week of things they've done or said that may have displeased God or hurt other people. (Parents can help nonreaders with their lists.) Ask members to bring their unsigned lists as a letter of confession to the service the following Sunday. After a brief prayer of confession, allow a time of silence in which young and old can remember the specific sins they wrote down and silently ask God for forgiveness. Then collect the papers and put them in a trash bag as a visible reminder that believers can throw their "lists" away after they confess their sin. This exercise helps children become more aware of things that may stand between us and God in worship. It also serves as a concrete lesson to all of us that God doesn't remember our sins after confession, and neither should we. After confession, we are free to worship!

Prayer is not only something we do for our children but also something we do with our children. We have much to offer the younger members of Christ's body, and they have much to offer us.

- Ask children during the church education time to think of things that people might do or say that hurt their friendship with God and with other people. Write down their suggestions and use them in the time of confession during the service: "Forgive us, God, when we . . ." This will help make the prayer of confession more accessible and personal to the children.

- If your congregation is small enough, you may regularly ask for prayer requests before the congregational prayer. Encourage parents to be aware of needs their children may want addressed (sick friends, problems at school, exam time) so that if the children are too shy to make the requests, the parents can do so. Or collect lists of concerns from the church education classes and include these in the congregational prayer. If the prayer time is opened up to the congregation, encourage children to offer prayers also.

Church school and other types of classes are settings in which prayer can be made an integral part of every session. Regularly give the children opportunity to share their joys and concerns. Encourage them to use all the elements of prayer (adoration, confession, thanksgiving, supplication, submission), not only requests (supplication). Encourage them also to pray as a group, offering sentence prayers in response to prayer needs shared within the group. Set an example of making the prayer needs personal rather than always on behalf of others. If your lesson focuses on a certain attribute of God or on a symbol of the Christian faith, occasionally give the children the opportunity to think quietly about that and to respond by writing a short prayer or psalm of praise that you can use at the end of your session or in a future worship service with the entire congregation.

Churches should also encourage their families to pray regularly together. Here are a few examples:

- Pray informally as a family at mealtime, holding hands as you do so. Ask one child to open or close the meal with prayer. Or perhaps your children would like to offer sentence prayers. You may want to combine your prayer time with sharing about the day's activities, talking about the most important things that happened in each individual's day. Then, when you're done, thank God together for the good things that happened and ask him for help with the problems mentioned.

- Regularly include a time of praise, perhaps by reading a psalm together as a "warm-up" to your own sentence prayers. You might choose to write your own psalms of praise as a family, with each person contributing lines or phrases that express who God is to him or her. Use these written prayers at special occasions.

- Light a candle during your family devotions to signify God's presence with you. Talk about the symbolism of light and darkness, and include these images in your prayers.

- Making a prayer list is a helpful way to give everyone something to pray about. If your children are too young to read, draw pictures that will remind them of various prayer needs. For older children, you may want to keep a basket on the table to collect any written prayer needs that family members might drop in. At Christmastime, save the cards you receive and make them a part of your prayers, praying for several families each night.

- Set up a private, quiet area in your home for individual prayer. Though you may not have an empty room to spare, any small space will do (a corner of the guest room or part of the dining room, for example). Set up a folding screen, if necessary, and include a comfortable chair, a Bible and notepad, a prayer list, a globe or map, a candle, and other symbols that speak to you of God's presence and of prayer. Though your children may not use it regularly, they will see your example of prayer and know that it has a priority in your home.

Churches can also provide resources for family devotions—prayer guides, mealtime devotional booklets, and books of family prayers. Books like Robert Webber's *The Book of Family Prayer* or *Family Worship Through the Year* by Kristen Johnson Ingram are valuable additions to any church or family library.

Prayer is not only something we do for our children but also something we do with our children. We have much to offer the younger members of Christ's body, and they have much to offer us. In prayer, we all join as children of the heavenly Father.

6

FAMILY PRAYER

Dear God,

I read that home is where God (that's you) is.

What does that mean, I wonder?

Does it mean if I am at religious school I am not away from home?

Do I have to be in our living room to be with you?

Are you everywhere?

I am not sure. I just know that you are in my heart.

David (age 12)

Dear God,

Thank you for my parents, my sister Anita, and for my grandma and grandpa. They are all real warm and special. I forgive you for my brother Phil.

I guess you didn't finish working on him.

Sean (age 12)

—from *Dear God*
by David Heller
(Doubleday, 1987)

Children pray to God in their own language—very honest, very direct, and sometimes (to adults) very humorous. Family prayers are one area in which parents can nurture the child's growing awareness of God's presence and budding sense of communication with God. During family devotions, children can learn to speak to God by listening to their parents pray. They often say their first prayers to God around the family dinner table.

The phrase "family prayer" brings to mind the picture of family members gathered for a meal, taking time to read the Bible and to ask God's blessing on the food and on the day's activities. Though family prayer is not limited to mealtime devotions, this scene conveys the warmth and togetherness that mark the family's time for prayer.

Family prayers are a time for real worship to happen in the context of the family. For that reason they include not only parents but also children. Sometimes the prayers are limited to a blessing before the meal; other times they include an opening blessing and a closing devotional time—a time to share joys and concerns and to read a Bible passage together. The closing prayer reflects not only the concerns mentioned but also the application of the passage that was read.

Frequently the opening prayer looks back on the day and ahead to the meal; the closing prayer looks ahead to nightfall and the new day coming.

Sometimes family prayer takes place in other contexts: in the evening before bedtime, on a specified day of the week, and so on. It's not limited to mealtime devotions, though the supper hour (or breakfast) is one of the few times that the family gathers regularly each day.

why have family prayers?

Family prayer time is a prime place to nurture spirituality. The time of spiritual togetherness creates a bond between family members, reinforcing the strength of the home.

The family is the most basic small group within the church's fellowship. As such, it's a natural place for children to learn to pray aloud and to join in with the prayers of others. Most children will learn to pray by modeling their parents. Family prayer time should be the place where they feel the safest and most secure in making up their own public prayers to God. (Not all families are safe places to be, however. As you promote family prayer in your congregation, be aware of family situations that will need healing before true prayer and worship can occur.)

Family prayer time also gives children the opportunity to air the concerns of their day, to talk about the needs of their friends, to share their feelings, and to reconcile tensions between family members.

Family prayer is not a magical guarantee, however, of your children's spiritual health and growth. Children learn much more about spirituality by the way we relate to them than by the words we say at family devotions. As Donald Sloat

points out in *The Dangers of Growing Up in a Christian Home,*

> *The way parents treat their children in daily living has more impact on their children's eventual spiritual development than the family's religious practices, including having a family altar, reading the Bible together, attending church services, and so on.*

> *Perhaps you're wondering if I'm saying that regular family spiritual activities are not important. No, that's not my point. They are important, but the way parents treat their children in everyday living can subtly undermine all their lofty spiritual aspirations.*

In *A Family Affair: Worshiping God with Our Children* (CRC Publications, 1990, 1994), Edith Bajema offers these insights into family prayer:

> *Children learn about God more through the nuances of family life and parenting than through even the most rigorous daily table devotions. But family worship and prayer is an important element of those nuances. What tone of voice do parents use when they pray to or talk about God? Do the words "God" and "Jesus" turn up only in prayer and Bible reading, or do they appear naturally in everyday conversations? Is the atmosphere at family devotions one of freedom or control?*

> *If the children experience support and warmth in the home, what they learn there about God will take root. Often it will grow into healthy, genuine faith and worship (though not always, unfortunately, as some parents have learned with pain). Family worship can be the single most effective way in which children experience the everyday reality of God. In family worship*

they can meet a God who loves them, who hears their prayers, and who becomes tangible in the affection and respect they show each other.

ideas for family prayer

What are some ways to make family prayer and worship a time that your children will enjoy and participate in? Much depends, of course, on the age of your children. The younger they are, the simpler and shorter this time should be. Mealtimes may be a test of your endurance at this stage in your family life; Bible stories and prayer time might best be kept for bedtime or early morning if the children are very young.

The way parents treat their children in daily living has more impact on their children's eventual spiritual development than the family's religious practices.

Including Bible stories as part of your prayer time, however, will hold the children's interest. Bible stories also help introduce the children to a God who is compassionate, powerful, and wise; to a God who hears the prayers of those who love him. These stories can help lead you and your children into worship. Several well-written Bible-story books include *The Bible in Pictures for Little Eyes* by Kenneth N. Taylor, *Bible Stories for Children* by Geoffrey Horn and Arthur Cavanaugh, *Keys for Kids* (Children's Bible Hour, Grand Rapids, Mich.), and *Theirs Is the Kingdom* by Lowell Hagan and Jack Westerhof. Refer to the stories in your prayers, thanking God for the qualities that have been revealed about him through the stories.

With older children, you might enjoy using short devotionals such as *Today: The Family Altar, Daily Manna,* or *Intermission* (by James C. Schaap, CRC Publications, 1985, 1987, 1997) to guide your Scripture reading and meditation before praying together. Use Scripture, especially the Psalms, as part of your prayer time. Regardless of your children's ages, be sure to include a time of sharing before you pray together as a family. Ask each member about the good and bad things they experienced that day, how they're feeling, and what things they think are important for prayer. This sharing time will probably open your eyes to a lot that is going on in your children's life, things that you may not have otherwise been aware of. But this time also teaches your family that prayer is about real things, the things that count, everyday feelings and needs and hurts. Your children learn that nothing is outside the realm of prayer.

Keep your family prayers specific. Record them, if possible, to see how God answers them. Howard Hendricks, writing in *Vinelife*, offers this insight from his experience:

> *Socrates once said, "Generalities are a refuge for a weak mind." I believe generalities in prayer are a refuge for a weak spiritual commitment. Years ago my wife and I got ourselves a little loose-leaf notebook. We opened it flat and on one side we wrote, "We asked," and on the other side we wrote, "He answered." I would not substitute anything for what this notebook did to teach my children the theology of prayer. Nothing is as exciting as writing down a specific request.*

Pick a special spot to pray together —the living-room couch, the family room, the den, the kitchen table, wherever you can all gather comfortably. Also pick a regular time to pray. Many people have family prayers at the end of the evening meal; others in the morning or on weekends. Whatever time you choose for prayer, keep it unhurried and upbeat.

Cultivate a sense of God's presence with you. For children, it helps to have a visual reminder of God's presence. Lighting a candle during family devotions and prayer time is one way to symbolize the presence of one who came as the light of the world. Welcome God as your friend, as someone you can talk with freely. Your children will learn to address God in the same way.

You might also try a time of silent prayer with your family. Toward the end of your prayer time, save a period of time for private conversation between each of you and God. You might introduce this time by saying something like, "Now let's go into our hearts and welcome God there." Introduce topics such as items of personal need or concern, praise for things God has done in your life today, and so on.

Be sure to end your time in a defined way each time: perhaps with the Lord's Prayer said in unison, with a hymn or the doxology, and with the extinguishing of the candle. (*A Family Affair* offers additional ideas on how to worship and pray as a family. Call 1-800-333-8300 for more information.)

how can the church get involved?

Churches can encourage family prayer time by emphasizing its importance in sermons and in special emphasis weeks on the family and spiritual growth.

Churches can instruct parents in how to lead family worship by offering an annual workshop on the subject, by teaching a course on children and worship (for example, *A Family Affair*), or by setting up a clinic for parents (and inviting people from the community as well). Christian speakers are available to speak on this subject, and there may be families in your congregation who can offer encouragement and inspiration through their testimonies.

Church libraries can provide resources for the family prayer time, offering Bible-story books, videos (such as John Maxwell's *The Family Altar,* available from Injoy Ministries, P.O. Box 7700, Atlanta, GA 30357-0700), and books, such as *To Dance with God: Family Ritual and Community Celebration* by Gertrude Mueller Nelson and *Family Worship Through the Year* by Kristen Johnson Ingram.

7

PRAYER GUIDES

After being members at First Church for three years, Vic and Sharon Vanden Berg decided they would pray regularly for the church and its needs. They set aside a half hour on Saturday evenings, after the children were in bed, to pray for the coming worship service, for special needs of members in the congregation, and for the church's leaders and ministries.

They found it difficult, however, to pray for more than five or ten minutes. Vic and Sharon didn't know many members well enough to be aware of personal or family needs. They weren't always sure of special events that were being planned for the worship service, or of the sermon topic for that Sunday. They gleaned what they could about the church's ministries and leaders from the Sunday bulletin.

Finally, Sharon approached the minister with a suggestion: she wanted the church to publish a prayer guide that would help people pray specifically and effectively for the needs of the congregation. She mentioned that Vic was willing to help set up a system by which these needs could be communicated every two or three weeks.

The result was a compact list, published every other week and included in the bulletin, that included updated information on all the areas that Vic and Sharon wanted to pray about. Instead of just praying, "God, please bless the church's used-clothing ministry," they could add specific requests like, "Help us find a store that will donate some winter clothing for children."

By using the prayer guide, Vic and Sharon were able to fill more than half an hour each Saturday evening with specific requests and thanksgiving for God's work of renewal and ministry within their church. When they explained the prayer guide to the congregation during Sunday-morning worship, others caught their enthusiasm and commitment to prayer and began prayer times of their own.

Of course, a prayer guide on its own won't bring a renewed commitment to prayer within your church. But it's a tool to guide those who have committed themselves to pray. And it reminds others of the great need for prayer. Publishing a prayer guide is one way to publicize the prayer needs, concerns, and answers to prayer of families and ministries within your church fellowship.

getting the requests in and getting them out

Many requests included in a congregational prayer guide come from church members themselves. Often the requests are communicated via cards that are placed in the pews for people to fill out and leave in prayer boxes or in the collection plate. Church leaders can also request prayer for the ministries and programs they're involved in. Requests also come from denominational newsletters, other prayer guides, and outside organizations.

Some prayer guides are published by smaller, more limited groups for use within their own fellowship: senior citizens, single parents' groups, support fellowship groups, and so on. Individuals, such as pastors, might also distribute a list of prayer concerns for their prayer support group to use (see chapter 20).

Some organizations publish prayer guides that focus on all the countries of the world, updating every few years with new information and prayer needs. *Operation World*, for example, is a daily guide giving the size of countries, demographics, economic data, religion, education, and so on, as well as very specific points for prayer. The following is taken from the section on Rwanda, a country in East Africa:

1. **Praise God for the open door for the gospel** and also for the noteworthy "Rwanda Revival" of the '30s in the Anglican Church, which spread to many denominations and lands in East Africa and beyond. Spiritual life is still evident, but much of the love and fire of that generation has gone. Pray that Christians may be an example to the nation that has been torn by the intertribal warfare and massacres of the '60s.

2. **There has been a fresh move of the Spirit** over the last ten years among young people in all churches. Pray that this may result in a breakdown of the "generation gap" between them and the older Christians and a

new vitality in all expressions of church life.

3. **There has also been a spontaneous movement of the Spirit in the Roman Catholic Church.** A very extensive network of prayer and Bible study groups sprang up all over the country. The emphasis on the Scriptures has gradually been replaced by increasing structure and control, and a reversion to a more conservative RC theological stance. Pray for the born-again believers within this church.

4. **Unreached People Groups:**

   a. The Muslims are a growing community. Much money has been poured into the country by Libya. Few Christians have either the burden or the knowledge to approach them with the gospel.

   b. The twenty-five thousand Twa remain unreached, and few Christians are concerned for them.

This kind of prayer guide is invaluable to groups praying for missions and for world evangelization. It provides detailed information on each country, as well as specific prayer needs.

Who should get the church's prayer guide? Often the entire congregation receives a copy by mail, or the prayer guides are left on a rack or table in the narthex for those who are interested to pick them up.

> **A prayer guide on its own doesn't bring about a renewed commitment to prayer within your church. But it's a tool to guide those who have committed themselves to pray.**

Prayer guides of general interest can also be distributed as part of the church bulletin. One church's bulletin includes a section entitled "We Believe in Prayer," listing prayer needs and answers to prayer. Even those who just scan the bulletin for church schedules and news grasp the idea that prayer is a priority in this church. Some churches include a regular prayer column in the church newsletter, incorporating prayer needs with thoughts on prayer and encouragement to pray.

Other prayer guides are distributed only to certain groups that have committed themselves to prayer: senior citizens, women's guilds, mission groups, and so on. Still other guides are prepared for a one-time occasion (prayer meetings, congregational meetings, prayer retreats, and more).

How often you publish such a prayer guide depends on the number of prayer needs within your congregation and how efficiently you are able to gather them. Some prayer guides are published weekly; others, monthly.

organization of the prayer guide

A standard format opens with quotations from Scripture that encourage regular, faithful praying; includes thanksgiving for answers received to previous prayer needs; then concludes with new requests for intercession, describing new concerns and situations that need prayer.

Other prayer guides are arranged by weeks or by the month and present one prayer request per day. This format works especially well with various mission agencies and denominational prayer concerns. A weekly prayer guide from the congregation might look something like this:

Prayer List for August 20

Prayer Scripture: *"Let us then approach the throne of grace with confidence, so that we may receive mercy and find grace to help us in our time of need" (Hebrews 4:16).*

Prayer Meditation: *Thank you, Jesus, for acting as a high priest on our behalf. Thank you for speaking to the Father on our behalf, with compassion and sympathy. Give us the confidence that we will find mercy and grace at your throne, both for our needs and for others' needs. Amen.*

Prayer Requests:

Praise God for the quick recovery that Jane Elmers is experiencing after her cancer surgery!

Gerald Smith has asked for prayers for his nephew's alcohol and drug addiction. His nephew, Paul, has checked into Glenwold Hospital for treatment.

Remember to pray for the mothers that meet for a community Bible study in the church basement at 10 A.M. on Tuesday.

Gene Pastoor asks for prayer for his sister, who faces a serious job decision this week.

The fourth grade church school class requests that we pray for the homeless people in our city and for the Agape soup kitchen's ministry. Pray for more volunteers and food donations for Agape's kitchen.

Prayer guides for missions can be organized by making a list of missionaries and ministries supported by the congregation. Try to get requests and updates from the missionaries and ministry leaders themselves. This gives those who are praying a greater sense of personal involvement and an assurance that the requests are accurate.

You might want to try the "prayergram" approach, publishing prayer requests on a small card that people can carry around with them during the day. You can also send the prayer-gram to homebound persons, college students, "snowbirds," and any others who are not able to regularly attend church services.

Here's a sample prayer-gram:

Front of card:

> PRAYER CARD for the week of July 17. "Always keep on praying for all the saints" (Ephesians 6:18).
>
> **Facility Expansion**—For continued progress toward our April groundbreaking, that God will keep us on schedule and in tune with him.
>
> **Ministry Development**—For the growth and development of children's ministries here at Our Savior's, that multitudes of children will be discipled for Christ.
>
> **Staff Leaders**—For our minister of discipleship, Dan Kane, that God would give him wisdom, power, and fruit for Christ in all that he does.

Back of card:

> Dear Member or Friend of Our Savior's:
>
> The other side of this card is this week's "Prayer-Gram," a means to ask your prayers daily for God's help with urgent needs and for God's direction for the ministries of Our Savior's. We sense more than ever the need for divine guidance and wisdom; your prayers are absolutely essential!
>
> May I suggest that you keep this card in your pocket or purse, over the kitchen sink, or in another place where it may easily serve as a reminder to pray? Thanks so very much.—Pastor Mike

Or you might choose to organize prayer requests by listing people's names under headings identifying specific needs: illnesses, ministry involvement, unchurched friends or family members, healing for substance abuse, and so on.

how can people use this guide?

Members of your congregation who have a high interest in its ministries should receive a copy of the prayer guide. So should others who have the gift of intercession.

Encourage all members to use the prayer guide in their private devotions. Suggest that they keep a copy of the guide in their Bibles to remind them of the church's prayer needs. It can also be used in family devotions, with each member praying for a specific need. Post a copy on the refrigerator door or bathroom mirror, where the entire family will see it often.

Small group fellowships and special-interest groups (those involved in evangelism, world hunger, or justice and peace issues, for example) may also be interested in using a prayer guide that highlights needs in their areas of interest.

Encourage people to use brief interludes in their day—standing in line at the post office, being put on hold on the telephone, waiting for a doctor's appointment—to take out the prayer guide and offer prayers to God. We don't have to pray for long periods of time before God will hear us; a quick "God bless" is heard and honored by the Lord (Ephesians 6:18; 1 Thessalonians 5:17). The Spirit hears brief prayers as well as lengthy ones.

You can also send the "prayer-gram" to homebound persons, college students, "snowbirds," and any others who are not able to regularly attend church services.

do's and don'ts

Do preserve the confidentiality of personal requests. If the prayer guide has a broad audience, you may wish to keep some requests more general than others for the sake of confidentiality. If the guide is given only to a small group, caution intercessors not to spread personal matters beyond their prayer closets.

Do be as specific as possible when writing out prayer requests. As Pastor Cho of Full Gospel Central Church in South Korea points out, it can be more effective and God-honoring to ask God for a women's ten-speed with wide tires than to say "Lord, we need a bike." Communicate with the Spirit, as far as is possible, about exactly what is needed. God delights to answer prayers lifted up in childlike faith.

We don't have to pray for long periods of time before God will hear us; a quick "God bless" is heard and honored by the Lord.

Do include answers to previous prayer requests, if possible.

Do mention items that call for thanksgiving and praise as well as needs and requests.

Don't wait too long between prayer guides to update information. If you do, the prayer list gets stale and people lose interest.

Finally, encourage church members to keep their own prayer lists. To do so, they might carry around small pads and pencils in their pockets or purses to jot down names and situations that God leads them to pray for.

And let members know that the incidents of the day can also serve as an unwritten prayer guide. While driving past a school, a government office building, a nursing home, or a hospital, pray for the people who work there or who are being cared for there. Pray for the grocery clerk who rings up your bill, the waitress who serves you, the person with whom you've just spoken, the one who will be receiving the letter you've just sealed and sent off. Using the events of your day as an unwritten prayer guide is a beautiful way to pray without ceasing (1 Thessalonians 5:17).

8

PRAYER TELEPHONE MINISTRIES

Second Baptist Church in Houston, Texas, measures its growth not in members or in worship attendance but in how many people attend the weekly Sunday school classes. In a period of eight years, Second Baptist's Sunday school attendance jumped from eight hundred to more than five thousand.

What accounts for this phenomenal growth? Second Baptist is very clear on what changed its growth patterns: prayer. They decided to take God's words literally: "My house shall be called a house of prayer" (Isaiah 56:7; Matthew 21:13). And the growth followed.

To emphasize its determination to become a house of prayer, Second Baptist set aside one room of its building specifically for prayer. The room is staffed with volunteers twenty-four hours a day. Prayers from that room undergird all the church's ministry and support its members and the people of its neighborhood during times of crisis.

A prayer telephone ministry is a vital part of Second Baptist's prayer room. The church has installed a phone in the room, and volunteers from the church are available around the clock to take calls, to pray with people on the phone, to refer them to counseling or help if needed, and to pray for their concerns. Though the church has never advertised its prayer telephone number in the community, news of its availability has spread by word of mouth. Recently fifteen thousand calls were received in one year.

Second Baptist of Houston uses its prayer telephone ministry to minister both to its members and its neighbors. For those who use it, the telephone number is a link to a listening ear and sympathetic prayer support.

A prayer telephone ministry can be an instrumental part of any church's decision to become a house of prayer. This ministry differs from a telephone prayer chain, which relays urgent needs within the congregation. A prayer telephone ministry invites those from the church or community to call in and request prayer for their needs. These needs are not distributed in the congregation but are prayed for by a team of people gifted in intercessory prayer.

how to set up a prayer telephone ministry

To set up a prayer telephone ministry you will first need to obtain a phone number dedicated exclusively for this ministry. You should install this phone in a private room, preferably within the church building, where the members who are taking calls aren't likely to be interrupted.

The prayer room should be appropriately outfitted for prayer: comfortable chairs, a Bible, a notepad, a filing system for tracking prayer needs and follow-up, a list of guidelines for prayer and for talking with those who call in, and so on.

To staff the prayer line, the church will need a number of people, each of whom are willing to cover the phone for at least one hour per week. Since these volunteers may receive only one or two calls during that hour, they should also be willing to spend the rest of that time in prayer for the needs that have been called in.

The number of people needed for this ministry will be determined by the amount of phone coverage you decide to offer and how many hours your volunteers can give. To cover the phone 24 hours a day, you'll need 186 person-hours each week. To cover the phone from 6 A.M. to 12 midnight each day, you'll need 126 person-hours.

The volunteers who staff this ministry are people touching people at their point of need. Because they will be responding to a wide variety of needs and problems, your volunteers will need some training or orientation before they take their place in the prayer room.

The volunteers must keep thorough records of each call received and the general content of the conversation. Your church may use this phone line as an extension of its pastoral ministry to the congregation; the needs that members express may be passed on to other members of the church pastoral team or to the elders. Good record-keeping also promotes effective prayer. Those who staff the prayer room later in the day or week will use the "quiet" time of their designated hour to pray for the requests that have been recorded. Detailed, specific records of each request allow these volunteers to pray more knowledgeably and to enter into the requests more personally.

You may also choose to publicize your prayer telephone ministry's phone number throughout the community as well as within the congregation. Some churches, like Second Baptist of Houston, rely solely on word of mouth. Other churches use newspaper ads, send out community flyers, post notices on community bulletin boards, rent billboard space, include the phone number in their community newsletter, or advertise the prayer telephone ministry on TV and radio. One church went so far as to print its telephone ministry phone number and a brief invitation on the grocery bags of a nearby store.

> **A prayer telephone ministry can be an instrumental part of any church's decision to become a house of prayer.**

guidelines for operation

At some point in the training, give your volunteers these guidelines to help them as they answer calls:

1. Listen sympathetically to each person who expresses a need or concern.

2. Write down the request, including all details the caller gives you. If necessary, ask questions to clarify the information and to get any further pertinent information (being careful not to probe too far).

3. Get the caller's name, address, and phone number, if possible.

4. Pray with each caller over the phone and inform the person that someone will be praying for his or her concern every hour throughout the next few days.

5. In the course of the conversation, inquire about the caller's spiritual needs with open-ended, nonthreatening questions such as

"Are you a religious person?"

"Where are you now in your spiritual journey?"

"Do you know that it's possible to have a real, person-to-person relationship with Jesus Christ?"

6. Based on what you learn in response to your questions, share the good news of Jesus and help the caller begin a personal relationship with him.

7. If the caller lives within your local community, ask if he or she would like a visit from the pastor or a church member. If so, complete an information card that you can pass on to the pastor or a member of the calling team.

8. Offer to send the caller appropriate literature that may be of help (for example, a short Bible study for new believers, such as *To Be Sure, Living in Christ, Assurance,* or *Meet Jesus Christ* from Church Development Resources; call 1-800-333-8300 for more information). When you finish the call, prepare the material for mailing.

9. Invite the caller to a particular church function—worship service, community Bible study, single parents' group, a class on marriage enrichment, and so on—if you think it will meet his or her need.

10. Immediately after the call, bring the person's request to God in prayer.

11. Write down the prayer need and the caller's name on a list so that others can also pray about the need during their time at the prayer ministry phone.

what to pray for

Those who staff your prayer telephone ministry will often have large blocks of time in which the phone is silent. Ask them to commit themselves to prayer during this "down time," and post a list of prayer items in a highly visible spot in the prayer room. The list should include at least some of the following (add your own items as well):

- Pray for yourself—your relationship with God, any personal problems, your spiritual struggles, your commitment to pray for others.

- Pray for your family needs, joys, unsaved members, relationships between siblings, between parent and child, between husband and wife.

- Pray for the requests that have been posted on the church's prayer-needs bulletin board. Include special needs of your congregation, such as retreats, fellowship events, members' surgeries, births and deaths in the congregation, and emergencies.

- Pray for the lost, especially those on the prospect list that has been gathered from families and acquaintances of church members.

- Pray for missionaries supported by your church or denomination. (Their needs should be described on posters or fliers that are kept in the prayer room.)

- Pray for the pastor and the church staff. (A staff-needs notebook, in which staff members record their needs and update the pages weekly or monthly, will help.)

- Pray for the church membership, family by family. (You may wish to do this on a rotation system, praying for one or two families per day. Each family should be invited to give the prayer team input on their prayer needs when it's their turn to be prayed for.)

- Pray for the needs recorded on the call-in sheet from the previous two or three days.

- Pray for those who telephone while you are on call.

- Pray for expectant mothers in the congregation, that both they and their unborn babies will remain healthy and have safe deliveries.

- Pray for public officials on the local, state, national, and international level.

- Pray the news. As you think about events in the news, both local and international, pray about them.

- Pray for leaders in your church and denomination.

- Pray for the church's ministry efforts. (Again, a list of ministries posted in the prayer room, complete with special prayer needs, will help your volunteers pray effectively.)

- Offer God praise and thanks for answered prayers.

9

PRAYER EMPHASIS WEEK

A 1912 conference of Dutch Reformed ministers in Stellenbosch, South Africa, took note of the generally low state of the church's spiritual life. Professor de Vos, speaking at the conference, pointed out the church's lack of spiritual power. He called those present to find out the cause of this spiritual apathy in the church.

"If only we study the conditions in all sincerity," Professor de Vos said, "we shall have to acknowledge that our unbelief and sin are the cause of the lack of spiritual power; that this condition is one of sin and guilt before God, and nothing less than a direct grieving of God's Holy Spirit."

The ministers at the conference responded to de Vos's invitation with a spirit of confession and repentance. As they began to look within themselves to find what blocked their spiritual power, God opened their eyes to what had been lacking.

A report of the conference stated, "The Lord graciously ordered it so that we were gradually led to [identify] the sin of prayerlessness as one of the deepest roots of the evil. No one could plead himself free from this. Nothing so reveals the defective spiritual life in minister and congregation as the lack of believing and unceasing prayer. Prayer is in very deed the pulse of the spiritual life."

The ministers took this word from the Lord to heart. They asked forgiveness and cried out for God's help in establishing faithful, fruitful lives of prayer for themselves and their congregations.

One outgrowth of this kind of revival in the Dutch Reformed Church was the practice of holding daily prayer meetings on the ten days between Ascension Day and Pentecost. This "prayer emphasis" time was used to call people back to God. It helped people focus on their commitment to God, on their life in the Spirit, and on the discipline of daily prayer.

a week focused on prayer

A prayer emphasis week is supposed to lift up prayer, to focus the church's attention on its primary connection with God. It is an annual time to reflect on the importance of prayer and to ask God to make prayer a more vital part of our relationship with him.

A prayer emphasis week also encourages people to confess and repent of the sin of prayerlessness, as did the Dutch Reformed ministers in South

Africa. This is an essential step in reclaiming the power of prayer and growing in its discipline. Without confessing our weakness in prayer and asking for God's help, we will remain stuck. No proven methods or surefire steps to success will enrich our prayer life until we are honest with God and with ourselves about the ways we've often put prayer near the bottom of our list of priorities.

Beyond that, however, a prayer emphasis week stirs up believers to take hold of God in prayer and to set new goals in the discipline of prayer. They will hear again the call to devote themselves to prayer, as did the believers of the early church (Acts 2:42). They can also set new goals in prayer as a congregation, committing themselves to making prayer a more vital part of their small groups, their outreach ministries, their committee meetings, and their worship together. Teachings on prayer and stories of how God has answered prayer will rekindle people's interest in prayer. And the commitments that members make together help to make prayer a vital part of their lives, not for just one week out of the year but for a lifetime.

Planning your prayer emphasis week for the fall (traditionally the time of new beginnings in the church year) helps emphasize the focus on a new beginning in prayer. Setting new goals as a congregation, planning new prayer groups or programs as an outgrowth of prayer emphasis week, adding new opportunities for prayer in worship—these are often best achieved at the beginning of the church year.

Use this week as an opportunity to begin new disciplines as Christians: a renewed commitment to personal, daily devotions; a more creative, inclusive approach to family devotions; a more personal time of sharing and prayer during council and committee meetings; and so on.

You might also want to combine an emphasis on prayer with your mission emphasis week, highlighting the vital importance of prayer with missions and outreach (see chapter 18). Or you might schedule it to coincide with a national day of prayer (see chapter 31), coordinating your prayer emphasis week with other local churches and connecting with a nationwide movement of prayer.

the prayer emphasis committee

A committee of three to five people should begin planning your church's prayer emphasis week several months in advance. This committee is responsible for planning events, scheduling speakers, and finding materials.

Just as important as planning, however, is the group's commitment to pray for the success of the week. Because it's easy to plan this kind of event without adequate prayer, a conscious effort should be made to bring each step to God in prayer. Members should request the Spirit's guidance in finding speakers and in choosing the theme. They should also pray regularly for the preparation of the hearts of those in the congregation so that people will come ready to hear what God is saying to them. At least part of every meeting of the planning committee should be set aside for prayer; members might also meet for the sole purpose of prayer from time to time.

"Nothing so reveals the defective spiritual life in minister and congregation as the lack of believing and unceasing prayer. Prayer is in very deed the pulse of the spiritual life."

This committee is also responsible for promoting the prayer emphasis week in the congregation. The date should be placed on the church calendar. The committee might ask creative members of the church to design banners that promote the prayer emphasis week. Colorful posters help church members take note of the week's events and remind them to write the events on their calendars. Advance announcements in the bulletin are also helpful, as well as a brochure or special bulletin insert that explains the purpose of the prayer emphasis week and lists the speakers, events, and dates.

The committee should integrate other church activities into its planning. For example, it should invite the pastor to preach a sermon (or series of sermons) on prayer prior to the scheduled events. Along with the events planned for the entire congregation, the committee should also ask existing Bible study and fellowship groups to focus on prayer for that week. They could also organize a congregational prayer meeting in which members gather to pray for open hearts and for God's Spirit to move through the speakers and the events of the week.

> **There's nothing like a true story of someone's experience of answered prayer to open people's eyes to the power of prayer.**

Follow-up is also an important part of the committee's responsibilities. The committee should talk to the church's council and ongoing fellowship groups about providing support in this area if necessary.

options for the prayer emphasis week

1. **Time to pray together.** This is at the heart of your church's prayer emphasis week. It's not primarily a week to talk about praying, to learn about praying, or to think about praying. It's a week to pray. This will be your most important activity during the week.

    You may need to help people overcome their natural reluctance to pray aloud with others. You might do this by planning a mini-course titled "Overcoming Hesitation to Pray Aloud." (You might also want to include mini-courses such as "How to Have a Personal Quiet Time" and "Learning to Pray with Your Family" for those who have had little experience with personal and family devotions.)

    In connection with the group prayer time, consider a special prayer project, one with an emphasis on outreach: missionaries, your city or neighborhood, social concerns that have become important to your church, political leaders on the local and national levels, and so on.

    You might best organize this kind of prayer time by scheduling daily prayer meetings throughout the week, with a special Sunday prayer time before or after the worship service (or in place of the evening service). You'll want to schedule the daily prayer meetings at a time when most people can come—probably in the evening (though you may want to provide a smaller early morning or midday prayer time for those who cannot come in the evenings). Offering childcare during these times is a big help for parents of young children.

2. **Preaching and worship.** Ask your pastor or an outside speaker to give a series of messages on prayer throughout the week. Acts 6:3-4 provides a fitting theme for this series: "We will . . . give our attention to prayer and the ministry of the Word."

    During the worship service, you may wish to introduce a time of sharing and prayer, dividing the congregation into small groups for this purpose. (For suggestions on how to organize this time, see chapter 3.) Or you may want to schedule a praise service devoted to prayers and songs of praise and adoration before God. Whatever you decide, make prayer a major part of your worship times during this week.

3. **Educational events.** If people gifted in teaching are available in your own congregation, consider asking them to teach mini-courses on prayer for one or two evenings of this week or to sponsor a seminar on prayer. You can insert lessons on prayer into existing study and fellowship groups: societies, catechism classes, church school classes, home fellowship groups, and so on.

Schedule midweek meetings to provide teachings on prayer as well. Consider using a video or film such as J. Edwin Orr's *Role of Prayer in Spiritual Awakening.*

4. **New forms of prayer.** Initiate programs or strategies for prayer that your church hasn't tried before: the ninety-day prayer challenge, prayer chains, prayer vigils, prayer triplets, prayer cells, and so on. All of these are described in this *Sourcebook.*

Give people the opportunity to experience forms of prayer that may be new to them: an extended prayer time at the church (perhaps on Friday night during your prayer emphasis week), where people can stay for several hours to pray together or alone; an all-night prayer vigil; praying together in small groups; and so on.

Don't forget the family worship time. Provide suggestions for worshiping as a family with children of various ages and for creative family worship. Encourage families who do not yet do so to establish a daily time of prayer, interaction, and Bible reading.

5. **Prayer retreat.** You might schedule one day of the week for a prayer retreat, encouraging all from the church to attend. Find a setting that gets people away from the busy, hurried pace of their lives. Give them plenty of time alone to pray and lots of opportunity to learn about prayer.

Or encourage people to get away for a short period of time—a morning or afternoon, or an entire day—to spend alone in personal prayer. A personal prayer retreat is a wonderful opportunity to get away from the pressures of one's daily schedule, to find peace and quiet, and to reflect on the importance of prayer in one's life. Again, the setting is important; suggest several places where people can go for this kind of individual retreat.

The stories will help people realize that ordinary humans can do extraordinary things when they commit themselves to prayer.

6. **Books, videos, and tapes.** To get people thinking about the power of prayer and how it connects in their lives, select a number of good books on prayer:

- *Prayer,* by O. Hallesby (a classic on the subject)

- *Too Busy Not to Pray,* by Bill Hybels

- *Effective Prayer,* by R. C. Sproul

- *The Kneeling Christian,* author unknown (Zondervan)

- *Prayer: Key to Revival,* by Paul Yonggi Cho

- *Touch the World Through Prayer,* by Wesley Duewel

Encourage people in your congregation to read one of these books during the weeks before the prayer emphasis week. You might alert people to these books by distributing a list of titles and authors, by placing books in the library, or by selling them on a table at the back of the sanctuary (see "Resources for Praying Churches" at the end of this *Sourcebook*).

If you have been helped by articles on prayer that have changed your own prayer habits, make copies of them for the congregation. (Be sure to get permission for reprinting.)

Again, several excellent videos on prayer are available through CRC Publications or your local bookstore. You might make these available for members to view at home during the week or to use in their small groups. Make audiotapes of your pastor's messages on prayer available for those who wish to hear them again or who missed them the first time.

7. **Stories of answered prayer.** Teachings on the principles of prayer are valuable, but there's nothing like a true story of someone's experience of answered prayer to open people's eyes to the power of prayer. In worship or in your prayer gatherings, ask people from your congregation to share their stories of answered prayer. You might also bring in others from outside your fellowship who have experienced the results of believing, persistent prayer. These stories will make the teachings and principles come alive. You can also use the stories provided in the "Stories of Praying Christians" section of this *Sourcebook* as a source of inspiration. The stories will help people realize that ordinary humans can do extraordinary things when they commit themselves to prayer.

8. **Memorization.** Encourage all the members of your congregation (children too!) to memorize verses on prayer, such as the following:

> *This is the confidence we have in approaching God: that if we ask anything according to his will, he hears us. And if we know that he hears us—whatever we ask—we know that we have what we asked of him (1 John 5:14-15).*

> *The prayer of a righteous man is powerful and effective (James 5:16).*

> *"I say to you: Ask and it will be given to you; seek and you will find; knock and the door will be opened to you. For everyone who asks receives; he who seeks finds; and to him who knocks, the door will be opened" (Luke 11:9-10).*

10
PRAYER CHAINS

One evening several years ago I received a long-distance call. My brother was on the line, frantic. "Shelley fell into the backyard pool, and we didn't find her right away. We rushed her to the hospital, but I don't know if she's going to make it—she's in a coma. Please pray!"

My mind raced to three-year-old Shelley, lying deep in a coma over a thousand miles away. I began to pray, but soon felt overwhelmed with helplessness. I felt alone, cut off from my family. Desperate, I called our church's prayer-chain coordinator. I poured out all my worry, fear, and grief. "Please get this message down the prayer chain as quickly as possible," I told her. "Every minute counts."

She did. Within twenty minutes, nearly everyone in our small church had been contacted and was praying for Shelley. As I prayed, pacing the room and pleading for Shelley's life, the awareness grew within me that my voice was not alone. Other voices were joining mine, asking God to keep Shelley alive, asking for strength for me and my family. These voices were coming from my fellowship, from people who knew and cared for me deeply.

I felt comforted, knowing that I was not alone in my worry and separation from family. My family was around me, praying.

Shelley did not come out of her coma. She died a week later. But the comfort and hope that sustained me through those first dark hours and the long weeks that followed taught me much about the power of prayer and the necessity of having God's people pray with each other.

what is a prayer chain?

A prayer chain is the alarm system for the needs of the congregation. It makes possible a concentrated prayer effort on any specific concern or issue, including emergency situations. The information is passed along by phone, and those who receive the call immediately make the concern a part of their prayers and pass it on to others.

"Carry each other's burdens," Scripture tells us in Galatians 6:2. Spreading news of a special need through a congregational prayer chain makes this kind of caring possible; everyone in the church can be involved in praying for a particular concern.

We need this kind of mutual burden-bearing. A prayer-chain ministry helps to build a healthy dependence within the body of Christ that counteracts our culture's spirit of independence and individualism. A prayer-chain ministry can also, as the story above shows, ease the load of those who are bearing difficult and painful burdens.

Not only does a prayer-chain ministry encourage extraordinary prayer for extraordinary needs, it also keeps a congregation praying regularly for daily or weekly concerns. "Pray in the Spirit on all occasions with all kinds of prayers and requests," God's Word tells us. "Be alert and always keep on praying for all the saints" (Ephesians 6:18). A prayer-chain ministry is an important way to help your congregation carry out this command.

Your congregation's prayer chain may take one of many forms. It can include all members, for example, or only volunteers. Some prayer chains are used only to pass along news of severe emergencies; others serve as an information system to remind people of prayer needs they may have forgotten or not thought about during the week. Some prayer chains are limited to people who are able to call each other at home during the day, others to people who are home only in the evening. Most prayer chains involve only one church; some, however, link two or more churches.

Prayer chains can also vary in structure. The word "chain" suggests one person linked to another, who is linked to another, and so on. This structure is often used in churches, though it is susceptible to the problem of weak links. The proverb "A chain is only as strong as its weakest link" is often true here. To avoid the problem of weak links, some prayer chains are actually structured more like inverted pyramids, with a smaller number of committed people making many of the calls.

suggestions for organization

Perhaps the most important question is whom to include on the prayer chain. Consider including every member of your church, since this reflects the ideal that your church is truly one body. Everyone can be a part of this prayer ministry; each member can love and serve others through prayer. Including everyone also emphasizes each member's responsibility to make his or her needs known and to pray for others' needs. If a member is contacted regularly on the prayer chain, that

A prayer chain ministry helps to build a healthy dependence within the body of Christ that counteracts our culture's spirit of independence and individualism.

person will also find it easier to ask the prayer chain to pray for his or her concerns, should the need arise.

You may also want to consider broadening the focus of prayer needs to include events or concerns that are important to Christ and his church. In other words, don't limit use of the prayer chain to emergencies. Births, deaths, important family events, ministry outreach programs, special congregational meetings or concerns—all these are important matters of daily prayer for all your members. You could also use the prayer chain to remind people to pray for things that are already public knowledge—a tragedy in the community, an international crisis, or a special congregational need. Your prayer chain does not have to be limited to unexpected emergencies.

You will probably want to appoint prayer-chain captains—a team of two or more persons responsible for maintaining the system once it's started. The captains can take the initial calls for the prayer chain, set the prayer requests in motion, see that new people are added to the chain, send letters and reminders to participants, prepare bulletin announcements, keep alert for special needs and for answers to prayer, write down people's requests concisely and clearly, and so on. Such a team of captains will be invaluable in keeping your prayer chain effective and efficient.

If you involve your entire church, be sure to emphasize that the prayer-chain messages are not just for the individual who takes the call but for the entire household or family. Ask those who receive the call to communicate the request to the rest of the family. Make it part of group devotions; encourage children to include the request in their bedtime prayers.

All of those involved in the prayer chain should receive some communication from the prayer-chain captains at least twice a year—reminding them of guidelines, thanking them for their prayers, encouraging their use of the prayer chain for special needs, reminding people again of the reason for the prayer chain, providing an updated chart of the prayer chain with new members and phone numbers, and so on. Don't assume that once your prayer chain is started, it will keep going on its own power. You'll need to affirm people regularly in order to keep them motivated and active.

Don't leave the phone until you have actually prayed for the request you've received. That's one of the main purposes of the prayer chain— immediate attention to a specific need.

To spread prayer requests as efficiently as possible, consider using a small number of committed people as the core of your prayer-chain force. This means using the "inverted pyramid" structure rather than a simple chain. Have the two captains each call four people, who each in turn call four more, who each call four more, and so on. At that point, you will have reached ninety households. At that point, the remaining families may need to contact only one or two other households, depending on the size of your church.

The inverted pyramid structure is helpful because you can concentrate most of the responsibility on twenty to thirty members who are committed to passing the message on as quickly and clearly as possible. You might consider requiring these key people to write down the prayer request word for word. This will do much to prevent a garbled message at the end of the line. The people at the start of the pyramid should be available throughout most of the day for calls. Since this core of key people is vital to the prayer-chain ministry, consider meeting with them once or twice a year for prayer, encouragement, and affirmation from the pastor or council.

Be sure to give people at least two or three names to call to start a prayer message—perhaps the team captains and the church-office secretary.

Try to get at least one item a week on the prayer chain. This practice keeps the machinery well-oiled; it's also a weekly reminder to your congregation of the need for regular, consistent prayer.

Also make sure that the prayer-chain messages include answered prayer and reasons for thanksgiving. All too often we pray for serious needs but don't hear how things turned out—and that discourages persistent prayer. The prayer captains should seek out answers to prayer and pass them along—through the prayer chain and through sharing with the congregation at times of worship.

Encourage all those involved to keep on praying. Sermons, studies on prayer, books, teachings on prayer through video or films—all these create an aura of encouragement and inspiration. You may want to ask your prayer-chain captains for help in organizing this part of your prayer-chain ministry.

guidelines for prayer-chain members

1. Write the message exactly as you have received it—then verify the information by repeating it to the person who

called you. This may seem a bit unnecessary at the time, but it will help prevent misinformation, partial messages, expanded messages, or unrecognizable messages at the end of the line. The prayer-chain captains, who receive the message initially, should write the message in clear, concise language.

2. Pray immediately. Don't leave the phone until you have actually prayed for the request you've received. That's one of the main purposes of the prayer chain—immediate attention to a specific need. Besides, it's easy to forget to pray later on.

3. Repeat your prayer throughout the day, every time you think of it. Make the request a matter of persistent, faithful prayer to God. Shoot up "arrow prayers" if you don't have time for longer, more intense prayer.

4. Share the prayer-chain message with others in your household. Make it part of your mealtime devotions, your family prayers, your children's bedtime prayers. And make sure everyone also hears about the answers to prayer that come later on. This is especially important for children.

5. Use the information as a matter of prayer, not gossip. This is especially important in cases of family trauma, relationship problems, or sensitive areas of concern within the church.

6. Report answers to prayer soon after they happen. This is one of the most important—and most neglected—elements of a prayer-chain ministry.

7. Never make a prayer-chain call after 10:00 P.M. unless the emergency warrants it or unless you are sure that the person you are phoning will welcome a late-night call.

8. Those who are part of the core group should inform the prayer captains when they are on vacation or when they'll be gone for long periods of time.

what to pray for

If you are planning to include more in your prayer-chain ministry than congregational emergencies, here are some things you might consider:

- All emergencies: illness, injury, death, hospitalization, divorce, family crises

- Stages of life when families or individuals have greater needs: birth, surgery, wayward family members, profession of faith, marriage, and so on

- Congregational, committee, or council meetings at which key issues are discussed, crucial decisions reached, and so on

- Special ministry efforts of outreach teams, Coffee Break, Men's Life, youth groups, church education, small groups, evangelism calling, church retreats, work trips, and so on (include problems as well as special events)

- Plans for the church's future (needs for new development, new ministry groups, unmet community needs, finding a cohesive focus of ministry for the church, and so on)

- Needs of the pastor and church leaders in the areas of counseling, busy schedules, new preaching series, leadership challenges

- Needs of people supported by the church—missionaries, long-term volunteers, volunteer work teams, and so on

- Needs of the broader community: community events, denominational events or concerns, broader ecumenical movements, efforts of neighboring churches, national or international needs

greatest difficulties and suggested solutions

1. Some churches find that their prayer chain is rarely used. One woman reported that she had not received one prayer-chain message in the past three years! People hesitate to use the prayer chain for their concerns if it's to be used only for emergencies, thinking, "Is this bad enough to warrant a call?" Most people will think twice before putting their requests through.

   Solution: Make the prayer chain available for any matter that concerns Christ and his church. Try to get at least one message on it weekly, and encourage people to use it freely if they have a need.

   The more people you can get to write the message down, the greater the chance that everyone will hear exactly what they're supposed to hear.

2. Prayer chains often break down at their weak links. If a key person is missing, the others further down the chain won't get called.

   Solution: Concentrate the calling responsibility on a smaller number of committed persons (see explanation of inverted pyramid structure above). Set up a fail-proof backup system, whereby the missing person's calls are automatically picked up by someone else if that person isn't contacted within six to eight hours. Ask key people to notify the prayer-chain captains

if they will be out of town for a few days.

3. Garbled messages and misinformation cause not only frustration but also hard feelings. We've all taken calls in which we remember everything perfectly—until we put the receiver down. Then we don't remember—was the baby a boy or girl? Did Mr. Smith have an appendectomy or a laparotomy? Sometimes, if we don't remember the details, we fudge a little. We exaggerate or downplay the emotions of the people involved. Messages get changed with each call, mainly because we hear only what we listen for.

   Solution: Prayer-chain captains should write down a clear, concise message when they get a call, and they should make sure the caller approves the wording. The next person to receive the message should write it down, word for word, and repeat it to the caller to ensure accuracy. The more people who write the message, the greater the chance that everyone will hear exactly what they're supposed to hear.

4. Without leadership, prayer chains can be a hit-or-miss affair. Procedures get fudged, no one follows up on people who complain that they never get called, people aren't sure whom to call or how to get things started.

   Solution: Appoint a prayer-chain team of captains to coordinate this ministry (see description of responsibilities above).

11

PRAYER TRIPLETS

A prayer triplet is made up of three home units who agree to pray daily for members of the other home units. The purpose of establishing prayer triplets in your church is to give each church member the opportunity to be prayed for daily by another member of the congregation. Though the members of the triplet do not get together to pray, they contact each other every one to two weeks with prayer requests and updates.

how do we structure our prayer triplets?

The prayer triplet has a simple format. Each triplet consists of three households (includes singles and families with or without children). These groups of three are put together by a prayer coordinator, who works from lists of those who have indicated—by signing a sheet or handing in a commitment card—their desire to participate.

Why do the prayer triplets pray separately, rather than gathering for prayer? First of all, the prayer triplet strategy is meant to be a basic, initial model that every congregation can use. Most families and singles have busy schedules that make even once-a-month meetings difficult—especially when coordinated with two other households. Also, a surprising number of people feel awkward praying in the presence of others. But the commitment to keep in contact with each other weekly or biweekly is crucial.

Also crucial is the confidentiality of prayer requests. Participants in this ministry are to understand clearly that they are not to discuss the prayer requests outside the prayer triplet. If confidentiality is not guaranteed, people will not feel free to share their struggles and needs with each other.

Another important reminder: Encourage people who may feel that a daily commitment to pray for others is intimidating. Acknowledge from the start that we can all forget to pray for each other on a given day; emphasize that prayer triplets *purpose* to pray daily, which means *aiming*, or *trying*, to do so. The only thing required is the willingness to try.

Families should include their children as part of their prayer triplet. Encourage use of family devotional time for remembering in prayer the requests of the other prayer-triplet families. Children may want to choose specific people in their family's prayer triplets to pray for; this may work especially well for children of similar ages.

what will prayer triplets do for our church?

They will **help people appreciate the meaning of Christian community.** Prayer, more than any other kind of contact, unites believers with other believers. The spiritual reality of prayer, according to Dietrich Bonhoeffer, provides us with our most direct link with another person. Daily prayer for other households in your church will bring a sense of community that is not easily broken.

Prayer triplets will also **help people to see that they are accountable to each other.** We are told, "Pray in the Spirit on all occasions with all kinds of prayers and requests. With this in mind, be alert and always keep on praying for all the saints" (Ephesians 6:18). God expects us to pray for each other; it is a gift he has given to the church. Prayer triplets bring this commitment to the forefront of the church's attention.

Also, **people's deep hunger to have others care and pray for them** will also begin to be filled. Churches don't often provide this kind of caregiving automatically. Many members feel that no one is in touch with their day-to-day needs. Prayer triplets provide a small support group for each member, a place where he or she can bring the smaller traumas and concerns of everyday life.

Satan tries to weaken the church by divisions, but "the church that prays together, stays together." In prayer **we learn to be tolerant of others' struggles.** As your members call each other weekly with concerns, they will be more and more open to sharing their own struggles and weaknesses, building a base of compassion and an awareness of their common struggle to live the Christian life. The resulting bond of unity in your con-

gregation will be able to withstand the storms of controversy that visit all churches from time to time.

And, of course, **God's power will be set at work in your church** through the daily prayers of your people. You will see answers to prayer that will strengthen your faith and bring a renewed awareness of God's presence in your midst. Faithful, daily prayer for each of your church's members is sure to bring visible results.

how do we organize prayer triplets?

First, you will need a prayer coordinator to help inform the congregation and then match people up in prayer triplets. (Finding a prayer coordinator at this point is a good way to initiate someone into the work of coordinating other areas of the church's prayer life as well.) The prayer coordinator would be responsible for working with the pastor or church council to raise people's awareness of this ministry and to oversee the organizational details.

You may want to follow a process something like this in starting up the prayer triplets: First, your pastor should preach a series of sermons on prayer, explaining the challenge of the prayer-triplet ministry and also its purpose—to give each member of

The purpose of establishing prayer triplets in your church is to give each church member the opportunity to be prayed for daily by another member of the congregation.

the congregation the opportunity to be prayed for daily.

The coordinator should then distribute information on prayer triplets— what they are, what purpose they serve, how they work, who will be involved— through the church bulletin, in flyers, and so on. A suggested sample letter introducing the prayer-triplet ministry to the congregation is included at the end of this chapter.

Two or three weeks later, after people have had time to read and think about this ministry, give them the opportunity to sign a commitment card and hand it to the prayer coordinator. You may want to do this on several consecutive Sundays in order to contact as many members as possible.

Once you have a list of people or households who wish to participate in this ministry, match them up in groups of three. **Don't be afraid to mix households of different ages, lifestyles, and backgrounds. This can be a wonderful opportunity for people to be in touch with others whom they wouldn't otherwise get to know.**

Once you've matched up the prayer triplets, send each person or family in a triplet a letter with the names of the others in their group. Explain again the purpose of the prayer triplets, and remind people not to be discouraged if they don't always remember to pray daily for their partners. Reinforce the expectation that they should be in contact with the others in their triplet at least once every two weeks; suggest that they share their prayer requests as freely as possible. It may help to designate a particular household as the one that will initiate the first phone call and see that regular contact is maintained. Use this letter also to encourage participants to keep track of answers to prayer. Remind them to keep all prayer requests confidential.

Because some participants may feel at a loss as to what to pray for, you might suggest a list of general concerns people can use in their prayer time (prayers for spiritual growth, for protection from Satan's attacks, for good health, for strong family relationships, and so on). Some Scripture references might be helpful as well. Send this list with the general letter of information mentioned above.

The prayer coordinator should work with the pastor on establishing a time during Sunday worship in which people can share what's been happening in response to prayer. Don't neglect this time of sharing; this is an important source of encouragement and inspiration for your church's prayer ministry.

Be sure to keep a list of all prayer triplets on file so that you can adjust them to include new members or to replace ones who have left.

Give people the opportunity to sign up again after three months. Use your judgment as to whether it would be more valuable to reassign participants or to keep the original groups together. You might ask participants for their thoughts on this matter.

sample letters

Here is a sample letter informing the congregation of the upcoming opportunity to be part of a prayer triplet:

Dear church family members:

With this letter, our church invites you to be part of a prayer triplet. A prayer triplet is made up of three home units (families or singles) who purpose to pray daily for each other. For a ninety-day period, you will have the opportunity to be involved in a daily ministry for our church—a ministry in which families and individuals in our congregation pray for each other every day.

Praying for each other in this way is one of the best gifts we can give each other. In fact, it's one of the most important gifts God gave the church. As we make use of prayer, we expect to see God at work in our church in answer to our prayers. And we hope to get to know and care for one another as we share requests and concerns for prayer.

You're not asked to pray for the entire church, just for two other persons or families who have agreed to pray for you as well. Your small group of three, called a "prayer triplet," will contact each other every week or two to pass along prayer concerns and to let each other know how God has been answering your prayers. You will not be expected to meet together to pray; each household purposes to pray daily for the needs of the other two.

If you're concerned about the daily commitment, don't be. None of us is perfect at remembering to pray consistently for a certain need or person. We're just asking that you purpose, or aim, to pray daily for each other. All that's required is the willingness to try. If you miss a day here or there, you haven't failed.

If you have children, this is an excellent ministry to include in your family devotions. Post the names of your prayer-triplet members on your bathroom mirror, over your kitchen sink, or on the dashboard of your car. Remember their specific requests and ask God to bless their lives. And rejoice that they're doing the same for you!

Participation in this prayer ministry is voluntary; you will have the opportunity to sign up a few weeks from now. We want to give you time to think about it before you respond.

As you consider this, think about God's words to the early church: "Pray in the Spirit on all occasions with all kinds of prayers and requests. With this in mind, be alert and always keep on praying for all the saints" (Ephesians 6:18). Let's begin to follow this command, unleashing God's power in this church through our prayers for each other!

Sincerely,

Here is a sample letter from the prayer coordinator to prayer-triplet members, telling them the names of their prayer-triplet partners and explaining the details of the ministry:

Dear prayer-triplet member:

I'm glad you have chosen to be part of the prayer-triplet ministry in our church! For the next ninety days, we'll be experiencing together this adventure in prayer. I think this will be a way for all of us to learn more of God's power in our lives through prayer.

Here are the names of the households you will be praying for each day:

_____

(name of each family member; phone number)

_____

(name of each family member; phone number)

You are asked to keep in touch with one another at least once every week or two. Try to call as soon as possible after receiving this letter in order to set up a regular time and date to call each other with prayer requests. If a need or concern should arise before your agreed-upon time, be sure to call your prayer partners to let them know about it.

What kinds of requests will you be sharing? Let your prayer partners know of important events coming up in your lives, of any sickness in the family, of special needs or concerns you may have, of unchurched neighbors or friends with whom you may have significant contact. The more specific you are, the easier it is for them to pray each day for you.

These concerns are, of course, confidential. Please keep them within the circle of your prayer triplet until a time when you agree to share God's response to your prayers with others. Knowing these requests are kept confidential will enable all of you to develop a relationship that is trusting and secure.

Don't be too hard on yourself if you forget now and then to pray for your partners. We all fall short in that area occasionally; that's why you've been asked to purpose, or aim, to pray daily. To help you remember, you might post the names of your prayer-triplet partners on your bathroom mirror, over the bathroom sink, on the dashboard of your car, or any other place where you'll be reminded to pray daily for them.

Post the names of your prayer-triplet members on your bathroom mirror, over your kitchen sink, or on the dashboard of your car.

Thank you for purposing with us to make prayer a central part of our life together.

"Is any one of you in trouble? He should pray. Is anyone happy? Let him sing songs of praise. . . . The prayer of a righteous man is powerful and effective" (James 5:13, 16).

In the name of him who answers prayer,

Prayer Coordinator

ideas on what to pray for

If you aren't sure what to pray for regarding your prayer partners, here are some suggestions that will get you started:

1. **Their physical health and well-being.** Pray for God's healing in their physical bodies and for faith and cheerfulness when they are suffering from injury or sickness. (And if they are ill, don't forget to add actions to your prayers by sending a card, bringing a meal, or doing anything else that says, "I care.")

2. **Their relationship to God.** Pray that God will help them experience and respond to his love. Pray, too, that they will allow the power of God's love to change their lives—healing broken relationships with family or friends, conforming them to the character of Christ, enabling them to reach out to others who don't know God.

3. **Their commitment to prayer.** Ask God to keep them praying faithfully for themselves and for the other prayer-triplet members. Pray that they will be encouraged with the answers they receive and that they will discover more of God's power in their lives because of prayer.

4. **Their awareness of needs around them.** Pray that God will open their eyes to the needs of people he has placed them with—neighbors, family members, coworkers, business contacts, classmates, friends. Ask God to help them be like salt and light to those who don't know God.

5. **Their involvement in ministries at church.** Wherever they are involved—choir, church school, adult education, church council, food

pantry, used-clothing store, or neighborhood outreach—ask that God will motivate them with love and with excitement for the gospel.

6. **Use Paul's prayers as your own,** substituting your partners' names in the appropriate places:

> *Ever since I heard about your faith in the Lord Jesus and your love for all the saints, I have not stopped giving thanks for you, remembering you in my prayers. I keep asking that the God of our Lord Jesus Christ, the glorious Father, may give you the Spirit of wisdom and revelation, so that you may know him better. I pray also that the eyes of your heart may be enlightened in order that you may know the hope to which he has called you, the riches of his glorious inheritance in the saints, and his incomparably great power for us who believe.*
>
> —Ephesians 1:15-19

> *Since the day we heard about you, we have not stopped praying for you and asking God to fill you with the knowledge of his will through all spiritual wisdom and understanding. And we pray this in order that you may live a life worthy of the Lord and may please him in every way: bearing fruit in every good work, growing in the knowledge of God, being strengthened with all power according to his glorious might so that you may have great endurance and patience, and joyfully giving thanks to the Father, who has qualified you to share in the inheritance of the saints in the kingdom of light.*
>
> —Colossians 1:9-12

do's and don'ts

Do try to match members appropriately. It's okay to put the more mature with the less mature, but don't let the gap be too wide.

Don't put people together who are obviously mismatched, resulting in a frustrating prayer partnership.

Do emphasize that people are *purposing* to pray daily.

Don't ask people for a daily *commitment,* in which failure brings guilt.

Do pray daily that God will move their hearts to become involved in this ministry.

Don't pressure people to become involved in a prayer triplet.

Do encourage people to keep prayer requests confidential.

12
PRAYER CELLS

The room is dark. Light from a single candle on the table creates an atmosphere of peace. One by one, members of the group take their places around the table. They pray silently. For ten minutes there is no sound save an occasional passing car, a ringing phone in a room far away, someone laughing on a front porch down the block, a barking dog.

No one speaks. All heads are bowed. Each member of the group is reflecting on the truth of the promise, "Where two or three are gathered together in my name, there am I in the midst of them."

Then, when he feels the time is right, the leader begins with the Lord's Prayer. All join together now in audible expression until the room literally seems to come alive with praise as they end together, "Thine is the kingdom, and the power, and the glory, forever. Amen." After a moment's pause, the leader says, "Now we will join hands around the table and pray for those with special needs. Are there any requests?" Gradually they come. A woman tells of her neighbor who faces an operation tomorrow. A man confesses his worry about a difficult decision that confronts him this week. Another asks for prayers for a church

program in which he is involved. The suggestions vary from intimate, personal matters to prayers for the coming election of public officials. Then the group prays. The leader has asked that they begin on his right and continue around the circle. He has also stated that whoever does not feel like praying may squeeze the hand he or she holds, indicating a wish to pass.

The prayers vary from halting, first-time petitions to [eloquent appeals by] experts in the art of public prayer. Some are set in the intimate terms of "you," "yours," and the ordinary language of simple conversation. Others use the familiar "thou," "thee," "thine"! Some use both. They pray for those requests that have particularly touched them. They pray for personal matters that reveal the hidden thoughts of the praying mind. When the circle has been completed, the leader prays. He seeks to summarize the feelings of all and remembers before God the unmentioned requests too. The session ends in silence, then the light goes on.

—Charlie Shedd, How to Develop a Praying Church, pp. 95-96

what are prayer cells?

Prayer cells are small groups that meet primarily for prayer. These groups have a limited size—usually about 8 to 12 members, though there can be as few as 4 to 6 members or as many as 15 to 18. The prayer cell meets at a time and place convenient for its members—mornings or evenings, weekdays or weekends, in homes, restaurants, or churches. In these ways prayer cells differ from prayer meetings, which are open to anyone, meet at a central location (usually the church), and are publicly announced from week to week. Also, prayer-cell meetings are very informal, whereas regular prayer meetings tend to be more structured and formal.

Prayer cells can be made up of a broad mix of church members—couples, singles, young adults, retirees, and so on. Sometimes, however, the prayer cell is an affinity group—one made up of young mothers, professionals, businessmen or women, young singles or couples, those in a certain ministry, or those who share a special concern (such as outreach to the unsaved, church renewal, world missions, and so on). In some prayer cells all members are of one gender; most, however, are of mixed gender.

In other words, no two groups will be exactly alike. Your church may have a number of prayer cells, some spontaneous and some planned. Some may be ongoing, while others may commit themselves to meeting together for two or three months. Prayer cells will share certain basic features, however, as described in the section below.

standard features of a prayer cell

- **A clear focus or purpose.** Many prayer cells gather for fellowship, shar-

ing, and Bible study as well as for prayer. However, prayer should always be the primary focus of your group. Don't let the other activities overshadow your prayer time together. Discuss together the purpose for your prayers: ministry to others. All believers are called to minister, and prayer is one of the believer's most powerful opportunities to minister in the lives of others. Don't lose this outward focus by praying only for the group's own concerns.

- **Regular meeting time.** This may be the most important "detail" decision your group has to make, since choosing a time that is inconvenient for some members means you probably won't see them regularly. Tailor the time to the special needs of

> **The prayers vary from halting, first-time petitions to [eloquent appeals by] experts in the art of public prayer.**

your group—mothers, business people, retirees, and so on. Early morning, midday, weekend, Sunday evening—try to find a time slot that everyone can make consistently.

- **Limited size.** The best size for a prayer cell is 8 to 12 members. However, it is not always possible to have exactly the right amount. If your group is smaller, that's okay. If it grows beyond 15 or 16 members, discuss the possibility of breaking into two groups. Having too large a group makes it difficult for everyone to have a chance to share; large numbers also break down the atmosphere of intimacy within the group.

- **Opportunity to pray aloud.** Though you may want to allow time for silent prayer, as in the example at the beginning of this chapter, you will also want to give every member of the prayer cell an opportunity to pray aloud. This praying together usually follows a time of sharing—requests, concerns, joys, answers to prayer. You may want to structure your prayer so that everyone has a chance to pray, as in the example above. Take care to avoid having prayer times dominated by the leader's prayers to the exclusion of others'.

- **An agreed-upon discipline.** As a group, decide what you will expect of each other: attendance, daily prayer for each other, confidentiality on personal matters, continuing prayer throughout the week for the concerns discussed, and so on. Do all members need to be present each week? Can each member expect his or her concerns to be held in confidence? Can every member know that he or she is prayed for regularly throughout the week? You may wish to express your commitments to each other verbally or in writing.

- **No pressure to pray aloud.** Don't force anyone to pray, of course; let people understand that they are free to remain silent. This is particularly important if you have newcomers or new Christians in your prayer cell. Some people have never prayed in front of others; it will take some time before they get the courage to do so. Using "popcorn prayers" (short, one-word or single-phrase prayers of thanksgiving or request) may make it easier for such people to contribute.

- **A defined list of prayer concerns.** When members of the group share prayer concerns, write them down so that no one's requests are forgotten. (The list is also essential for prayer throughout the week.) If you sense, however, that your list of concerns is getting too long and covering too broad a spectrum of needs, talk about how you might focus your prayers on more specific areas of need.

- **Short, succinct, specific prayers.** Long, rambling prayers can bog down a prayer meeting and keep others from contributing their prayers. It's a good idea to agree beforehand that members' prayers will be kept under one or two minutes at the most and will focus on only one need at a time.

- **Limited time of commitment.** A small group needs to give members opportunity to reaffirm their commitment or to withdraw from the group. It should be established at the outset that the members' commitment is requested for only nine weeks, two to three months, half a year, or whatever you agree upon. This limited commitment enables people to join without feeling like they're signing up for life. It also enables the group to rethink its purpose and commitment regularly.

- **Prayer for each other's needs.** A prayer cell is a group in which we learn to bear one another's burdens—not with superficial sympathy but with God's love and power, made available to us through prayer. We all have needs; or, as one person expressed it, "Everyone has a problem, is a problem, or lives with a problem." Divorce, illness, death, family tensions, financial worries, questions about God, unsaved family and friends—all these touch our lives from time to time. These may not always be shared aloud in the prayer cell. But we need to be aware that each member needs our prayers, for the unspoken needs as well as the spoken. That awareness should call us to pray regularly for each other.

- **High priority on attendance.** Again, discuss as a group your expectations for commitment. Remember that the priority you give to gathering for prayer reflects how much you believe in the power and necessity of prayer. Don't put God's business too easily aside.

- **Love for each other.** As one prayer-cell member put it, "When we meet one another on the street or at church or casually at social affairs, there is an instant bond. We share a secret. We know that our relationship is more than casual, more than that which springs up between people with mutual board-member or church-organization interests, more than those with similar social interests. In some cases it is deeper than the bond of family." You will know the presence of God's Spirit by your deep love for one another.

leading a prayer cell

The leader's job is to make the prayer cell effective, to avoid pitfalls in the group. He or she can do this by keeping the following suggestions in mind:

Pray for a deep love for the members of your prayer cell. Are you deeply interested in each member? Do you draw the members out, getting to know them as well as you can? Displays of affection are indispensable in effective prayer leadership. Members will respond to this much more readily than to any other qualities you may bring to your leadership.

Prepare for each prayer-cell meeting. Intercede for other cell members during your daily private devotions. Depend on God to show you which items need to be shared or prayed about during your cell meetings. Give careful thought to any struggles or temptations your prayer-cell members may be facing.

Find appropriate passages to share from the Scriptures. Though your prayer cell is not a Bible study or preaching service, it's valuable to read a few verses and make brief, appropriate comments on what you've read. Your comments should

lead into the group prayer time, not detract from it.

Above all, teach your members how to pray. This is especially important for beginners. Encourage them by asking for one-sentence prayers at first or for a verse of Scripture or a quote that has helped their prayer life. Be sensitive to the terror that some people feel about having to pray aloud in front of others. You might even ask a few of your group members to write out prayers during the coming week so that they can read their prayers aloud at the next meeting. Gradually they will learn to pray more spontaneously.

Remember that your aim as leader is twofold: To nurture members' spiritual development and to link the prayer cell to the church. Don't let your cell become self-sufficient and ingrown. Remind your members of the church's needs; set aside the time each week to pray for concerns in the greater fellowship.

> **Prayer-cell meetings are very informal, whereas regular prayer meetings tend to be more structured and formal.**

Encourage the prayer cell to fertilize the church, to generate spiritual vision and power.

Finally, work toward nurturing other leaders in your group who will gather other prayer cells around them. As these groups multiply in your church and community, the whole atmosphere can be changed.

the value of prayer cells

Prayer cells will enrich your church in many ways. One outstanding benefit is the **development of each member's spiritual time in prayer,** both alone and together. It gives them a rare gift: time with God. Members begin to deliberately cultivate the life of Christ within them.

In the midst of their busy schedules, they take the time to grow spiritually. They begin to trust each other. They learn the value of strength in numbers, strength in depending on the body of Christ. They learn that action and prayer go hand in hand.

Prayer cells also **raise the spiritual life of the congregation.** Not only will prayer-cell members stimulate others in the church to more faithful prayer by their example: they will also nurture the church by praying for its ministries and outreach. Their prayer unleashes spiritual power and grace within the congregation.

Long, rambling prayers can bog down a prayer meeting and keep others from contributing their prayers.

Finally, prayer cells **help make the church part of God's answer to the world's need.** They encourage members not only to bring their family and work concerns to the prayer group but also to bring Christ into their daily family and work activities. The two go hand in hand. And the cell's prayers for the needs of its community and the world will result in answers from God that will bring healing and hope to others.

13
PRAYER MEETINGS

Does your church presently have a prayer meeting, or are you thinking of starting one? If so, here are some words for you from C. John Miller, author of *Outgrowing the Ingrown Church:*

> You are in the toughest battle facing the Christian church. Prayer meetings constantly tend downward, to become either intellectualistic Bible studies or anxiety-sharing sessions where religious arguments break out. Christian people and their leaders are ready to do almost anything except get down to praying with power and authority in the name of Christ.

George Verwer of Operation Mobilization echoes these thoughts:

> If there is any part of our church life that seems to be in trouble, it is the prayer meeting. The fact is that in an increasing number of churches, for all practical purposes, there is no such meeting. Ministering in thousands of churches over the past twenty-two years around the world, I have never ceased to be amazed at the neglect of true, heartfelt, corporate prayer.

Gloomy words. But both writers also give glowing accounts of prayer meetings that are bursting at the seams with people and filled with fervent prayer—meetings to which people come expecting to be changed and to encounter God. The church parking lots are crowded, rooms are filled to overflowing, people profess their faith, some are converted or healed, and specific answers to prayer come every week.

What makes the difference between a live prayer meeting and a dead one? The touch of the power of God, says Miller. And the expectation that God will be present, healing and changing those who come.

This chapter will deal with prayer meetings. The structures suggested here, however, will not ensure a prayer meeting that is alive with God's power. No structure can do that. Even the most well-planned structure cannot replace these essentials: the conviction that prayer is the church's lifeblood; the expectancy that God will be present with power and healing; a commitment to doing God's will, whatever the cost; and the prayers of the leaders before the prayer meeting itself.

Building on these essentials, then, your church can use the structures suggested below to help make its prayer meetings more effective and smoothly run. Intertwined with a firm belief in the power of prayer, these structures will help you organize prayer meetings in which

God's power is present and his name is glorified.

what is a prayer meeting?

A prayer meeting is not primarily a Bible study. It is not a share-and-fellowship time. It is not a teaching time. A prayer meeting is a regularly scheduled meeting with one central purpose: prayer.

This may seem obvious. However, as Miller notes above, prayer somehow seems to get neglected in the prayer meeting. It often takes a backseat to other activities—all related to prayer, of course—that keep us busy talking about prayer but not actually praying. Singing and teaching have a rightful place in a prayer meeting, but prayer is always to be dominant.

Other characteristics of a prayer meeting: it is publicly announced, open to all, and can range in size from a few people to a large crowd. These qualities distinguish a prayer meeting from a prayer group or cell, which is usually a "members only" group that meets in a person's home or in another private place for prayer.

Other elements of the prayer meeting can vary: the time can range from one to several hours, for example; and the focus can be strictly on prayer or can include teaching, singing, and praying. The location need not be limited to the church building, and frequency can vary from once a week to once a month.

what will prayer meetings do for the church?

Jesus said to his followers, "If two of you on earth agree about anything you ask for, it will be done for you by my Father in heaven. For where two or three come together in my name, there I am with them" (Matthew 18:19-20).

There is phenomenal power generated through a group that meets to pray. There is no power like it—not wealth, not social position, not political clout. It is the power of God, who created the universe and keeps it running by the word of his power. God's strength moves obstacles and brings changes that no other force can. This awesome power is available to even the smallest group of believers through prayer.

Praise is a must. Giving praise to God will warm your spirits like the sun on a gloomy day. It will help break through the clouds of doubt and hopelessness that sometimes overshadow prayer.

Fellowship and unity also come through the prayer meeting. How can it be otherwise, when Jesus is there among those who pray? The awareness of Jesus' presence and the knowledge that their prayers are heard bring people together with a new excitement, a sense of expectancy and joy. There is an undercurrent of life and anticipation in prayer meetings where people take Jesus' words in Matthew 18 seriously.

Prayer involves listening as well as talking, and God speaks to people gathered to pray. Our willingness to listen to God is one way in which we acknowledge his presence among us. As we silently wait on God, we can often sense his guidance. God speaks especially through others, as they share the burdens God has placed on their hearts and the insights they have gained through his Spirit.

Vital prayer meetings also stimulate Christians to spread the word about prayer. As people are moved by the force and excitement of a prayer meeting, they communicate their enthusiasm by recruiting others to come and pray. Prayer meetings can thus be the source of renewal, encouragement, and faith in the life of your church.

A word of explanation: These benefits come through frontline, not *maintenance* prayer meetings. Maintenance-style prayer meetings are aimed at preserving the status quo of the church. Their main purpose is to maintain the existing life and ministry of the congregation. In maintenance prayer meetings members meet to pray for the church's internal needs. They do not come expecting God to change them, to change their church, to challenge and break down any rigidity present in the church, to turn them outward to the needs of the community.

Frontline prayer meetings, on the other hand, are seen as battle stations in which the prayer warriors themselves are changed. People come expecting to meet God and to be changed by their encounter with him. From him they find grace to confess the sins they struggle with. From God comes life-changing love for other people. From God comes an energetic desire to "put feet on their prayers" through outreach ministry. Frontline prayer meetings turn the church outward to face its community. Those who come look for revolution, not maintenance, within the church and within their own lives.

> "Christian people and their leaders are ready to do almost anything except get down to praying with power and authority in the name of Christ."

how to organize and lead a prayer meeting

You can use the following procedure for starting up your prayer meeting, but keep in mind that it is only one among several possible procedures. Choose what fits for your church; feel free to adapt or change these ideas according to your needs and experience.

1. **Begin by praying for the Lord's guidance.** Ask the Spirit to show you the best time and place for the meeting, what agenda he wants you to have, how often you should meet, and how to prepare the church for this prayer ministry. As you and other leaders pray together, use a pattern of praying that encompasses all elements of prayer—adoration, confession, thanksgiving, supplication, and surrender (ACTSS)—since you will want to incorporate this breadth of prayer into your prayer meeting as well. Ask the Spirit to show you areas of your life in which you have not surrendered to God's will. Pray for openness, for a sense of expectancy and eagerness.

    Pray, too, that God will prepare your congregation for this adventure in prayer, helping them to hunger for a deeper experience of God's power and ministry.

2. **Announce the prayer meeting with expectation.** Let your faith and excitement be visible every time you speak of the meeting. Personally invite all kinds of people to the meeting, not just your church's faithful "pray-ers." Businesspersons, people who come to you for counseling, teenagers, young mothers, retired people—invite them all to come. Tell them, "This is the best meeting in the church. Come and expect great things to happen!" Those who respond will most likely be those who feel a need to know God better, who are open and teachable.

3. **Begin the meeting by reading some Scripture passages on prayer or quoting an author or two on God's power in prayer.** Focus people's attention on God, not on themselves. Sing some simple worship songs that people already know or can learn easily. Keep this opening time brief—perhaps ten or fifteen minutes. Close it with a prayer for the Lord's blessing and presence during your prayer meeting.

4. **Next, share with the group some answers to things you've prayed about in past meetings, as well as reasons for thanksgiving.** Open the sharing time to anyone who can report on answered prayer. Follow this sharing with prayers of praise and thanksgiving. Allow the entire group to participate in these sentence prayers. It's important to begin your prayer meeting with a tone of praise and thanksgiving, affirming your faith in a God who hears and answers prayer. Praise is a must. Giving praise to God will warm your spirits like the sun on a gloomy day. It will help break through the clouds of doubt and hopelessness that sometimes overshadow prayer.

5. **Give a brief teaching on prayer, filled with excerpts, quotes, and stories on prayer.** To do so, you will need to become more familiar with the Scripture's teaching on prayer, with current literature on prayer, and so on. You could also ask some individuals to share insights on prayer from God's Word—anything that would train and stimulate the church to pray. Though this teaching time should be kept brief, it's an excellent opportunity for people in the congregation to use their gifts to teach and encourage each other.

6. **Give individuals the opportunity to present personal needs at this point, as well as the broader needs of the community and the world.** You may want to ask a few participants beforehand to share their vital, recent experiences of involvement with God. Such fresh stories of faith will testify to the reality of God's presence and his willingness to interact in our lives.

Ask individuals to report on specific ministries of your church: Coffee Break, Men's Life, vacation Bible school, a neighborhood calling program, and other outreach ministries. These people should make short, specific requests regarding the mission needs of each ministry. An individual should also report on the latest news and prayer needs of each missionary your church supports.

Record these requests and needs (in abbreviated form) on an overhead projector so that everyone can see them. Or provide pencils and notepads so that people can record the requests themselves. You may also ask someone to write these out in greater detail; you can then copy this request sheet for distribution after the prayer meeting for use throughout the week.

Make sure your requests cover not only your church's internal needs but also community and international needs. Mention requests for personal acquaintances who are not saved, for problems your community faces, for the poor in your area who struggle to survive, for international crises, for the agencies and people who work to help in these crises, for the schools in your area, for local government and **As people leave, encourage them to take home the list of prayer concerns and to make these a part of their daily conversations with God.** international leaders. Encourage people to share needs for physical, emotional, and spiritual healing. Encourage them also to pray for an increased willingness to follow God's will without hesitation or reservation.

7. **Break into small groups of four to six for this part of the prayer time,** but keep the groups within the main hall or sanctuary. Appoint a leader in each group and set a time (about 30-45 minutes) for the groups to spend in prayer. Encourage each member of the

group to pray, audibly but in a low voice, for the requests mentioned in the sharing time. Members of the groups may also feel more comfortable sharing personal needs just within the small group they're praying with. If so, encourage them to do this. Though you may vary the format of this prayer time occasionally, remember to keep a balance of spontaneity and planned direction.

8. **Close your meeting on a note of confidence that God has heard your prayers and has already responded to them.** Reassemble as one group and sing together a few songs that inspire faith and confidence in God's power to answer prayer. Again, read or repeat a passage of Scripture or a particularly encouraging quote on prayer or on the believer's relationship with God.

> **The Spirit is constantly seeking to turn us outward toward our neighbors and to alert us to areas within the church that need change or healing.**

As people leave, encourage them to take home the list of prayer concerns and to make these a part of their daily conversations with God.

ways to kill a prayer meeting

As with any effort or undertaking, there are pitfalls to be avoided if you want an effective prayer meeting. Some are listed here; others you will learn through experience.

1. **Praying too long at one time.** Some people dominate a prayer meeting or small group by praying for five to ten minutes at a time. Their desire to pray is laudable; but they forget that others are waiting to pray. They also forget how difficult it is to concentrate on one person's prayer for more than a few minutes.

To avoid this pitfall, establish guidelines at the outset of the meeting that limit prayers to no more than one or two minutes. If individuals cannot express all that they want to during this time, encourage them to pray two or three times—but to keep each prayer brief. You may need to kindly but firmly remind participants of this if one or two people still tend to dominate the prayer meeting.

2. **Preaching at people through prayer.** This is a great temptation, especially when the prayer is focused on controversial issues or matters of spiritual growth or church direction. Often, because we tend to be more aware of others' presence than of God's, we tend to address our words to those around us. However, this creates resentment and division among those who are gathered for prayer. It dishonors God by pitting one believer against another and by setting up subtle distinctions.

Prevent this problem in your prayer meeting by leading an open discussion of this kind of prayer. Emphasize that our prayer is directed to God alone. In his presence we come to realize that all of us have weaknesses, have wrong perspectives, make wrong choices. Our prayers should be humble and should acknowledge our own weaknesses as well as those of others.

3. **Praying only for things that pertain to your church.** Again, this mistake is easy for believers to make. We are proud of our church programs, and we feel comfortable in our fellowship and ministry. It is natural to ask God to bless what we've already begun to do in his name. However, this kind of ingrown vision will quench the Spirit

of God in the prayer meeting, because the Spirit is constantly seeking to turn us outward toward our neighbors and to alert us to areas within the church that need change or healing.

To avoid this pitfall, use some of the suggestions for prayer requests listed in step 6 above.

4. **Not changing anything from week to week.** Though a good basic structure to the meeting is essential, people welcome change and variety. Some prayer meetings can focus on one main concern or emergency (personal, community, or international). Others can be led by a visiting missionary or someone from a local ministry who can convince people of the need for prayer through their personal stories and experiences. Vary the format also; ask people for suggestions as to what changes they would welcome.

5. **Looking down on those whose English or theology is not perfect or who pray with more enthusiasm than others.** Your prayer meeting should be a community that welcomes people from all backgrounds and from a wide social spectrum. You will discover that often it is those with the least polish whom God chooses to gift with wisdom and spiritual depth. Allow for different prayer styles—from the most reserved European tradition to the more energetic Pentecostals. None should look down on or offend another.

6. **Not really believing or expecting specific answers to prayer.** This problem is perhaps the greatest impediment to the prayer meetings' coming alive with God's power. This lethargic attitude toward prayer is best combated with solid, biblical teaching and with true stories of God's faithful answers to our specific prayers. Once people begin to realize how powerful and

effective prayer is, watch their eyes light up and their excitement begin to grow! You won't be able to stop them from coming to the prayer meeting. It will truly be, as Miller suggests, "the best meeting of the church."

14

PRAYER VIGILS

vigil \ 'vi jəl \ n (ME vigile, OF, fr. LL & L; LL *vigilia* watch on the eve of a feast, fr. L, wakefulness, watch, fr. *vigil* awake, watchful . . .) 1 a: a watch formerly kept on the night before a religious feast with prayer or other devotions b: . . . a day of spiritual preparation c: evening or nocturnal devotions or prayers . . . 2: the act of keeping awake at times when sleep is customary . . . 3: an act or period of watching or surveillance
—*Merriam-Webster's Collegiate Dictionary*, 10th ed.

Roger shifted his position a little, stretching his legs out under the pew in front of him. He listened to the murmur of voices from four others scattered throughout the sanctuary, then checked his watch: 1:15 A.M. Fighting sleep, he shook his head to clear his thoughts.

On the pew beside him was a sheet of paper—a list of prayer concerns handed to him when he entered the church at 12:30 A.M. It was Maundy Thursday, and Roger had just finished the midnight shift in the pediatric unit at the hospital. Now it was the early hours of Good Friday. He had volunteered for an hour-and-a-half slot in the Maundy Thursday-Good

Friday prayer vigil. His time was half gone.

Roger read the next item on the list: "Pray for the neighborhood outreach of our church during Holy Week, especially for the calling teams that will be inviting people to the Easter sunrise service and breakfast." His wife, Margaret, would be on one of those teams.

Roger closed his eyes again. He envisioned Margaret and others going from door to door, shaking hands, warmly extending invitations. He thought about the inner-city problems that plagued the church's neighborhood, and he remembered the words in the Gospel of Mark about people being like sheep without a shepherd and the compassion Jesus had on them. Roger prayed for the people who lived around the church, asking that God's Spirit would persuade them to come to church at Easter to hear about the risen Lord, who cared about them.

Others in the sanctuary were praying for various concerns on the prayer list: for the renewal of the church's vision for neighborhood ministry, for the pastor and worship team as they prepared for the Good Friday and Easter services, for a child who had been born that day with a heart defect. Roger knew that the newborn child's situation was critical; surgery would have to be performed within one or two days, if the infant was strong enough. He prayed intently for the child's health.

At 1:45 the group gathered for a time of praise together. They shared their experiences in prayer, the insights that had come during their vigil, the struggles they had in concentrating and staying awake. They laughed and hugged each other. At 2:00 A.M. Roger and two others left. Several more came to take their place.

Roger found out the next morning that the infant's health had improved during the night; the surgery was scheduled for noon. He hugged his wife. "I wasn't sure about this prayer-vigil thing before I did it," he said. "But I'm glad I went. I feel much more a part of what the church is doing this week, and spending that much time in prayer has helped me focus more on what God wants for me and the church. It reminded me again of what the church is all about."

what is a prayer vigil?

A prayer vigil is a concentrated prayer effort by a number of believers who agree to pray about specific needs for a definite period of time. As suggested by the definition above, it can also be a time of watchful prayer before an important holy day, such as Easter or Christmas.

How did the idea of a prayer vigil get started? One memorable New Testament prayer vigil took place when the believers prayed all night for Peter's deliverance from prison (Acts 12:5, 12). And Jesus himself is our prime example: he spent nights in prayer before making key decisions (whom to choose for his disciples—Luke 6:12-16) or at crucial points in his ministry (the watch in the garden of Gethsemane with his disciples—Luke 22:39-46). Old Testament believers were often called to fast, watch, and pray before national crises or important decisions. Nehemiah and the workers kept

watch on the walls of Jerusalem as they were being rebuilt, with one hand raised in prayer and the other on their swords (Nehemiah 4). "Watch and pray" has been a password for believers through the centuries.

different kinds of prayer vigils

Prayer vigils are not limited to one prescribed pattern or routine. When you plan a prayer vigil for your church, you'll have to consider a number of variables. For example, some churches conduct prayer vigils at the church building, while others simply ask participants to pray in their homes for a specified time period. Some vigils go around the clock, day and night, for one or more days; others last only for eight, twelve, or sixteen hours. Some churches ask participants to come for the entire time; others have members sign up for different time slots.

Some prayer vigils focus on emergency concerns: an important legislative decision that will affect the nation, a church member whose life has been endangered by a serious accident, and so on. Others are planned to coincide with the church year (during Lent or Advent, for example) and to focus on spiritual renewal and community outreach. Some are open to a wide variety of congregational and community prayer concerns; others focus on a specific need.

what will a prayer vigil do for your church?

First of all, prayer vigils will focus your church's attention on the importance and power of prayer. A prayer vigil gives a strong message to your church about the priority of prayer in its life and ministry. In doing this, it will create an atmosphere of expectancy and urgency. People will begin to sense that the church is really serious about its belief that God works through prayer. When you stop merely talking about prayer and begin to do it, people will respond in ways like this: "Let's get down on our knees and start praying! I know of a real need here."

Prayer vigils focus everyone's prayer on a specific concern. Such concentrated prayer is powerful; it releases God's power in people's lives—power for healing, for conversion, for change. For example, one church's twenty-four-hour prayer vigil group decided to pray for the police force in their small city. Within two months, two of the policemen—without any direct invitation from the church—began to attend the church and were baptized within a few weeks. After six months, the crime rate in the city had dropped from an average of twelve violent crimes in a six-month period to only two such crimes.

> **In a day when we put high priority on church programs and high-tech productions, prayer vigils remind us of the church's dependence on God.**

God has worked in amazing ways in response to prayer vigils in times of crisis. Your people will begin to look forward to these prayer events, since they know that something significant happens each time they meet to pray in this way.

Prayer vigils can be a testimony to your church's neighborhood as well, as you send out a letter to your community asking for prayer concerns. If you explain the nature of your prayer vigil and provide a postcard that people can fill out and return (or a phone number they can call), many will respond with personal needs and community concerns. What better way to tell your neighbors that your church really cares about their welfare?

Prayer vigils will also help forge a deeper sense of identity within the church. In a day when we put high priority on church programs and high-tech

productions, prayer vigils remind us of the church's dependence on God. We are faced with our ineffectiveness apart from God's power—and our tremendous potential through joining with his purpose and Spirit in prayer. We begin to see afresh that our identity is rooted in God, not in our programs.

how to organize a prayer vigil

No matter what format you choose for your church's prayer vigil, there are some steps you can follow to make sure everything is clearly explained and smoothly executed.

1. **Establish the reason for the prayer vigil** (a special need or crisis; future planning for the church's mission, vision, and goals; an upcoming evangelistic meeting; preparation for special days such as Easter and the annual day of prayer, and so on). Make sure the congregation is informed with as much detail as possible. Setting up a vigil for a sick member of the congregation may simply require a call on the church's emergency phone chain. A vigil for legislative issues or evangelism outreach, however, may require printed materials and several messages during the Sunday worship services to alert people to the need for such prayer.

2. **Choose a period of time for the prayer vigil** (from two to forty-eight hours, or even longer).

3. **If you're planning on an extended prayer vigil, divide the time into smaller segments that people can sign up for.** To fill the time slots, you may wish to circulate the sign-up sheet in a council meeting to get a strong representation from your church's leaders.

This sets a good example for the rest of the congregation. You may ask several groups in the church to fill a specific portion of the sign-up sheet (not necessarily with members from their group).

If you ask participants to pray for 15-minute segments, you will need 32 people for an 8-hour vigil each day, 64 for a 16-hour vigil, or 96 for a 24-hour vigil (assuming that each person signs up only once). If the vigil takes place at the church, you may want to designate half-hour or one-hour time slots, since people may not want to come all the way to church for just 15 minutes of prayer.

4. **Provide helps and direction on how to pray and what to pray for.** For example, you could hang an informational poster or two on the wall of the sanctuary or prayer room, or type up a handout to give to people as they come in. These informative pieces could include some Scriptures on prayer or praise, suggestions on how to divide the prayer time (for example, adoration, confession, thanksgiving, supplication, surrender), and a list of prayer concerns.

The list of prayer items should be as specific as possible. If you are praying for an upcoming evangelistic outreach, name the people involved, the details of operation, and the specific goals of the outreach effort. If you are praying for missionaries or special speakers, gather as much information on them as possible. The same is true for legislative issues and national/international crises. The more people know about a prayer need, the more specifically and personally they can pray.

5. **Prepare the building for the prayer vigil.** Make sure the doors are unlocked and a notice is posted to tell people in which room the vigil is being held. Even details like heating and air-conditioning can affect the success of a prayer vigil. If you are not meeting in the sanctuary, make sure the room has comfortable chairs or pillows, pleasant lighting, and a Bible available. You may also want to set out a notebook that people can use as a prayer journal to record thoughts and insights that come to them during the vigil.

6. **Close the prayer vigil with a time of praise, prayer, and celebration, if appropriate.** Use songs that express a vibrant trust in God's power to act in response to prayer. The end of your vigil may flow right into the Sunday worship or an evangelistic or worship meeting.

examples of prayer vigils

As mentioned above, there is no set procedure for a prayer vigil. Reading about the following churches' experiences with prayer vigils may help you develop some ideas of your own.

• One church in Michigan, for example, holds two overnight prayer vigils each year—some from Friday night to Saturday, some from Saturday night to Sunday. The Sunday prayer vigil concludes with a breakfast at 8 A.M. and a time of prayer before the Sunday-morning service. Church members sign up for as many time slots as they wish (the pastor first circulates the sign-up sheet among council members to make

The more people know about a prayer need, the more specifically and personally they can pray.

sure the elders and deacons are well represented). Young people and singles usually "adopt" the hours between midnight and sunrise.

The vigil is held at the church building. The participants gather in the sanctuary each hour for five to ten minutes of praise, led by the pastor or another leader. Then everyone goes off alone in the sanctuary to pray for about half an hour, at which time the leader calls everyone back together for a time of sharing, praise, and group prayer. A writing tablet and pen are available for people to record their prayer thoughts and insights during this time.

These prayer vigils always have a specific focus. One vigil, held during a designated "Faith-Promise Week," concentrates on prayer for missionaries. The leaders gather and distribute as much information as possible on the various missionaries beforehand. The vigil held during Easter week focuses on community outreach, with a special praise time for the entire church from 11:30-12:00 P.M. During Lent the church sends out letters to the people in its neighborhood, explaining the prayer vigil and asking neighbors to submit prayer concerns. These concerns are then incorporated into the prayer list.

- One church in Minnesota holds a prayer vigil once a month, from 9 P.M. to 2 A.M. The focus of the vigil is church growth. The people pray, sing, and worship together. Attendance at the vigil started small, but is growing steadily. "Whatever you do, don't give up," said the pastor. "Many prayer vigils start with only two or three people. But if the vigil

is a positive experience for them, the word will spread, and others will start coming."

- A Canadian church holds a twenty-four-hour prayer vigil once each year. Sometimes members focus on a specific concern; other times the focus is general. One room in the church is set aside for the vigil, and only one person at a time is present to pray (people can sign up for half-hour time slots). A Bible is placed in the room, along with a list of suggested passages to look up. Participants are encouraged to write their thoughts and prayers in a prayer journal in the room. "I have found this prayer time extremely worthwhile," wrote one person. "It has given me the opportunity to think and pray about the areas of this church that touch my life."

- A church in Texas maintains a constant twenty-four-hour vigil. At least one church member is always in the church's prayer room, praying and ready to answer the church's prayer phone line. The phone number to the church's prayer phone is publicly advertised throughout the city; members of the community are encouraged to call and talk about their problems or crises. Someone will always be there to listen, to pray with them, and to pass the message on to other "pray-ers." The listener always asks for the person's phone number and address and prays with that person over the phone. Participants in the prayer vigil call back later to follow through on answers to the prayer requests or to mention new developments to pray for. Routinely asking, "Are you a Christian?" has opened the opportunity to lead many to Christ. Thus the church's prayer vigil has become an outreach ministry to the community as well as a source of power and praise for the church's worship.

Prayer vigils don't have to be limited to one church. During times of community or national crisis, a prayer vigil is an excellent way of getting together the churches of your community to join in prayer for a specific need. Such a vigil promotes fellowship between churches and emphasizes their common faith in a God who hears and answers prayer.

Nationwide prayer vigils are another expression of this common faith and sense of mission. In one effort, groups of intercessors from various denominations committed themselves to an unbroken day-and-night prayer vigil for the U.S. Supreme Court and for the abolition of abortion in the United States. People gathered each day to pray for three to six hours at a site within view of the Supreme Court and capitol buildings. Individual churches were also invited to commit themselves to week-long fasting and prayer vigils for this cause. The prayer vigil remained unbroken for more than two years—at the end of which the Supreme Court agreed to hear a case that would reopen the issue of legalized abortion in the United States.

15

SENIOR INTERCESSORS

Martha Valens is seventy-six years old. She lives alone, loves to garden, and attends church whenever she can get a ride back and forth. Failing eyesight makes it impossible for Martha to drive a car, though she can still distinguish between a weed and a tomato plant. Apart from gardening and occasional church activities, Martha stays at home in familiar surroundings.

Until last year, Martha felt frustrated with being a "fringe" member of a church she had been active in all her life. Then the pastor dropped by one day and began talking about her obvious love for the Lord and her keen interest in the families of the church. He suggested that Martha be part of a prayer team of seniors in the church.

"More and more I am convinced that the church needs the power of God through prayer," he told her. "God really moves in response to prayer—prayer that comes to him out of compassion for others and out of faith in God's ability to act in people's lives. I need people in this church who have that kind of faith and that interest in other people—and who are willing to commit time every day to pray. You're one of the first people I thought of. I've been praying that you'd join us—will you help us in this ministry?"

Martha was more than willing. Since that visit, she has spent a large part of each day in prayer, asking for God's intervention in family crises in the church, in the lives of members' unchurched family and friends, in the problems and challenges of her local community. Martha and the others on the seniors' prayer team get updated prayer lists every week (Martha gets hers on a cassette tape, since reading is difficult for her). The prayer ministry has benefited Martha as well as the church. She enjoys being a vital part of ministry once again.

"I won't be able to garden much longer," she said, referring to her failing eyesight. "But some days that doesn't matter any more. I'm tending the Lord's garden too."

why use seniors?

Seniors aren't the only potential prayer warriors in the church, of course. Every member should be encouraged to cultivate a vital prayer life and to pray for the church's ministries. But there are several reasons why involving the senior members of your congregation is especially beneficial.

First, it helps them understand how valuable they are to the church. In a society that tends to treat "unproductive units" as castoffs, this is a strong statement of the values of God's kingdom, where individuals are valued simply because God made them and they belong to his family. Many seniors are healthy and active well into their nineties, but others are forced into early retirement, homebound, or moved to a nursing home because of illness or increasing weakness. These members particularly feel frustrated by their inability to do much. A vital prayer ministry can turn a life of forced inactivity into a space for prayer. It can also help these seniors understand how valuable they are to the church.

And they are valuable. They are among the most spiritually mature members of your congregation. Through years of church membership, most seniors have learned the hard lessons of faithfulness, commitment, and discipline. They have experienced much over the course of a lifetime—youth, parenting, pain, illness, sorrow, the struggle to know God's will for their lives. This often makes them sympathetic to the prayer needs of others who are going through similar struggles. Seniors have a heart for the church, a knowledge of God's promises, a lifetime of experience in prayer, and a faith that has endured the test of years.

Finally, the most compelling reason to recruit retired and elderly members of your church in the ministry of prayer is that prayer is the most important thing we can do. "Ask and you will receive," says Jesus (John 16:24). "Always keep on praying," writes Paul (Ephesians 6:18). "In everything, by prayer and petition, with thanksgiving, present your requests to God" (Philippians 4:6). God's power enters our human programs through the door of prayer. Unless the church's ministry is bathed in prayer, it remains merely a human endeavor. Your senior members can be a vital part of the powerhouse of prayer that energizes your church with God's power and guidance.

how do we get a senior prayer ministry organized?

The basic principle is to let seniors organize this ministry themselves. If your church already has a prayer coordinator, ask one or two seniors to work with him or her on the details of organization. If there is no prayer coordinator, find two or three seniors willing to set up this ministry on their own.

You might suggest several different structures for the coordinators to consider. For example, the format of **prayer cells** may be the most beneficial for the seniors in your congregation. You could structure different prayer cells with regard to location (for example, those who live in a certain area or who reside in retirement homes), kinship (widows, widowers, those who share similar situations or similar interests in ministry), and more. See "Prayer Cells" (chapter 12) for further suggestions and guidelines.

> **"More and more I am convinced that the church needs the power of God through prayer. God really moves in response to prayer."**

As an alternative, you might consider setting up a **prayer chain** for seniors. Again, you will need at least one person to set up the structure of the prayer chain and keep it moving. To make the chain effective, it should be used for prayer requests at least once a week (see guidelines for prayer chains in chapter 10).

Prayer guides are another way to involve your seniors in a prayer ministry. A prayer guide put together by seniors and published for their use could include the church-ministry calendar for each day of the month, background on your church's missionaries and their needs, and denominational prayer concerns—as well as the weekly needs of church families and the community. A biweekly letter can serve as a reminder to pray and can give updates on current concerns.

In some congregations, seniors might prefer to work as **prayer partners.** Sometimes these partners are the young people of the church, with whom they keep in contact for special needs and for whom they pray daily. Each senior might also be asked to pray for a specific individual—a church member with special needs, a member who is wayward or no longer attends church, an unsaved person in the community, a new or prospective member, someone who struggles with illness, an evangelism prospect, or someone with another need. Each member of the prayer ministry is committed to praying daily for the person assigned to him or her. Though they don't necessarily contact the person prayed for, they are given as much information as possible so that they can pray specifically and compassionately.

Prayer meetings are another option for a seniors' prayer ministry. Gathering monthly, bimonthly, or even weekly for prayer enables them to be involved with the church's ministry and outreach on a continuing basis. It also provides fellowship and a place where they can bring their own prayer needs. Consider combining the prayer meeting with a luncheon or supper, coordinated by the organizers of the prayer ministry. If possible, the seniors should have the opportunity to pray both as a large group and in smaller groups. See "Prayer Meetings" (chapter 13) for more specific guidelines and suggestions.

> **God's power enters our human programs through the door of prayer. Unless the church's ministry is bathed in prayer, it remains merely a human endeavor.**

what other churches are doing

A Christian Reformed church in Hudsonville, Michigan, began a program of "secret senior intercessors" a few years ago. Those senior members who volunteered were assigned a young person in the church (more than sixty participated). They prayed as specifically as possible for their young partners throughout the year and sent cards and notes of encouragement—but never identified themselves. (See the sample letter at the end of this chapter for guidelines and suggestions on keeping in touch.)

At the end of the school year, the adults got together with the teenagers for a supper and a sharing time at church, and the young people got to meet their secret prayer partners for the first time. Here are some of the comments that came from the young people:

- "It's nice to know someone cares and is praying for *me*."

- "It helped me through the year."

- "Good to be thought of specifically with prayer."

- "Makes me feel special."

- "It's comforting to know that someone besides my family is praying for me."

The adults also had positive comments:

- "This has created a special bond between me and my partner."

- "It's been a great experience!"

- "Prayer is more powerful than I realized."

- "I really learned to love my prayer partner."

Another church in Grand Rapids, Michigan, not only involves its seniors in a secret intercessor program but also has a group of about thirty seniors who are committed to praying for the church's needs. They receive a monthly intercessors' guide that lists congregational needs and items for thanks and praise.

One program, started by the Church of God, is called "The 88th Prayerborne Division of God's Intercessors." Named after America's military airborne division, the 88th Prayerborne sees itself as a spiritual strike force—an army of volunteer senior citizens, led by retired ministers, who do daily battle through prayer. The leaders are asked to recruit and train as many members as possible to pray on a regular basis—at least once a week together (possibly at the church with a lunch or supper) and daily at home. They pray by name for their pastor and staff, for government officials, for their family and friends, asking that God's will prevail in every aspect of their lives and in their work for him.

what's the value of such a ministry?

A senior prayer ministry capitalizes on the spiritual maturity and prayer power that often belongs to senior citizens. Being involved in this ministry may also open some of their eyes to the power of prayer in a way they had not experienced before. Seeing God's answers to their prayers will not only encourage the entire church but will also stimulate the faith of these elderly believers.

In so doing, it provides seniors with a ministry in which they can be effective—even when they're unable to be physically active or engaged in ministries that require lots of energy. This involvement combats the low self-esteem that many older people suffer when they sense

that society (and in some cases their own families) has put them on the shelf.

A prayer ministry keeps seniors involved in a positive way. If older members remain relatively uninvolved, they'll find it easier to feel critical of the "younger generation's" ways and ideas. Prayer links between old and young will help build a bridge across the generational gap. As older people pray for young people and their activities, they gain more of a sympathetic interest and a desire to understand and get to know the young people better. This bridge works two ways, also allowing younger people to appreciate the humor, wisdom, and experience of the young at heart.

A prayer ministry also gives seniors good reason to be together at a time of life that is often lonely. Anna, who is in her nineties, often remarks that most of her friends have died. Brothers and sisters are also gone, and her children live out of state. Anna feels left alone in the world, especially since she finds it difficult to attend church. If it weren't for the senior prayer ministry, she would have very little heart-to-heart involvement with anyone. In the biweekly prayer meetings, Anna can talk about some of the worries she has and the problems she faces living at home alone. She keeps up with others' prayer concerns and prays faithfully for

A senior prayer ministry capitalizes on the spiritual maturity and prayer power that often belongs to senior citizens.

their needs. This newfound fellowship of prayer has reassured Anna of the church's support for her and has strengthened her lifelong faith in God.

keeping the ministry going

As in any prayer ministry, it's vital to communicate regularly about prayer concerns and answers. Sharing answers to prayer is particularly important, since there is nothing more discouraging than never hearing the results of one's prayers. Hearing about God's answers to prayer, on the other hand, can rejuvenate people's faith and help them pray with greater spirit and intensity.

If you have a prayer chain, you can communicate answers as well as requests via the phone. Or, as with the prayer guide, you can send out biweekly or monthly reports on what's happening with the prayer concerns. Members of prayer cells or participants in the prayer meeting can do their own reporting when they meet as a group. You might also consider sharing some of these answers to prayer with the larger congregation during a worship service.

This newfound fellowship of prayer has reassured Anna of the church's support for her and has strengthened her lifelong faith in God.

Any ministry in the church needs affirmation to keep going. The pastor and the spiritual leaders of the church should let the seniors know how much their prayer ministry is appreciated. From time to time the pastor should mention this ministry in the worship service; perhaps an appreciation banquet or luncheon would also be in order. Notes of thanks from the council members would convey this affirmation in a personal way, acknowledging that the leadership benefits greatly from the seniors' efforts in prayer.

The ministry will need some organizational help from the pastor or a staff person, especially as it sets up the times and places to meet, plans food or refreshments, puts together a prayer guide, and connects with the church's youth.

To keep the program going, you will also need to make an effort to pull in others who are not yet members: recent retirees, new church members, those who have been previously unmotivated, and so on. Establish an atmosphere of openness and welcome. Encourage those involved in the prayer ministry to keep it from becoming a clique, since new members bring fresh insights and needed stimulation.

Finally, provide training for those involved in the prayer ministry. No matter how much experience we've had with prayer, there's always more to learn. So provide your seniors with outside speakers, videos on prayer, a five- to ten-week course on prayer—anything that will help them deepen their understanding and practice of prayer. See "The School of Prayer" (chapter 4) for more ideas.

sample letter to secret senior intercessors

THANK YOU SO MUCH for your willingness to be a prayer partner for one of the young people in our church family. It will mean more to that person than you will ever know. Prayer does change things, and it also promotes unity in the family of God. Read on to find out from last year's prayer partners how much it meant to them:

- *"Glad to know someone is praying for me."*
- *"I've seen how God provides through the love of others."*
- *"Prayers appreciated."*
- *"Nice that someone takes the time to pray for me."*
- *"Felt the power of prayer."*
- *"Especially in hard times it's good to know someone is thinking and praying for me."*
- *"Had answers to prayer."*
- *"Makes me feel special."*

It's exciting to know how much prayer means, right? We also know that some of you are new at this and may not know exactly what to do. Here are some guidelines to help you effectively pray for and keep in touch with your prayer partner:

- *Write the person's name on a 3" x 5" card and tape it, as a reminder to pray, to the inside of a cupboard door you open daily.*

- *Talk to a family member of the young person at church or by phone to find out what extracurricular activities he or she is involved in and would need prayer for. If in school, what subjects are most difficult?*

- *Get a copy of the school calendar to become aware of special events or activities such as music performances, plays, sports events, exams, and so on in which your young person might need special prayer support.*

- *Make an effort to send your person a card at least once a month so that he or she knows you haven't forgotten your prayer commitment. Write it on your calendar so you don't forget. Holidays, birthdays, special events, and so on are good times to send a card. Say something like, "Just to let you know I'm praying for you."*

Be creative; let the Holy Spirit lead you. Remember, prayer is a vital link to growth in our walk with God. By praying for one another, we are drawn closer to one another and to him. Enjoy!

16

CHURCH PRAYER SUPPORT GROUPS

what do church prayer support groups support?

These prayer groups support the church—its ministries, its activities, its members. A church prayer support group is a number of people committed to praying daily for their church's life and health. Their focus is inward; their purpose is to nurture and support the body of Christ through prayer.

Church prayer support groups keep well-informed of prayer needs, especially of the ministries and weekly activities that go on inside the church. Though group members usually pray as individuals, the entire group can also gather to pray for the common concern that has drawn them together: the church's health, vitality, and growth.

This kind of prayer support group is distinguished from other prayer support groups (groups that support the pastor, for example, or the church's missionaries, or individual members within the church through prayer). While these other groups have much the same purpose, their focus is narrower than that of the church prayer support group, which is concerned broadly with all of the church's ministries and activities. (For more information on

these other, more specific prayer support groups, see related chapters in this book.)

what's the goal?

"Praying the church to health"— that's the goal of the church prayer support group. Its members pray for specific ministries and activities operating each day of the week.

On Sunday, for example, each member of the team prays silently during the worship services for guests, for the worship leader, for the musicians, for the worshipers, and so on. On Monday they may pray for the council meeting that evening; on Tuesday, for the food pantry's staff as it serves the community; on Wednesday, for the weekly evangelistic Bible study groups as they meet, and so on.

If the church prayer support group is large enough, members may also choose to organize their efforts so that each member of the congregation is prayed for every day. This involves taking separate sections of the membership list and rotating them every week or so, if the group desires. It might be helpful to list beside each member's name the ministries that he or she is involved in—from cleaning the church kitchen to evangelistic calling. Members with special care needs should also be prayed for daily.

Of course, you'll want to let the people in ministry know that this team is supporting them in prayer. Not only will it boost their morale, but it will also help them begin to look for the ways in which God is answering those prayers. Encourage the persons in charge of each ministry to let the prayer support team know of special needs, of answers to prayer, and of their appreciation for the prayer team's support.

examples of church prayer support groups that work

First Christian Church in Pampa, Texas, was struggling. Though worship services were going well, though stewardship was fair to good, and though nothing was particularly wrong, the pastor sensed a feeling of stagnation and dwindling enthusiasm.

The pastor realized that although the church had a lot going for it—great doctrine, intelligent and creative people, solid education programs—the sense of victory in Christ was not present. The excitement of winning battles against the realm of darkness was missing.

As a result, he decided to get back to the basics of life in Christ: strong Bible study, meaningful worship, and *prayer*. He told his congregation that they had gotten too far from the fundamentals, and he began to preach and teach on the need for prayer, among other things.

He wrote personal letters to all the members, stating his firm belief in the power of prayer. He asked all those who were willing to pray every day for an entire year—for the church, for its minister, for its leaders, for its daily witness and growth—to sign the letter and return it to him.

The response was overwhelming. Almost a hundred people of all ages gathered for a meeting in which they decided to form a church prayer support group: the "Prayer Power People." Membership was open to all who signed a "prayer covenant."

The group decided to do the following:

- Establish four classes on intercessory prayer, using Maxie Dunnam's *Workbook of Intercessory Prayer*.

- Set up a phone chain so that members could be contacted for prayer in emergencies.

- Establish a special telephone line called the CareLine (669-CARE), on which members could call up to receive a daily recorded prayer message that included new requests and updates to previous prayer concerns.

- Meet for prayer every Sunday for fifteen minutes before church school begins, with the prayer time focused on the minister, the service, the guests, and the church education teachers.

As a result of this prayer group, everything in the church began to pick up steam. Concern for prayer continued to build. People became much more positive about their church.

> **The excitement of winning battles against the realm of darkness was missing.**

The number of new members quadrupled in one year. New music groups sprang up, additional young adult and youth groups were added, and church attendance and giving slowly rose.

"What is going to happen next? Who knows? I don't," the pastor admits. "I just hope and pray that this movement never stops, that God will grant us the wisdom and insight to become more and more involved in his hidden agenda for us."

Another pastor in San Jose, California, faced the reality that most in his congregation were spiritually apathetic and immature. A faithful few were doing much of the work and were growing spiritually, but the church was becoming lopsided in its spiritual growth.

"Give me one hundred preachers who fear nothing but sin and desire nothing but God, . . . such alone will shake the gates of hell and set up the kingdom of heaven on earth. God does nothing but in answer to prayer."

After studying principles of spiritual renewal in Scripture, the pastor challenged his people with the theme of "God's Awesome Few"—the remnant whose faithful prayer would be the key to revival and renewal. He took to heart John Wesley's words:

> Give me one hundred preachers who fear nothing but sin and desire nothing but God, and I care not a straw whether they be clergymen or laymen: such alone will shake the gates of hell and set up the kingdom of heaven on earth. God does nothing but in answer to prayer.

So the pastor set about to find, motivate, and train that "remnant" in his church. He began with seven who were willing to pay the price of meeting each week for prayer and to fast from at least one or more meals on the day they met to pray.

The pastor built up their faith in the leavening power of God's remnant, the few through whose prayers God's power would be released to work on the apathy of many in the church. He sent out monthly letters to focus their prayers on critical issues in the church. He invited the entire congregation to join this small group once a month for prayer.

The result? After one year, the group of "God's Awesome Few" had grown to forty-five persons, making up eleven smaller prayer bands meeting weekly. Church attendance swelled from 235 to more than four hundred; and for the first time in the church's history, attendance rose rather than declined in the two months after the Christmas season and during the summer.

keeping the group going

Several key factors will make the difference between a lively, vital prayer group and one that slowly fades out. Consider the following as you establish your church prayer support group:

1. **Members must be convinced of the value and importance of prayer.** Only a strong personal conviction will keep them praying through the times when nothing seems to happen and when others get discouraged and drop out. Search the Scriptures together to strengthen your conviction that God places his faithful remnant in groups and churches as a "power point" for renewal.

2. **The group will need regular encouragement from the pastor, the staff, and key leaders in the church.** These should also participate in the prayer support group when possible. The pastor should lead the group—or at least actively share in assuming responsibility for this faith venture.

3. **Provide a yearly time of recommitment, when members can feel free to end their participation and others can take their place.** Make sure that you let all newcomers know what you will expect of them (for example, faithful attendance, fasting from one or more meals, faithful daily prayer). Remember that it's as important to let

people out of this commitment as it is to bring others into the group.

4. **Clear communication is vital.** Set up some way of communicating prayer requests quickly and effectively. Take time to share in your group the answers God gives. Allow group members to offer their own needs and requests so that they feel supported and cared for. Encourage feedback from group members so that you can correct things that aren't working and improve things that are.

As you communicate prayer needs, be as specific as possible. Set prayer goals that you can trust God to meet within a specified period of time. Target your prayers to specific people and events. The more particular and concrete your prayer goals and requests are, the better.

5. **Keep group members aware of the presence of the entire prayer team.** If you meet weekly in smaller groups, be sure to meet once every month or so as an entire group. It's also important that you stay united in spirit as a group. Work out any difficulties or tensions that arise within the group; don't let anything hinder the effectiveness of your prayers together.

17
EVANGELISM PRAYER GROUPS

Plans and programs in evangelism are necessary and good, but it is only God's power that will actually win people to Christ. No expenditure of time, effort, and money can replace the convicting and calling of souls by God.

In our evangelistic efforts, as in all work for him, God is able to accomplish through us only "according to" the power that works in us (Ephesians 3:20). This power is appropriated and released by praying. In evangelism, our prayer is for people to find Christ.—Evelyn Christenson

In the sweltering heat of July 1857, a businessman named Jeremiah Lanphier walked the streets of New York City. For two months he knocked on office doors in the neighborhood, inviting businessmen like himself to join him in prayer on Wednesday afternoons for spiritual revival.

On September 23, the date of the first prayer meeting, Lanphier opened the door of the Dutch Reformed Church at twelve noon. No one was present. He waited and prayed. At twelve-thirty the first person appeared. A few more joined them before the hour was ended.

Undaunted, Lanphier persisted in prayer. Every Wednesday found him in the church building, praying with a small but growing number of local businessmen.

Six months later, ten thousand businessmen were gathering throughout New York for daily prayer. They prayed for revival, for the spread of the gospel, for a growing love for God. As a result of this prayer movement, which eventually spread across the country, more than a million converts were added to American churches within two years of Lanphier's first prayer meeting in New York City.

Throughout the history of the church, great revivals have all been preceded by prayer—beginning small and mushrooming into a movement of repentance and revival that have spread across denominational and national boundaries. Jeremiah Lanphier is just one example of a small group of believers who took prayer seriously enough to begin a revival.

As your church becomes more active in prayer, you should not overlook God's call to pray for conversion and repentance among the people of your neighborhood. Praying for the unsaved and the unchurched is a vital ministry. God uses prayer to prepare people's hearts and to stir in them a hunger for the gospel. Thus an evangelism prayer group is vital for any church that wants to reach its community for Christ.

what is an evangelism prayer group?

An evangelism prayer group is one that reaches out in prayer. It's a group of people who have covenanted with God and with each other to pray for unsaved people. They pray for people to whom their church is reaching out and for the evangelistic ministries of the church. Their primary concern is for people to be led into a vital relationship with Christ.

Several qualities make for an effective evangelism prayer group. First, the members should covenant to make prayer for the unsaved a regular discipline in their lives. While avoiding guilt-producing rules when members don't live up to them, group members should at least have the intention of daily prayer for the unsaved.

Second, because this kind of prayer is an important and daily commitment, members should limit their commitment in the group to a specific length of time (six months, one year, and so on). After they have fulfilled that commitment, they are free to leave the group or renew their covenant of prayer, if desired.

The prayer outreach team should get together as a group at least once every two weeks, in addition to individual daily prayer. Praying together and talking about God's answers is powerfully motivating for people involved in an outreach ministry. They should keep tabs on the people they pray for, since their greatest encouragement will come from seeing God's intervention as a result of their prayers.

For that reason an evangelism prayer group should have a good communication system. It should have ready answers to questions like these: What prayers were answered? How did God answer them? What new developments in people's lives and in the church's ministries need to be lifted up in prayer? This kind of information is vital to the success of the prayer group. A prayer chain, a weekly newsletter, a meeting just prior to the Sunday morning service—all of these can keep members informed of how God is working through their prayers. Make sure the information is fresh and complete; members will find it discouraging to pray for a vague request or one that's a week or two old.

what are some ways to organize this group?

An evangelism prayer group can be organized to pray for church outreach in a number of ways. Here are some suggestions:

1. **Your group may simply commit to pray for each of the church's outreach ministries and for the people who work in these ministries.** As they do, group members actually participate in the ministry of outreach. They have joined as partners with those who work in outreach, with just as vital a role to play. As Paul wrote to his praying supporters in Rome, "I urge you, brothers, by our Lord Jesus Christ and by the love of the Spirit, to join me in my struggle by praying to God for me" (Romans 15:30). In the unseen realm of prayer, we can actually share in others' struggles to present the gospel to the unsaved.

Praying together and talking about God's answers is powerfully motivating for people involved in an outreach ministry.

This kind of prayer support is tremendously heartening to the church's outreach ministries. The leader of one church's Congregational Evangelism Training (CET) said of his church's prayer outreach team, "I can't imagine doing what we're doing without this group of people. Visitation evangelism can be pretty scary work; we put ourselves on the line every time we knock on a door. We never know exactly what will happen on each visit. But knowing that the team has already prepared a way for us, through the Spirit, is tremendous. Only God can open the doors of these people's lives, and he's doing it through our prayer outreach team."

> There is a power in prayer that helps get through the defenses people raise when they meet someone on their doorstep.

2. **The prayer group may choose to pray for people on your church's evangelistic prospect list.** The names on this list can come from several different sources. First, those directly involved in outreach can share the names of the persons they are working with or hope to reach. Second, the congregation can supply a good list of evangelism prospects. Ask members to share the names of the persons they know who don't have a living relationship with Christ: family, friends, neighbors, coworkers, and so on. Such prayer brings surprising results. One Baptist church gathered a list of sixty names from its members and began praying for each of those people in September. By the following February, thirty of the people on that list had come to Christ (and most became members of that church).

Other prospects on your list might come from those who have visited your church more than once. The evangelism prayer group commits itself to pray for these people and their families daily, asking that they be led into a vital relationship with Christ and that they find the church of their choosing. Those who join your church will be deeply impressed with mem-

bers' commitment to pray for them while they were still outside the fellowship of God's family. One man, who learned that he had been prayed for, said, "When I thought about someone who didn't even know me praying for me and my family every day, I got the feeling that I had to know more about what makes people do things like that." He eventually joined that church and became one of their most effective leaders.

3. **Instead of using a prospect list, the evangelism prayer group might pray for your church's neighborhood, block by block.** One church in a small New York town, for example, decided to canvass its community without brochures, newsletters, or tracts. No one pressed a single doorbell. All the church did was pray.

Street by street, with map and red marker, church members prayed weekly for the people on each of the town's forty streets. They named no individuals and prayed only that God would touch the lives of those who lived on a particular street.

What happened? People started visiting the church "out of the blue." One Sunday four families came soon after the week the church had prayed for their street. "I think some of our people were genuinely surprised at the results," said the pastor. "They supported the canvass, but they were still amazed when visitors began showing up."

Your church may want to combine this kind of canvassing with the more conventional kind: passing out leaflets for a special event or Bible study at your church, calling door-to-door for Coffee Break invitations or evangelism, handing out flyers that welcome people to worship at your church, or whatever. It's a good combination. There is a power in prayer that helps get through the defenses people raise when they meet someone on their doorstep.

4. **Your church may want to form prayer outreach triplets**—groups of three people who covenant to pray regularly for specific family members and acquaintances. Each member entrusts to the others the names of three people whom he or she wishes to see saved. The group prays for the relationship between group members and the unsaved persons, asking God to work through them to show the love of Jesus and the truth of the gospel.

Group members should pray not only for these unsaved people but also with them, presenting their needs before God. They pray not only for salvation but also for all the needs in these people's lives: family problems, financial worries, relationships, and so on.

The prayer triplet members should pray not only individually but as a group, keeping in contact regularly on the needs of the persons they are praying for. They also should use this group time to hold each other accountable in these relationships. Are they being supportive? Are they reaching out? Do they follow through on needs that come up from week to week? In other words, the prayer triplet prays not only for the nine unsaved persons but also for the relationships they have with those nine.

Prayer outreach triplets differ from the prayer triplets described elsewhere in this sourcebook by their clear focus on evangelism and on the nine people for whom they pray. You might establish prayer outreach triplets in connection with a Friendship Sunday in your church, with your church's Coffee Break or Men's Life program, with an evangelism crusade, or with another special evangelism effort. For more information, see "Prayer Triplets" (chapter 11).

how do we pray for the unsaved?

Pray first of all for what God wants to do in the lives of unsaved persons. If you aren't sure what specifics God wants to accomplish, use these more general requests, drawn from Scripture:

- That God will draw them to himself (John 6:44).

- That they seek to know God (Acts 17:27).

- That they believe the Word of God (1 Thessalonians 2:13).

- That Satan is bound from blinding them to the truth (2 Corinthians 4:4).

- That the Holy Spirit works in them (John 16:8-13).

- That they turn from sin (Acts 3:19).

- That they believe in Christ as Savior (John 1:12).

- That they obey Christ as Lord (Matthew 7:21).

- That they take root and grow in Christ (Colossians 2:6-7).

Second, pray with the conviction that God is able to accomplish great things in the life of another person. Paul told the early Christians, "I pray also that the eyes of your heart may be enlightened in order that you may know . . . his incomparably great power for us who believe" (Ephesians 1:18-19). God made the world and the universe in which we live; he holds everything together by the word of his power. God has promised to work in response to our prayers when we pray within his will. Pray full of faith and expectancy; God will move people's hearts, awaken their souls, and use the circumstances in their lives to bring them into his kingdom.

Third, pray that the works of Satan in people's lives will be demolished. "The weapons we fight with are not the weapons of the world. On the contrary, they have divine power to demolish strongholds. We demolish arguments and every pretension that sets itself up against the knowledge of God" (2 Corinthians 10:4-5). The strongholds that Satan has built up in people's lives—false teaching, unbelief, hatred, self-centeredness, lust—are torn down by the power of prayer. In prayer, believers fight the powers of darkness on behalf of their unsaved family members, coworkers, and friends. Our prayer against Satan must be persistent because Satan doesn't give up easily. If believers do not fight this battle, no one will.

In prayer, believers fight the powers of darkness on behalf of their unsaved family members, coworkers, and friends.

You may have to do some talking to get people involved as part of your church's evangelism prayer group. But once they begin to see God's answers in response to their prayers for the unsaved, they'll be full of enthusiasm and excitement. This kind of prayer is an adventure that won't let you go once you've begun.

18

PRAYER GROUPS FOR MISSIONS

"World evangelism!" When we hear that slogan, we think of a whole list of things related to evangelism: missionaries, organizations and structures, the philosophy of missions, mission strategy and fund raising, and literature crusades.

But something is missing in that list: prayer. Prayer is more vital than money, personnel, organizations, or philosophy. Prayer is the most vital force in world evangelism. Do we believe that? Do we practice it? As Wesley L. Duewel observes, "Has any missionary organization done more than make token efforts to build prayer into all its annual plans, all its structures, all its strategies, all its promotion, and all its financing?"

Prayer groups for missions fill in the gap that is left amid all our organizations, annual reports, and fund drives. Prayer groups provide the spiritual power for changing people's hearts. Praying believers are vital to a missionary's success in the spiritual warfare that takes place on the mission field. As Eugene Rubingh says,

> All the earth is the Lord's; the nations are being placed in line for that great and final day, in this global arena. If we can see that, so can Satan. At very crucial points where Satan's bondage is being challenged today, where light is shining into the dark-

> ness, there his energies are concentrated in counterattack. Disease crops up in especially bizarre and disheartening forms; demon possession is virulent; disorder and evil appear constantly and often visibly and audibly. The authority that Christ has provided his people must now be unleashed and aimed at these powers. It is time to break through in these places, a time when the very lives of missionaries and new Christians are at stake.

To perform our mission, we must surround, permeate, and energize our efforts with the power God has in store for his praying people.

A prayer group for missions meets this need. It's a group of people who are committed to praying daily (or at least regularly) for a missionary, a mission cause, or a specific mission field. It's a group of people united in spirit, convinced of the need for and the power of prayer. They are aware of specific needs on the mission field, for which they pray as a group. And they are willing to pay the price of faithful intercession.

what forms can a prayer group for missions take?

Prayer groups for missions can take many differing forms. For example, the prayer cell structure (described in chapter 12) easily lends itself to a missions focus. If your church already has prayer cells, you may want to ask each one to "adopt" a missionary or mission endeavor for their weekly and individual prayer times. Or you may want to form prayer cells whose primary purpose is to pray for missions.

A prayer chain also works well among a group that is interested in praying for missions. They may meet once a month or so to pray together as a group, but mainly they commit themselves to praying daily (or regularly) for missions, using the prayer chain to pass along weekly updates as well as emergency requests.

Or your church may wish to organize an all-night prayer vigil once or twice a year (perhaps in connection with a mission emphasis week), in which each hour of the vigil is devoted to a specific missionary or mission field supported by your church or denomination. Members of the congregation can sign up for the hours they wish to participate. It's helpful if printed sheets are distributed that provide a description of each missionary, including general information about the country and the history of the mission endeavor there, plus a list of prayer requests written by the missionaries themselves. For more suggestions on how you might organize such a prayer vigil, see chapter 14.

If you have a regular group praying for missions, make sure members are in regular contact with the person or the cause for whom they are praying. This contact is important not only to keep the group informed of the concerns that need to be lifted up in prayer, but also to encourage them with reports of how God has answered their prayers.

how should the group focus its prayers?

Your prayer groups for missions can focus their prayers in a number of ways. The most obvious way is to **assign each group a particular missionary.** Some churches ask their prayer groups not only to pray for their assigned missionaries but also to write letters of encouragement, send needed supplies, and learn about the needs, daily routines, and cultural difficulties that the missionaries encounter. This involvement helps make the prayers more specific, more heartfelt, and more of a priority in the prayer group.

> Some churches ask their prayer groups not only to pray for their assigned missionaries but also to write letters of encouragement, send needed supplies, and learn about the needs, daily routines, and cultural difficulties that the missionaries encounter.

Another way to focus prayer is to **assign each group a specific country or mission field.** This can be an effective way to pray:

- The group can focus on what's going on in a given country or region by following the newspapers and reports of political, social, economic, and agricultural news. They can pray for the specific needs of the entire area.

- People in the congregation who have a special interest in a certain country or area will often join the prayer group and help maintain a high level of interest in the group.

- Group members who may be considering missionary work themselves will find support and direction from the prayers of the group.

- Members of the prayer group may actively support a missionary in the assigned region; their involvement in the group will give them a greater appreciation for their missionary's situation.

- This group may find a resource such as Patrick Johnstone's *Operation World: A Day to Day Guide to Praying for the World* (WEC Publications) helpful in obtaining basic information about their assigned country or region.

A third option is to **assign the group a different missionary each month.** If your church does not support at least ten or twelve missionaries, you might ask your denominational mission board to send you information packets on a number of its missionaries.

- Prior to the beginning of each month, send copies of the information packet to each member of the prayer group. (If the group is large, you may want to divide it into four subgroups, assigning each a specific week of the month for prayer.) A month or two before you do this, however, notify the missionary and family that your group will be praying for them. Invite them to submit special prayer requests from the field and to send any recent newsletters. Many missionaries respond enthusiastically, and often group members become so interested that they write the missionaries back.

- This kind of prayer group for missions is especially effective for a young people's group. It gets young people to think about needs outside their own circles and culture, it encourages them in the discipline of

regular prayer, and it teaches them the crucial importance of mission work. Personal involvement with the missionaries and thoroughly researched information packets are vital, however, for maintaining high interest in the prayer group.

Your prayer group for missions may want to adopt a language group as a focus for their prayers, perhaps in connection with a ministry such as the Wycliffe Bible translators. Wycliffe sponsors the Bibleless People's Prayer Project, through which prayer groups can request to be assigned to a language group that has not yet had the entire Bible translated into their language.

Is there a need for this kind of prayer? Yes! Of the 6,703 distinct languages in our world, only 308 have the whole Bible published as of 1996. (About 760 more have the entire New Testament, and 1,014 more have at least one book of the Bible.) These languages encompass more than 90 percent of the world's population, but there are still at least 440 million people who have no part of the Bible available in their own language.

Prayer reaches even the remotest and smallest of these language groups. One prayer group was assigned a tribe in an African country that was closed to mission work. Another was asked to pray for a nomadic people, the Nahuas, in the Amazon rain forest whom no outsiders had ever seen—or at least returned alive to report about. Both prayer groups were discouraged by the difficulties their assignments presented, but they agreed to pray. And God worked in response. Not long after, several Nahuas appeared out of the Amazon and asked for someone to come help their tribe. Before the Wycliffe translators could translate a single verse, there were already believers among the Nahua. As for the African nation, it was quickly opened up for mission work, and

Wycliffe workers received permission to begin translation there.

George Cowan, president emeritus of Wycliffe, said this about his experience with praying for a language group:

One can't know the excitement and joy of answered prayer unless personally involved. Stories of answered prayer from others won't do it. My wife and I discovered this when we committed ourselves to pray daily for the two hundred thousand Sinti gypsies of Europe. We prayed faithfully for three-and-a-half years, with no indication that anything was happening.

Then, quite unexpectedly, we learned that Wycliffe had accepted a new member from Austria who was analyzing the Sinti language for a Ph.D. in linguistics. But God had done far more than we had asked or even dreamed. Two Sinti men, on their own initiative, had already begun translating Mark's gospel for small, struggling groups of Sinti believers in Germany who desperately needed it.

Other prayer groups may want to adopt a people as their focus of prayer. For more information on this kind of linking between prayer groups and people groups who have yet to be reached with the gospel, write to the Adopt a People Clearinghouse, P.O. Box 17490, Colorado Springs, CO 80935.

precepts for prayer groups

1. **Churches that haven't learned how to pray often show little interest in missions and evangelism.** Make sure that the prayer group or the entire congregation is well trained in the basics of prayer and knows what kind of commitment they're making. The result: a vital prayer life that brings with it a sense of outreach.

2. **Churches often learn fastest by example.** If the pastor has a keen interest in the work of missionaries and prays for them regularly, his example will get the church involved more quickly.

3. **The missions prayer group will have a broader impact on the life of the congregation than they may think.** Like a pebble that falls into the water and creates ever-widening ripples, their strength in prayer will gradually become a resource of spiritual power for the life of the whole church.

4. **Retirees may have the greatest amount of prayer time available.** It's vital to encourage the church's older members to enter retirement anticipating a life of intercession. Target this group especially in your workshops and seminars on prayer.

5. **Remember always that the key to prayer is love: our love for Jesus, and Jesus' love flowing through us.** If we do not love those for whom we pray, our prayers will lack the warmth and power of God's Spirit. Remember, praying for missions means praying for people's souls.

> Like a pebble that falls into the water and creates ever-widening ripples, their strength in prayer will gradually become a resource of spiritual power for the life of the whole church.

6. **Do you feel that asking Christians to pray places a burden on them?** You can do a person no greater favor than to help him or her enter a regular discipline of prayer. You are helping Christians in their spiritual growth

when you encourage them to pray daily for others.

7. **Perhaps one of the greatest regrets we will have at the end of our lives is the amount of time we spent in activities far less important than intercession.**

Are we making full use of the power of prayer in missions? How much power lies untapped in our churches? What might five minutes of prayer a day accomplish?

There are about 70 million evangelical Christians in North America. If only one million believers spent five minutes a day praying for unreached peoples, a powerhouse of over eight years of cumulative prayer would break loose over the world each day.

Five minutes a day. That's only two percent of the amount of time that most evangelical Christians spend watching TV and shopping every day. Our prayer groups for missions can help congregations begin to see the deep need for prayer and the great difference that even five minutes a day can make.

19

SUPPORT FELLOWSHIP GROUPS

John and Elaine's relationship with their two teenage daughters had been difficult in the past year and a half. Their daughters, ages 17 and 15, had fallen into the wrong group of friends and were dating boys whom their parents suspected of using drugs.

John and Elaine were especially worried about the girls' reluctance to talk with them. Jill and Karen still confided in each other, but only behind closed doors. They no longer talked to their parents about school, about their friends, or their plans for college.

"I just don't understand what they're rebelling against," said Elaine. "We've always been a close family and never had any big quarrels or a lot of anger. I feel like I don't know my daughters anymore. They seem like strangers."

John and Elaine received counseling together and persuaded Jill and Karen to join them several times. But things were progressing slowly. John felt there was a spiritual battle going on that needed fighting through prayer. Elaine agreed that they should share their family problem with their support fellowship group from church. "I'm coming to trust the members in our group more and more," she told John. "Something like this is personal, but enough of them have shared their own family problems that I know

they'd understand. And I'm beginning to see that prayer really changes things."

When John and Elaine shared their situation with the support fellowship group, they were overwhelmed by members' responses. The group promised to pray daily for John and Elaine's relationship with Jill and Karen. They agreed to pray specifically against Satan's influence through the girls' friends and to ask God for healing through the family counselor's advice.

But what surprised John and Elaine the most was the support they received through phone calls, encouraging notes, and the people who listened and understood their struggle and anxiety. They hadn't realized how alone they had felt before sharing their concerns with the group. "The prayers and the support have made a big difference in my attitude alone," said Elaine. "I can see God working in all of our lives through this. I'm just so grateful for a place where I know people care about us and pray."

what is a support fellowship group?

A support fellowship group is a small group of believers who covenant to meet regularly for fellowship and to pray with and for each other. They pledge their mutual support in personal, family, and vocational life. They're a group of people who are committed to the Lord and to each other.

Support fellowship groups accomplish several important goals that unite a church in supportive prayer and fellowship. A support fellowship group

- gives believers strength to serve Christ in all areas of their lives.

- creates an atmosphere of interdependence within the body of Christ. This is especially important in a culture in which many people suffer from loneliness and alienation.

- provides a place where believers can share their convictions and experiences, thus enriching their own and others' faith.

- enables Christians to find support and strength in each other.

- helps members grow spiritually and develop basic spiritual disciplines.

- encourages believers to develop vision and outreach beyond themselves, thus heeding Christ's command "Obey everything I have commanded you" (Matthew 28:20).

Who needs this kind of group? It's for Christian business professionals, parents, pastors, young couples, homemakers, college students, and any other group of Christians who want to support each other in spiritual and personal growth.

Because of its inward focus, a support fellowship group differs from prayer cells and church support groups, which are more outward looking. The size of the group should be kept small—five or six members—to allow for deep fellowship and involvement in each other's lives. New members are allowed to join only at the invitation of the group.

Is this kind of group necessary in the church? Surveys show a great need for supportive fellowship within our churches and culture. An average of one-third of any group experiences a major economic or vocational upheaval at any given time; another 20 percent face domestic crises. That means more than half of a given group of people are facing severe tests in their lives. A support fellowship group gives these people a place to share their burdens and receive prayer support and encouragement.

how do we form support fellowship groups?

Your church may choose to explain what such groups are and why they are valuable, then formally invite its members to form support fellowship groups. You may want to use sign-up sheets or structure the formation of such groups in another way.

The most effective way of forming support fellowship groups, however, happens when two people discover in each other a common loyalty to Christ and a common desire for mutual support. To form their group, they ask God to help them discover others of like mind who might join them. Those who come together agree on such things as where and when to meet, how often they'll get together, and how long they will meet before reevaluating their commitment as a group. (There should always be a set period of time from six months to a year or so after which group members can decide to drop out of the group or to renew their commitment.)

A support fellowship group requires deeper commitment from its members

A support fellowship group is a small group of believers who covenant to meet regularly for fellowship and to pray with and for each other.

than other prayer groups might. The group should give careful thought to the following commitments:

- to attend all meetings (or to make attendance a high priority)

- to be sensitive and supportive of the others to the best of one's ability

- to trust oneself to the others by sharing, as freely and honestly as possible, what one's life is like (This may happen by degrees, not all at once.)

- to faithfully support other group members in prayer

- to build relationships with group members outside of the group meeting itself

- to keep confidential what is shared in the group

- to always affirm the other group members, expressing unconditional love to each other (Members should renew this covenant of affirmation with each other on a regular basis, following Jesus' example of unconditional love and affirmation. See John 1:40-42, 47-51; Luke 7:36-47; 19:1-10.)

- to be committed to each other in the spirit of Christ, regardless of each other's differences

- to pour out hearts sacrificially for each other and for the world of human need, as led by the Lord

Early in their meetings, members should review a brief history of their lives, share their feelings about their roles in life, talk about their strengths and weaknesses, and do some thinking aloud with the group about their personal goals. Why is this sharing necessary? Because you can't support each other without knowing each other.

This trust and openness come only by degrees. You don't have to trust all of your private life to the other members at this time. In fact, you may want to spend about five weeks gradually getting to know each other, using the following sharing questions each successive week:

1. **Review your personal history, answering questions like these:** Where were you born? What is your family like? What schooling have you had? If you're married, how did you meet your spouse? How did you decide on your present vocation? How would you describe your spiritual pilgrimage? What special interests do you have?

2. **Tell how you feel about your role** as a spouse, parent, employer/employee, friend, son/daughter, church member, child of God, or whatever role is important in your life right now.

3. **What weaknesses and strengths do you see in yourself?** How do these affect your life right now? Your family and friends? Your vocation?

4. **Share with each of the group members a strength or quality that you see in him or her.**

5. **What are two or three personal goals you'd like to achieve in your life?** In what areas do you want to grow and develop relationships with family members, personal devotions, vocation, and so on? Share these goals with the group and explain each one.

This time of sharing is very important. The relationships we find in our culture often yield only superficial conversation. Though we fear getting hurt, we long to know and to be known by others at a deep, personal level. The questions above allow us to get beyond superficial chitchat and talk about things that matter to us. We're no longer talking just about ideas and concepts; we're talking about ourselves, our hopes, our history, our feelings, our faith journeys, our day-to-day experiences. Such sharing brings the risk of rejection, but without this sharing we risk losing the love of those who can support and encourage us.

what's the best format for a support fellowship meeting?

Your group may choose one person to lead the discussion, to introduce the prayer time, and to keep the meeting moving. You may consider rotating leadership. Be creative with your meeting time. You might meet over a meal, perhaps getting together for breakfast in a local restaurant. Homemakers might arrange for childcare during one morning or afternoon each week or have a weekly night out together. You might also include getting together for various ministry activities, Bible study, recreation, and so on.

The central purpose of your meeting is sharing your joys and concerns and praying together about what you've shared. If this time is shortened by Bible study, group activities, or casual conversation, you're losing your focus as a support fellowship group. The leader should be ready to steer the group away from detractions.

Members should also try to pray for each other every day (but avoid laying guilt on yourself or others if this doesn't always happen). If a member is going through a particularly rough time, remember that person during the week with a phone call, note, or other way of telling them that you care for them.

Your sharing time will focus on a number of areas in your lives:

- your calendar or weekly schedule: upcoming events, meetings, challenges, and so on

- relationships: What am I working on this week?

- goals: What am I trying to achieve in my life?

- ministries: How has God been calling me to use my gifts in the church and community? What has been happening?

what types of support fellowship groups are possible?

Professionals. This group of people have special needs that can be met in a support fellowship group. They need support with evangelism in a secular work environment; they want to learn how to balance work and family; and they need encouragement to lean on God in a world of competition and affluence.

To meet these needs, group members must be committed to listening to each other and to encouraging each other to get involved in group discussion and prayer. This group should probably rotate leadership. Members should work together to find the right level of accountability for each person—accountability that challenges but does not threaten.

This trust and openness comes only by degrees.

The group should also motivate its members to model the truth of God's Word in their lives and professions and make it easy for them to talk about the times they've failed. The group should allow members to express their individuality in the group. And it should draw on each member's gifts and talents to challenge and edify the other members. In so doing, group members will find that their needs bring them together in a special kind of unity in Christ.

Couples. This is a natural way to choose members for a support fellowship group, though the group should not be larger than four couples. Their purpose should be to support each other so that each member will be more effective in caring and in sharing the love of God in the workplace and at home.

> The relationships we find in our culture often yield only superficial conversation. . . . We long to know and to be known by others at a deep, personal level.

Often the couples who make up a group will be about the same age and situation in life—for example, young marrieds, parents of young children, middle-aged couples, or retirees. However, couples may find it stimulating to be in a group with couples of differing ages and lifestyles. One group of four couples did just that and found their fellowship enriched by the diversity. They took turns leading (desiring to develop leadership skills within the group), met once each week for two hours, and also gathered for social occasions and ministry projects. After one year of meeting together, they reevaluated their experience and decided to make some changes: more outreach, greater accountability, and more spiritual disciplines.

Post-college singles. Members of this age group may feel a need for greater commitment to other believers and more challenge in their walk with Christ than they are finding in their church fellowship group. Their commitment to each other in a support fellowship group will help them set healthy directions and grow stronger in their faith at this important time in their lives.

One group of twelve post-college singles met every week for two hours of Bible study, sharing, and prayer. They often began around the piano, singing hymns of praise to prepare them to hear God's Word. They found that their sharing times were more meaningful after this kind of preparation.

After a month and a half, however, it became obvious that the group was too large for in-depth sharing. They divided into two groups of six, which proved to be much easier to handle. They also found it important to be accountable to each other: to consistently read the Word and pray during the week and to come prepared to tell the group how God had worked in their lives that week.

Fathers. "Going it alone" may be the way of the American male, but it's a risky business. Even the best father has his blind spots and vulnerable moments, so it's good to seek out three or four other fathers for candid sharing and accountability. This will perhaps be the single most important parenting step these men will take. Men who are interested in such a group should look for two to five others who might also be interested, whose fathering responsibilities are similar to their own, and whose faith they respect.

Group members should commit themselves to meeting for six weeks before reevaluating the group and their commitment to it. You might assign each member to come with a personal fathering struggle. Be sure to spend at least fifteen minutes of your meeting in prayer for each other (this may be the most difficult discipline to keep). Here are some helpful starter questions:

- Describe your father (or the strongest father figure in your life). How are you and he alike? How are you and he different?

- What does each of your children need from you most at this stage of his or her life?

- What's the biggest barrier you face in being a good dad this week?

- How well do you and your wife work as a parenting team? What are your strengths and weaknesses?

Pastors. Though a group of caring elders can help a pastor immeasurably, most pastors have few or no peers with whom to confide or pray. Meeting together with a few local pastors can offer these leaders security, support, a safe listening ear, and powerful prayer partners.

There are other benefits to a pastor's support fellowship group as well:

- the ability to sense God's leading not only in one church but also in the entire community

- the growth of conviction that pastors need to pray for revival

- a growing unity between leaders and churches that had formerly looked on each other as rivals

- the recognition that Christians of every denomination need each other

A pastor's prayer group needs several qualities to achieve the right chemistry. Humility is perhaps the most important—the ability to put aside a competitive spirit and to share weaknesses with each other. A second quality is kingdom vision—a perspective on the church of Christ that transcends the narrow focus of a single church or denomination. Third, the pastors need to see this meeting as a priority, as essential to their ministry in the church and community. Finally, they need to recognize and put to use each other's gifts: coordinating, teaching, discerning, saying a prophetic word, and so on.

The examples above are only a few of the types of support fellowship groups possible. As you promote this kind of prayer group in your congregation, ask God to help you find the right combination for the people who make up your church.

what makes a support fellowship group attractive?

Such a group meets personal and spiritual needs by helping many members discover the meaning of the term "communion of the saints." It moves them beyond superficial conversation into the important issues of their lives and faith.

Also, this kind of group has the freedom to set its own schedule, meeting format, leadership structure, level of commitment, and so on. Members can agree together on the structure that they feel most comfortable with.

Being involved in a support fellowship group draws the members out of their self-centered approach to faith and life. It wakes them up to the need to respond to others, to support and care for each other as Christ calls them to.

> **Being involved in a support fellowship group draws the members out of their self-centered approach to faith and life.**

This group also brings its members into a deep, thoughtful commitment to each other. This is a refreshing change from other relationships in which there is no accountability, little honesty, and uncertain commitment.

Here's what some people said about their support fellowship group:

"The sharing is what made the group special. It allowed love to flow, where normally one might keep the relationship very businesslike. I found that the more I could share, the more I understood myself. On the other side, when I was able to listen and support a brother, I received as much as he did. I felt worth and joy within myself that I could reach out and touch or help someone else. I can feel the love of Christ."

"Many times in the group prayers, I sensed the real power and presence of the Holy Spirit. The prayer times were the most meaningful parts of the support fellowship groups in that our needs truly were taken in God's hands and he answered them."

"I received support from the group in various ways. Prayer support was meaningful, especially in times of stress or crisis. Also, the opportunity to develop deep-level friendships with others in a similar family and business position was important. Spiritually I have grown in many ways, including the area of devotions and in my concern and love for others in Christ's family."

what are some dangers in this kind of group?

Spiritual pride may creep into a support fellowship group when members view themselves as superior to those who are not in such a fellowship. Other members may seek the limelight in group discussions and prayer or may be judgmental of someone who has shared a problem or weakness. Members should be aware of the danger of spiritual pride and make it part of their evaluation process every six months or so.

Breaches of confidentiality can also destroy the trust in a support group. Group members learn much about each other's lives: their dreams, their failures, their problems and griefs. It's easy to let that information slip out—often under the guise of prayer requests to others. Members need to guard against this by reviewing their commitment to confiden-

tiality regularly. They need to realize that if they have a concern for someone's problem, the place to talk about it is in their private prayer closet.

A support fellowship group can also lose its momentum if its focus is exclusively inward. Members may come only to receive, not give, support. Discussion and prayer also tend to get stale if the group is not concerned with people outside of its circle. Members should trust the Lord to lead them in ways of reaching out as a group to others with the love and support they've found together.

20

PASTOR'S PRAYER SUPPORT TEAM

Intercession for Christian leaders is the most underutilized source of spiritual power in churches today.
—C. Peter Wagner

Intercession for the pastor? Isn't the pastor supposed to be praying for the congregation? Of course, but the role of pastor or pastor's spouse can be one of the most demanding and lonely positions in the congregation. Ministers are pulled in many directions as they try to involve themselves in all aspects of the church's ministry. They are at the forefront of the church's spiritual battles, yet they often feel a step removed from congregational members, with no safe place to bring their personal needs.

That's the purpose of the pastor's prayer support team. It's a group of church members who are committed to praying specifically and regularly for the pastor and the pastor's ministries in the church. These church members recognize the special demands that ministry places on pastors and their spouses. They commit themselves to praying for the pastor's personal needs and ministries. This prayer support team is designed to give pastors and their spouses the spiritual and emotional rapport they need to minister effectively in the church.

the need for intercession

Peter Wagner uses a passage from the Old Testament to highlight the need for prayer on behalf of church leaders, who are at the forefront in the battle against spiritual opposition:

The Amalekites came and attacked the Israelites at Rephidim. Moses said to Joshua, "Choose some of our men and go out to fight the Amalekites. Tomorrow I will stand on top of the hill with the staff of God in my hands."

So Joshua fought the Amalekites as Moses had ordered, and Moses, Aaron and Hur went to the top of the hill. As long as Moses held up his hands, the Israelites were winning, but whenever he lowered his hands, the Amalekites were winning. When Moses' hands grew tired, they took a stone and put it under him and he sat on it. Aaron and Hur held his hands up—one on one side, one on the other—so that his hands remained steady till sunset. So Joshua overcame the Amalekite army with the sword.—Exodus 17:8-13

This story emphasizes the power behind the battle—the power of prayer. Moses saw that his primary duty was to uphold Joshua in prayer on the hilltop. How much praying was Joshua able to do in the heat of battle? Little or none. His power came through the constant intercession of others. Many Christian leaders are like Joshua—busy, active, fighting. But there are often few intercessors to give their ministry the spiritual power for victory.

Many leaders today could echo the apostle Paul's desperate pleas to the New Testament Christians:

I urge you, brothers, by our Lord Jesus Christ and by the love of the Spirit, to join me in my struggle by praying to God for me.—Romans 15:30

Pray in the Spirit on all occasions with all kinds of prayers and requests. With this in mind, be alert and always keep on praying for all the saints. Pray also for me, that whenever I open my mouth, words may be given me so that I will fearlessly make known the mystery of the gospel.
—Ephesians 6:18-19

Brothers, pray for us.
—1 Thessalonians 5:25

Pastors and leaders need intercession because they are especially visible and especially vulnerable in God's kingdom—making them one of Satan's primary targets. Satan can most easily discredit God's church by discrediting its leaders. And he has been quite successful at that in past decades. Newspapers and magazines regularly carry stories of leaders who have fallen prey to greed, lust, financial mismanagement, and a host of other sins. Following are a few factors that make Christian leaders especially vulnerable.

First, leaders have more responsibility than the average Christian, and, as a result, they're held more accountable.

"Not many of you should presume to be teachers, my brothers, because you know that we who teach will be judged more strictly" (James 3:1). When they fall, the crash is louder.

Second, pastors and leaders face more temptation than other Christians. They are higher on Satan's hit list, and he'll try anything to thwart them: greed, power, pride, lust, demonic activity, mental and physical disorders, and so on.

Third, Christian leaders are targets of spiritual warfare. Most Christians may not realize this, but Satan worshipers also practice prayer. For example, a group of Satanists in London committed themselves one year to pray to Satan for the elimination of a number of evangelical leaders throughout the city through the breakdown of their marriages and families. Later that year, the group was honored at one of its conventions for being the most successful; they had succeeded in aiding the downfall of five significant leaders through immorality and marital breakdown.

On a flight from Detroit to Boston, a Baptist church leader sat next to a man whose head was bowed in prayer for much of the flight. Impressed, he asked his neighbor if he was a Christian. The man replied, "Oh, no. You have me all wrong. I'm not a Christian; I'm actually a Satanist." Asked what he was praying for, the man responded, "My primary attention is directed toward the fall of Christian pastors and their families living in New England." With that, he returned to his work of prayer.

A fourth factor that makes pastors and leaders in greater need of prayer is their influence on others. Many believers may have been converted and discipled through their ministry. When leaders fall, believers are more ready to

Being a pastor or a pastor's spouse can be one of the most demanding and lonely positions in the congregation.

hear Satan's accusation that the gospel is also false. Satan knows how to play his cards. When leaders fall, they pull many down with them.

Finally, pastors and leaders have the greatest visibility within the church. Like all public figures, they are subject to more gossip and criticism. Because their message often nudges individuals out of their comfort zone, people are out to get them. This puts leaders in greater need of prayer.

Pastors and leaders need intercession because they are especially visible and especially vulnerable in God's kingdom—making them one of Satan's primary targets.

Unfortunately, pastors themselves often don't recognize their need to have others interceding for them. Jimmy Swaggart, before his fall from a reputable ministry, wrote,

I have always taken pride in my spiritual strength. I have believed that in my relationship with God, if He promised me something, I could have it. I can't recall, in all of my life, ever going to anybody and asking them for help.

—*The Evangelist,* March 1987

After the scandal was exposed, he penned these comments:

Maybe Jimmy Swaggart has tried to live his entire life as though he were not human. And I have thought that with the Lord, knowing He is omnipotent and omniscient, that there was nothing I could not do. . . . And I think this is the reason (in my limited knowledge) that I did not find the victory I sought because I did not seek the help of my brothers and sisters in the Lord. . . . If I had sought the help of those that loved me, with their added strength, I look back now and know that victory would have been mine.

—*Charisma and Christian Life,* April 1988

how do pastor's prayer support teams get started?

Some prayer support teams are initiated by members of the congregation who sense their pastor's need and are willing to help.

Take the case of Ben and Jan, for example. Ben was discouraged. He was beginning his third charge, a one-hundred-family church that had been split over several controversial issues. He and his wife, Jan, found that most church members tried to find out their opinions on the issues and then either treated them as enemies or friends. As a result, Ben began to feel that his ministry was ineffective at best.

Then a small group of church members approached Ben and said that they wanted to support him and his wife in prayer. They were concerned about the church's health and about the pressure Ben was feeling. "Do you have any specific requests we can pray for?" they asked.

Ben and the prayer support group met over coffee, where he talked about some of the tensions he was dealing with and asked for prayer regarding some specific ministries he was involved in. Ben was careful not to criticize church members or tell too much in his prayer requests, but he was grateful for a group of people who were there to listen to his concerns and accept him as he was. Even more rewarding were the subsequent meetings at which he shared God's answers to the group's specific prayers. Healing in church relationships was one evidence of the Spirit's work in response to their prayer.

Jan was drawn into the group after a few months, and she found a place where she, too, could relax and be herself. The group prayed that she would find her own place in the church's ministry, and Jan found the confidence to suggest that she start a singles' support group from the families in the church and the neighborhood. Jan had a special burden for single parents, having come from a broken home herself. She worked hard at promoting the group and was pleased when both church and community people responded. Three unchurched women joined the church's Bible study group as a result of Jan's group, and two neighborhood families began coming regularly to church. All were prepared through the daily prayers of the prayer support group.

Ben especially appreciated the support group's prayer for him on Saturday evenings and Sunday mornings. He saw it as an essential source of power and inspiration for preaching God's Word. He knew that the group was committed to praying during the sermon especially, asking that God's Spirit would use his words to touch people's hearts. They were also committed to praying for any visitors who might be present that Sunday. Feeling confident that God heard and answered those prayers, Ben preached with an enthusiasm and conviction that he had not known earlier.

Pastors can also initiate the formation of a prayer support group. John Maxwell, former pastor and founder of Injoy, Atlanta, Georgia, offers the following suggestions and guidelines for establishing an effective and lively pastor's prayer support group:

- Work with people from the church who show solid, committed spiritual leadership or the potential for it. Invite them to share in your ministry, committing themselves to be your prayer partners for at least one year.

- Explain that the commitment requires praying daily for the needs of the church. It also means praying

one day each month (or each week, depending on the number of people involved) specifically for the pastor. (If monthly, ask each prayer partner to pray on the day of the prayer partner's birthday; i.e., if the prayer partner was born on August 7, she prays for the pastor on the 7th of each month.)

- Some prayer partners will be scheduled each week to lay hands on you and pray for you before the service, then to pray in a separate room for you during the worship service.

- Begin the year-long commitment in September with a prayer partner retreat—one day set aside for teaching, intensive prayer, and personal sharing and testimonies. For those who have participated the previous year, give opportunity to renew that commitment for another year.

> **The prayer partnership is a two-way relationship—you as pastor also commit to praying for your partners each month on the date of their birthday.**

- Ask all prayer partners to meet monthly or quarterly for a prayer breakfast, which serves as the teaching and prayer time together. You might give a teaching on prayer, show a film, or discuss a book you've read together, but be sure to allow plenty of time for praying with each other!

- The prayer partnership is a two-way relationship—you as pastor also commit to praying for your partners each month on the date of their birthday. (Again, for a smaller group, you may want to do this weekly instead of monthly, assigning each partner a specific day of the week.)

- To communicate prayer needs, you may want to send out a weekly schedule of church ministry activities, your weekly schedule, and any upcoming decisions that face you and the church leaders. Also, give your prayer partners the opportunity to let you know their needs for prayer. For special needs or emergencies, establish a prayer chain among the prayer partners so you can pass the information on quickly.

- The larger the church, the more organization and scheduling are required for the pastor's prayer support team. If at all possible, appoint a coordinator who has not only a healthy prayer life but also the ability to lead people and oversee details. The coordinator schedules people for prayer during the services, writes to remind them of their commitment, sees that prayer requests are passed along, sets up the prayer chain, and serves as a contact person when prayer partners have questions or are unable to reach the pastor.

- The size of your pastor's prayer support group will depend on the size of your church. If your church is small, try for seven people (to cover each day of the week) or thirty people (to cover the days in a month). Larger churches will be able to sign up two or three people for each day of the month.

Whatever form your pastor's prayer support team takes, it will be a multifaceted blessing to your congregation by giving prayer warriors the opportunity to exercise their gifts, by developing spiritual maturity and prayer disciplines among those who participate, and by unleashing the power of prayer on the front lines of your ministry. Begin with whatever core members you have to work with. Challenge them to see the scope of their ministry: what you need from them as a pastor, what they can become through the discipline of committed prayer, and how they can serve the church through their spiritual leadership.

21

CONCERT OF PRAYER

I sat in the third row at the local symphony last week. I was close enough to see the musicians shuffle their feet on the floor as they played, moving back and forth in time to the music as if nothing else mattered. Led by the conductor, each part joined with another, forming melody and countermelody, until the music of individual instruments blended into beautiful harmony.

This is the image behind a concert of prayer—individuals gathering to pray under the direction of one or more leaders, blending individual voices into a single offering of prayer to God.

The concert of prayer is distinct from all other gatherings, including the prayer meeting (described in chapter 13). Prayer leaders offer direction in the way the prayers are orchestrated, suggesting different kinds of prayer (such as thanksgiving, praise, repentance, intercession, and so on). Leaders also suggest various themes, such as personal ministries, awakening in the church, world evangelism, and so on. But mainly it is the people who do the praying—often aloud.

Just as a full orchestra can be broken down into soloists and smaller musical ensembles, people gathered for a concert of prayer are often asked to pray in different kinds of small groups—as individuals, as prayer partners, in groups of five or six.

Prayers are always kept short to allow everyone to participate. Sometimes just one person leads the whole group in prayer. Other times they pray through song or through the Scriptures. Prayer is thus interspersed with music and Bible reading to allow God to speak to the people as well as the people to God. In quiet listening times, people are encouraged to hear the inner voice of the Father.

There's another meaning to the word *concert*, implying a *concerted* effort. In this respect, the people are united in their sustained commitment to seek God in prayer. God's Spirit, who orchestrates all the prayers that are offered, unites God's people with one heart and mind to rejoice, to repent, to make requests, to intercede for others.

Jonathan Edwards provided an accurate, if lengthy, description of the term *concert of prayer* in the title of his book written in the 1740s to equip Christians for prayer: *An Humble Attempt to Promote Explicit Agreement and Visible Union of God's People in Extraordinary Prayer of the Revival of Religion and the Advancement of Christ's Kingdom on Earth.*

There's now a renewed interest in concerts of prayer throughout much of the world, particularly in the United States. This broad movement (1) crosses denominational lines by including believers from different churches, ministries, social levels, generations, and even doctrinal camps; (2) focuses on spiritual awakening and world evangelism; and (3) rejoices in hope that God's promises will be kept and that he will answer prayers for spiritual awakening and world evangelism.

As we mentioned in chapter 13, after initial feelings of discomfort with praying aloud during a concert of prayer, your church members may find it to be an invaluable and uplifting experience. Hearing others pray aloud around us encourages our own participation in prayer; the reality and power of communal prayer sinks in as we hear our voices joining with others in petition, adoration, and thanksgiving. There is a dynamic here that is entirely missing from our usual ways of praying together. Everyone is focused at once; everyone participates in verbal prayers, which hold their attention more easily than mental prayers.

If members worry about the distraction caused by the multitude of voices, remind them that God doesn't find it disconcerting in the least. Hearing many prayers at one time has never seemed to be a problem for God.

what's the value of a concert of prayer?

First, a concert of prayer is a way to network the body of Christ within a particular church, denomination, city, college campus, and so on. It provides a neutral meeting ground in which believers of different traditions are united in an overarching concern for God's kingdom through mutual prayer. They can sharpen each other's prayer ministry and help everyone involved to see that we need each other—leaders, laypeople, mission workers, youth.

Second, a concert of prayer is a good training ground for those who wish to mobilize prayer throughout the body of Christ. Concerts of prayer should be organized so that participants can adapt what they've experienced to fit the situations in which they pray with others. A concert of prayer is meant to be a workshop as well as a ministry.

Third, concerts of prayer provide a sustaining foundation for ministry. United prayer is our base of operations; it taps into the power of God's Spirit to equip believers to become more spiritually attuned and more committed to Christ's cause. A concert of prayer can become a vital source of power for all local ministries.

> **God's Spirit, who orchestrates all the prayers that are offered, unites God's people with one heart and mind to rejoice, to repent, to make requests, to intercede for others.**

where can we use a concert of prayer?

In addition to the broad-based concerts of prayer that gather people from all over the continent or throughout the world, concerts of prayer can also be organized on a local scale.

For example, individual churches can organize a concert of prayer for their congregations, perhaps as part of a larger worship service. You can adapt the concert of prayer into your service by asking people to pray on a number of different themes, interspersed with Scripture readings and songs. You can also ask the congregation to pray alone, in pairs, or in "huddles" of six persons to cover different topics and prayer needs.

A church can also use the concert-of-prayer format in its prayer service, such as one held on the National Day of Prayer. A standard format includes a number of basic components: celebration, preparation, dedication, seeking fullness, seeking fulfillment, testimonies, and closing. Here's one sample two-hour format, suggested by David Bryant in his book *Operation: Prayer.*

I. CELEBRATION (15 min.)
—Praise in hymns and choruses, focus on awakening and mission
—Reports of God's answers to prayers offered during previous concerts
—Prayers of praise for God's faithfulness, for his kingdom, for his Son

II. PREPARATION (20 min.)
—Welcome to the concert!
—Overview: Why are we here?
—Biblical perspective on what we're praying toward (spiritual awakening, world evangelization)
—Preview of the format
—Teaming up in partners and huddles

III. DEDICATION (5 min.)
—Commitment: to be servants through prayer and to be used in answer to our prayers
—Thanksgiving: for the privilege of united prayer and for those with whom we unite
—Invitation for Christ to lead the concert and to pray through us
—Hymn of praise

IV. SEEKING FOR FULLNESS/ AWAKENING IN THE CHURCH (30 min.)
—In partners: for personal revival
—In huddles: for awakening in our local churches and ministries
—As a whole: for awakening in the church worldwide
—Pause to listen to God
—Chorus

V. SEEKING FOR FULFILLMENT/ MISSION AMONG THE NATIONS (30 min.)
—In partners: for personal ministries
—In huddles: for outreach and mission in our city or campus
—As a whole: for world evangelization
—Pause to listen to God
—Chorus

VI. TESTIMONIES: WHAT HAS GOD SAID TO US HERE? (10 min.)
—On fullness (awakening)
—On fulfillment (mission)

VII. GRAND FINALE (10 min.)
—Offering ourselves to be answers to our prayers and also to live accordingly
—Prayer for God's empowerment in our own lives for ministry
—Prayer for prayer movements locally and worldwide
—Offering praise to the Father, who will answer our concert of prayer in wonderful ways
—Leave to watch and serve "in concert"

This format can also be used on the occasion of a church's designated prayer meeting to draw together people involved in prayer ministries—prayer cells, meetings, classes, telephone ministries, and so on. You might also include those involved in education, evangelism, fellowship, service, and administration. Though the concert of prayer is generally open to everyone, make sure that people in key ministries are encouraged to attend and that the issues and concerns close to their hearts are included in the prayer time.

Concerts of prayer also work well as a joint effort between two or more congregations. In fact, they can be ideal for the churches located in a classis, presbytery, conference, or region of the country. A concert of prayer gives these churches the opportunity to share their mutual concerns for building up the church, for ministries they share, for issues they face, and so on. It gives the churches in a given community or area a chance to focus prayers on their common warfare against Satan. For such a gathering, a church building may not be sufficient; look into renting an auditorium of the appropriate size.

City-wide concerts of prayer can focus on neighborhood outreach, concern for schools and drug abuse, local government, and other matters of mutual concern. You can seek leadership from local churches or from a national prayer concert headquarters.

Conventions and college campuses are other arenas well-suited for a concert of prayer. Conferences for youth, for education leaders, for evangelical leaders, or for mission groups can benefit from a concert of prayer that focuses on their unique issues as well as on the broader issues of spiritual awakening and world evangelism. On high school and college campuses, a concert of prayer can increase depth of unity and spiritual awareness for believers from many different backgrounds.

guidelines and suggestions for your concert of prayer

This section assumes that you will follow the basic pattern described earlier in this chapter. Feel free to adapt these guidelines to fit your particular situation.

During the *celebration* time, focus your praise on God's character as revealed in Christ. Highlight God's desire for spiritual awakening and world evangelization. Do this through hymns and choruses that you've chosen to reflect the major themes in your concert of prayer. Don't preach; simply introduce each song with a few brief comments. At the end of this time, have three or four participants lead the entire group in brief prayers of praise for what has already happened in your time together.

For the *preparation*, welcome everyone and explain the unique purpose and character of a concert of prayer. Give a brief biblical perspective on the hope that we have as we turn to God in prayer, seeking spiritual awakening and world evangelization. As you introduce everyone to the format for the prayer concert, you may want to distribute a printed program. Explain the flow of what's happening and the importance of each part of your prayer time. Suggest that participants be sensitive to each other in how long their prayers are, how loud, and so on.

Help people get to know one another by asking what church or ministry they're from, if they've been to a concert of prayer before, and so on. Then ask them to find partners, giving them a minute or two to get acquainted. Next ask the pairs of partners to gather in groups of three pairs to form a huddle of six people. Inform the group that throughout the evening they'll be praying as individuals, as partners, as huddles, and as an entire group.

The *dedication* is a short time in which the leadership team guides the entire group through a time of silent prayer. Give the group a brief time to offer silent prayers after you introduce the following topics: reaffirming their desire to serve God through a ministry of intercession, confessing any known sins and asking God's forgiveness, asking for the Spirit's filling and guidance, thanking God for everyone else gathered and for his ability

> **A concert of prayer can bring a greater depth of unity and spiritual awareness to believers from many different backgrounds.**

to blend them all into one symphony of prayer. At the end of this time, the leader should offer a prayer that invites the Lord Jesus to take up his role as high priest among his people.

In the half hour or so allotted to *seeking for fullness*, everyone unites in prayer to seek the fullness of Christ in the church's life—both locally and worldwide. First, ask partners to pray together after a brief time in which they share areas in which they need personal revival and renewal. Prayers for each other should be brief.

What does God want me to do to fulfill his desires in the areas of spiritual awakening and world evangelization?

After three or four minutes, ask the people to form huddles and pray for awakening in their own church fellowships and throughout their city or campus. Remind participants that prayers should be brief, based on Scripture, and as specific as possible. After about seven minutes, call everyone back to pray as an entire group. Ask a few people to lead this time, offering short and specific prayers for spiritual awakening worldwide.

Finally, ask the group to sit in silence, listening to what God might want to say to them personally about the issue of spiritual awakening. Conclude by standing to sing a song or chorus that focuses on the themes you've touched on.

In the next half hour, designated as a time for *seeking fulfillment*, choose another leader to help guide the group into seeking the fulfillment of Christ's cause throughout the world and throughout your community.

Follow the same pattern as in the previous section, using partners, huddles, and group prayer to pray for mission outreach; for the three billion in our world who have not heard and received the gospel; for victims of world hunger, war, injustice, poverty, disease, immorality, and so on. Prayer partners should pray for each other's ministries. You might also ask any missionaries present to stand while the entire group offers a special prayer on their behalf. Close with the two minutes of silent listening, as before, and with a song that focuses on the theme of missions.

Use the *testimonies* time to share what God might want you to do in response to your prayer time. In huddles, participants can share their thoughts on this question: What does God want me to do to fulfill his desires in the areas of spiritual awakening and world evangelization? Am I willing to serve him in this way? This might involve a new dream or vision for ministry or a renewed commitment to an already existing ministry. Remind the group to keep testimonies short and to focus them on the question you've given them.

In the *grand finale*, ask everyone to move into a time of personal, private prayer, offering their lives for God to use in any way he chooses. This prayer time should end after about two minutes, when people get back into their huddles to pray for each other's lives. Ask for the Spirit's power in each other's lives, to begin the work of awakening and of bringing forth new ministries.

Then ask everyone to stand as one body while three people from the leadership team lead the group in prayer for a prayer movement that grows throughout the country and the world. Conclude with songs of praise, anticipating the answers that will come in response to your intercession.

Urge people to greet each other as they leave, and provide them with information on the next concert of prayer.

n

22

PERSONAL PRAYER RETREAT

"Take a whole day out of my busy schedule to pray? I just don't have the time!" That's the instinctive response most of us would give if someone encouraged us to spend a day alone with God in prayer and reflection.

But those who have made the effort to carve time out of their demanding, sometimes hectic schedules have found this extended time alone with God to be one of the most refreshing, important, and helpful experiences they've ever had. "I never thought a day could make so much difference," one writes. "My relationship to everyone seems improved," says another. "Why don't I do it more often?" Still another person comments, "A day alone with God helped me focus my life with a saner, more biblical perspective—something my busy life had crowded out."

Jesus knew the necessity of an extended time alone with God. So did his apostles. So have the men and women God has used throughout the church's history to build his kingdom and to awaken people to the gospel.

And so can you if you put aside the matters that seem pressing and give priority to the most important times in your life: your prayer times with God.

why spend an extended time alone with God?

First, we need times of deeper, more intensive fellowship with God beyond our morning devotions. We need time just to think about and be with God. God has called us into *fellowship* with him and his Son; this fellowship is nurtured by being together. "Come near to God and he will come near to you," writes James (4:8). We need time in God's presence. "As for me, it is good to be near God," sings the psalmist (Psalm 73:28).

Second, extended time alone with God gives us opportunity for personal reflection and renewal. We're alerted to our need for deeper prayer when our spiritual wells run dry, when we're running on our own energy, not God's. At such times we desperately need refreshment for our weary spirits. In times of doubt or despair, we need to receive once again the inner assurance of his promises to us. When we face major decisions, we need to steep ourselves in Scripture and in prayer to discern God's guidance. Prolonged time with Jesus will give us personal revival, a new sense of peace, and steadiness of soul amid pressure and confusion.

We may also need to find a clearer sense of God's will for our lives, "asking God to fill [us] with the knowledge of his will through all spiritual wisdom and understanding." Can we hear God's voice amid the constant pressures of our daily routine? Yes, but often faintly. In extended times alone with God, we can more clearly hear his Spirit teaching us, perhaps revealing a new direction for our lives or a deeper understanding of spiritual truths. Especially in times of difficulty, we need to sharpen our vision of the unseen, gaining a new perspective from God's vantage point.

A fourth reason for an extended time alone with God is the need for focused intercession for others. Can we change people and influence events through prayer? Yes, but this fact, though well known among Christians, is not often put into practice. We need to get serious about the needs of our non-Christian friends and relatives, the missionaries we support, our pastors, families, marriages, and government leaders—the list goes on and on. Our daily prayer times often don't give us opportunity to wrestle in prayer with others' needs. The spiritual warfare taking place in our world calls us to longer, more extended times of intercessory prayer.

Finally, a day in prayer alone with God will prepare us for service. God gives us plans in this time spent with him. He sharpens our purposes so that when we're faced with an opportunity for service, we'll be ready. We'll also be prepared for the attacks of our archenemy, the devil. Through prayer we remain one step ahead of him, attacking his defenses first instead of waiting for his attack on us.

getting ready for time alone with God

First, set aside time in advance. You might begin with two half-days if a full day seems too difficult to manage. You could also take turns with your spouse or with another couple if you'll need childcare in order to get away. If you're employed, use part of your scheduled vacation, or choose an office holiday for a longer retreat. Sunday afternoon may be a good time for a shorter prayer retreat; or engage in a half-night of prayer beginning at suppertime. You may want to skip the evening meal, strengthening your prayer time with a brief fast.

Choose a place where you can pray undisturbed. One pastor notes that he has spent his days of prayer in unusual places—in a railway waiting room, on an isolated mountainside, in an empty warehouse storage room, in a church prayer room just big enough for one person. You might choose a wooded area near home or even your own backyard. If you sincerely desire to spend time with God, he'll lead you to the right place.

Don't forget to prepare yourself as well. For several days in advance, ask God to prepare your heart, to give you the desire for fellowship with him, to keep your scheduled retreat time open, and to give you blessing on that day. **We need time just to think about and be with God.** Begin the retreat as rested as possible. (Take a brief nap during your prayer time if you need to, so that you can return to your meditation and prayer properly refreshed.)

Take along items you may need for your prayer time: a Bible (perhaps several translations), a hymnbook, a notebook and pen, your current prayer list, a sack lunch, a concordance, a devotional book, a flashlight (if necessary), a cushion to kneel on, a watch or alarm clock, a calendar, a family or personal budget, adequate wraps for warmth, your prayer diary, anything else that may be useful. Thinking ahead about what you plan to do will help you decide what to take along.

Finally, inform someone where you can be reached in case of an emergency. Don't publicize your time alone with God, but do notify those who may need to get in touch with you.

some general guidelines

Let the Word of God speak to you. Read Scripture to inform yourself of God's nature and his will, to stimulate your own thinking. Use it throughout the day, allowing God to speak to you during various moments of prayer. You will find that listening to God is as important as speaking to him; feasting on his Word is as essential as interceding for others. Use the Bible in your prayers as well, letting the prayers you find there shape your own. Pray on the basis of the promises you find. Read aloud, even as much as an entire book of the Bible, and consider how those words apply to your life. Read with a receptive, teachable mind. As you are exposed to God's Word, that Word will lead you in prayer.

Write your thoughts in a journal. Answer these questions: What do I see God teaching me at this point in my life? How do I feel about my experiences? What insights have I gained from the reading I've done? What specific sins do I need to confess? If it is helpful, write down your prayers for healing, for forgiveness, and for insight into God's grace through Christ. At the end of the day, sum up in writing the key points of your time alone with God. Jot down how these might be translated into a new perspective for your daily living. This journal will serve as a record, a bridge, for your next time of prayer. It will

Repenting of sin and really seeing it for what it is may take longer than a half hour of quiet time. We must ask God himself to search our hearts.

also help you clarify your thoughts and make your plans definite.

Plan for variety during your prayer time. Extended prayer can be exhausting. To avoid fatigue, change your posture, get up and walk around, sing a song, say your prayers aloud as well as silently, read awhile, eat a small snack. God understands your physical needs—be free and relaxed in his presence.

Be willing to pay the price. Extended time alone with God will take sacrifice. If you're looking for a comfortable time and place to pray, you'll not become a person of prayer. You will also pay an emotional cost: identifying with God's grief of spirit at the sin that destroys the world he has made. Too often we don't pray because we don't share God's passion of heart. But when we become connected with God in an entire day of prayer, we begin to feel things the way God wants us to, and we sense a new burden for prayer.

Take time to listen to the Lord. Let the Holy Spirit teach you throughout the day. Read the Bible, respond to truths that come alive to you, and apply what you've learned in your own life. Thank the Lord for what he has shown you; let him know specifically what you intend to do in response. Remember, too, that although God never contradicts what is in his Word, he may speak to you through other ways as well—through song, nature, others' testimony, and the still, small voice of his Spirit within you.

a plan for your prayer time

1. **Begin by focusing on God.** We are told to enter God's presence with thanksgiving. Take time to thank God for who he is, for his love, for his power at work in the world and with-

in you, for his death and resurrection, for the fellowship he's given you in the church. Consider using Psalms 103, 111, and 145 to praise God for his greatness and might. Lose yourself in the wonder of God.

Express your joy in God's presence through song as well. Bring a hymnal along and sing a few songs of praise, changing the "we" to "I." You will find that others have put into words and music the feelings that you sometimes strain to express. Memorize verses or choruses that particularly move you to praise.

2. **Deal with barriers of sin.** An overwhelming sense of personal, group, or national sin can drive us to our knees. Often this may be the very first part of our prayer time: confessing sins that stand in the way of God's hearing our prayer. Humility and submission prepare the way for our intercession.

This may take longer than we think. Repenting of sin and really seeing it for what it is may take longer than a half hour of quiet time. We must ask God himself to search our hearts. We need time to get to the root sin, to deal with how we've cherished disobedience in our hearts, to yield our wills to God. Reading Psalms 32 and 51 and 1 John 1:9 may be worthwhile here. It may be helpful also to write down specific steps of correction and recommitment.

3. **Pray for yourself.** You are God's child, and everything that concerns you also concerns God. Nothing is too big or too small. You pray not to inform God of something he doesn't know but to share your heart with him. Pray from the list of personal needs and problems you wrote down prior to your retreat. Spread it out before the Lord, asking for his help and guidance.

Your perspective during this time should be "Lord, what do you think of my life?" Ask yourself if you truly want God's will more than anything else. Examine your goals, vision, and self-evaluation in light of these questions. Ask God for a renewed vision from Scripture. Write down your thoughts in your prayer journal.

4. **Pray for others.** You have time now for unhurried, more detailed prayer for those whom you usually just mention briefly in your morning devotions. Pray for God's will to be done in their lives, focusing your prayers on God's interests. If you remember specific requests from various people, jot them down and bring these before God. Pray especially for missionaries' physical strength, courage, stamina, and mental alertness. Try to imagine yourself in the situation of those you are praying for, and pray accordingly.

> **Your aim in this day should be to come away with some newly driven stakes in your life—new conclusions and insights, renewed convictions, specific promises to claim, definite directions in which to move.**

You might also trace your way around the world in prayer, bringing to God the needs of countries currently in the news. Pray also for revival among Christians worldwide, for the spread of God's kingdom, for holiness and love to replace apathy and division in the church. Intercession for the lost should also be a vital part of your prayer time.

5. **Drive some stakes.** Your aim in this day should be to come away with some newly driven stakes in your life—new conclusions and insights, renewed convictions, specific promises to claim, definite directions in which to move. Don't be discouraged if you haven't achieved this at the end of the

day. But write these things down in your prayer journal if you have been given them. Summarize on paper the things God has spoken to you in this day.

6. **End with praise.** Close your day with a time of doxology, of expressing love and adoration to the God who has given you life. Even if you cannot see God's answer or be sure of how he will work in answer to your prayers, you can return with a heart that sings in praise and thanksgiving. You may want to use some of the songs that you've found meaningful during your retreat. Take with you a renewed sense of God's presence.

making time

Days of prayer don't just happen. Our culture offers us many distractions to keep us busy and forgetful. Our enemy uses every ploy he can to keep us from prayer and from closer fellowship with God. So it's no wonder that we have to fight to make time for an extended prayer time alone with God.

Plan ahead to schedule a day of prayer and reflection into every two or three months of the coming year or as often as you feel God is nudging you to set aside time for him. Remember that this time alone with God won't just appear in your schedule. Planning for it in advance ensures that it will happen.

These days of prayer may well prove to be among the deepest and richest of your life. You will probably ask yourself, "Why didn't I do this sooner?"

23

DAY-OF-PRAYER RETREAT

A day-of-prayer retreat is an entire day spent with others *in prayer*. It's not a day to talk about prayer, to hear about prayer, or to think about prayer. It's a day *to pray*. As the following material emphasizes, about three-fourths of the day is spent in actual prayer.

A group of ten to fifteen people is ideal for this kind of retreat. If your group is larger, you should spend most of your prayer time in small groups. This not only gives individuals more opportunity to pray aloud; it also helps people who find it difficult to pray in large groups feel more comfortable.

The best location for your day of prayer is a retreat center or another out-of-the-way place where you can pray uninterrupted, without the distractions of telephone, street noises, people coming and going, and so on. You'll probably want a place where meals are prepared and served for you (or a location where you can serve meals with little fuss).

The prayer retreat will generally last from 8:30 A.M. to 9:00 P.M., though it can be shorter or longer to meet the needs and purpose of the group. Members must be committed to stay with the prayer group for the entire time. Be sure that group members understand this before they agree to participate. Those who run in and out destroy the sense of unity and purpose that slowly builds in a group of this kind.

What is the purpose of a day-of-prayer retreat? It's for believers to be together before God, concentrating prayer on the kingdom of God. This day is set aside to seek God's face regarding things that you know are important to God: his glory, his kingdom, his will done in your lives and in the world. As a group, you will pray for renewal in your own lives, in your families, in the church, and in world evangelism.

There is really no more important thing you can do to renew the church and advance Christ's kingdom than to spend extended time in prayer. Prayer is the moving force behind the kingdom of God. If you bypass the power of prayer, you bypass God's power in your life and ministry. The day-of-prayer retreat is one way of focusing your energy and attention on prayer and giving it the priority it needs.

gathering to pray

Your day of prayer may take different forms, but it should include the following basic elements of prayer:

1. **Prayers of praise and thanks.** Even before you spend time in personal sharing with members of your group, it

is important to focus on God and to praise him. Begin with songs of praise, selecting those that will best direct your thoughts to the person and work of God.

Depending on the makeup of your group, you'll want to choose traditional hymns, contemporary praise choruses, or a combination of the two. Some of the following well-known hymns of praise are effective in helping to set a tone of praise and awe at God's majesty:

- "How Great Thou Art"
- "Holy, Holy, Holy"
- "Praise to the Lord, the Almighty"
- "Crown Him with Many Crowns"
- "Beautiful Savior"
- "Oh, for a Thousand Tongues"
- "All Creatures of Our God and King"

A number of contemporary choruses and Bible songs have also become so familiar in many churches that you can sing them by heart:

- "Eight-fold Alleluia"
- "To God Be the Glory"
- "I Exalt Thee"
- "Glorify Thy Name"
- "We Bring the Sacrifice of Praise"
- "He Is Lord"
- "Majesty"
- "Open My Eyes, Lord"
- "Father, We Love You"

Allow the songs you sing to bring you into the presence of God himself. As you sing, let your spirit move into prayer, into praise, into adoration of the God who has given you life.

Your prayers of praise should focus on God, telling him what it is that you appreciate about him. Many people find it difficult to keep the focus on giving praise; they often quickly move into other elements of prayer. To encourage a longer time of praise, give everyone a Bible passage that focuses on God. Have them read it in silence and then, as a whole group, praise God by reflecting the truths you've just read about in those verses. Following are some especially helpful passages to begin your praise time:

- 1 Chronicles 29:10-13
- Psalm 33:1-9; 103:1-6 (or all the verses); 145:3-13
- Isaiah 6:1-4; 40:28-31
- Romans 11:33-36
- Ephesians 3:17-21
- 1 Peter 1:3-5; 2:9-10
- Jude 24-25
- Revelation 4:8-11; 5:12-14; 7:9-12; 15:3-4; 19:1-2, 5-8

2. **Sharing your lives.** Getting to know each other is an important part of the day-of-prayer retreat, especially when members are drawn from diverse backgrounds and occupations. Ask each person to give a three-minute personal biography that includes a testimony of faith and a brief sketch of his or her journey into the discipline of prayer. Because these can become long stories instead of brief sketches, and because your time together is limited, allow only three minutes per person (you may want to use a clearly visible timer so that those who speak can see how much time they have). Use the following questions to help people organize their sharing:

This day is set aside to seek God's face regarding things that you know are important to God: his glory, his kingdom, his will done in your lives and in the world.

- Where did you grow up, and what was life like for you as a child?
- What high and low points do you remember from your journey through life?

- What place has prayer had in your life throughout the years?

Members may feel a bit intimidated by this exercise at first, but encourage everyone to participate. It's simply the best way to begin to get to know each other and to break down barriers that may exist in any group.

After the sharing time, consider singing a song or two that expresses the common pilgrimage of your faith:

- "Amazing Grace"
- "Surely Goodness and Mercy"
- "Safe Am I"
- "Yesterday, Today, and Tomorrow"
- "Fill My Cup, Lord"

3. **Prayers of repentance and recommitment.** This segment of your prayer time is meant to be a cleansing experience, one that prepares you for the work of prayer and intercession that lies ahead.

Two Scripture passages that are especially pertinent here are 2 Chronicles 7:14 and 1 John 1:9, which urge believers to humble themselves and to confess their sins, praying for each other's healing and restoration.

After the group is prepared for the time of confession, form prayer triplets and spend time confessing before God the sins that stand in the way of your work of prayer today. Ask God to reveal the things that stand between you and him, and pray for each other's recommitment and healing.

After your prayer time, join in singing songs that emphasize God's grace, mercy, and forgiveness, such as

- "When Peace, Like a River"
- "There's Power in the Blood"
- "Revive Us Again"
- "And Can It Be"

- "My Jesus, I Love Thee"
- "Man of Sorrows"
- "Spirit of the Living God"

End this time by reading Scripture passages that speak of the assurance of pardon, such as Psalm 103:9-13; Isaiah 43:25; 1 John 1:9.

4. **Prayers of intercession.** Use this time to pray as one group (unless you have more than fifteen people, in which case you should form two or more groups). Your intercession will center on the health and mission of the church and on the personal ministries of each person present. Following are some suggestions as to how to break down these general areas into more specific topics for prayer. Encourage members to pray as specifically as possible for the needs they are aware of.

Pray for the health of the church (the local congregation, the denomination, and the church worldwide)

- that God will clarify the vision of the church, strengthening its commitment to ministry and reawakening believers to the awareness of why God has called them together. Mark 4:30-32 and Ephesians 1:9-10 are helpful passages to read as you focus your prayers on this area of the church's health.

- that God will provide visionary, Spirit-filled leadership to stir God's people on to ministry and to spiritual warfare

- that God will build up the ministering body so that it is fully equipped for ministry and develops a servant's heart for God and others. Romans 12:4-8 and 1 Peter 4:10-11 should be part of your prayer time as you focus on this topic.

- that the church will respond to God in celebrative, Spirit-controlled worship (see John 4:23-24; Acts 6:4)

- that the church's efforts in education will produce mature, well-trained members (see Colossians 1:28)

- that the fellowship of believers will be characterized by genuine love, by caring for one another, by a spirit of unity (see John 13:34-35; 17:20-23)

- that believers will support the church's ministries with faithful, love-motivated stewardship (see Malachi 3:10; 2 Corinthians 9:6-11)

To close this segment of your prayer time, you might sing a hymn such as "Jesus, with Your Church Abide," "I Love Thy Kingdom, Lord," or "The Church's One Foundation." Believe that God will respond to your prayers by working mighty things in his church.

Pray for the mission of the church on the local, denominational, and worldwide level

- for an outpouring of God's Spirit to enable believers to be Jesus' witnesses (see Acts 1:8)

- for commitment to the mission task, working as willing laborers in the harvest (see Matthew 9:37-38; Luke 24:46-49)

- for a worldwide vision of evangelism that moves beyond our own culture (see Isaiah 55:5)

- for a burden for the lost (see Matthew 9:36-38). Nearly 3,000 language groups have not heard God's Word in their own language, and nearly 12,000 people groups have not been reached with the gospel.

- for open doors (Colossians 4:3) and great boldness (Ephesians 6:18-20)

- for compassion for the needy; that those of us who live in comfort may feel others' needs as our own (see Matthew 25:34-36; 1 John 3:17-18)

- for new believers who are being gathered into the church (see Acts 2:41, 47)

- for the evangelization of North America and the world (see Matthew 28:18-20; Acts 1:8)

You might choose from the following songs to conclude this part of your prayer time:

- "He Is Lord"
- "I Love to Tell the Story"
- "O Zion, Haste"
- "Our God Reigns"
- "Victory Song"
- "In Christ There Is No East or West"
- "Go, Tell It on the Mountain"
- "Jesus Shall Reign"
- "From Ocean unto Ocean"
- "Where Cross the Crowded Ways of Life"
- "Come Labor On"

Pray for the personal ministries of each person present. At this point, suggest that individuals spend personal time in conversation with the Lord, seeking his will by asking the following questions:

- What am I most thankful for?

- What would I like others to pray for?

- What are my goals for the future?

After people have gathered again, you might sing a song such as "Standing in the Need of Prayer." Then, in groups of six, members may share briefly their "life and ministry" prayer requests and receive prayer from the group.

Ask God to reveal the things that stand between you and him, and pray for each other's recommitment and healing.

A fitting way to close this time would be to sing one or more of the following:

- "O Master, Let Me Walk with Thee"
- "The Bond of Love"
- "O Jesus, I Have Promised"
- "Spirit of the Living God"
- "When We Walk with the Lord"
- "O for a Closer Walk with God"
- "We Are One in the Spirit"

5. **Reflection and sharing time.** This time is divided between individual and group activity.

Personal reflection. Ask each person to write a brief, three-paragraph journal entry based on these two questions:

- If you were to write a letter to God based on your experience in prayer today, what would you say to him about yourself, your ministry, your future, and so on?

- Write a letter from God to you. What do you sense he is saying to you?

Share time. When you gather again as an entire group, ask each person to share briefly from his or her journal by reading a portion of what they've written or by summarizing the thoughts they've jotted down.

6. **Future commitment.** As you come to the close of an intense day of fellowship in prayer, you will want to consider making future prayer commit-

ments. Look especially at these ways to do so:

- *Do members want to commit themselves to pray for each other?* Group members should consider making a covenant among themselves to pray for each other regularly, remembering the specific needs that have been mentioned in your prayers for each other's personal ministries.

- *Do members wish to continue meeting regularly as a prayer support group?* You may wish to pass around a sheet on which those who are interested can sign their names and list phone numbers so that such a group can be set up in the future.

7. **Closing.** Give your closing moments together a sense of liturgy, a flow between yourselves and God, just as your prayers have done during the day. You may wish to use something like the following exercise:

Our word to God:

"To him who is able to keep [us] from falling and to present [us] before his glorious presence without fault and with great joy—to the only God our Savior be glory, majesty, power and authority, through Jesus Christ our Lord, before all ages, now and forevermore! Amen."

—Jude 24-25

God's Word to us:

Read 1 Thessalonians 5:16-19, 21-24 as a summary of God's will for each member as you disperse and take up the ministries God has given you.

answering questions about a day-of-prayer retreat

You may find that some people may be hesitant to take part in this kind of retreat—for all kinds of reasons. To overcome people's natural reluctance, it's best to be prepared for their questions. Here are some of the questions most frequently asked:

What would a person possibly pray about all day?

Sometimes people have a hard time praying for fifteen minutes. They fear that an all-day prayer retreat would be an intimidating experience. What if they're all prayed out after the first hour? Reassure participants that the time spent in prayer will pass so quickly that they'll be surprised when the day is over. Time after time, those who have taken part have said with chagrin at the end of the day, "But there's still so much to pray for!" The variety in forms of prayer—group prayer, singing, private meditation, Scripture-led prayer—breaks up the longer periods of prayer. Group members have often mentioned that rather than feeling drained at the end of the day, they feel filled, focused, and energized for ministry.

Will I feel uncomfortable in such an intimate setting with people I hardly know?

The format of the retreat is designed to break down the barriers that exist in every group, to make sharing easier, and to focus people's attention away from themselves and toward the ministry of prayer. As one participant wrote afterward, "The atmosphere was relaxed, cordial, and nonthreatening. . . . No one felt ill at ease. The times of conversation, fellowship over food, private meditation,

singing, and, above all, prayer were a genuine blessing to me."

Rather than feeling like strangers, group members will be strengthened in the common faith that makes them brothers and sisters. They will be refreshed by the prayers that others offer for them. They will experience the relief that comes when they are able to share their burdens in ministry in prayer with others.

Isn't an all-day prayer retreat a bit pietistic, bordering on the charismatic?

Jesus, who has set us an example in everything, spent hours and days in prayer. It was essential for his ministry, and it is essential for ours. Setting aside long periods for prayer has characterized all great men and women of the faith. Doing this

> **Time after time, those who have taken part have said with chagrin at the end of the day, "But there's still so much to pray for!"**

with a group of other committed Christians is a matter of common sense and practical faith, as well as of obedience to scriptural principles.

Do I really have time for this?

The answer is an unequivocal "yes." God gave us time, intending it to be not our master but our servant. We make time for the things we know are important. When sickness or a broken transmission keep us from our daily routine, we discover that the world can get along without us for a day. Clearing our schedules for a day of prayer may not be easy but certainly is possible. Perhaps a better question to ask would be, "Do I really believe prayer is important to my spiritual life and to God's kingdom?"

the value of a day-of-prayer retreat

A day-long retreat spent in prayer with others stimulates our own prayer life.

We come away with a new awareness of the power of prayer and with spirits that have been refreshed through an extended time in God's presence. These effects carry over into our private prayer habits, motivating us to be more disciplined and more eager to spend time with God in praise, confession, and intercession.

We also find support, strength, encouragement, and a deeper sense of community. We experience prayer more directly as a ministry for others—and as a lifeline of support for our own personal ministries. Group members come away with a new appreciation for the community of believers, for bringing each other's needs before God in intercession. A sense of community remains long after the group has dispersed, and some groups decide to continue meeting on a regular basis.

We come away with a new awareness of the power of prayer and with spirits that have been refreshed through an extended time in God's presence.

The greatest value, of course, lies in learning from God and being in his presence. We learn from God through his Spirit, who speaks through us and through others during prayer. Prayer is meant to be a two-way conversation, and listening for God's guidance through prayer and Scripture is one of the most important parts of this retreat. Even entering God's presence through prayer is enough in itself, for it is in God's presence that we are changed within. Prayer is a spiritual discipline that brings us to a place where God can change us, mold us, put his thoughts and spirit within us. A day spent in prayer with others will put the weeks and months that follow in a new perspective—one that grows from hearing God's voice and being with him.

strategies

169

DAY-OF-PRAYER RETREAT

24

PRAYER MINISTRY TEAMS

what is a prayer ministry team?

A prayer ministry team is a group of two to six people with a special interest or special gifts in prayer. This team meets regularly to pray with others for inner healing, for physical and spiritual healing, for deliverance from Satan's oppression, for guidance and spiritual blessing.

This team is committed to praying with hurting people—both churched and unchurched. The members work only as a team, praying along with at least one or two others from the team. They are available to go out and pray with the sick and those who are homebound, with people in the hospital, and with families in times of crisis.

The prayer ministry team is also available to pray with those who come forward for prayer during or after worship. Often the church provides a prayer room for this purpose, a place where the prayer team can meet privately with those seeking prayer. Other churches, however, provide an area at the front of the sanctuary or to the side, where people can pray with relatively little interruption.

The team may also be present at the church for a specified time during the week in order to meet with people for prayer, especially those who have been referred from a counselor or pastor. The team is also present at healing services or other prayer services to help individuals who may need special or follow-up prayer.

Some churches have found it helpful to include both men and women on their prayer ministry teams. One pastor cautions that it's important to have a woman present on the team if the person being prayed for is also a woman (and vice versa). This is not only a safeguard but also an attempt to be sensitive to the feelings of those for whom you are praying.

A church's prayer ministry team may consist of the same people or may rotate its members from a larger pool of trained volunteers. Or a church might train several prayer ministry teams and schedule them on a rotating basis as needed.

qualifications of team members

Because the prayer ministry team deals with many different kinds of people, with complex or crisis situations, and with all the dangers that accompany spiritual warfare, it's important to choose the team members carefully. Look for people with the following qualities:

1. **A strong personal prayer life.** The key ingredient in praying successfully

with others is a life of experience in the ministry of prayer. Each member of the team must have the ability to listen to the Holy Spirit's promptings and direction in order to pray effectively for another's problems.

2. **A firm understanding of the place that God intended prayer to have** in the church and in the Christian life. Are the members of the prayer team convinced that God wants to give them his blessings in response to their prayers?

3. **Experience in lay counseling.** As mentioned above, many people may seek prayer because of long-standing emotional or spiritual problems. It's important that team members be able to recognize these problems and, by way of questioning, get at the root problem behind the surface symptoms.

4. **Love for people.** A prayer ministry for others is based on a sensitivity to people's needs, a compassion that reaches out to them, and a willingness to serve them in prayer.

5. **Spiritual maturity.** Spiritual warfare through prayer can be dangerous or overwhelming for those who are young in the Christian life. Participating in a prayer ministry team requires strong faith and maturity in the Word.

6. **A consistent Christian lifestyle.** Because the members of the prayer team will often be influential in the lives of those they pray for, their commitment to an obedient walk with Christ must be without compromise.

7. **Spiritual gifts** of intercession, faith, healing, encouragement, or insight. God uses these gifts in the realm of prayer to combat Satan's oppression.

8. **Willingness to support team members in ministry.** At times, members will need to support each other in prayer or to put aside personal differences in order to do God's work together.

9. **The ability to keep confidences.** Those who come for prayer will often unburden their hearts of their deepest, most well-kept secrets. Any betrayal of confidence could shatter the trust that is essential for healing.

No one, of course, measures up to the task perfectly. This list is meant to offer guidelines. Assure members who wish to participate that they are able to serve even if they feel they fall short of these standards.

training for prayer ministry teams

Volunteers for the prayer ministry team will need training to help them deal with the wide variety of situations and problems they will face. This training might take different forms: a list of books to read on prayer and healing, for example, or a workshop or seminar. Two excellent books on the subject are *Christianity with Power* by Charles Kraft (Servant Publications) and *The Healing Team* by Leo Thomas (Paulist Press). Compile a list of key Scripture passages for your volunteers to read and study.

The pastor or others qualified in the church community could also meet with the volunteers for teaching and training. (Rev. David Beelen of Madison Square Christian Reformed Church in Grand Rapids, for example, has developed this kind of training session for prayer ministry teams. For further information on this kind of training, contact him at 1434

This team meets regularly to pray with others for inner healing, for physical and spiritual healing, for deliverance from Satan's oppression, for guidance and spiritual blessing.

Madison Ave. SE, Grand Rapids, MI 49507, (616) 245-7791.)

Once a prayer ministry team has been trained, you can train new volunteers by linking them with experienced members of the team. Trainees can learn from being present at the prayer sessions, from debriefing and discussion afterward, and from general teachings given by team members. This on-the-job training is often the most effective.

Don't expect prayer to be a magic tool. All God asks is that you expectantly believe in his powerful love.

ongoing support for the team

Because this ministry can be intense and demanding, team members will need ongoing support and opportunity to evaluate their own commitment and involvement. Ideas for support should include the following provisions for prayer ministry team members:

- regular team meetings to maintain clarity of focus

- communication with the pastor about the people they've ministered to in prayer, problems they've encountered, and so on

- the opportunity to review and evaluate their ministry and to address practical questions (for example, "How do we handle this situation?")

- prayer and ministry to other team members, especially in areas of spiritual growth or in personal crises

- regular training opportunities in new areas, using resources such as books, copies of articles, tapes by knowledgeable speakers, and so on

- meetings specifically focused on plans for the future—training new

volunteers, adding more teams, ways to expand the ministry, and so on

guidelines for prayer

Though each team member will bring to this ministry his or her own approach to spirituality and prayer, certain guidelines are important to remember as you're praying for others:

1. **Ask the person to state the prayer request simply and clearly.** Keep conversation about peripheral things (life history, symptoms, points of interest, and so on) to a minimum. When the person has verbalized the request, repeat what you've heard to confirm that you understand what the person has said.

   One congregation asks those who come forward for prayer to write down their requests. This forces people to express what they want with clarity; it gives focus to their thoughts and emotions. (The written requests are returned to each person after the prayer time to avoid any problems with confidentiality.)

2. **Bring to prayer this confidence: God is with you.** He is able to give you anything you think you may lack. Through Christ you are qualified to pray. But don't try to do too much in one prayer session. Recognize that there may be limits to what God wants to accomplish in that session; agree to meet and pray in subsequent sessions, if necessary.

3. **Communicate the love and compassion of Christ.** Many who are involved in healing ministries today strongly emphasize the importance of compassion for the one you are praying with. It is through this "feeling with" (the literal meaning of compas-

sion), this empathetic love, that God's healing power flows.

4. **Allow room for the Holy Spirit to lead.** The Spirit may give you a greater knowledge of the person's true needs, a knowledge that enables you to pray differently than you had first intended. Listen to the Spirit's promptings.

5. **When you are finished praying, allow a brief time of quiet,** then ask the person to thank God (silently or aloud) for loving him or her through the prayer time.

6. **It may become obvious that the person or family needs help in addition to prayer.** Encourage the person to seek guidance from a qualified counselor or from the pastor. Remember, you are not expected to solve every problem through prayer.

7. **Don't expect prayer to be a magic tool.** All God asks is that you expectantly believe in his powerful love. You serve as an assistant who places one hand in God's and the other in the person's for whom you are praying. You are there to help someone "make the connection" with God.

8. **Follow through.** Continue to pray for the person and his or her needs after the initial time of prayer. Follow up with repeated times of prayer with each individual (if you've established this kind of initiative as the team's responsibility).

9. **Maintain confidentiality.**

laying the groundwork

Some churches may not understand the necessity for a prayer ministry team or how it fits into the church's life and ministry. How can you sensitize people to the need for this prayer ministry? Here are a few ideas:

- *Preach and teach on prayer and healing.* These are prime ways to help your congregation see the importance of prayer ministry. Present a scriptural perspective and emphasize that the team simply prays and leaves the results to God. Stress that God wants to operate in response to our prayers.

- *Do what you can to create an atmosphere of acceptance and openness to this kind of ministry.* Help the members of your church understand that it's okay to be vulnerable, to admit we have problems that need prayer. Emphasize that we are here to help each other cope with our needs, that God gave us the gift of prayer for that purpose.

- *Start low-key.* Involve members who are respected in your congregation and try to acclimate people gradually to this ministry. Especially at first, avoid anything that might be considered too out of the ordinary, threatening, or emotionally high-key.

- *Finally, demonstrate that pastors and other key leaders are also willing to receive prayer* from the team. This gives the congregation an unmistakable message: this ministry is not just for crisis situations, not just for the spiritually weak, not just for emotionally unstable people—it's for everyone. To achieve this, pastors could begin setting the example by asking for prayer from council members. Council members can set the example for the congregation by praying for each other and by being willing to be prayed for. Along with this, the congregation needs to hear the pastor say from time to time, "I really need prayer."

benefits of a prayer ministry team

The most obvious benefit is answered prayer. Your church will see and experience the power of God's Spirit at work in the church as he heals and changes lives. This can help create a sense of expectation within the congregation, a feeling of "What will God do among us next?"

Another benefit of this prayer ministry is that people will be set free from sin, from hurtful memories, from bondage to temptation or weakness, from illness. As they are set free, their spiritual life will deepen and their faith in God and his promises will be strengthened.

Beginning a prayer team ministry is also a wonderful way to use members who have the spiritual gifts of intercession, healing, faith, discernment, encouragement, and so on. God's gifts will not lie idle; they will be used to strengthen the body and to reach out to the unchurched and unbelieving.

This ministry may help to create within your church a great openness to the Holy Spirit and to his healing work. Faced with the reality of God's presence among them as his power is released, people will become more alive to the Spirit's work in their own hearts as well.

Beginning a prayer team ministry is also a wonderful way to use members who have the spiritual gifts of intercession, healing, faith, discernment, encouragement, and so on.

Finally, this ministry will give your congregation another concrete experience of love in the community of Christ. Sharing burdens in prayer, asking together for God's healing, making other's concerns your own—all these will give renewed meaning to Christ's blueprint for the church: "Love each other as I have loved you" (John 15:12).

25

PRAYER MINISTRY FOR HEALING

Reformed churches are generally uneasy with the idea of a healing ministry. We think of the fraud associated with some superstar "faith healers" in our culture and the megabucks they've made peddling their wares.

True to John Calvin's belief that certain gifts of the Spirit went out of practice after the apostolic age, Reformed believers have avoided prayer ministries for healing that include such practices as anointing with oil and laying on of hands. Sometimes we view claims of miraculous healing with suspicion.

In the past several decades many people in the church have begun to think again about healing and its many forms. We recognize that all healing comes from God and that beyond healing for physical ills there is also a need for inner healing and the healing of relationships. Along with many in the healing professions we recognize the need to consider the whole person and the fact that healing has physical, emotional, and spiritual dimensions.

The church's healing ministry takes many forms. A church may have one or more support groups for people with common life situations; regular healing worship services may be scheduled; prayer teams may be trained and deployed; or members with the gift of intercession may be praying regularly for and with people in need of healing.

This chapter introduces the subject of healing and highlights the service of healing. We are grateful to John H. Timmerman, professor of English at Calvin College, for much of the material contained in this chapter (adapted from an unpublished article titled *The Healing Service: A Report to the Council of Alger Park CRC*).

is prayer ministry for healing biblical?

Though this is a very broad and sometimes controversial subject, let's look briefly at three basic biblical foundations for the ministry of healing today.

First, God is a healing God. This truth is clear from both the Old and New Testaments. In the Old Testament, healing is linked with humility, seeking God in prayer, and repentance:

> *"If my people, who are called by my name, humble themselves and pray and seek my face and turn from their wicked ways, then will I hear from heaven and will forgive their sin and will heal their land."*
>
> —2 Chronicles 7:14

This text also shows that healing is a sign to God's people—a sign of his grace and his enduring love for them. This teaching echoes the words of Exodus 15:26, where God identifies himself as Jehovah-Rapha, "the Lord, who heals you."

The New Testament tells us that healing was one of Jesus' primary ministries:

> *News about him spread all over Syria, and people brought to him all who were ill with various diseases, those suffering severe pain, the demon-possessed, those having seizures, and the paralyzed, and he healed them.*
>
> —Matthew 4:24

Jesus also healed people from the disease of sin—through his crucifixion and resurrection.

Second, God bestows his healing power for people to use. Again, this is evident in both the Old and New Testaments. Elijah, Elisha, and other prophets received healing powers. One of Jesus' first commands to his disciples was "Heal the sick, raise the dead, cleanse those who have leprosy, drive out demons" (Matthew 10:8). He instructed the group of seventy, "Heal the sick . . . and say to them, 'The kingdom of God is near to you'" (Luke 10:9).

Jesus passed on his ministry to us, his disciples. The question is, Does that ministry include healing? When we pray for healing, are we stepping into forbidden territory? Or are we obeying a command from God that we dare not break? The Scriptures support the latter, suggesting that we are to carry out the work of a healing God in a broken and sinful culture.

Third, this healing ministry has never ceased within the church. Throughout the Christian era, pastors and others have prayed for the sick. Prayers for healing are often offered from the pulpit. In fact, in earlier days the church was often the only institution in society that offered hope for the hurting and was instrumental in establishing hospitals. To this day, the church continues this tradition in medical missions to Third World countries. At times in the history of the church, however, belief in God's healing power has been accompanied by abuses and manipulation. The Reformers reacted to such abuses by emphasizing again the gospel's central message of justifying grace and its call to thankful obedience. At the same time, the church has not ceased to pray "Your kingdom come." Throughout its history, the church has been privileged to see evidences of the kingdom's powerful presence in answer to prayers for healing.

All that we find in Scripture supports the belief that the church has been given the power and mandate to heal. In his farewell address to his disciples (John 14-17), Jesus promised the Holy Spirit's power not only to the twelve disciples but to all his followers. He also promised the twelve disciples and all who would come after them, "I tell you the truth, anyone who has faith in me will do what I have been doing. He will do even greater things than these, because I am going to the Father" (John 14:12).

We recognize that all healing comes from God and that beyond healing for physical ills there is also a need for inner healing and the healing of relationships.

At Pentecost the Holy Spirit was given to all 120 of the followers who were gathered, not just to the twelve apostles (Acts 2:1-3). And the New Testament epistles are clear about the mandate to heal. Paul describes healing as one of the ministries of the church (1 Corinthians 12). James gives this spiritual prescription, not just for the apostles but for the church universal:

Is any one of you in trouble? He should pray. Is anyone happy? Let him sing songs of praise. Is any one of you sick? He should call the elders of the church to pray over him and anoint him with oil in the name of the Lord. And the prayer offered in faith will make the sick person well; the Lord will raise him up. If he has sinned, he will be forgiven. Therefore confess your sins to each other and pray for each other so that you may be healed. The prayer of a righteous man is powerful and effective.

—James 5:13-16

It is true that a good practice can go bad. John Calvin no doubt reacted to excesses and misuses in the church of his day. But we must recognize that the practice of healing is biblical.

basic principles in healing

We are often called to pray not only once but perhaps many times for healing. Some Christians believe that a single prayer that accomplishes its desire immediately is a sign of one's faith in God's power to heal. But persistence is also a sign of faith. And God's answer may come in the form of patience, or healing may come in a way that you did not expect. We should take this as encouragement to pray repeatedly—bathing the condition or problem in prayer.

Be sensitive to the possibility of receiving a Scripture passage, message of encouragement, hope, rebuke, and so on from God to give to that person.

We must also *see the healing ministry not as a series of proper techniques but as a result of God's powerful ability to heal.* A list of the "right" things to do may be of some help in learning to follow biblical princi-

ples. But a powerful prayer life goes far beyond technique; it is a complete relationship with God. Is the continual experience of God as vital to us as the air we breathe? Or are we looking at the healing ministry as a new twist or spiritual diversion?

Finally, *we don't heal as lone rangers but as members of an entire body.* Experiencing dramatic results in healing prayer can lead a person to believe he or she is a spiritual superstar. This opinion is deadly. It leads to spiritual unwholeness, to excesses, and to manipulation. Remaining merely a small part of the whole body of Christ, however, focuses attention on the true source of healing power. It also emphasizes the power that lies within a group of believers—a power that exceeds that of any individual. A healthy prayer team consists of two or three spiritually mature men and women who are trained for this purpose. In some churches prayer teams are made up exclusively of the elders.

the healing service

A healing service begins and ends much like any other worship service. The sermon might deal with one of the many biblical texts or stories that involve healing. Following the sermon, teams of two or three people station themselves in the sanctuary. Those who would like to make a request for healing for themselves or for someone else join one of the teams for conversation and prayer.

While the prayer teams pray with people, the congregation quietly and prayerfully sings a series of psalms and hymns until the last person who has requested prayer has been prayed for and everyone has returned to their seats. The service concludes with a word of encouragement from Scripture, the doxology, and the benediction. A sample liturgy for a healing service may be found in *Reformed Worship* 11 and 26 (CRC Publications, 2850 Kalamazoo Ave. SE, Grand Rapids, MI 49560; call 1-800-333-8300 for more information).

suggestions for leading a healing service

1. **Before you actually begin the healing service, make a few brief remarks** that prepare people for what will be happening (especially if this is your congregation's first healing service or if there are people new to the experience).

   First, stress the need for healing. Explain that prayers for healing address not only physical illness but also other hurts in our lives, as shown in broken marriages, disturbed relationships, depression, guilt, and so on. Offer Jesus' invitation: "Come to me, all you who are weary and burdened, and I will give you rest" (Matthew 11:28).

   Second, emphasize that healing is an action of God's grace. Those who pray are merely the ones through whom God's grace comes, like an electric current through a metal rod. The grace of healing comes when we trust in God's authority and power to heal.

   Third, remind those present that God answers prayers in his own way. Sometimes healing is instantaneous. But other times we do not understand God's answers to our prayers for healing. Healing can come very gradually. Therefore, our prayers should be persistent and continual. They should be "soaking prayers."

2. **Interview the person who desires prayer for healing.** Ask, "What do you want us to pray for?" Often people don't have a clear idea of their need. Give them time to describe it specifically—the location, symptoms, and root of the pain. Are the complaints physical? Spiritual? If the problem lies in a relationship, the person may need time to identify the areas of need. As the person talks, listen to what is being said "between the lines." Listen to God's Spirit within you.

3. **Discover any barriers that may block the prayer for healing.** Ask the person, "Is there any unforgiven sin that may be a barrier to God's answering our prayer for you?" and encourage the person to confess any known areas of sin.

   Remind each person of the Bible's teaching that sin often hinders God's answering of our prayers: "If I had cherished sin in my heart, the Lord would not have listened" (Psalm 66:18; see also Isaiah 58:2). More specifically, unresolved conflict in relationships can block our prayers (Matthew 5:23-24), as can an uncaring attitude toward others (Proverbs 21:13), inadequate faith (James 1:5-8), and selfish motivation (James 4:3).

   Jesus often associated healing with forgiveness. Are there any sins the person needs to confess? Is there someone who needs to be forgiven? As you talk and listen, do not prod, and remain gentle at all times. Be sure to retain confidentiality. Seek to discern the deeper roots of the problem with the Holy Spirit's guidance. Identify any areas of resentment or anger, and pray that these may be released by God's power. You might lead the person through such a prayer, asking him or her to repeat the prayer after you. Then in prayer claim the forgiveness that comes through heartfelt confession.

4. **When people are ready to be prayed for, you might ask them to sit or kneel as you place your hands on them.** Touching is important because in the prayer for healing, the one who prays is representing Jesus to that person. Many healings in Scripture are accompanied by touch (see Mark 5:23, 41; Luke 4:40; 8:43-48). When praying, it is best for the "pray-ers" to place their hands on the person's head and/or shoulders.

5. **Determine what kind of prayer is needed to help the person.** Ask, "What would you like God to do for you?" Ask the Spirit to guide you as you pray. Identify the person by name before God and pray specifically for the complaint (using the person's own words, if possible). Be sensitive to the possibility of receiving a Scripture passage, message of encouragement, hope, rebuke, and so on from God to give to that person.

We are to rejoice with those who experience God's healing in response to prayer. But we are also to weep with those who experience disappointment.

6. **Assessing the results of your prayer will help you know what further prayer is needed.** Obviously, if the healing is immediate, you can stop and give thanks. If the healing has just begun, however, you may need to continue praying or to encourage the person to return for more prayer later.

If you can see no evidence of healing, further conversation might be necessary. Or you may have to concede that God has said "no" for the present. Whatever the case, don't give up on the need for prayer and for healing.

7. **Follow-up visits are important.** People may need subsequent prayer for healing, and they may need constant encouragement in their faith. What do these people need in order to remain healed? If the prayer for healing has not dealt with the root of their problems, the symptoms may return, revealing the need for deeper, more focused prayer.

People also need to talk about their experiences with healing—and possibly to become involved in their own ministry. Follow-up might include counseling, developing spiritual disciplines, a change in relationships, reevaluating one's lifestyle, and so on.

8. **Fundamental to developing healing services is growth in openness and sharing in worship.** This growth inevitably results in more praying for each other. And nothing encourages fervent prayer like the sharing of answers to prayer. Be sure to leave time for such sharing in your weekly worship as well as in the healing service itself.

cautions

One question that Christians raise frequently is this: Can we always expect a miraculous healing in response to a prayer of faith? Lewis B. Smedes, professor of theology and ethics at Fuller Theological Seminary, has some realistic cautions to offer regarding this question. Miraculous healings are certainly a cause to celebrate, he says. But, in the face of much human suffering that still remains on this earth, "we should see miraculous healings not as a way of solving human suffering, but as . . . signals that God is alive, that Christ is Lord, and that suffering is not the last word about human existence."

We are to rejoice with those who experience God's healing in response to prayer. But we are also to weep with those who experience disappointment. Smedes recounts the following incident that illustrates this need for caution and compassion:

> Not long ago, I received a phone call from a newspaper reporter who told me of a healing that he and his wife had experienced. They had wanted a child for several years, but were unable to conceive. Then, in a "what-have-we-got-to-lose" mood, they went to a healing service and were prayed for. The minister there assured them that they would soon conceive a child. And in four months, his wife was pregnant.

> I told him I was glad about his miracle, but then I got a memory jolt, a stab of pain. I thought about three other Christian couples I know who also had been barren and who had prayed even longer for a child and who gave thanks to God when he answered their prayers with the gift of conception. But then . . .

> One woman [carried] the fetus through the fifth month, and at that point the heart stopped beating, and the child lay dead in the womb. Another woman bore her child to term, only to deliver a baby boy who was almost unbearably malformed. The third couple's baby was born too early, seemed fine, but died within two days because her lungs were too small. Yet each couple had prayed for a child and for a while believed that God had given them one.

> The healings that are given to some individuals are almost like a rescue at sea; we are glad that God allowed our family to survive, but our survival makes us all the more sensitive to the suffering of the many families who have lost their loved ones (The Reformed Journal, February 1989).

Finally, nothing in this chapter should lead anyone to neglect the ordinary means of healing available in our society. All genuine healing is a gift from God. We are thankful for the skills of the medical profession, for compassionate physicians, counselors, and other therapists. Prayer teams must encourage people to seek out these means of healing and must never suggest that they should disregard the advice of physicians. When God is pleased to grant healing in response to prayer, the person so blessed should seek confirmation of the healing from his or her physician.

Until Christ returns, all healing is temporary and partial. But the rule of God is eternal. As important as a ministry of healing is, the church does not exalt the healing or those who prayed for it, but only the triune God, from whom all blessings flow.

26

PRAYER IN ECCLESIASTICAL ASSEMBLIES

In many denominations, representatives from individual congregations gather periodically to make decisions, to report on their churches' situations, and to determine the Holy Spirit's leading in the denomination as a whole. Synods, classes, presbyteries, assemblies—whatever they are called, these ecclesiastical meetings are common to almost every church structure.

Traditionally these assemblies include an opening and closing prayer led by one person. Recent years, however, have shown an increasing interest in prayer sessions in which all present have the opportunity to participate. Delegates are beginning to see prayer not only as the way to open and close the meeting but also as a vital part of their work sessions in between.

the value of group prayer in assemblies

Group prayer is a valuable experience in itself. Things happen in group prayer that don't happen in individual prayer or in prayer led by one person.

Group prayer in ecclesiastical assemblies creates a greater sense of involvement among the participants. Group prayer recognizes that the contribution of each person is not only valuable but also vital. It calls on each one present to use his or her spiritual gifts—discernment, wisdom, intercession, leadership, compassion, and so on—in the realm of prayer. It recognizes the uniqueness of each delegate's role in the gathered assembly.

Group prayer means an increased amount of time spent in prayer—and usually an increased intensity in prayer as well. Some, of course, may see this as a liability. After all, who wants to take time away from the business at hand? But for those who have come to see prayer as the primary way in which God accomplishes his work in this world, the greater amount of time given to prayer is an asset that makes group prayer an attractive option.

Opening prayer up to all the delegates also gives the Spirit freedom to work in people's hearts, bringing to mind a variety of concerns and a burden for prayer. As these are verbalized in prayer, the attention and prayers of the entire group are focused on the concerns that the Spirit has made known.

In group prayer, the whole assembly tends to be lifted in prayer, and "unity of the spirit through the bond of peace" becomes a reality (Ephesians 4:3). This often becomes most evident in the business meetings that follow group prayer.

Delegates who have been given the opportunity to pray together before a meeting report less division, fewer self-oriented comments, less criticism, and more inclination to listen to the Spirit's leading as opposed to their own inner dissenting voices.

options for group prayer

1. **Prayer and share time for the entire group.** Before you pray, invite delegates to give reasons for thanks or to mention requests for prayer before the entire assembly. After this time of sharing, everyone is invited to contribute to the prayer time as the Spirit may lead.

To facilitate these prayer requests and items for thanks, one classis asks its delegates ahead of time to be prepared to share a concern and/or a reason for thanks from their churches. Another classis asks half of its churches to submit written reports on their work and ministry, which then go into the classical agenda. At the classis meeting, a representative from each reporting church may highlight or update items in its report, then delegates unite in prayer for the ministries and churches that have been mentioned. Though specific people are appointed to pray for the reporting churches, all delegates are free to participate as well.

The leader's responsibility during this time is to invite contributions for the sharing time, make arrangements to begin and conclude the time of prayer, and to introduce songs and Scripture at appropriate points. Here are some suggestions to help make the prayer time more effective and meaningful:

- As part of the sharing and prayer, choose some Scripture passages and a few familiar songs that help people focus on God's presence and what he wants to accomplish among them.

- Keep everyone close to each other, not spread out in a large room. This helps to create a sense of unity.

- Designate one person to begin and end the prayer time.

- Remind delegates of the confidentiality of some of the requests they will be praying for.

- Suggest an approximate amount of time for the prayer so that everyone knows how long this time will last.

- Encourage brief prayers, explaining that this gives more people an opportunity to pray.

- A brief agenda for prayer is helpful. Include, for example, local churches, classical ministries, denominational ministries, the worldwide church, and the present meeting. You might also include common concerns of the churches—concerns that you will respond to God's call, that churches may reach out more effectively, that members will practice financial stewardship, that churches will be well-staffed, that Christian education will flourish, that moral battles and issues of justice will be won, and so on.

2. **Small group prayer.** After opening with songs of praise and a Scripture reading, invite delegates to pray together in groups of three to five persons. Each group should have a brief agenda for prayer, supplied by the leader. For example, you might ask each group to divide their time between the following topics:

praise and thanks

prayer for churches of the assembly and their ministries

prayer for the denomination (including issues, agencies, and so on)

prayer for the worldwide church and world evangelization

prayer for the present meeting and for agenda matters

You might hand out a printed agenda or have each group write down these categories. Or you may wish to introduce these prayer topics yourself during the prayer time, giving the groups a few minutes to pray for each one.

The leader's responsibilities include setting the tone by means of appropriate songs and Scripture readings. Along with introducing and explaining the agenda for the prayer time, the leader should also serve as time-keeper, letting the groups know how long they can be in prayer and signaling the end of that period.

The whole assembly tends to be lifted in prayer, and "unity of the spirit through the bond of peace" becomes a reality (Ephesians 4:3).

Here are some suggestions for a small group prayer time:

- Keep everyone in the same room. It's not necessary to separate the groups into different rooms since the noise level of everyone praying at once will cover up individual voices and give each group a sense of privacy. At the same time, delegates will feel part of a larger, combined prayer effort.

- Suggest that each group choose one of its members to make the transitions between prayer topics.

- Encourage brief prayers rather than long ones so that more people can participate.

Options for closing the prayer time:

- Encourage small groups to quietly leave the room when they have finished. They can go to another room for a coffee break, lunch break, or other activity.

- Ask group members to continue to pray silently after their group has finished praying aloud together, or to sit quietly until the rest of the groups are done.

- Play some quiet music to signal the end of the prayer time. Those who are already finished may listen to the music or join in a song that continues until every group is done praying.

3. **Concert of prayer.** Explain the concept of a concert of prayer to the assembly (see chapter 21), saying that the group will form into prayer triplets with people from different churches as well as elders and pastors in each group. Their purpose will be to pray for the health and ministries of their local churches.

Begin your concert of prayer with songs of praise, focusing your attention on the wonderful character of God. Follow your singing with a prayer of praise and thanks and Bible readings on prayer.

Divide the assembly into triplets (groups of three) and begin with a few minutes of sharing—identifying the church they're from, a few concerns they've come with to the meeting, and so on. Then ask the groups to spend about five minutes in prayer for each person's personal ministry, including concerns for family and friends.

Next ask the prayer triplets to pray for local churches, incorporating some of the following concerns into their prayers: Christ's vision for the church, strong and visionary leadership, the power to mobilize members for ministry, strength in God's Word, a strong prayer life, celebrative worship, the opportunity to help children and youth grow spiritually, a greater sense of hospitality and caring, the ability to assimilate new members into the fellowship, effective evangelism, greater church growth, and so on. You might close this segment with the song "Jesus, with Your Church Abide," using only piano at first and asking everyone to join in quietly the second time.

Then pray for the health and ministries of the denomination and of the church worldwide. For this prayer time, combine triplets to form groups of six. Ask groups to pray for the ministries and programs of the classis or assembly (you might list these before prayer) as well as denominational ministries. The prayer might touch on these topics: educational ministries (colleges, seminaries, local schools, youth federations, and so on), missions ministries (both domestic and world missions), world care and relief ministries, and literature ministries.

Prayer for the worldwide church should include a focus on efforts to bring the gospel to all nations, churches that are experiencing persecution or repression, and the need for unity among denominations. An appropriate song to close this time is "I Love Your Kingdom, Lord."

For the close of the concert of prayer, the leader should lead in prayer for the delegates as they offer themselves to God for his empowerment and they praise him for being a God who hears and answers prayer in powerful ways.

An alternate program for the concert of prayer from a classis in Kalamazoo, Michigan, is given below:

concert of prayer

1. *Introduction—Explanation—Break into triplets*

2. *Scripture: Psalm 111:1-3*

3. *Songs: His Name Is Wonderful; Jesus, Name Above All Names; Praise the Name of Jesus; Father, I Adore You*

4. *Prayer of Praise*

5. *Scripture: Psalm 139:23; Joel 2:12-13*

6. *Song: Spirit of the Living God*

7. *Individual Silent Confession*

8. *Personal Concerns (in triplets)*

9. *Renewal in the Local Church*

10. *Renewal in the Church Worldwide*

11. *Prayer for the Meeting Today*

12. *Song: Jesus, with Your Church Abide*

The leader's responsibility in the concert of prayer is to direct the various sections of the concert, making sure that everything flows smoothly. The leader should arrange for music: selecting the hymns, choosing music to open and close each section, and so on. He or she should also appoint those who will be leading the whole group in prayer.

other classical prayer activities

1. **The assembly or classis can produce a monthly prayer guide**, prepared by a prayer coordinator, that describes prayer concerns from its churches and reasons for praise and thanksgiving. This prayer guide can be sent to all the pastors, clerks, and church secretaries for distribution in their congregations (see chapter 7).

2. **An assembly or classis might sponsor a workshop or speaker** to equip its leaders and members in the discipline and ministry of prayer, as well as in the dynamics of group prayer. It might also consider recruiting a prayer trainer from its churches for this purpose, rather than bringing in an outside speaker.

The assembly or classis can produce a monthly prayer guide, prepared by a prayer coordinator, that describes prayer concerns from its churches and reasons for praise and thanksgiving.

3. **The assembly or classis could also include instructional and inspirational articles on prayer** in its newsletter in order to continually encourage prayer.

4. **Establishing prayer partnerships between churches promotes prayer and fellowship between congregations.** Churches that sign up for this ministry would commit themselves to

   • monthly, pastoral prayer for each other, with an emphasis on members' renewal and spiritual growth

   • sharing specific needs with each other (perhaps through an intercessor's newsletter, published by the church)

   • prayer for the community in which each church ministers

5. **The assembly or classis could also send each member church a list of classical ministries to include in its bulletins, requesting prayer for the people involved in those ministries.**

27

THE PRAYER ROOM

The prayer room described in this chapter is not a quiet place in which people stop in to pray whenever they feel the need. Nor is it the same as a room off the sanctuary, set aside for people who need the ministry of prayer after a worship service.

The prayer room suggested here is a quiet room in which continuous (or nearly continuous) prayer is offered for the church, the community, and the world. Those from the church who come to pray have pledged themselves to a regular time to pray (such as from 3:00-4:00 P.M. on Tuesdays) and are committed to keeping it.

Such a room becomes a place where church members come to engage in such vital ministries as

- battling the powers of darkness
- bearing the burdens of the hurting
- reclaiming broken lives
- releasing the power of God in the church and its leadership
- lifting up the communal experience of worship
- increasing the power of the spoken Word in worship
- supporting the work of missionaries around the world

what to include in the prayer room

What kind of place would make an effective prayer room? It should be simply furnished—plush furniture is not needed. Carpeting should be thick enough to make kneeling comfortable. Cushions are also helpful to use when kneeling in prayer. Low-level lighting is recommended to help create a meditative atmosphere. Be sure to place a globe or wall map of the world in the room to remind people to pray for missionaries and for countries other than their own. Also include such items as hymnbooks, wall plaques, desks, and appropriate filing systems.

You'll want to keep at least three boxes—simple filing boxes or baskets will do—in which to keep requests to be prayed for, requests that have been prayed for, and answers to prayer. When people enter the room for prayer, they can go immediately to the request cards in the "Pray For" box to bring those requests to God in prayer. As they pray for each request, they place it in the "Prayed For" box. When the "Pray For" box is emptied, someone can take the cards out of the "Prayed For" box, turn them over, and place them in the "Pray For" box to begin again. (You'll find, however, that the box containing answers to prayer will be the most popular spot in the prayer room. It encourages members' faith and inspires further praying.)

If your prayer room is large enough, you may want to make several prayer stations, each one for a different prayer concern: crises, unsaved friends and relatives of church members, missionary needs, pastor or staff needs, church activities and ministries, social problems in your community and nation, government leaders, and so on. People may choose to move from station to station if they would like, or, if several come to pray at one time, each can choose a station.

how to set up the prayer ministry

The first step may seem obvious, but it is crucial: *As a church, first decide that you need a prayer room.* Without the ownership of church members, the prayer room will remain unused. Study God's commands concerning prayer; look also at the need for prayer in the world, in your nation and community, and within your own church fellowship. Let God's Word and the need for prayer convince your church council and the entire congregation that a prayer room is a vital ministry for your church.

Second, choose the location for your prayer room. It's wise to choose a room separate from any other church activities that might intrude on the prayer that takes place. Consider using a room that has an outside entrance—so that the entire building need not be open just for this one ministry. The room should be accessible both day and night, clearly marked with signs to guide those who come to use it.

Third, print the cards to be used in this prayer ministry: (1) commitment cards on which volunteers can indicate the day

and time at which they will pray, (2) prayer concern cards on which people can write their prayer needs, and (3) prayer notecards to be sent to those who are being prayed for. See sample illustrations at the end of this chapter.

Fourth, enlist leaders for the prayer room ministry. The most strategic person is the director, who should have the gift of organization as well as a heart for prayer. Choose this person only after much prayer. If possible, free him or her from any other responsibilities in the church; enable the director to focus solely on mobilizing members for prayer. A prayer secretary is helpful in keeping the requests filed, recorded, and current. (This position may not become essential until after the ministry has been established.)

Finally, select eight prayer captains to assist the director. Each captain will be assigned a three-hour period for each day and will be responsible for finding church members to fill those slots.

These people—the director, the prayer secretary, and the captains—form the prayer-room team. Once chosen, they should spend much time in prayer to discern how God wants them to function and act. Don't begin this ministry too quickly. Take time to train and organize prayerfully (minimal organization is best).

Finally, enlist your volunteer intercessors. Do this by setting aside one Sunday for prayer mobilization. Focus everything—Sunday school classes, sermon, worship songs, choir music—on the topic of prayer. After the sermon, hand out the volunteer intercessor commitment cards to everyone, teenagers and older. Urge people to give an hour or more per week to the prayer-room ministry. Ask them to write down the time and the day that is best for them,

A prayer room helps a church look beyond itself, motivating it to unleash prayer power for the unsaved, the community, the nation, the church's missionaries, and the world.

along with their name, address, and telephone number. Remind them that this commitment is just for three months; they will have an opportunity to discontinue or to renew their commitment after each three-month period.

Collect the commitment cards and ask the prayer-room team to come forward, along with others from the congregation, to pray for those who wish to join the team. Use this time to emphasize the crucial nature of the prayer-room ministry.

Prayer captains should call the people who have signed up for their respective time slots. Together they agree on a specific prayer commitment each week. Some people may not be able to give a full hour; others' commitments may overlap. That's okay; take whatever time the people can give and assure them that more than one person can be in the prayer room at the same time.

> **The church that prays for the needs of the unsaved, the unchurched, and the hurting in its area sends out an important message to its community.**

Mention the volunteer commitment cards frequently from the pulpit during the months that follow, urging others to join in the prayer-room ministry. As you receive more commitment cards, follow up on them within a week, scheduling them into the ministry as quickly as possible.

week-to-week operation of the prayer ministry

Prayer concerns will come in as church members are encouraged to use the prayer-request cards in the pews. They can use these cards for their own prayer needs or for the needs of others (friends, relatives, neighbors, especially the unsaved). Encourage members to give blank prayer-concern cards to people outside the church membership so that they can send in their own prayer requests. If your church has a prayer hotline for the community (see chapter 8), you can also gather prayer concerns from this ministry. The director or the secretary (described below) can see that these requests are placed in the proper boxes in the prayer room.

Volunteer intercessors will come in to pray as scheduled. You will not be able to monitor everyone's presence, of course, but it is helpful to know when people show up and when they don't. To keep track, post a sign-up sheet in the prayer room and ask people to use it.

The volunteer intercessors are to pray for the needs on the prayer-concern cards, which will have been organized and put into the proper boxes and/or stations. Ask them, as a general rule, to begin with crisis needs and then to move to the church's leaders and ministries, the long-term ill, the unsaved, and so on.

Remind the volunteers that one person need not pray for all the concerns in the box. If there are many cards in a category, several intercessors may be needed to go through the entire collection. (The church membership list can be covered once a week.) After a person has prayed for the concern of a specific card, he or she should initial and date that card so that others are aware that it has been brought before God in prayer.

The director or the secretary should pull the cards after an agreed-upon number of days in order to keep the requests file current. He or she should also move the prayer-concern cards to the "answered" box when those prayers have been answered. It's helpful to write the answer on the back of the card. (If you haven't received an update on prayer requests after three months, the director or secretary should call the person who submitted the request to find out any new information. If some requests go unanswered for a long time, they should be placed in a more permanent file.)

Encourage your volunteer intercessors to occasionally send prayer notes to the persons they pray for. This is an effective way of keeping in touch with those who are distant or who are in particular need of encouragement. The homebound, the lonely, missionaries, public officials—all these can be cheered by the knowledge that someone is praying consistently for them. Prayer notes like these should include the church's name, address, and phone number, along with an appropriate Bible verse on prayer. Leave room for personal notes from the volunteer intercessors. Remind the intercessors to make a note on the prayer-concerns card whenever they've sent a prayer note to someone.

The persons who submit prayer requests should be informed that the cards will be pulled after a number of days (for example, 30, 60, or 90). Encourage these persons to resubmit their requests after that time if they want intercessory prayer to continue.

You may want to add a prayer telephone ministry to the prayer room's activities. This will extend the prayer room's effectiveness beyond the church family and out into the community. If you are interested in doing this once your prayer-room ministry has been established, read chapter 8 in this manual for suggestions and guidelines.

long-term efforts that keep the ministry going

Because church members' interest and involvement are crucial factors in the continuation of this ministry, you will need to keep it in front of people. You can do that in a number of ways:

- Set up a prayer board showing the hours of the week that you hope to fill and the hours that are already filled by volunteer intercessors. Make this prayer board large (perhaps 4' x 8'), and place it in a prominent location—perhaps the narthex or fellowship hall. In this way you can remind people of the prayer ministry and of the hours that are still unfilled.

  You may want to place a box of volunteer commitment cards near this board, along with a basket in which new volunteers can place their completed cards.

  Don't write the names of volunteer intercessors on this board, only the names and phone numbers of the prayer captains responsible for each time slot. You may want to place asterisks in certain time slots to indicate how many people have committed to pray during that period.

- Use posters, signs, and other displays to let people know of the prayer-room ministry. Colorful, quality banners and posters will keep the importance of the prayer room before the congregation.

- Include at your central display a bulletin board that lists answers to prayer. These answers can be taken from the cards in the "answered" box, but be careful to maintain confidentiality. If it's impossible to word an answer to prayer in such a way as not to "give it away," it may be necessary to call that person and ask for permission to post the answer to prayer. Other requests and answers will be sensitive enough that they should not be brought out of the prayer room. One church posts "thank-you" notes that people send after receiving specific answers to prayer.

- Mention this ministry often from the pulpit during Sunday worship, include it in the congregational prayers, and use the bulletin to remind people that this ministry needs their support.

- Mention the prayer-room ministry in each issue of your church's newsletter.

- Keep blank prayer-concern cards and volunteer-intercessor cards available in your sanctuary and fellowship hall at all times. Make sure that you clearly designate baskets in which people can put their completed cards.

- Every three months, give your volunteer intercessors the opportunity to renew their commitment. Use this time to challenge the rest of the congregation to participate in the ministry as well.

- Celebrate the gift of intercession at least once a year, perhaps with an appreciation banquet, with recognition in the worship service, or with some other public acknowledgment.

duties and responsibilities of the prayer-room team

The **director** has a key position in this ministry, since he or she oversees the total ministry of the prayer room. This person should work closely with the pastor, informing the pastor of important prayer needs and reminding the pastor to keep the prayer-room ministry before the congregation frequently.

The director should meet regularly (monthly or weekly) with the rest of the team to pray together and to evaluate the ministry. Staying in regular contact with the prayer captains is important, especially to encourage them to fill the time slots they have been assigned.

In general, the director should offer help to all who participate in the prayer ministry. Encouragement, sharing results, seeking to enlist new members, overseeing a monthly news bulletin, suggesting great books on prayer for the church library, working with the church council on matters of budget—all these are duties of the director.

Organizing a semi-annual prayer rally is another way in which the director can promote prayer in the church. Meant for those who have participated or who will participate in the prayer-room ministry, this rally can be a time of instruction as well as inspiration, including a time for singing, for sharing outstanding answers to prayer, for sharing about conversions that happened as a result of prayer, for asking people to tell what the prayer-room ministry has meant to them, for relating special prayer needs; for praying together in small groups, and for enlisting new volunteer intercessors.

In addition to the rally, the director should see that the church offers ongoing teaching about prayer, encourages an annual prayer retreat, and monitors the sign-up sheet.

Prayer captains are responsible to enlist, supervise, and encourage the volunteer intercessors who fill the hours of their sections. Captains should try to have more than one volunteer praying during each one-hour period. They should also consider taking an hour of that section themselves, setting an example in prayer.

Captains encourage, inspire, and lead their volunteer intercessors, rejoicing with them when prayers are answered. Captains might consider getting together once a month with their volunteers to pray together about needs and to praise the Lord for what he is doing through their prayers. They should stay in touch with each other by phone.

The **prayer secretary** is responsible for keeping the prayer-concern cards in order and in the right place. Any card left in the "Pray For" box over the specified length of time should be pulled, and the secretary should call the person who submitted the request for an update. The secretary is responsible for keeping track of answers to prayer and should write them on the backs of the cards. Those that do not receive answers should be placed in a long-term file for further prayer (for example, concerns for unsaved friends or relatives).

Volunteer intercessors should be faithful in their commitment to come and pray during their time slot and should remember to record their names on the sign-in sheet. If they cannot come at the time they have promised to pray, they should find a replacement or switch with someone else.

When intercessors come to the prayer room, they should spend some time alone in prayer. If others are present, however, they might also pray together regarding some of the requests that have come in.

One more important duty: intercessors should keep the prayer requests confidential. Each prayer-concern card is a sacred trust to be shared only with God.

Each **church staff person** should commit to at least one hour in the prayer room. These staff persons should also see that the outer entrance to the prayer room or church has a key lock or combination that is available to those who come to pray at night. The church staff should encourage and promote the prayer-room ministry in any way they can.

the value of a prayer room

A prayer room ministry

- calls forth the intercessory gifts of church members and greatly increases the prayer efforts of a church.

- gives tremendous prayer support to church ministries and leaders. It undergirds every aspect of a church's prayer life. A prayer room ministry is to the church what the heart is to the body.

- unleashes God's power and grace on people with all kinds of needs.

- helps a church look beyond itself, motivating it to unleash prayer power for the unsaved, the community, the nation, the church's missionaries, and the world.

- develops and strengthens the prayer lives of those who participate.

- restores the balance of a healthy prayer life, which God intends for the church.

- raises the image of a church in its community. The church that prays for the needs of the unsaved, the unchurched, and the hurting in its area sends out an important message to its community.

Note: *A Room That's Like a Mountain*, a comprehensive guide for starting a 24-hour prayer room in the local church, is available from Rev. Don Miller, Bible Based Ministries, Box 8911, Fort Worth, TX 76124.

prayer-concern card (side one)

my prayer burden

File
□
Letter

Check if
□
Request
for
Salvation

Pray for: _____
_____
_____
_____
_____
_____
_____

Is request for   ___Yes
CFBC member?   ___ No

Is it O.K. to send   ___Yes
Prayer Lines?   ___No

Date _____

| Submitted by: | Phone: |

Prayer Lines - Please Print:

Name _____

Address_____

City, State_____Zip_____

Date Prayer
Lines Sent
_____
_____
_____
_____
_____

"If two of you agree on earth about anything that they may ask, it shall be done
for them by my Father who is in heaven." Matthew 18:19

prayer-concern card (side two)

How God Answered . . .

Date _____

prayer notecard (outside folded card, inside is blank for note)

prayer line

You were remembered in prayer today . . .

commitment card

To help make CHAMPION FOREST BAPTIST CHURCH a "HOUSE OF PRAYER"
(Matthew 21:31) I will be in the Prayer Room praying . . .

Write in the spaces below your 1st, 2nd and 3rd choice for the day and prayer time you desire.

My Prayer Offering

Time	Day	Choice	Time	Day	Choice	Time	Day	Choice	Time	Day	Choice
Mid - 1 AM	___	___	6 AM - 7 AM	___	___	Noon - 1 PM	___	___	6 PM - 7 PM	___	___
1 AM - 2 AM	___	___	7 AM - 8 AM	___	___	1 PM - 2 PM	___	___	7 PM - 8 PM	___	___
2 AM - 3 AM	___	___	8 AM - 9 AM	___	___	2 PM - 3 PM	___	___	8 PM - 9 PM	___	___
3 AM - 4 AM	___	___	9 AM - 10 AM	___	___	3 PM - 4 PM	___	___	9 PM - 10 PM	___	___
4 AM - 5 AM	___	___	10 AM - 11 AM	___	___	4 PM - 5 PM	___	___	10 PM - 11 PM	___	___
5 AM - 6 AM	___	___	11 AM - Noon	___	___	5 PM - 6 PM	___	___	11 PM - Mid	___	___

*My Commitment = 30 min. ___ 60 min. ___ (Check One) This is a 4-month commitment.

Name _____ Phone _____ Date _____
Address _____
Street   City   Zip

This Prayer Offering is a = Continuation of my present commitment _____ (Check one)
Change in date or time of my present commitment _____
A new Prayer Offering _____

28
HOUSES OF PRAYER

"Love your neighbor as yourself" (Matthew 22:39). This command applies to everyone on your block, including the family across the street who never returns your greeting. And, yes, it even applies to the guy living next to the church who runs his power saw during the morning service. It applies to neighbors of all shapes and kinds. God places us next to these people so that we can show his overpowering love to them and pray for their needs—spiritual and physical. By this means we can bring them into the kingdom.

This is the heartbeat of the church: reaching out to our neighbors. And this is what neighborhood houses of prayer are all about: praying faithfully and consistently for the neighbors on our streets and in our apartment complexes, college dorms, and workplaces. Your congregation's outreach can be revitalized by this kind of prayer ministry.

what is a house of prayer?

Very simply, a "house of prayer" is two or more people who commit to pray regularly for their neighbors. It can be a husband and wife, or it can be two or more Christians living in the same neigh-borhood or working for the same employ-er—any believers who share a concern for the people they live or work with. The "house" can be a home in the neighbor-hood, an apartment in a complex, a room in a college dormitory, or a meeting place at work. Or it can simply be the Christians' commitment to pray for their neighbors' needs, without necessarily meeting together to do so.

Prayer is not the only activity, how-ever, that takes place in a neighborhood house of prayer. Houses of prayer become channels of God's blessing and love in many different ways: through intercessory prayer, through meals brought to the sick or lonely, through cards filled with encouragement, through childcare offered or leaves raked and bagged. Through prayer and acts of kindness, God's power and grace are released into neighbors' lives like soft rains on dry and thirsty ground.

We may ask, "Who is my neighbor?" Jesus answers, "Those people whom I put in your life every day: the ones who live next door, the family on the corner of the block, the person who delivers your mail, the one who works at the desk next to yours, your college suite mate, the people around your church. Each one is your neighbor. Love these neighbors as you love yourself."

Jesus' command rings clear in the matter of prayer: "Believers, if you pray for yourselves and your own needs, do the same for those who live around you. Do the same for those you work with. Do the same for those God puts in your path each day." The "nations" start at our doorstep.

how to organize a house of prayer

First, as your church leaders consider this as a possible ministry, provide information in the form of a video-based training seminar and printed materials. These are available from Mission 21 HOPE, P.O. Box 141312, Grand Rapids, Michigan 49514 (toll-free: 1-800-217-5200). Invite anyone who is interested to an informational meeting, and spend time in prayer with the pastor and/or other leaders to make sure you have felt the burden of God's heart for your neighbors and caught his vision for prayer.

Choose a person to coordinate this ministry—preferably one with proven gifts of organization as well as a passion for prayer. (If no one seems an obvious choice, make a temporary assignment.) Set up a timetable for introducing this vision to the congregation, for training participants, and for launching the neighborhood prayer ministry. Again, be sure to prepare for each of these stages with intercessory prayer to head off Satan's inevitable opposition.

When you inform the congregation of this new outreach, make good use of the flyers and videos available from Mission 21 HOPE (the acronym HOPE stands for "Houses of Prayer Everywhere"). Ask your pastor to preach a series of sermons on prayer and evangelism, ending with an invitation for people to sign up. Or present this ministry at a congregational meeting or informational session.

Training takes place in three evening sessions, using the videos provided by Mission 21 HOPE. (You can also make use of the booklet "How to Pray for Your Neighbors" and the 28-day "Neighborhood Prayer Ministry Devotional Guide.") Those who attend the video sessions will be prepared, at the end of the training, to begin their own houses of prayer. Ask them to make a commitment for thirty days, giving them the opportunity to try out the ministry before making a long-term commitment.

Pray for the Spirit to give you ideas on how to keep reaching out with small, natural acts of kindness.

When you are ready to launch your houses-of-prayer ministry, ask the congregation to pray over the participants publicly, perhaps as part of a dedication or commissioning service. Then ask the leader of each house of prayer to meet with his or her group to choose a specific neighborhood or prayer focus and to determine how they will achieve at least one hour of prayer each week.

organizing a house of prayer

Leadership and structure are key ingredients to a successful house-of-prayer ministry. From the start, it's important to designate a point person—someone to convene the group, schedule meetings, distribute information, keep records, order materials, and generally help members to be effective and fruitful in this ministry. It is the point person who lifts up other team members in prayer, supporting them as they do spiritual battle against powers of darkness. Overseeing this team of point people is the church's house-of-prayer coordinator.

Because their position is crucial, point persons of each group in the church should meet monthly to help each other in this role. At these meetings they can share answers to prayer, receive training and motivation, and find the support and resources they need. Without these meetings, most neighborhood prayer groups will eventually fail because of our built-in resistance to serious prayer and to Satan's vigorous opposition. A supportive team meeting is a strong counterforce to both of these obstacles.

how the ministry evolves

In the first year, your houses of prayer will develop into outreaching ministries with a life of their own. But this happens gradually, as members build relationships with the people they pray for.

This should happen in a very low-key, nonthreatening way. In the first two or three months, your only contact with your neighbors may be regular prayer, along with a letter introducing yourself and letting them know that you are praying for them and for others who live or work in the same area. Keep this a short, informal note that is not "preachy" but warm and friendly. Invite anyone who is interested to join you in praying for the neighborhood.

It's a wonderful thing to pray God's thoughts back to him on behalf of your neighbors.

During these first months, create a prayer map that shows each neighborhood unit and lists the needs of each unit, along with as much family or personal information as you can gather.

Also, lay a strong foundation of prayer that will make your neighbors' hearts sensitive to God's working in their lives and will help prepare the way for them to receive your future acts of kindness in Jesus' name.

Then, during the next few months, you may want to establish further contact by means of door hangers (available from Mission 21 HOPE) and cards that neighbors can fill out and mail back to you, informing you of any special needs they would like prayer for. Do some prayer-walking around your neighborhood (see chapter 30), asking God to give you insight into each family's needs as you pass their home.

It may not be until several months later that you make a planned personal contact. At that point you should offer a gift—a small loaf of homemade bread, a simple devotional or inspirational booklet, some extra produce from your garden, a flower-seed packet, a neighborhood directory.

Now may also be a good time for a small community get-together—an open house, block party, backyard barbecue, or Super Bowl party. Pray for the Spirit to give you ideas on how to keep reaching out with small, natural acts of kindness.

After the bridge of friendship has been built, you can perform the kindest act of all, sharing the gospel. There are many ways to do this—by personally sharing the story of what God has done in your life, with a booklet or cassette that explains the good news, by inviting neighbors to church. Your pastor or minister of evangelism can suggest other methods as well.

This process of building bridges may be much shorter, of course, if God works quickly in response to your prayers. Families may respond immediately with prayer needs and may clearly be open to the message of the gospel. By all means follow God's leading. But be patient with those neighbors who seem reserved, who hold back and prefer to keep their distance. Wait for God's timing, and continue praying.

what and how to pray

First of all, keep your focus on neighbors. Serious prayer for neighbors is one of the most neglected ministries in North America. Don't dilute the focus of your house of prayer by making it a catch-all for other intercessory needs. Some houses of prayer may choose to intercede for a specific group: the local police force, civic leaders and judges, and so on. Whatever your focus, remember to "keep the main thing the main thing": your neighbors' needs.

You may not know particular needs of the neighbors you are praying for. But Scripture gives us a wealth of things to pray for, things that God clearly wants to do for people:

- meet their life needs
- draw them closer to himself
- protect them from the evil one
- maintain strong and healthy marriages
- convict people of sin
- give them an opportunity to hear the good news of Jesus
- turn them from darkness to light
- establish good parent-child relationships
- bring good friends into people's lives

Use Scripture passages such as the Lord's Prayer, the listing of the fruits of the Spirit, the "love chapter" (1 Corinthians 13), and the Ten Commandments as a basis for your requests as well. It's a wonderful thing to pray God's thoughts back to him on behalf of your neighbors.

God will move powerfully in response to these prayers. It can be difficult, however, to keep a record of answers, because these prayers are more general in nature.

Therefore it's important to keep track of neighbors' specific prayer requests when you are able to get them. Because most people believe that spiritual powers affect our lives, they will be convinced through answered prayer that God is alive, that he is powerful, and that he is involved in their lives. Through this means God gets people's attention and opens a door to their hearts. As you and your neighbors see specific prayers answered, you will have an open door to tell them about the One who has answered.

In addition, it's important to keep track of Spirit-prompted prayers. At times when we are in tune with God's mind and heart, we may receive impressions from the Holy Spirit on how to pray for a specific person. Such communications often reveal how God desires to act, and they are among the prayers he is most quick to answer in an obvious way.

You and the other members of your house of prayer will be partners with God.

a neighborhood ministry, a spiritual battle

The houses-of-prayer ministry operates in a spiritual realm, between two spiritual kingdoms. Christians are called to build bridges to people outside of God's family, to "turn them from darkness to light, and from the power of Satan to God" (Acts 26:18). Satan doesn't take this assault lying down, of course. He will try to steal the seed of God's Word from hearts that aren't prepared to receive it. He will try to blind their minds. He will deceive, accuse, and create fear.

Prayer is our most powerful weapon in defeating Satan. Our prayers are what will build the kingdom of God on our streets. They are the weapons that will destroy the kingdom of Satan. All true prayer is spiritual warfare, because Satan opposes everything God wants. So expect Satan's opposition to your prayers—

through interruptions, blocked relation-ships, tiredness, busyness, forgetfulness. Pray your way through these, and encourage each other—especially as you discern the designs of the enemy, who will use any means possible to discourage you.

The result of your perseverance and faithfulness in prayer is the building of God's kingdom on your streets and in your neighborhood. You will see people's lives brought closer to God, families changed, friendships built. You will see people starting to attend church, to rebuild their marriages, to learn how to show God's love to people who have hurt them, to find the great healing of God's forgiveness in their own lives.

In other words, you and the other members of your house of prayer will be partners with God. There's no greater joy than to see God's hands working through your own to change and heal people's lives. This is the heart of the houses-of-prayer ministry, and it can revitalize not only your neighborhoods but also your church.

29

SOLEMN ASSEMBLIES

a time for repentance

It's not easy to say, "I'm sorry." It's often hard to say, "Forgive me." But there are times when this is necessary.

This is true of churches as well as individuals. We aren't used to repenting as a group. In fact, it rarely happens. But there are times when a congregation needs to say to God and to each other, "We are sorry. What we have been doing is wrong, and we need God's help and forgiveness." Then is the time to call a solemn assembly.

what is a solemn assembly?

Solemn assemblies are called specifically to confess any known sins, to restore a right relationship between God and the church, and in some cases to bring healing and restoration to troubled churches.

First, the matter of repentance. Though Christians are more used to dealing with personal rather than corporate (or group) sins, these also must be dealt with. As the name suggests, a solemn assembly is marked by seriousness, reflection, and a sense of awe before God. It's a time for believers to listen to what God has to say to

them through Scripture, to confess together where they have missed the mark, and to renew their covenant with God.

Because these times of listening to God and of confessing sin make believers more sensitive to God's holiness and his love, solemn assemblies historically have served as catalysts for restoring people to God. They have often sparked revival and renewal in the church.

A solemn assembly may be the tool by which the Holy Spirit will heal and restore your church when it is troubled and divided. In this setting, a congregation has the opportunity to come to terms with its destructive behaviors, its toleration of sin, or its spiritual apathy.

A solemn assembly can be described as a divinely ordained process for corporate repentance. It is the urgent call of leaders for the people of God to gather and to

- humble themselves before God by prayer and fasting
- ask for God's presence among them
- listen to God's Word
- turn away from the things that displease their Lord
- worship God with true hearts
- pledge a new commitment to their covenant with God
- dedicate themselves to being God's vessels in this world

when to call a solemn assembly—and why

Sometimes as a congregation struggles with a crisis or drifts away from God's will, the Holy Spirit may impress a message on the leaders' hearts through Scripture or prayer. It may be inappropriate to share a message like this from the pulpit in a public worship service, since visitors may be present. In such cases, a solemn assembly may be a very effective setting for communicating and dealing with the congregation's struggle, especially if the congregation is well prepared before the assembly gathers.

The need of a solemn assembly most often arises when a church is facing deep spiritual problems. It is not uncommon for a church to be marked by bickering, unfair treatment of its pastors, divisiveness over unimportant issues, spiritual indifference, mistrust of leadership, or other deeply rooted problems.

In one congregation, a powerful member tried everything he could to dislodge a new pastor who had been voted in by a large majority of the other members. This member rallied support from inactive members, threatened lawsuits if the pastor was not fired, and demanded that the church facilities be turned over to him and his friends. Eventually the church removed him from membership. In response, he sued.

The new pastor called a solemn assembly of the entire congregation. "It was a response to this season of testing, asking God to protect us from bitterness, to keep us broken before him, and to guard us from anger and hatred toward those who were suing us," says the pastor. "We also honestly sought to know specific ways we had grieved those who had turned against us."

Solemn assemblies can also be a proactive, preventive measure to keep dissat-isfactions from taking root and growing into problems. A church that had been losing its younger members steadily for a decade took time in a solemn assembly to reflect on its congregational history. Members discovered negative patterns that had hindered their growth: a tendency to limit God, the desire to remain within comfort zones, an unwillingness to accept those who were different, a mistrust of their spiritual leaders, and critical speech against one another. Once they let God show them their weaknesses, they were ready to ask forgiveness and to covenant to begin more holy living.

Solemn assemblies may also be a way to bring healing for past mistakes. One congregation, during its solemn assembly, realized that it had inappropriately fired four pastors. Members repented from the heart and sent letters to each former pastor, requesting forgiveness for all the pain that had been caused. Another congregation recalled, during the course of its service of repentance and reflection, that it owed a former pastor some compensation. So it wrote a letter of apology on the spot and sent him twice what they owed.

People should understand, from the first, that the assembly will be an encounter with God.

A solemn assembly can be a cry for guidance from the Lord as well. The congregation that was faced with lawsuits had first felt that they should give up the building without a fight. But after their assembly, during which they spent nine-and-a-half hours in prayer, they were convinced that God wanted them to stay and to watch him act in response to their prayers.

what scripture says

When the people of Israel angered God by worshiping the golden calf, Moses pitched the tent of meeting outside the main camp, away from the place of sin.

He commanded that every Israelite who sought the Lord come out of the camp for a solemn assembly, to meet God in his tabernacle and to hear what he had to say to them (Exodus 33:7-11).

To help the Israelites prepare themselves for the return of the ark of God, the prophet Samuel called a solemn assembly. None of the people ate that day, and they spent the time confessing what they had done to displease the Lord. They asked God to take them back as his people and to put them under his protection (1 Samuel 7:5-6).

Asa, Jehoshaphat, Jehoiada, Hezekiah, Josiah, Zerubbabel, Ezra, Nehemiah, and Joel all proclaimed solemn assemblies throughout Israel's history, calling the Israelites to return to the Lord with all their hearts, to separate themselves from the sin of the nations, and to recommit to their covenant with God.

In Joel's day, God said to the prophet, "Declare a holy fast; call a sacred assembly. Gather the people, consecrate the assembly; bring together the elders, gather the children. . . . Let the priests, who minister before the LORD, weep between the temple porch and the altar" (Joel 2:15-17). Although Israel had committed horrendous sins, God wanted to meet with them: "Even now, return to me with all your heart, with fasting and weeping and mourning" (2:12). Although in the Old Testament and today it is the spiritual leaders who call a solemn assembly, in a deeper sense it is God himself, calling out to his people to return with all their hearts. This is the biblical vision of the solemn assembly.

preparing for a solemn assembly

People should understand, from the first, that the assembly will be an *encounter with God*. It must be guided by God's agenda, not theirs. God is calling the assembly together, and the people are to stay until God is through speaking to them.

Because this is an unfamiliar concept to many Christians, take the time to prepare them for this encounter with God. Begin such preparation weeks beforehand with an extended period of teaching, using sermons, devotional materials, church-education lessons, and biblical exposition. You might consider preparing a one-page handout for all members to take home and use during their quiet times, giving them Scripture passages to focus on and specific issues to bring to God in prayer. Include open-ended questions, based on the Scripture passages you've chosen.

Ask everyone—especially council members—to pray daily for the upcoming assembly, asking that the Holy Spirit prepare their hearts to listen. One pastor requested that his congregation pray intensively at home for three weeks, then fast for three days before the assembly. Another church shut down every other ministry for the week preceding the assembly, giving people more time for reflection and prayer. One pastor noted after such a time of preparation, "By the time we got to the solemn assembly, the anticipation had been building. People were ready; I mean really ready. It was now something they owned."

conducting a solemn assembly

There is no one right format for such a gathering or service. Ask God to guide you in your planning beforehand, and be flexible if during the service itself the Holy Spirit seems to be moving powerfully through such elements as singing, confession, group prayer, or silent listening to God. Be willing to take more time at that point, allowing the Spirit to do convicting work.

Solemn assemblies usually include most of the following elements:

- **A formal call to assemble** before God and to seek his face.

- **Scripture readings,** especially those that focus on renewing our relationship with God and those that list specific sins that are offensive to God.

- **Prayer,** which should make up the greatest part of your time together. "Nothing is discussed more and acted on less than prayer," notes one pastor. Make sure that this is not true of your solemn assembly. Individual, small group, or corporate prayers are all effective in this setting. You may want to read some prayers from Scripture, such as Daniel 9:4-19; be sure to give adequate time for prayers of confession and repentance.

- **A time of confession,** both corporate and personal. This is vital. Though personal sin can be confessed privately and silently, sins that affect the entire congregation should be confessed publicly. You may want to do this in small groups or as one assembly, all together. Using an open microphone for all prayers is often a good idea, especially if the group is large.

- **A time of commitment,** both corporate and personal. This should be expressed as "sacrifices and offerings," as in Old Testament times. Today our sacrifices and offerings consist of presenting ourselves back to God, holy and acceptable, in response to Christ's sacrifice for our sins. Allow people to express how they feel God is calling them to commit themselves as a congregation.

- **Celebration and praise.** Give the people time to celebrate and praise the Lord in song, Scripture reading, and personal testimony. If the Spirit has been at work and people have responded to God with all their hearts, they will want to voice the thanks they feel.

- **Renewal of the covenant with God.** This is a fitting close to the solemn assembly. Consider reading a passage such as Hebrews 10:15-25, or asking the assembly to voice its commitment by reading responsively Joshua 24:14-24 (with the leader reading verses 14-15). Or you may, as did the people of Israel, agree to a covenant based on God's promises.

practical suggestions

- Don't hesitate to include children in your solemn assembly. Scripture indicates that all ages were present for such assemblies, and with good reason. A solemn assembly is a wonderful opportunity for children to see their parents and elders demonstrating their faith at its deepest corporate levels. Teens and adolescents can be deeply affected by the Spirit's work and by the congregation's response to God. You may want to ask outside baby-sitters to look after the youngest children so that parents are free to give their full attention to the assembly.

- Consider making fasting a part of your spiritual preparation. Much has been written about fasting in recent years; ask for good references at your local Christian bookstore if you would like to learn more about the biblical basis for fasting. In brief, however, fasting is a way of acknowledging to God that there are issues vastly more important than the meeting of our physical needs. It's an outward demonstration of our willingness to give our full attention to spiritual needs.

- Sacrifice is an important element of the solemn assembly (see, for example, Numbers 10:10 and 15:3). The people of Israel offered to God what was most valuable to them—their flocks and grain harvest. Today perhaps our most valuable commodity is time. What sacrifice could be more significant in today's pressured schedules than to set aside an entire day for listening to the Lord and seeking his face? Encourage people to look on this day as a sacrifice honoring God.

A solemn assembly is a wonderful opportunity for children to see their parents and elders demonstrating their faith at its deepest corporate levels.

- Coupled with the idea of sacrificing our time to God, consider setting the solemn assembly to last for at least a day. Some solemn assemblies in the Old Testament met for as long as seven to fourteen days. Your congregation most likely is used to worship services that last for about an hour. A solemn assembly, however, requires a prolonged period of time for God to accomplish all he wants to do.

- Make preaching an integral part of your solemn assembly. The assembly provides a meaningful opportunity for Spirit-anointed sharing of God's Word, which can lay bare the secrets of the heart. The sermon(s) should deal specifically with the issues of the day and help people to see how they can respond to God's call upon their lives.

what can we expect to happen?

In a solemn assembly, there are many unknowns. It is impossible to know beforehand, for example, what issues God may lay on people's hearts, what Scriptures or songs will prove most powerful, and what parts of the service may need to be prolonged or expanded to allow the Spirit room to work.

But you can count on some things. Both ancient and recent history show God's wonderful response to his people's heartfelt repentance and recommitment. If you are seriously seeking God, you can expect God to answer your prayers for guidance, reveal hidden sins, move individuals to speak his truth, and send spiritual refreshment and healing where it is needed most.

Congregations that have been going through spiritual struggles may feel as the Israelites did when locusts and drought ravaged their once-fertile land. God's promise to his people still holds true today: "Return to me with all your heart . . . [and] I will repay you for the years the locusts have eaten" (Joel 2:12, 25). God will send abundant showers and make the dry places alive and green.

Call your solemn assembly and prepare together to listen to the Word of the living God. Then wait and see what the Lord can do.

30

PRAYERWALKING

The word *prayerwalking* may be new to you. It describes a new way of praying for your community. By targeting the streets around your home and around your church, prayerwalking enables you to intercede for each home and place of business as you walk by.

Here's how one pastor was introduced to prayerwalking:

"Not long ago, God spoke to my heart and gave me a very simple yet powerful word: 'You do not have the right to evangelize your community until you have effectively prayed for your community.' After seeking God as to how this was to be accomplished, we began to 'Take Prayer to the Streets.'

"At first, we did not have a clue as to how to go about doing this. I had never been involved with anything like this. It was about this same time that I came across several books dealing with the idea of prayerwalks. I read each page with great interest as the words confirmed to me the call to pray for our community.

"Since then we have been out on the streets about seven or eight times. Each time those who were on the streets with us were blessed and energized. As many were praying, God

touched their hearts with the spiritual condition of our community. They began to feel the pain and the hurt of the community."

praying on-site with insight

How does God's Spirit get ingrown churches to grow outward, to reach beyond their doors and into their streets and neighborhoods? By helping them to see firsthand the plight of their communities. By putting feet to their prayers. By moving them to pray for very specific homes and places of business and families.

Prayerwalkers go out on the streets in order to get nearer to the problems, to pray more clearly for them. It's usually a low-profile affair: friends or family walk two-by-two through their own neighborhoods, schools, or workplaces, praying quietly as they go. Or church members go in pairs or small groups through the streets around their church.

Though they usually walk unnoticed, prayerwalkers quickly become aware of the realities and needs of their neighbors. They rely on the Holy Spirit to give them insight into what needs to be prayed for. That's why some describe prayerwalking as "praying on-site with insight."

As the pastor above notes,

"Through God's inspiration we were able to discern certain areas that we should concentrate our prayer toward. Before we went out, we listed key areas where we knew crime was high and drugs were a problem. We made a list of most of the bars in the area. We targeted spiritual strongholds such as shops that sold pornographic materials and places where the occult was being promoted. When this list was completed, we had a good list with which to target our prayers."

the spiritual value of prayerwalking

Prayerwalking yields a variety of spiritual benefits. It's like a tractor, used by the farmer for many different tasks: plowing up hard ground, sowing seed, cutting down weeds, harvesting. Because the tractor does so many different kinds of work, once around the field is never enough.

In the same way, the Holy Spirit uses our on-site prayers to cultivate and prepare the resistant hearts of our neighbors, to sow small seeds of influence, to restrain evil spiritual forces, and to help us encounter neighbors at the ripe moment with an invitation to follow Christ.

The primary value, of course, is answered prayer. But there are other long-term benefits:

1. **Prayerwalking involves every church member in united prayer.** While out prayerwalking, each person focuses on the neighborhood and its needs. For an extended period of time you are all in prayer before God, asking that his will be done in the homes and businesses that line your streets. For an even greater display of unity, you can invite neighboring churches to join you on the streets.

Prayerwalking can involve everyone, no matter what their age or physical condition. Children can walk with adults. Teens can cover the hardest terrain. Those unable to walk can pray from church or from home while others are covering the community.

2. **Prayerwalking prepares the way for the gospel.** When we pray before doing the work of evangelism, we put the focus on God as the main evangelizer. Without a doubt, God will respond to our prayers by opening minds and doors for gospel contact.

But there's more. The most immediate result you will see in a prayerwalk is the impact it has on the "pray-ers" themselves. The act of venturing closer to neighbors invariably puts them in sync with God's "seek and save" mission. Not only are your neighbors being prepared to hear the gospel, but

Prayerwalkers go out on the streets in order to get nearer to the problems, to pray more clearly for them.

your walkers are being prepared to share it. One businessman put it this way:

"I was a bit skeptical, thinking that surely I could pray any of the same prayers from home. But I was amazed to find myself looking into the faces of kids and praying for them in ways I know I would never have done in the routines of my household and business at home. Especially when I realized that some of these kids hadn't been prayed for by a Christian ever, and may not get prayed for again for years. It was definitely worthwhile for them. But I think I got the most out of it."

3. **Prayerwalking trains church members in prayer.** Some may feel at a loss when praying for their neighbors: "What can I pray for? What do they need?" We get close so that we can get clear. The Holy Spirit provides the insight. In addition, people learn to pray aloud, explicitly, creatively, conversationally, and sensitively.

4. **Prayerwalking creates opportunities for contact.** Prayerwalking opens divine encounters. People ask, "Why are you walking here?" A forthright answer usually leads to an opportunity to pray directly with people for their felt needs. Your neighbors will be surprised to find Christians who, instead of preaching them a sermon, warmly ask about their needs and pray for their problems.

5. **Prayerwalking roots church members to their neighborhood.** What pastor hasn't bemoaned the fact that some members will pick up and move each year? Part of this is unavoidable in our society, of course. But some relocation happens when Christians fail to take into consideration God's calling and mission when they plan their move. Prayerwalking gives church members a sense of mandate for service in a particular location, a feel for God's call to pray and minister on the streets where they are. They often develop a growing determination to bear spiritual fruit right in their own neighborhood.

how to lead your church in prayerwalking

1. **Begin with a few.** It usually takes a while to get people to accept a new idea or way of doing things. So start

behind the scenes without a great deal of fanfare.

Find the active "pray-ers." You'll usually find a few folks who have already been praying in their own neighborhoods. Or set out on a series of short prayerwalks with a few friends whom you personally invite. You will find that prayer is often mobilized one friendship at a time. You will build your vision for prayerwalking in your church by multiplying the practitioners.

2. **Involve leaders.** If you are not a pastor, be sure you talk to your church's pastor(s) about what you and the other prayerwalkers are doing. Invite them to join you as they have opportunity.

Also keep them posted with a one-page summary of what's been happening on your prayerwalks: who, what, where, when, and why. Describe a few of the prayers. These kinds of details are highly effective; it's far better to "tell" a vision than to try to "sell" it. And this kind of detailed communication will enable your pastors to recommend prayerwalking to the congregation with confidence.

3. **Lift your vision Christ-ward.** Keep your prayerwalkers' focus on what Christ is doing, not on what they are doing, in your city. Don't inflate people's expectations of sudden and dramatic results; don't present prayerwalking as a sure-fire technique. Instead, focus as a group on what God may want to do city-wide. Look further into the future than just the few days following your prayerwalk, and think of your prayers as helping to effect a city-wide revival and renewal. It's like praying, "May your kingdom come *in this zip code* as it is in heaven."

4. **Link prayerwalking with your church's existing program.** Prayerwalking can be seamlessly integrated into many ministry efforts:

- If your church has a prison ministry, prayerwalk around the prison several times before a crucial time of outreach.

- If you are targeting a part of your neighborhood or an apartment complex for a Bible study, prayerwalk in that area before knocking on doors and distributing flyers.

- Your church may be located in or near a troubled neighborhood through which you can prayerwalk with candles on weekday evenings. One church that did this weekly found that members are invariably asked to pray for specific needs as their candles burn into the night.

- A youth leader challenged his high school youth group to walk around their campus a few times in prayer. Within days some of the least likely students were asking questions about the gospel.

- Taking very small groups of children on a prayerwalk around the neighborhood can make a very deep impression on them. In one church that did this, parents reported that their children's prayers at home were more thoughtful and specific as well.

There are scores of ways to pray onsite, and many of these will fit into your church's existing ministries. Prayerwalking is particularly valuable before you begin a new ministry, especially a fresh gospel outreach. Some churches prayerwalk an area carefully before laying any plans at all, in order to better sense God's mind and timing.

how to lead a first-time prayerwalk

1. **Clarify the invitation.** Make sure that people know what they're getting into. If they have not done something like this before, they may not understand what it involves. Some have imagined kneeling in people's driveways and praying with a megaphone. Others may think of it as a walk-athon, or as a loud public event like March for Jesus, or simply as a door-knocking evangelism campaign.

So explain it in simple terms. The best one to help you do this may be a layperson who can tell people what his or her own experience has been, describing a typical prayerwalk in detail. This will help to decrease the apprehension and guesswork of first-time prayerwalkers.

2. **Prepare the routes.** Plan a few different routes, but make sure that each begins and ends at the same place. In addition, try to start people in a place other than their own home turf. Sometimes familiarity with an area can frustrate early attempts to express kingdom-size prayers. Prepare hand-drawn maps to distribute before everyone starts, and be sure to keep the routes limited to a mile or less. You can expect people to cover a mile in about half an hour.

3. **Form teams.** Ask first for those who will stay in the spot where you've convened to support the prayerwalkers in prayer. Then have the rest of the group members pair off in twos or threes. Identify those who don't have partners, and link them with each other.

4. **Provide a prayer theme.** Emphasize prayers of blessing on behalf of people,

directed toward God. You may be focusing on a specific need—crime, drug trafficking, spiritual emptiness, family breakdown—in your neighborhood. If so, encourage your prayerwalkers to pray in positive terms, focusing on what God can do rather than on the problems themselves.

In addition, use Scripture in your prayers. You may want to distribute appropriate verses printed on small cards or slips of paper. For example, use the Lord's Prayer or Psalm 23 to pray for people without a shepherd. Scripture will provide you with no end of powerful ways to pray for your neighbors.

5. **Regather and report.** Coming together afterward to evaluate what you've done will encourage long-range prayerwalking. Testimonies of what people have experienced can be powerful and moving. Talk about what you prayed, who you met, what you saw, and what you sensed God's Spirit telling you. Then be sure to explore future efforts by asking, "What's next?"

There are scores of ways to pray on-site, and many of these will fit into your church's existing ministries.

6. **Continue what you've started.** Encourage members to identify an area of fifteen to twenty homes that they will prayerwalk two or three times a week—perhaps for a period of forty days. Your prayerwalkers will always refine the idea and suggest their own changes, but giving them a specific challenge will help them get started.

7. **Connect with other evangelistic efforts.** What organized campaign for evangelism or outreach can your church initiate or join? When your church gets involved in such a campaign, offer to prayerwalk through the targeted areas of your city.

side by side, city by city

Organizations such as Prayerwalk USA have made it their goal to see every community in North America covered in prayer by caring Christian neighbors who will pray for every home on every street in America. Their vision is to prayerwalk through every zip code in the United States by the year 2000 and beyond.

As local leaders, you can mobilize the churches in your area to pray in creative ways for your whole city. Eventually we may see every home upheld in prayer by caring Christian neighbors every day.

For more helpful information about prayerwalking, see *Prayerwalking: Praying On-Site with Insight* by Steve Hawthorne with Graham Kendrick (Creation House, 1993) and *Prompts for Prayerwalkers* by Steve Hawthorne (published by WayMakers, P.O. Box 203131, Austin, TX 78720; phone 512-419-7729).

31

NATIONAL DAY OF PRAYER

a spiritual legacy

Prayer is part of the lifeblood of much of North America. From 1775—when the First Continental Congress of the United States convened—millions of people across North America have observed national days of prayer. In 1952 the U.S. Congress passed a joint resolution declaring that the U.S. would observe a National Day of Prayer each year. In 1988 this day was designated as the first Thursday in May.

Many North Americans have long recognized the rich heritage of prayer in their history. Since the day John Hancock signed the first congressional order in the U.S., establishing a day of prayer "throughout the country," leaders have invited citizens to join them in acknowledging their dependence on the highest government of all. State legislatures have the right to begin each day with prayer. The U.S. Congress and the Supreme Court both start their days in prayer.

George Washington, in his inaugural address to Congress, declared, "It would be particularly improper to omit, in this first official act, my fervent supplication to that Almighty Being, who rules over the universe, who presides in the councils of nations, and whose providential aids can supply every human defect, that his benediction may consecrate to the liberties and happiness of the people of the United States."

A later president, Benjamin Harrison, added, "It is a great comfort to trust God—even if his providence is unfavorable. Prayer steadies one, when he is walking in slippery places—even if things asked for are not given."

During one of the darkest hours of U.S. history, Gen. Robert E. Lee said, "Knowing that intercessory prayer is our mightiest weapon and the supreme call for all Christians today, I pleadingly urge our people everywhere to pray. Believing that prayer is the greatest contribution that our people can make in this critical hour, I humbly urge that we take time to pray—to really pray. Let there be prayer at sunup, at noonday, at sundown, at midnight. . . ."

gathering as "one nation, under God"

What is the value of a national day of prayer? How is it different from individual prayers raised on a nation's behalf? Private prayers are heard by God; there is no doubt of that. But a special national day set aside for prayer is a unique and public way to honor God and to ask for his presence, wisdom, and direction in our government and in our homes.

A national day of prayer lifts up the nation to God. The moral fabric of Western society has been crumbling, bit by bit. Families, the foundation of our communities, are unraveling in record numbers. God gave the family unit as a blessing, as a safe place in which small children—the next generation of leaders—can be trained to live good and upright lives. But divorce rates, abuse, violence, crime, drugs, suicide, and abortion continue to increase.

President Ronald Reagan said, "Without God there is no prompting of the conscience . . . without God there is a coarsening of the society; without God democracy will not and cannot long endure. . . . If we ever forget that [the U.S. is] 'one nation under God,' then we will be a nation gone under."

If we are to survive, we must return to God for the same reasons our nation's leaders have looked to God: to honor him, offer thanksgiving, seek safety, ask forgiveness, and rely on him for all we need.

A national day of prayer gives people the privilege of gathering and praying for the nation all together, in many different places of worship and public office, across state or provincial lines and time zones.

adding your voice to the nation's

All churches are invited to take part in a national day of prayer, but it's up to each one to decide how. When you participate in a national day of prayer, your first step should be to approach the prayer coordinator or prayer leaders in your congregation. These people will be essential in contacting other churches in the area about community activities, in planning your church's involvement, and in promoting your plan within the congregation.

The next step—one that will save you hours of groundwork—is to order a resource kit from the National Day of Prayer (NDP) Task Force (see information below). This wealth of information and ideas will provide an excellent foundation for your planning.

As you decide how your congregation can best be involved, keep your mind open to suggestions you may not have tried before. Here are a few ideas:

- *A prayer-related concert.* Invite local church choirs to perform music with patriotic and prayer-related themes. If weather permits, hold the concert in a local park, and invite people to bring picnic suppers.

- *Prayer breakfast or luncheon.* Invite your community to listen to a well-known speaker who will focus on prayer. The resource kit mentioned below offers NDP prayer guides for all participants, as well as camera-ready art to promote your event.

- *Youth prayer rally.* Involve your youth pastor or leaders, and invite area youth groups to join you. A Youth Resource Kit is also available from the NDP Task Force address listed below.

- *Nationally televised concert of prayer.* A station in your area may be carrying the live broadcast of this televised event. If so, consider making this telecast a part of your evening prayer activities.

The National Day of Prayer gives Americans the privilege of gathering and praying for the nation all together, in many different places of worship and public office, across state lines and time zones.

- *Request distribution of prayer guides.* Ask different groups from church—church school, youth group, men's or women's groups—to distribute NDP prayer guides to shut-ins and the elderly. At the same time, they can collect prayer requests to be prayed for during the week of the National Day of Prayer.

- *24-hour prayer vigil.* Ask people to sign up for a period of time, during which they will pray at home or at church. Consider leaving the church doors open for those who wish to pray in the quiet of the sanctuary.

Most churches include a worship/prayer service as part of their involvement. Below is a sample service suggested by the NDP Task Force. It gives you an idea of how much time to give to music, message, and prayer, and it suggests songs that focus on themes of praise, honor, and prayer. You may adapt it to fit your congregation's needs.

Minutes	Event	Notes
4	Opening worship	"I Will Call Upon the Lord" "Ah, Lord God"
2	Welcome	Pastor/Leader
3	Scripture reading	Choose from suggested list below.
12	Worship	"How Majestic Is Your Name" "Heal Our Land" "Praise to the Lord, the Almighty" "I Worship You, Almighty God" "I Sing Praises to Your Name"
14	Message	Theme: "Honor God" (1 Samuel 2:30; Jeremiah 33:3, 6-9)
2	Song of response	"Be Exalted, O God"
20	Prayer	That God would be honored . . . among our leaders in our families in our churches in each individual life (Select a leader for each topic, 5 min. each.)
3	Closing	Challenge to "carry the light" (Isaiah 60:1-3)

Here are some alternate Scripture passages you can use as the focus of your service or activities:

Leviticus 10:3	"I will be honored."
1 Chronicles 16:23-33	"Declare his glory among the nations."
1 Chronicles 29:10-18	David's prayer at the end of his life: All comes from God.
Nehemiah 9	Israelites confess their personal and national sin.
Psalm 8	"How majestic is your name."
Psalm 34:7-10	"God protects those who fear him; they lack nothing."
Psalm 66	All people should praise and glorify God.
Psalm 85:9	"His salvation is near . . . that his glory may dwell in our land."
Psalm 86:9-12	"All the nations you have made will come and worship before you."
Psalm 96	"Declare his glory among the nations."
Isaiah 60:1-3	"Nations will come to your light."
Daniel 4:37	"Glorify the King, because everything he does is . . . just."

You may also want to make use of the brief prayer guide provided by the NDP Task Force. Not only does it list by name the top U.S. federal officials; it also suggests ways to pray for their needs. The guide gives excellent suggestions on how to pray for churches, ministries, families, the media, and personal renewal in the country. It encourages Christians to remember prisoners and those persecuted for their faith.

a complete resource kit

The NDP Task Force has also put together a valuable resource booklet that expands on the ideas listed above, adding the following:

- dozens of suggestions for family observance of the National Day of Prayer

- concrete ideas for youth groups and students from preschool through college

- creative ways to get congregations involved with their communities, including plans for worship/prayer services

- ideas on how to get businesses involved in promoting the day of prayer

- proven ways to get the attention of your community through advertising and group activities

- media publicity ideas, including camera-ready art, radio spots, and banner designs

- historical background to the National Day of Prayer, including a listing of books, pamphlets, and tapes on the subject

- a list of further resources offered by the NDP Task Force

You can order this kit by contacting

National Day of Prayer Task Force
P.O. Box 15616
Colorado Springs, CO 80935-5616
(719) 531-3379
Fax: (719) 548-4520

a variety of options

Let these ideas, taken from the resource booklet described above, stimulate your creative thinking:

- **Families.** Decorate the outside of your home with red, white, and blue streamers, and display a NDP poster on your front door. Use your nightly devotional time to talk about stories from the Bible that show how prayer changes people's lives, and memorize Scripture passages on prayer together. Take a prayerwalk around your neighborhood; and as you pass neighbors' homes, leave an NDP bumper sticker on each doorstep, along with a note telling your neighbors that you've been praying for them.

With the wealth of ideas available, you have the opportunity to do something different each year with your congregation and community.

- **Youth and schools.** Make a prayer list of your friends, teachers, and school administrators. Use this for your private prayers, or publish a school prayer guide with requests from various families in the school. Invite the teachers and administrators to a special prayer breakfast that focuses on the needs of the school. Teachers can assign short papers on the role of religion (or prayer) in the lives of prominent Americans (Washington or Lincoln, for example). For preschoolers, hand out helium balloons with prayer requests tied to the bottom of the strings; after you've prayed for each request, release the balloons! On college campuses, bring in Christian musicians and ask them to help promote national prayer in their concert.

- **Community organizations.** Ask local businesses to sponsor an ad for the NDP on grocery and shopping bags. Request a donation of space from billboard companies, and use the free billboard art offered by the NDP Task Force. Organize a "ring around the city hall" (or court house), in which participants encircle the building and hold hands to pray for God's direction and blessing on all that happens inside.

- **Adopt-a-leader.** Ask individuals and families to select one leader (local, state, or national) and to commit to pray for that leader regularly for a year. Encourage them to contact the leader they've chosen for the purpose of encouragement and requesting information on prayer needs. Small groups—such as youth groups, Bible study groups, church school classes, Boy Scout or Girl Scout troops—can do the same as a group project.

With the wealth of ideas available, you have the opportunity to do something different each year with your congregation and community. And with the helpful resources put together by the NDP Task Force, you have most of the groundwork laid already. This year, add your voice to the prayers of Christians all over this nation. As S. D. Gordon wrote, "The great people of the earth today are the people who pray. I do not mean those who talk about prayer; nor those who can explain about prayer; but I mean those people who take time and pray."

32

MARCH FOR JESUS

what is a march for Jesus?

A new phenomenon that first appeared in London in 1987, the annual March for Jesus, is a day when Christians of different nationalities, cultures, and church backgrounds join to sing, pray, and celebrate Jesus publicly through the streets of their cities. It is a grassroots movement that has become a joyous, worldwide expression of faith in Jesus Christ.

Though it began in England, the march has become an international event, encompassing cities in almost every nation of the world. Christians march in every time zone, filling a 24-hour time period with continuous praise and prayer. More than fifty nations and millions of people join on the same day to proclaim in their cities, "The earth is the LORD's, and everything in it, the world, and all who live in it" (Psalm 24:1).

Imagine a crowd of fifteen thousand people walking through the streets of your city, singing songs of praise to God. Children walk beside their parents, banners wave overhead, and balloons and streamers add splashes of color. As the followers of Jesus pass through areas of business and residences, doors open and people come out onto their front porches to see and hear this unusual event. Shoppers pause on the sidewalks and listen to the songs of praise as the people march by. They see Christians who are smiling, singing, and unafraid to publicly praise their God.

This is a wonderful opportunity to take the church outside of its walls, to break the world's stereotypes of solemn Christians, to introduce a joyful company of people who are full of life and praise. It's a place for believers to proclaim their faith openly, without shame or fear of intimidation.

The March for Jesus is different from many of the other marches that have taken place in the past decades. It is not a protest march. Though protest has its place in our imperfect world, the focus of this march is a positive declaration of whom we are *for*, not what we are against. It is not

- an "issues" march. No matter how passionate Christians may feel about certain issues, Jesus is to remain center stage during this march, unifying believers from many different traditions and cultures.

- a march focusing on personalities. There are many Christian leaders worthy of respect, but on this day all praise, honor, and thanks go to Jesus.

- a media event. Though it may attract media attention, this march is clearly meant as a public witness to the city's inhabitants of Jesus' supremacy and glory.

march with a vision

The March for Jesus was born of a vision—a desire to see Christians united in public worship of their Lord, Jesus Christ. The hope is that believers will work together to make an impact on their city with their prayers, their songs of praise, and their bold proclamation that Jesus is Lord.

This march has one primary purpose: to worship Jesus. It is this purpose that spans the globe and unites Christians in different countries, languages, and time zones. To lift the name of Jesus, to give living testimony to our faith with lavish praise, and to do so in full public view—that is the one focus. Though the march can help bring renewal to the local church and create an atmosphere for evangelism, Jesus is still the center of attention. The agenda is simply this: to praise the living Lord.

the march is . . .

- *Praise*. Jesus Christ, the highest authority in this universe and beyond, deserves extravagant praise. We can adore him as individuals in our prayer closets and also in parades of praise that spill out into the streets. Both have their place in the Christian's life.

- *Prayer*. At the end of each march, participants gather for a prayer rally. They join to intercede for their cities and for the unreached people of the world. Marching through the streets of their city should move

Christians to compassion and a feeling of urgency to meet the needs around them. Prayer is a natural—and effective—response to those needs.

- *Proclamation*. Good news is proclaimed on this march: Jesus has risen; he is alive! And it is proclaimed with singing, with smiles, with enthusiasm, with unity. It is a powerful visual witness to the truth of the gospel in the lives of many city inhabitants.

- *Unity*. All races, ages, cultures, and denominations are represented in this march through the city, united by one aim: praising Jesus. It's a wonderful opportunity for different church fellowships to show the strength of their common bond in Christ. It is also a powerful witness for reconciliation in cities where racial tensions run high.

- *Repentance*. We take this promise seriously: "If my people, who are called by my name, will humble themselves and pray and . . . turn from their wicked ways, then will I hear from heaven and will forgive their sin and will heal their land" (2 Chronicles 7:14).

- *Spiritual warfare*. We know that Satan has strongholds in many places in our cities. As we focus on Jesus and praise the power of his name, God's light moves in to destroy the strongholds of spiritual darkness. Marchers should remember that "our struggle is not against flesh and blood, but against the rulers, against the authorities, against the powers of this dark world" (Ephesians 6:12).

- *Evangelism preparation*. Christians who may have been silent about their faith, due to fear of ridicule, can be stirred by their participation in this march to be more bold and open in their witness to Jesus' life-changing power and God's offer of salvation.

from grassroots to global

In the 1980s several congregations in England wanted to take what they were experiencing in their churches—a joyous spirit of praise—into the streets of their cities. Graham Kendrick, a Christian songwriter and musician, helped to provide music for these public celebrations.

The first formal March for Jesus was held in London in May 1987 under the leadership of Ichthus Fellowship, Youth With a Mission, and Pioneer Team. The team who planned the prayer and praise march through the streets of London was amazed to see more than fifteen thousand people participate, in spite of pouring rain.

The annual March for Jesus is a day when Christians of different nationalities, cultures, and church backgrounds join to sing, pray, and celebrate Jesus publicly through the streets of their cities.

The next year's march drew a crowd of 55,000 believers. And in 1989, a March for Jesus was held in forty-five cities across the British Isles—including Belfast, Northern Ireland, where more than 6,000 Catholics and Protestants marched together. By 1990, over 200,000 British Christians were marching for Jesus in six hundred cities throughout the United Kingdom.

In 1990 the movement also had spread to the United States, where 1,500 believers marched through the streets of Austin, Texas. The next year 15,000 participated in Austin and 7,000 in Houston. The March for Jesus idea had taken root in the United States and was flourishing.

England, the United States, and Europe joined hands in 1992 for the first truly worldwide March for Jesus. It was a phenomenal success. In the U.S. 300,000 people marched in 142 cities, while 300,000 believers did the same in 25 European countries.

In 1993, the number of participants exploded to 1.7 million worldwide, marching on all continents except Antarctica. The largest March for Jesus took place in Sao Paulo, Brazil, where 300,000 shouted and sang of the lordship of Jesus Christ. Even in countries where Christians are persecuted, believers walked down sidewalks or drove through their cities, praying with their brothers and sisters around the world.

The number of participants continued to mushroom. In 1994, in the third March for Jesus in the U.S., 1.5 million believers marched through 550 cities, in every state in the nation. Worldwide, 10 million people from 178 nations—more than 4 million in Latin America alone—proclaimed that "from the rising of the sun to the place where it sets, the name of the LORD is to be praised" (Psalm 113:3).

The following year saw a profoundly symbolic event take place in Selma, Alabama, where the infamous "Bloody Sunday" had occurred thirty years earlier. Across the same bridge where African Americans had been beaten by law officers as they marched for voters' rights, blacks and whites marched together in loyalty to Jesus, singing and affirming his rule over their lives and hearts. "It was fantastic to see this march result in a new beginning and victory over our past," said one of the organizers.

The 1996 Global March for Jesus drew 10-12 million Christians together in marches of praise and triumph through more than 2,000 cities in 170 nations. That year in Nashville alone, 40,000 marched for Jesus. Governors in six states proclaimed May 25 as "March for Jesus

Day," as did mayors in dozens of states. And throughout the world, war-torn countries such as Croatia, South Africa, and Northern Ireland participated in heartfelt prayers for Jesus' rule to come to their people and government.

The future holds great promise, especially as we move into the 21st century. The church worldwide is becoming more aware of the urgency of Jesus' call to harvest souls. The landmark year A.D. 2000 is a signal, a wake-up call that his second coming is closer. With the unknowns that lie ahead of us, there is no better time to affirm before the entire world our faith in Jesus' rule over our homes, our cities, our nations, and the universe. We expect continued growth in the March for Jesus participation as we enter the "Bimillenial Era."

making city-wide preparations

The first crucial step is gathering the pastoral leaders in your community to head up the vision and planning. Before you do so, contact the March for Jesus office at the following address, requesting a packet of information:

March for Jesus USA
P.O. Box 3216
Austin, TX 78764
(512) 416-0066

Distribute these at a pastor's dinner in January or February, at which time the leadership team should be formed and the coordinators identified. If you think it helpful, request a speaker to come in during these first two months for a coordinator's workshop. Also invite the youth leaders in your city to a luncheon, where you can brainstorm ways to involve the young people in your city's March for Jesus.

Identify participating churches during these two months and distribute copies of the praise music that will be used during the march. Encourage congregations to begin learning the music already at this point in the preparations. Gather your musicians and set up a schedule of city-wide praise rehearsals.

During March and April the training begins. Along with the praise rehearsals, you will want to form praise teams to help lead sections of the march in singing and music. Use evening services as opportunities to teach the music as well as the vision and aim of the March for Jesus.

In May and June you mobilize! City-wide youth rallies, pulpit announcements, bulletin inserts, newspaper ads, and radio spots will help to get the word out to everyone who may wish to be involved. Focus on volunteer training at this point for those who will be helping with the march.

involving the local church

The key is to begin early. During the month of February, link up with the city-wide effort. Show your pastor and church council the video on Marches for Jesus (available from your city's coordinator or from the Austin office), and ask what involvement they can commit to.

You will need a group of people who will take leadership in planning your church's involvement. A natural place to look is the evangelism committee or worship committee—or a combination of both. Or you may feel it best to form a new task force to take the leadership in this once-a-year event.

Take advantage of the materials available from Marches for Jesus (again, available through the city's march coordinator or the national office). They include handouts, posters, music, and other resources.

You will want to use the following planning guide as you set up your church's countdown strategy:

January/February (Awareness)

- Schedule the Saturday of the March for Jesus (usually in early June) on your church's calendar.

- Obtain the Global March video and show it to the church staff; discuss the Public Praise book as well.

- Form a task force to meet periodically as needed.

- Post March for Jesus posters on your church bulletin boards.

March/April (Orientation)

- Show the Global March video to youth and adult education/fellowship groups.

- See that the appropriate people from your church attend the citywide Praise Leader rehearsals.

- Use selected March for Jesus songs during your worship services.

May/June (Involvement)

- Use the March for Jesus bulletin announcements and inserts for six weeks before the march takes place.

- Encourage participation through the pastor's and other council leaders' enthusiastic recommendations.

a march around the world

In 1996 Tonga was the first nation to begin the celebrative March for Jesus. Near to the international date line in the Pacific, the people of Tonga were the first to see the day dawn. The king and queen of Tonga led the march in their capital, then hosted a banquet for all who participated. The organizer of the event commented, "People want to follow the king's example and conviction to lift Jesus higher, and he has quite an impact on his people." Throughout the country of Tonga, almost 40,000 people took part in the six marches.

Japanese Christians marched in 29 cities, with 1,000 in Tokyo alone. "Japan is marching to show people a taste of real Christianity. We want them to see something very lively and bright, something full of life and very positive," said the nation's organizer.

The war-torn country of Croatia had 1,000 people marching in the city of Zagreb—a crowd that swelled to 3,500 in the Prayer Rally that followed.

The city of Sao Paulo, Brazil, usually has the honor of holding the largest March for Jesus each year. In 1996, 1.5 million people marched through the streets of that city, praising the name of Jesus.

The small island country of New Zealand held 90 marches within its boundaries, with 20,000 marching in Auckland and 7,000 in Christchurch. The nation had "an unprecedented show of unity as Catholics and Protestants marched together."

London, England—the city where these marches were first organized—had 23,000 turn out on the streets to celebrate the lordship of Jesus Christ. In other marches held in Belfast, Cardiff, and Glasgow, children led the prayers, which were broadcast by satellite throughout Europe.

The international sweep of this celebrative march is growing each year. As you prepare your own congregation and community to take their places on the streets of your city, remember the millions of Christians who are marching with you—in different time zones, praising in different languages, belonging to different denominations, but all with one voice lifting up the honor and glory of Jesus Christ the Lord.

33

PREACHING ON PRAYER

one pastor makes the difference

Dee Duke was a pastor who had almost given up. This dairy-farmer-turned-pastor was an exceptionally hard worker who had brought a struggling church up from twenty members to two hundred and fifty—and up and down again to one hundred three times. Frustrated and burned out, he almost quit the pastorate.

At the time of this crisis, he attended a prayer summit, desiring mainly to get away from the pressure of his work. There, however, his entire ministry focus was changed. He became convinced of the power and priority of prayer: "Devote yourself to prayer" was the theme that kept coming to his mind. He decided to make prayer the focus of his own life and of his leading in his church.

Among the goals that Duke set for himself at that summit was to preach on prayer for three months out of every year. He coupled this with a commitment to pray for an hour by himself daily, as well as to spend one hour at church in prayer daily with whoever wished to join him.

Duke's congregation saw a visible transformation when their pastor returned. Not only did he set an example for prayer in his own personal life, but he taught and encouraged from the pulpit as well. The combination was powerful. As they heard scriptural truth on prayer being taught and explained, as they heard stories—from the Bible and from the twentieth century—on what God can do through prayer, they began to catch the vision and to join their pastor in the work of prayer.

Through Duke's preaching and example, members were motivated to begin a 24-hour prayer room. They began to pray for other church members, for their friends and family members, for the people in their neighborhood. They formed groups to walk around local schools and pray, to go around businesses belonging to members and pray for blessings, to go into hospitals and nursing homes to pray. Encouraged by Duke's preaching, the church is continually saying in prayer to God, to each other, and to outsiders, "I love you!" As a direct result, church membership now numbers 1,300 in a town of 1,700!

Dee Duke's experience illustrates the power of the example of a pastor's prayer life, coupled with strong teaching and preaching from the pulpit. This chapter offers suggestions on topics for preaching on prayer, resources to use, and ideas for getting your congregation out of the "listening" mode and into the "doing" mode.

But this chapter also reminds you that what will give your preaching its power is this: living out the words that you preach in daily, committed, and believing prayer.

hitting the issues

Your choice of topics for preaching on prayer will be directed by your congregation's needs at the time, along with the Spirit's leading as you study Scripture. The following issues, however, are ones that Christians often struggle with in relation to prayer, and these issues should be addressed in your teachings on prayer.

- **Prayer: Making a Difference** "If God is sovereign, why should I pray?" This question expresses how a number of Christians feel about prayer. They are confused by the seeming contradiction in the picture of a God who is all-powerful and has his mind made up, and the picture of a God who has chosen to act in response to the prayers of his children. They cannot reconcile the two ideas of God, so they opt for the first one. In his book *Intercessory Prayer,* Dutch Sheets gives a clear, straightforward, and biblical answer to this question. A chapter titled "The Necessity of Prayer" is an invaluable resource as you address this topic in your preaching.

- **Prayer: Intimacy with God** God's children can get caught up in lists and requests and formulas for prayer, making prayer a mechanical duty to perform. When that happens, they lose sight of their Father and the fact that he simply wants them to spend time with him, telling him what's on their hearts and accepting

his love for them. Prayer is essentially relationship, not a grocery list. It is the talking part of our love relationship with God. If the people in your congregation seem to feel that their prayers are insignificant and their time spent in prayer doesn't make a lot of difference to God, then they need teaching on the relationship part of prayer.

Some Christians may fear intimacy with God, especially if there is hidden sin. Help them take a look at Genesis 3:8, which tells of Adam and Eve's hiding from God. Do we hide when we hear God calling us by name? If so, why? Can we pray with David, "Earnestly I seek you; my soul thirsts for you, my body longs for you" (Psalm 63:1)? Teach your congregation how Psalm 63 and Hebrews 4:16 can describe their prayer relationship with God.

- **Prayer: Struggle Against the Spiritual Forces of Evil** Christians today are beginning to awaken to a foundational truth: all true prayer is spiritual warfare. This is true because all of our aims in prayer—closeness with God, spiritual refreshment and growth, other people's forgiveness, blessings from God, forgiveness, peace, joy—are contrary to Satan's design. When God gives you the vision to pray for your neighbors, he says, as he said to Paul, "I am sending you to them to open their eyes and turn them from darkness to light, and from the power of Satan to God" (Acts 26:18). In prayer you are moving out into enemy territory.

North American Christians lag far behind their counterparts in other countries, where believers often start their prayer commitment at one hour per day, and increase as they grow spiritually.

As your enemy, Satan will oppose your church's efforts to reach out. Prayer is your most powerful weapon in defeating him. You will want to take a careful look with your congregation at Paul's teaching in Ephesians 6:10-20. In calling us to do battle against principalities and powers, he commands us to "pray in the Spirit on all occasions with all kinds of prayers and requests." Challenge your congregation to join you in doing this.

- **Prayer: A Time to Talk, a Time to Listen** We are often used to doing all the talking during our prayer time. But we should be listening fully as much as we talk. Jesus is our best model in this exercise; he often slipped away before daybreak to ask his Father's advice and listen for instructions. The prophet Isaiah was moved to describe Jesus' attitude this way: "[My Father] wakens me morning by morning, wakens my ear to listen like one being taught. [He] has opened my ears" (Isaiah 50:4-5).

Encourage your congregation to use Scripture during their prayer times, reading it as a back-and-forth dialogue in their conversation with God. Psalm 119 is a celebration of the life-giving power of listening to God's Word in prayer. Teach your congregation, using stories of Old Testament prayer heroes, to wait for God's leading in prayer, through the voice of Scripture and the inner promptings of the Holy Spirit.

- **Prayer: Giving Up the Controls** Listening in prayer is only the first step. Doing what God tells you to do is equally as important. If members of your congregation have used the acronym ACTS (adoration, confession, thanksgiving, supplica-

tion) in prayer, add a final "S" to the acronym: submission.

Perhaps the most compelling picture in Scripture is that of Jesus in Gethsemane's garden, praying, "Not my will, but yours" (Luke 22:42). There are dozens of other pictures of submission, from Abraham's obedience in going to sacrifice Isaac (Genesis 22) to Samuel's "Here I am" (1 Samuel 3). As you look at these examples, focus on the prayer challenge of Romans 12:1: "Offer your bodies as living sacrifices . . . this is your spiritual act of worship." As you lead your congregation in this by your example, you will see a deepening of spiritual growth and excitement.

- **Prayer: Purely Petition or Powerful Praise?** Listen closely to your own prayers. Many Christians find that their praise is often limited to the first sentence or two; then they get down to the "real business" of prayer. However, Scripture teaches a different emphasis. Ephesians 1, for example, repeatedly emphasizes that we were blessed by God "to the praise of his glorious grace," chosen "for the praise of his glory," and marked with the Spirit "to the praise of his glory." Giving glory to God and enjoying him forever— that is our "chief end," as the Westminster Catechism puts it.

The power of praise becomes evident as you look at the Old Testament stories of warfare. Israel's most amazing victories were accomplished when its leaders (and sometimes even its armies) were engaged in prayer and praise.

Use the Psalms as your pattern for prayer. Many psalms start with the injunction "Praise the Lord, O my soul." Challenge your people to make this the hallmark of their prayer times. During this prayer series, spend much of the actual service in praising God, particularly through prayer.

practical prayer problems to overcome

As you preach and motivate your congregation to pray more, be aware that you will have to help them overcome some hurdles:

- **We are not a praying culture.** North American Christians lag far behind their counterparts in Korea, Argentina, India, and other countries, where believers often start their prayer commitment at one hour per day, and increase as they grow spiritually. Many groups meet daily for an hour or more of prayer in addition to their individual prayer time. In contrast, we average four minutes a day in prayer. Giving prayer top priority in our often hectic schedules is perhaps the greatest challenge we face in bringing God's kingdom to our neighborhood and nation.

- **Many of us are afraid of praying aloud in the presence of others.** This is an unfortunate result of our strongly individualistic culture, in which we pray alone (when we pray) and rarely ask others to pray with us. We also rarely reach out to offer prayer for someone else in need. As a pastor, you may not relate to this fear, but you must take it into account as you encourage more prayer participation in your services and in small group settings.

- **We feel little responsibility to pray for others.** As mentioned above, we are an individualistic culture. We are not used to being regular intercessors for others' needs. You may have to work hard at helping people move beyond such "safe" requests as the health needs of their neighbors (cancer, surgery, and so on) to pray for salvation, for healing in relationships, for changed lifestyles.

preparation for preaching on prayer

Your preparation and involvement in prayer is an essential part of your sermon series. This preparation time may take several weeks or several months. Don't rush it; give the Spirit an opportunity to work in your heart, mind, and imagination, and to prepare you spiritually to lead your people in this adventure.

Following are some suggestions for preparation. Some are personal; some will help prepare a support group of prayer leaders who will be invaluable in implementing your teachings on prayer. This preparation time is especially important because your goal in preaching is not merely to increase knowledge but to move your

Encourage your congregation to use Scripture during their prayer times, reading it as a back-and-forth dialogue in their conversation with God.

people to action. And when they begin to move in prayer, you want to be ready!

- *Personal study of the Scriptures.* As you read Scripture stories and teachings on prayer, both knowledge and conviction will grow in your heart regarding the powerful gift of prayer that God has given us. Out of your conviction will come your sermons, and it is your passion about prayer that will speak to your people. So take the time to immerse yourself in Scripture's teachings, paying special attention to the following:

— *The great prayers and "pray-ers" of the Old Testament.* You will want to include the stories and struggles of people like Abraham, Jacob, Moses, Joshua, Hannah, David, Solomon, Daniel, Jehoshaphat, Nehemiah, Ezra, Hezekiah, and Job. As you study, let the Spirit of God make these people come alive for you and help you to connect with the way they wrestled with God in prayer. Herbert Lockyer's book *All the Prayers of the Bible* is a useful resource here. You may also want to look at "Notable Prayer Passages from the Old Testament" at the end of this chapter.

— *Jesus' prayers and his teachings on prayer.* These are invaluable to us because they show that Jesus shared wholly in our humanity and that he accepted all the limitations of being human, including depending on the Father and having to communicate with him through prayer. As E. M. Bounds wrote, "Prayer was the secret of his power, the law of his life, the inspiration of his toil, and the source of his wealth, his joy, his communion, and his strength" (*The Reality of Prayer*, p. 73). See "Jesus, Man of Prayer" at the end of this chapter for Scriptures that portray this side of Jesus' ministry.

— *Paul's life of prayerful ministry.* This great apostle is another vivid example of the power of prayer. Let Paul be your mentor as, through the study of Scripture, you listen to his teachings and observe the role that prayer played in his mission as an apostle. As C. Samuel Storms puts it, "Much of Paul's success in ministry is traceable to the fact that before he was a man of the miraculous, before he was a man of reputation and fame, Paul was a man of prayer. His power of discernment and insight, his conviction and courage, his commitment and fidelity to the gospel, are intelligible once we realize that he spent as much time on his knees as on his feet."

• *Good books on prayer.* There are many such books. See "Recommended Reading" in the Resources section of this *Sourcebook* for a listing of classic and contemporary books to help you get started.

• *Your own prayer life.* There is no substitute for developing your own prayer relationship with God. You must preach out of your own experience and struggles, or people will instinctively sense that you are not genuine. Ask God to help you set a healthy goal of time spent in prayer each day; then ask his help also in spending that time with him. Record faithfully your successes and failures; such personal notes will make your preaching much more accessible to the people who are listening.

• *Key congregational leaders.* Ask those who are most effective as leaders to join you in seeking a deeper prayer walk. Commit to holding each other accountable to what you feel God is asking you to do; pray for each other's needs in the area of prayer growth. Share regularly with each other what you've learned over the course of one to three weeks, and incorporate these insights into your sermon series.

- *Chief intercessors*. Every congregation has them; your job is to find out who they are and to enlist their help in planning the prayer messages. Meet at least once with them to brainstorm ideas and to seek God's leading on the movement of prayer in your congregation. Also be sure to secure their commitment to pray for you and for the congregation during this time. Be as specific as you can about your own needs in this area.

- *Past sermons*. Review the sermons you've preached on prayer during the past two years. What topics or questions have you touched on? What passages have you given your people to reflect on? What was their response? Plan your upcoming series on prayer with all this in mind.

- *Asking questions*. Don't take for granted that you know your members' degree of knowledge and practice of prayer. Find out the questions they have about prayer. What problems have they struggled with? What are their hopes and their desires for their prayer relationship with God? Don't guess at these things; most likely your guesses will be wrong. Even in Bible-preaching churches, the prayer life of members is surprisingly weak and sporadic. A large church in North America recently polled its members, asking how they saw themselves as "pray-ers." Of the three hundred that responded, only twenty-four classified themselves as "committed" in their prayer life. The other 276 saw themselves as "casual" or "crisis" "pray-ers." Another group that participated in a prayer survey revealed

that, on the average, members spent only 4.5 minutes each day in prayer. So you may assume that your congregation is—unfortunately—probably not far from the norm.

preaching on prayer

Listed below are some ideas for a sermon series that focuses on specific issues while giving a broad overview of prayer. These will work best for you if you adapt them to your congregation's needs and allow them to be shaped by the struggles and insights you have gained in your own prayer life.

- The Lord's Prayer—there is no better place to start than with this prayer, which Jesus gave to his disciples in response to their request for teaching on prayer. Your Christian bookstore or distributing company can give you a long list of resources on this topic.

- Jesus' teachings on prayer (see conclusion of this chapter)

- Jesus' practice of prayer (see conclusion of this chapter)

- The prayers of Paul (see conclusion of this chapter)

- The elements of prayer (ACTSS: adoration, confession, thanksgiving, supplication, submission)

- Old Testament heroes of prayer

- Scriptural promises to those who pray (for example, Psalm 145:17-19; John 14:12-14; James 1:5-8; James 5:13-18; 1 John 1:9; 1 John 3:21-24)

- Prayers of the Psalms—as much as two-thirds of the Psalms are directly addressed to God. They are prayers full of emotion, imagery, pleading, praise, and struggle. Many of these can serve as models in your preaching series. You may find Eugene Peterson's paraphrase of the Psalms—*The Message*—a helpful resource.

- As always, add stories to your sermons that will illustrate your teaching. Many of these can come directly from Scripture; however, there is a wealth of stories on prayer from Christians of all times and places. Many of these are recorded in the "Stories of Praying Christians" section of this *Sourcebook*.

opportunities for response

You cannot teach your people about prayer by simply giving them theory. They will not grasp the reality of the power and passion of prayer until they really do it. For this reason, require some kind of active response whenever you preach on prayer. Though it may feel risky, this will actually guarantee a success far greater than if you had just imparted head knowledge.

The responses you call for can vary; avoid asking the congregation to participate in the same activity each time. This chapter provides some suggestions to get you started; you will find yourself supplementing these as you consider how much you can ask of your people and what their greatest needs are. Here are what some preachers have done:

Give your congregation a practical assignment after the sermon.

- Model what you are preaching. "Show and tell" is an excellent motto for all preachers; it is just as effective for adults as it is for first-graders. Actually doing what you are teaching will help the message sink in. For example, if you are preaching on praise as a vital element of prayer, model a prayer that is purely praise. People don't hear such a prayer very often; it will lift their hearts and minds to God and give your listeners the experience of how praise revitalizes our relationship with God.

- Give your listeners the opportunity to apply immediately what they've heard you preach on, perhaps through a time of private prayer or by participating in group prayers that focus on what you've been teaching. If you are touching on several themes during your sermon, consider stopping after each point to pray in response to the teaching.

- Ask the congregation to form small groups in the pews, and assign them topics to pray for, such as local, national, and international concerns on World Hunger Sunday or a national day of prayer.

- Suggest the use of personal devotional materials, such as *The 28-Day Devotional Guide*, based on the Lord's Prayer (Mission 21 HOPE, 1-800-217-5200) or *Patterns for Prayer* (CRC Publications, 1996).

- Suggest study materials on prayer for those who wish to study prayer in small groups: *Experiencing God: Discover Prayer* by Henry Blackaby; *Prayer Life* by Hunt and Walker (Southern Baptist Sunday School Board, Nashville, TN 37234); or *Passion and Power in Prayer* by Alvin J. Vander Griend (CRC Publications).

- Give your congregation a practical assignment after the sermon. For example, you might organize into a prayerwalk around your neighborhood (see chapter 30) or challenge each family to start a neighborhood house of prayer in their home (see chapter 28). If you do, make sure your directions are clear and specific; provide handouts, maps, prayer suggestions, and anything else that will help people feel prepared to join in the activity with enthusiasm and confidence.

- Most important, follow through on your preaching by building new prayer ministries into the life of your congregation. This book was written to help you do that. It is designed to give you the teaching, suggestions, and resources you will need to introduce prayer ministries into your church's structure. Be sure to rely on God's leading when choosing which ministries to begin; the Spirit's timing is essential.

Enjoy preaching on prayer. Of all the activities suggested in this *Sourcebook*, this may impact you most deeply and personally. It is certainly true that the one who prepares and teaches on a subject is the one who learns the most through the process. You will be changed, and your congregation will be blessed as it follows your example and preaching into a deeper prayer life and ministry.

notable prayer passages from the Old Testament

Genesis 3:8-13; 18:16-33; 32:22-31; Exodus 17:8-13; 2 Chronicles 6:12-7:3; 20:1-30; Psalm 51:1-17; Nehemiah 1:4-11; 4:4-9; Daniel 9:1-14; Habakkuk 1-3: complaint and response.

Jesus, man of prayer

Eighteen references to Jesus' praying:
Matthew 19:13; 27:50; Mark 1:35; 6:41; 6:46; 7:34; 8:6; Luke 3:21; 5:16; 6:12; 9:18, 29; 11:1; 22:17-19, 32; 24:30, 50; Hebrews 5:7

Eight recorded prayers of Jesus:
Matthew 26:39; 27:46; Luke 10:21; 23:34, 46; John 11:41-42; 12:27-28; 17:1-26

Four references to Jesus' heavenly intercessory ministry:
Isaiah 53:12; John 14:16; Romans 8:34; Hebrews 7:25

Jesus' teachings on prayer:
Matthew 6:5-13 (see Luke 11:2-4); Matthew 7:7-11; 9:37-38; 18:19-20; 21:21-22; Mark 9:26-29; 11:17, 25; Luke 6:28; 11:5-13; 18:9-14; John 15:7; 16:23-24

Paul, the man who prayed continually

Constantly in prayer:
Romans 1:9-10; 10:1; 1 Corinthians 1:4; Ephesians 1:16; 3:14; Philippians 1:3-4, 7-8; Colossians 1:3, 9; 1 Thessalonians 1:2; 3:9-10; 2 Thessalonians 1:3, 11; 2 Timothy 1:3; Philemon 4

Practicing and teaching thanksgiving:
Philippians 4:6; Colossians 1:3-5; 4:2

Praying for his congregation:
Romans 1:9-10; Ephesians 1:16-19; 3:14-21; Philippians 1:3-4, 9-11; Colossians 1:9-12; 1 Thessalonians 3:10-13; 5:23; 2 Thessalonians 2:16-17; Philemon 6

Depending on the prayers of others:
Romans 15:30-31; 2 Corinthians
1:10b-11; Ephesians 6:18-20;
Philippians 1:19; Colossians 4:3-4;
2 Thessalonians 3:1-2

STORIES *of* PRAYING CHRISTIANS

INTRODUCTION

There's nothing like a good story to bring home a point. The stories you'll find in this section are varied, lively, and pertinent. You'll find them an invaluable resource in your preparation for teaching and preaching about prayer.

"Oh, that I may be a man of prayer," was the cry of Henry Martyn. Others throughout the ages have had similar desires, as do men and women today. The following are true accounts of ordinary people transformed into extraordinary tools in the Master's hands because of their commitment to and understanding of prayer.

ANSWERED PRAYER

mother/daughter/ Christ

One mother spent every Wednesday for years in prayer and fasting for her children. Here's what happened to one of them. One day, this college-aged girl seemed to hear a voice. The idea of it being God didn't cross her mind at first because for years she had been leading a life of rebellion.

"My life was in reality a miserable one. But I loved it because I did what I wanted, and I didn't want to change." Rock music was playing over her stereo, but she seemed to hear the voice again. She looked around; no one. She checked the entire house, but no one else was around. "If no one was in the house, but someone was looking at me, it had to be God. So I asked if he was the one."

"Yes" was the clear reply. Within moments, she broke down and invited the eternal King into her life. When her mother came home later, the girl said, "I have something to tell you!" Apprehensive, her mother prepared herself for terrible news. "I just gave my life to God. I love God and I love you."

—Ann Shields, *God Answers Prayer* (Servant Publications, 1984)

"God answers prayer"

Mary Slessor, the well-known missionary to West Africa, was once asked what prayer meant to her. "My life is one long, daily, hourly record of answered prayer for physical health, for mental overstrain, for guidance given marvelously, for errors and dangers averted, for enmity to the gospel subdued, for food provided at the exact hour needed, for everything that goes to make up life and my poor service. I can testify with a full and often wonder-stricken awe that I believe God answers prayer. I know God answers prayer."

a ray of light

The great explorer H. M. Stanley wrote, "I, for one, must not dare to say that prayers are inefficacious. Where I have been in earnest, I have been answered. When I prayed for light to guide my followers wisely through the perils that beset them, a ray of light has come upon the perplexed mind, and a clear road to deliverance has been pointed out. You may know when prayer is answered, by the glow of content which fills one who has flung his cause before God, as he rises to his feet. I have evidence, satisfactory to myself, that prayers are granted."

thrice granted

A group of missionaries had the opportunity to buy a much-needed home, but weren't sure if it was the Lord's will. So they prayed much, asking that the needed sum of one hundred pounds be granted if that's what the Lord wanted. The money came at once. Still, they hesitated. Two months later, another one hundred pounds came, earmarked for the house. Still, they hesitated. A few days later, another one hundred pounds arrived specifically for the house. What a wonderful display of God's kindness. "How precious is your loving kindness, O God" (Psalm 36:7).

—*The Kneeling Christian*
(Zondervan, 1971)

angels watching over me

Sadhu Sundar Singh was an Indian evangelist to Tibet. While preaching the love of Christ to those on the lonely, windswept, snow-covered hills of the Himalayas, Singh had many wonderful experiences of God's protection and aid. One of the most amazing happened in the town of Rasar. There the head Buddhist lama became incensed over Singh's bold preaching, had him arrested, and sentenced him to death. The method: slow death in a deep well. The evangelist sank slow and deep into the sticky, nightmarish quagmire of bones and rotting flesh of those who had died there before him. The stench was overwhelming; every move brought him into contact with flesh; consciousness eluded him for almost three days.

On the third day, as he prayed, he heard a key turning in the lid. To his surprise, it opened. A rope was lowered and a voice told him to grab hold. After being gently drawn out, the lid was replaced and locked, and instantly Singh's rescuer vanished. Sundar Singh praised his God and went right back to preaching. The lama had him arrested and demanded to know who had stolen the key and rescued him. After searching, the only key to the lid was found hanging on the lama's belt. In fear of the power of this evangelist's God, he asked Singh to leave town before all were killed by this mighty power.

—Wesley L. Duewel, *Touch the World Through Prayer* (Zondervan, 1986)

prayer through the ages

Throughout history, God has been answering prayer. The following is a litany of God's faithfulness to ordinary people made extraordinary through prayer.

- Job prayed for his friends, and they were helped; then he himself was healed.

- Moses prayed, and God delivered Israel from slavery in Egypt.

- Hannah prayed, and God gave her a son who became a high priest in Israel.

- David prayed, and God delivered him from his enemies. He prayed, and God forgave him his sins of murder and adultery.

- Samson prayed, and God gave him enough strength to kill a thousand Philistines with the jawbone of a donkey.

- Elijah prayed, and God restored a young man's life.

- Elijah prayed, and it didn't rain in Israel for three years.

- Elijah prayed, and it rained.

- Hezekiah prayed, and one of God's angels killed 185,000 Assyrian soldiers in one night.

- Ezra prayed, and Judah and Jerusalem had a revival.

- Nehemiah prayed, and the king released him, allowing him to go back to rebuild the walls of Jerusalem.

- Solomon prayed and received wisdom.

- Daniel prayed and was freed from the lions' den.

- Daniel prayed and interpreted Nebuchadnezzar's dream.

- Paul and Silas prayed and were set free from jail.

—Vonette Bright and Ben A. Jennings, *Unleashing the Power of Prayer* (Moody Press, 1989)

During his lifetime, George Müller recorded more than fifty thousand answers to prayer. He prayed for two men daily for more than sixty years. One of these men was converted shortly before Müller's death, and the other, about a year later.

even the little things

Is the Lord interested in the little things too? Consider this. When I was a freshman in college, I lost my fountain pen. It was in the days of the Great Depression, and I had no money. I was walking across a field where I thought I might have lost it, and being young I said, "Lord, help me find my fountain pen." I walked across that field, and there in front of my face was my fountain pen. God is interested in fountain pens as well as anything else. He wants me to come to him in everything!

—Vonette Bright and Ben A. Jennings, *Unleashing the Power of Prayer* (Moody Press, 1989)

the miracle of Salerno

During World War II, Rees Howells was burdened to pray for Salerno, the pivotal point for Italy. In September 1943, Allied troops arrived there in preparation for an attempted enemy push to Rome. During one of those crucial days, a student at Howells's college gave this eyewitness account.

"We had the first evening prayer meeting as usual in the conference hall, and gathered again at 9:45 P.M. The meeting had a solemn tone from the outset. The director's, Mr. Howells, voice trembling with the burden of his message and scarcely audible, said, 'The Lord has burdened me between the meetings with the invasion of Salerno. I believe our men are in great danger of losing their hold.'"

The student body began to pray. Howells writes, "The Spirit took hold of us and suddenly broke right through in the prayers, and we found ourselves praising and rejoicing, believing that God had heard and answered. We could not go on praying any longer, so we rose . . . the Spirit witnessing in all our hearts that God had wrought some miraculous intervention in Italy. The victory was so outstanding that I looked at the clock as we rose to sing. It was the stroke of 11:00 P.M."

Meanwhile in Salerno, a frontline reporter was with the troops in combat. His report stated rapidly advancing enemy troops and "increasing devastation was evident." The British troops were weakening. The only hope was a miracle that would allow them to establish a beachhead. Quite unexpectedly, all gun-fire stopped. A death-like stillness descended on the battlefield while every-one waited.

"We waited in breathless anticipa-tion, but nothing happened. I looked at my watch—it was eleven o'clock at night. Still we waited, but still nothing hap-pened; and nothing happened all night, but those hours made all the difference to the invasion. By morning the beachhead was established."

—Dick Eastman, *No Easy Road* (Baker Book House)

"then sings my soul . . ."

God is not a God for the good times only. In history's darkest times, he is there. During the dark night of the indi-vidual soul, he is there.

"I tell the Lord my troubles and dif-ficulties, and wait for him to give me the answers to them," says one man of God. "And it is wonderful how a matter that looked very dark will in prayer become clear as crystal by the help of God's Spirit. I think Christians fail so often to get answers to their prayers because they do not wait long enough on God. They just drop down and say a few words, and then jump up and forget it and expect God to answer them. Such praying always reminds me of the small boy ringing his neighbor's doorbell, and then running away as fast as he can go."

Johnny Bartek, a sergeant and close friend of Captain Rickenbacker, tells of his experience when lost at sea. "As soon as we were in the rafts at the mercy of God, we realized that we were not in any condition to expect help from him. We spent many hours of each day confessing our sins to one another and to God . . . then we prayed, and God answered.

"It was real. We needed water, and we got water—all we needed. Then we asked for fish, and we got fish. And we got meat when we prayed. Seagulls don't go around sitting on people's heads waiting to be caught. On that eleventh day when those planes flew by, we all cried like babies. It was then I prayed again to God and said: 'If you'll send that one plane back for us, I promise I'll believe in you and tell everyone else.' That plane came back, and the others flew on. It just hap-pened? It did not. God sent that plane back."

—Dick Eastman, *No Easy Road* (Baker Book House)

canceled cancer

A twenty-three-year-old mother of two had a cancerous growth on her brain. "It was the type that had spread like the tentacles of an octopus, and her doctors gave her only a few weeks to live." Christian women who knew of her plight went to prayer, and God heard. A few weeks later, they learned that the tumor was shrinking and there were no cancer-ous cells anywhere. Doctors gave her a normal life expectancy.

—Evelyn Christenson, *What Happens When Women Pray?* (Victor Books, 1989)

supernatural "greenbacks"

A teacher of a Bible conference was getting ready to print more syllabi for an upcoming conference when he discovered there was only $37 left in the checkbook. Not willing to accept defeat because of his conviction of the worth of the conference and the conviction that God wanted him to lead it, he and a few friends resolved to tell no one of the need except God. Soon after, a check for $1,000 arrived at the church—about what it would cost for printing.

Three weeks later, the bill for printing came—$1,097—$97 more than was on hand. The teacher was dismayed at the thought of having to give up because of such a small amount. But another letter in that morning's mail contained a check for $100 from someone who wrote: "I heard you speak . . . and have been praying for your ministry. This morning as I prayed, the Lord told me you had a need. Then he impressed me to fulfill that need, so here is the check."

—T. W. Hunt and Catherine Walker, *Prayer Life: Walking in Fellowship with God* (The Sunday School Board of the Southern Baptist Convention, 1987)

rained out

The first priority after Charles Stanley and his family moved to Atlanta was finding a suitable house. They looked for several weeks before finding just the right one, then they applied for the loan. They prayed daily that the loan would be approved; they even thanked God ahead of time for doing it. Then the bank called: "loan denied."

They felt let down, couldn't understand why such a thing would happen. Then the next day a tremendous rainstorm broke out, flooding the storage and study areas of the home they had hoped to buy. A week later they found a home that they really enjoyed.

—Charles F. Stanley, *Handle with Prayer* (Victor Books, 1982)

fight the enemy!

In the spring of 1588, the Spanish Armada set out to conquer England. But in the United Kingdom, congregations everywhere were on their knees in urgent prayer. Back in the English Channel, the Armada fared poorly against the English, and before long, strong winds and terrific storms whipped up the sea and drove them off.

ANSWERS DELAYED

sixty-three years and counting

George Müller, an Englishman of the nineteenth century known for his prayer and his concern for orphans, recognized that a delay in answered prayer is not a denial from God. He had to pray for more than sixty years for the conversion of a friend.

"The great point is never to give up until the answer comes," said Müller. "I have been praying for sixty-three years and eight months for one man's conversion. He is not converted yet, but he will be! How can it be otherwise? There is the unchanging promise of Jehovah, and on that I rest." We don't know if the delay was caused by a mighty wall thrown up by Satan, an extended attack by Satan to wear down Müller's faith, or what, but no sooner had Müller died—even before he was buried—and the friend became a Christian.

Müller knew he could count on God. That's why he said, "Oh, how good, kind, gracious, and condescending is the One with Whom we have to do! I am only a poor, frail, sinful man, but he has heard my prayers ten thousands of times."

—*The Kneeling Christian* (Zondervan, 1971)

answered, at last

The Connecticut mother was heartbroken when her son left for the army. He wasn't a Christian. Day after day she prayed for his salvation, and day after day she heard no word from him. Finally, she was notified by a hospital: "Your son has died."

Try as she might, the mother could find out nothing about his final moments on earth. Years went by, and she finally gave up hope. Years later, a friend of the dead son stopped by for business and, seeing the soldier boy's picture on the wall, asked, "Did you know him?" "That young man was my son," replied the aged lady. "He died in the last war." "I knew him very well; he was in my company." The mother asked, "Do you know anything about his end?" He replied, "I was in the hospital, and he died a most peaceful death, triumphant in the faith."

She had given up hope of ever hearing about her son, but before her time on earth was done, she had the satisfaction of knowing that God had heard her prayers.

—Dwight L. Moody, *Prevailing Prayer* (Moody Press)

BOLDNESS IN PRAYER

bold approach

Frederick Myconius wrote his friend, Martin Luther, in 1540 to tell him that he was deathly ill and would soon die. The following is Luther's response:

"I command thee in the name of God to live because I still have need of thee in the work of reforming the church. . . . The Lord will never let me hear that thou art dead, but will permit thee to survive me. For this I am praying, this is my will, and may my will be done, because I seek only to glorify the name of God."

By the time Myconius got the letter, he was already too weak to speak. Yet within a short time he recovered and lived two months longer than Luther.

To pray in God's will is to know God's will; to look the Creator in the eye and say, "You know I'm not praying for my own personal advantage, but only that your most holy name be glorified." Such praying lends great boldness to our ability to intercede for others and for the work of the kingdom.

—Donald G. Bloesch, *The Struggle of Prayer* (Harper & Row, 1980)

out of Burma

Ouan Lei, a Burmese Christian, had tried unsuccessfully for a year to get permission to leave the country, but time after time his visa was rejected. Meanwhile, at a conference in the States, friends aware of his situation were suddenly startled by a missionary who stood up and, believing God wanted Lei at that conference, began to pray. For twenty minutes this saint prayed. He began by binding Satan, then asked that the officials change their minds. He sat down, and the conference resumed.

An hour and a half later, a woman from the kitchen came running into the room. Someone called from Burma saying Ouan Lei had just received permission to leave the country.

—Charles F. Stanley, *Handle with Prayer* (Victor Books, 1982)

BURDENED TO PRAY

I feel like I know you

Ann Shields, noted Christian speaker, remembers an encounter she had with a woman about three years after she began public speaking.

"Sister," said the woman, "you don't know me; we've never met. But I feel like I know you. One evening three years ago I was praying, and I sensed the Lord telling me that I was to commit myself to intercede for you. And I want you to know that night and day for the last three years I have prayed, and I have often fasted, asking the Lord to give you the grace to remain faithful to him, to do what he wants you to do."

Shields went on to say, "I know that I would not have been able to do the things I have done, to be helpful to God's people in the ministries he has called me to, if it were not for people like that woman, praying and interceding for me."

—Ann Shields, *God Answers Prayer*
(Servant Publications, 1984)

the long arm of prayer

Talk about the long arm of the law—consider the long arm of prayer. In June of 1962, Wesley Duewel was summoned to a meeting in Los Angeles from where he was staying in the Himalayas. On the day he was to leave, he began to feel ill: raw throat, aching body, headache, fever. Duewel continued to work and prayed that his family wouldn't notice for fear they would not allow him to go. As they walked down the mountainside to the bus stop, he fought his fever and the family never caught on.

Once in the bus, Duewel dropped his head back, too weak to hold it up anymore. At the next town he boarded the train to Delhi and continued to suffer in a car that had neither fans nor lights. "My fever rose as I struggled with nausea and headache. I thought, 'If I could only find one Christian and ask him to pray for me!'"

Suddenly, from out of the darkness of that hot train car, a cool, human hand wiped the sweat from his face with a damp, refreshing washcloth. Instantly, his fever, headache, nausea, and sore throat were gone. He was completely healed.

At stopovers in Hong Kong and Tokyo, Duewel relayed the story to coworkers. Each time he told of the experience, he said, "I am here today because someone prayed for me. I don't know who it was, but I felt that one's hand."

One day, at the meetings in Los Angeles, a letter arrived addressed to him. The person writing it said that at 9:15 P.M.

on the day Duewel left the Himalayas, that person had a burden to pray for him. "Whether I had felt the actual hand of the prayer, or whether it was the hand of an angel in answer to the prayer makes no difference. Prayer spanned the miles and left its healing touch on a speeding train that hot June night."

—Wesley L. Duewel, *Touch the World Through Prayer* (Zondervan, 1986)

angelic intervention

"A sudden premonition of terrible danger swept over me. I began to plead God's mercy, lifting my hands in agony of prayer," wrote Wesley Duewel. He and his wife were praying in the home of his parents while they were at a church meeting. While kneeling with his wife, he experienced that sudden feeling of urgency. "I did not know what the danger was and thought perhaps a robber was outside our window. For ten minutes or more I could only plead the blood of Jesus and claim the name of Jesus.

"Then the burden lifted. My wife could not understand what had happened to me, and said my face was as white as a sheet. She asked me what I thought it was. I replied that I did not know, only that I was sure God had delivered from some great danger."

Soon after, Duewel's mother returned. "Oh, Wesley, God has been so merciful to us tonight! When Papa and I were driving home on the highway, the bright light of an oncoming car blinded our eyes. The car was coming at high speed straight at us. At the last moment it swerved and just missed us. When it was past, we realized that we were on the wrong side of the road!"

What happened? Did the hand of prayer guide the steering wheel of the other car? Did the prayer release a heavenly angel to right the situation? We do not know. What we do know, however, is that God alerted Duewel to a critical need and then responded to his prayers.

—Wesley L. Duewel, *Touch the World Through Prayer* (Zondervan, 1986)

a mother's prayers

Corporal Jacob DeShazer was one of the men shot down over Tokyo in the Doolittle raids of World War II. On the night of his capture, his mother felt compelled to pray, even though she had no idea of where her son was or what he was doing. "I awakened suddenly one night with a strange feeling like unto being dropped down, down, down through the air. Oh, the terrible burden that weighed my soul! I prayed and cried out to God in my distress. Suddenly the burden was gone." Meanwhile, at that precise time, her son was parachuting from his falling plane.

After his capture and imprisonment, his mother again felt compelled to pray for her son. It was later learned that at that precise time, God spoke to DeShazer in his prison cell and he surrendered his life to Christ. Soon after, it was announced that all prisoners would be executed. His mother cried to God to watch over her son, and again her intense burden lifted. Of the four men that were to be executed, three were, but Jacob was released. God didn't just save DeShazer's life, he saved it for a purpose. After the war, DeShazer used his life to preach Christ in Japan.

—Wesley L. Duewel, *Touch the World Through Prayer* (Zondervan, 1986)

the Spirit's plea

The body of Christ has needs galore. Often God wills to use us as channels of blessing, protection, and intervention for other members of the family. Judson Cornwall knows this.

While constructing a new church, Cornwall crawled through the steeple onto the new roof to see if it was safe. It was a cold, icy day, and Cornwall lost his footing. He landed on his chest and began a headlong slide down the steep church roof directly toward a pile of bricks on the ground far below. The crew of volunteers watched in horror, helpless to do anything about it. Just as Cornwall's head cleared the edge of the roof, he stopped. Not a gradual slowing down; an abrupt stop. Slowly, he turned himself around, then slid back to the peak of the roof. Shakily, he worked his way down to the ground.

Not until Sunday services did he learn what happened. While doing dishes the previous week, a member of his congregation suddenly felt the Spirit command her to pray. With soapy hands, she rushed into the bedroom, knelt, and prayed. When the spirit of intercession lifted, she asked the Lord what it was she was praying for. In a vision, she saw Cornwall sliding towards a fall, and the hand of God stop him at the edge and push him back up.

What would have been the outcome had she not listened to the Spirit's plea to pray? The body of Christ needs those who will listen.

—Judson Cornwall, *The Secret of Personal Prayer* (Creation House, 1988)

the real story in world news

In the late '70s, China opened up to Western travelers, trade was reestablished with the West, relations were improved, and the government of China even offered to restore to mission boards property that had been confiscated by the Communists some twenty-five years earlier.

That's what the world heard. Here's the real story. For twenty-five years, a group called Operation Sunrise had been praying for China. B. J. Willhite came on the scene a little late, but in 1979, he too had a tremendous burden to pray for China. "My heart broke as I thought of that land's spiritual darkness and oppressive government. As I prayed, the tears flowed down my face; I was sure that I had entered into the heart of God about China, feeling in a small measure as he did. At some point, I prayed in a language which sounded Oriental to me. It was like being a Chinese Christian crying to God for deliverance from oppression."

Apart from Willhite and members of Operation Sunrise, who knows how many others of God's prayer warriors were battling it out with the powers of darkness. Willhite was convinced there were many. "I've learned that when one feels such a burden, one can be sure that others who are in tune with God are feeling the same load. Knowing this can keep one encouraged—and humbled."

The newspapers and news broadcasts showed us the results. The stories of burdened "pray-ers" tell us the means used to get those results.

—B. J. Willhite, *Why Pray?* (Creation House, 1988)

spirits unified

Rev. Bailus was eating lunch with his family on a Sunday afternoon when an urge to pray became so powerful that he left the table and went to his prayer room. He didn't know what he was praying for, but for half an hour he prayed in tongues and with such fervency that he was soon soaked with sweat. Then, burden lifted, he went back to lunch and a normal Sunday afternoon routine.

Later in the day he visited a shop in town. The owner, surprised to see him, said his parents had been involved in a serious accident—at the very time Bailus was under the conviction to pray. He rushed to the scene of the accident and saw their Volkswagen—crushed flat against a truck loaded with building materials. The police officer standing there said, "I haven't seen such a miracle in my twenty years on the police force. In this kind of accident, everyone is always crushed to death under the truck, but these two elderly people were pushed out—as if somebody had held them in his arms."

Bailus rushed to the hospital and found his parents—fine except for a few scratches.

Listen to the Holy Spirit, let him lead you in prayer and intercession. The results of the Holy Spirit uniting with our spirit can be powerful indeed.

—Paul Yonggi Cho, *Praying with Jesus* (Creation House, 1987)

the copilot

Praying with a burden is probably the most neglected aspect of prayer. As a result, we often pray burdenless prayers. We repeat the same old requests over and over, but with no heart or sense of urgency.—Charles F. Stanley

It was 4:00 on a Monday afternoon, and the woman was preparing dinner for her family. As she worked, she became aware of Jack, a friend. Lots to do caused her to try and put him out of her mind, but she couldn't. She left the kitchen, went into the bedroom, and prayed. As she prayed, she wept. She pleaded with God to sustain Jack in whatever crisis he was going through. This went on for thirty minutes; then it was over. She resumed her duties and thought very little of it again till the next week.

Meanwhile, Jack was flying his single-engine private plane from Miami to Ft. Pierce, Florida. Because of time constraints, he had failed to check his fuel supply. At precisely 4:00, the engine began to sputter. Jack looked for a suitable place to land, but there was none. Far ahead was a freshly plowed field—perfect for landing—but he knew he could never make it that far. He prayed, acknowledging that he was totally in God's hands. He made it to the field and settled in the soft dirt with the nose of the plane gently resting against a tree. Neither he nor the plane were damaged. As the dust settled around the aircraft, he looked at his watch—it was 4:30.

—Charles F. Stanley, *Handle with Prayer* (Victor Books, 1982)

CHURCH AND PRAYER

united we pray

Many pastors acknowledge the effect a praying congregation has on their preaching. One preacher said, "I am very sensitive, and know whether you are praying for me. If one of you lets me down, I feel it. When you are praying for me, I feel a strange power. When *every* person in a congregation is praying intensely while the pastor is preaching, a miracle happens. If it does not happen today, somebody has failed to pray. Let us make it unanimous, and see what happens when everybody is praying."

In one church, the congregation had reached a point of such training and unity in their prayers that the pastor felt he was lifted out of himself—as if he was possessed by Christ, was being spoken through by Christ. Many in the audience shared those feelings. Afterward, six people said, "We saw Christ standing by you." As the minister left the church, he passed a woman with head down, sobbing. "I don't believe in such things," she said, "but what can I do? I saw Christ myself."

A praying congregation can be a powerful force in the spiritual realm. When the audience is melted into one by prayer, the invisible is made visible to the spiritual eye, hearts of lead are made pliable, the Holy Spirit makes himself known, and lives are changed.

—Frank C. Laubach, *Prayer: The Mightiest Force in the World* (Spire Books, 1959)

the way of the spirit

The Welsh revival began in 1904 as a result of united prayer. Here's how it happened.

Seth Joshua was a Presbyterian evangelist on his way to Newcastle Emlyn College in Wales. One of the students who would hear him there was Evan Roberts, a former miner preparing for the ministry.

During Joshua's visit to the campus, students were so stirred to pray that they asked for time off to hear his series of meetings in the city. Permission granted, all classes were canceled, and the entire student body attended. At the meetings Joshua prayed, "O God, bend us." Young Evan Roberts went forward crying out, "O God, bend me."

When classes resumed, Roberts had a hard time concentrating. "I keep hearing a voice," he told his principal, "that tells me I must go home to speak." He wondered if it were from the devil or the Holy Spirit. The principal answered,

"The devil never gives orders like that. You can have a week off."

Robert's pastor wasn't sure he liked the idea of a young, inexperienced man preaching on Sunday morning. So he allowed him time at the very end of the Monday night prayer meeting. "Our young brother, Evan Roberts, feels he has a message for you, if you care to wait," was Robert's introduction. Only seventeen people stayed. "I have a message for you from God. You must confess any known sin to God and put any wrong unto man right. Second, you must put away any doubtful habit. Third, you must obey the Spirit promptly. Finally, you must confess your faith in Christ publicly."

By 10:00 P.M., all seventeen had responded. The pastor was so moved by his testimony that he asked him to speak the following night and the following. More and more meetings were added; then it was decided to continue a second week when the heavens seemed to open.

So many people came that the road was plugged. Shopkeepers even closed early to get a seat in the church. Newspaper reporters began covering the situation and before long, the awakening spread over Wales. In five months one hundred thousand people met Christ in the immediate region. Judges had no cases to try. Police had no policing to do because there were no burglaries, rapes, or crimes.

"Before the revival," responded a policeman when asked what they did with their time, "we had two main jobs: to prevent crime and to control crowds attending the soccer games. Since the revival there is practically no crime. So we just go with the crowds [to the churches]."

"But how does that affect the police?" asked the reporter.

"We have seventeen police in our station. Five do nothing but control crowds on their way to prayer meetings." He said the other twelve were organized into three quartets and were singing at the churches.

—Dick Eastman, *Love on Its Knees*
(Fleming H. Revell Co., 1989)

church built up

Prayer is striking the winning blow; service is merely gathering up the results.—S. D. Gordon

Just prior to the Civil War, Zion Church in Charleston, South Carolina, was one of the largest Presbyterian churches in America. John L. Girardeau was the white pastor of this mostly black church. In 1858, they felt the need for revival. They and their pastor wanted the Holy Spirit for themselves and for Charleston. So they prayed.

George A. Blackburn, Girardeau's son-in-law, recounts from his father-in-law's diary how their prayers for the Spirit were answered:

This began with a prayer meeting that constantly increased until the house was filled. Some of the officers of the church wanted him to commence preaching services, but he steadily refused, waiting for the outpouring of the Spirit.

His view was that the Father had given to Jesus, as the King and Head of the church, the gift of the Holy Spirit, and that Jesus in his sovereign administration of the affairs of his church, bestowed him upon whomsoever he pleased, and in whatever measure he pleased. Day after day [the pastor], therefore, kept his prayer addressed directly to the mediatorial throne for the Holy Spirit in mighty reviving power.

One evening, while leading the people in prayer, he received a sensation as if a bolt of electricity had struck his head

and diffused itself through his whole body. For a little while he stood speechless under the strange physical feeling. Then he said: "The Holy Spirit has come; we will begin preaching tomorrow evening."

He closed the service with a hymn, dismissed the congregation, and came down from the pulpit; but no one left the house. The whole congregation had quietly resumed its seat. Instantly he realized the situation. The Holy Spirit had not only come to him—he had also taken possession of the hearts of the people.

Immediately he began exhorting them to accept the gospel. They began to sob, softly, like the falling of rain; then, with deeper emotion, to weep bitterly or to rejoice loudly, according to their circumstances. It was midnight before he could dismiss his congregation. The meeting went on night and day for eight weeks. Large numbers of both white and black were converted and joined the various churches of the city. His own [church] was wonderfully built up, not only in numbers, but also in an experience that remained in the church.

He was accustomed to say that he could always count on those who were converted in that meeting. This was probably due to the deep work of conviction of sin, the protracted period of the conviction, the clear sense of pardon, and the joyful witness of the Spirit to their adoption.

—Douglas F. Kelly, *Why Pray?*
(Wolgemuth & Hyatt, 1989)

strategy for church growth

Aldersgate United Methodist Church in College Station, Texas, consisted of eight members and a budget deficit of $150,000. That was May 1979, the year Terry Teykl arrived to make it grow.

"I realized we were in trouble. We needed outside help desperately. I had always believed in prayer, preached on it, and read books about it. Suddenly, I found myself in a desperate situation, and desperation seemed to lead us to pray fervently!"

The next month, Teykl and the eight members covenanted to become a church of prayer. They really worked hard at it by appointing a coordinator, setting goals, preaching on it, and most importantly, doing it. To their amazement, results trickled in. In seven years, they grew from eight members to twelve hundred members. They went from a budget of $0 to over $600,000 a year. "It is my conviction that many church growth books do not say enough about prayer as a means of reaching the unchurched. Many are the methods, goals, and plans needed for growth, yet without a strong soaking in prayer, these church growth principles may become dry and short-lived."

—Terry Teykl, *Pray & Grow*
(Discipleship Resources, 1988)

COMFORT IN PRAYER

forgiveness

It's been said that forgiving someone is like lifting a heavy load from one's shoulders, or relieving a great weight from one's heart. Corrie ten Boom would agree.

Corrie and her family were sent to a Nazi concentration camp because of their role in helping Jews. Her father and her sister both died at Ravensbruck; Corrie alone survived. After the war, while she was preaching, God said to Corrie, "The German people are suffering from the deep scar of the war. Go and preach the gospel to them." Corrie went. After a sermon on forgiveness, many people were weeping and confessing their sins. Several stopped afterward to shake her hand and thank her, including a man she recognized. As he stepped out of the line with hand outstretched, she recoiled in revulsion. He had been a guard at Ravensbruck. The prisoners had had to pass naked before him and he had frequently cut their food supply.

The memories of those days passed before Corrie like a picture book. He didn't recognize her, but she could never forget him, not even in a dream. He broke through her revery by saying, "I've become a Christian since leaving Ravensbruck as a guard. I know that God has forgiven me for the cruel things I did there, but I would like to hear it from your lips as well. Will you forgive me?"

She saw an image of her sister's dead body. She remembered her dead father. She felt again the pain and humiliation that she endured at that hellish camp. Finally she prayed, "Lord, I cannot forgive this man. Help me!"

When it seemed like she could not acknowledge his request or his presence, she managed to lift her hand. As she did, the resurrection life of Jesus flowed into her heart, and she forgave the former guard. All the feelings of hate and bitterness disappeared and were replaced with joy through the power of the Lord. She later said she felt as though she were ten years younger. For years after that, Corrie traveled the world and told about the love and forgiveness of Christ.

—Paul Yonggi Cho, *Praying with Jesus* (Creation House, 1987)

evangelical hit list

A successful pastor in Miami found his way on to Terry Muck's "hit list": a list of names that Muck needed to pray for because of his own inability to deal with feelings of jealousy, anger, and so on. This particular pastor was doing very well with his church, and Muck was jealous. So he prayed for the man for several weeks before he was able to go to that pastor and say, "I want you to know what's been going through my mind. You don't have to respond to it, but I just want to confess it to you." They ate lunch, talked, and said nothing more about it. They had a good relationship after that.

—Terry Muck, *Liberating the Leader's Prayer Life* (Word Books, 1985)

COMMITMENT IN PRAYER

surrender the need

Phil was having a hard time with his daughter, Cindy. Her life reflected values he didn't share, and his life seemed old, out-of-date, and worn to her. The tension between them was visible. Phil prayed for his daughter's problems daily. He had no doubt in his mind what she should do and how she should do it, and he constantly told God what he thought. At one point, Phil took his "impossible problem" to his pastor, who immediately diagnosed the underlying problem between Phil and Cindy. Phil had never surrendered the need to the Lord, asking what God wanted him to be as a father and a communicator of love, encouragement, and affirmation to his daughter as she went through the difficult years of trying to find who she really was.

Phil stopped telling the Lord what to do and committed the broken relationship to him. As he did so, he began to see the qualities he needed to be an effective father. The result was empathy instead of criticism, patience instead of impatience. And she began to love her father, to respect his opinions, to listen to him.

Many praying Christians are holding in tight-clenched fists needs that must be given to God. If only they could realize that he is trustworthy, that he has been dealing with people's problems for centuries, and hasn't made a mistake yet.
—Lloyd John Ogilvie,
You Can Pray with Power

COMMUNION WITH GOD

pray in all places

Thomas Brown, a physician, made a vow "to pray in all places where quietness inviteth; in any house, highway or street; and to know no street in this city that may not witness that I have not forgotten God and my Savior in it; and that no town or parish where I have been may not say the like. To take occasion of praying upon the sight of any church which I see as I ride about. To pray daily and particularly for my sick patients, and for all sick people, under whose care soever. And at the entrance into the house of the sick to say, 'The peace and the mercy of God be upon this house.' After a sermon to make a prayer and desire a blessing, and to pray for the minister."

CONDITIONS FOR PRAYER

Müller's method

Believing, childlike prayer brought George Müller more than a million dollars to support his orphanages—and countless souls to salvation (Müller believed the Lord had given him more than thirty thousand souls in answer to prayer). Here are five pillars to which Müller anchored his firm convictions regarding assurance in answered prayer:

"There are five conditions which I always endeavor to fulfill; by observing these, I have the assurance of answer to my prayer:

1. *"I have not the least doubt because I am assured that it is the Lord's will to save them, for he willeth that all men should be saved and come to the knowledge of the truth (1 Timothy 2:4); and we have the assurance 'that if we ask anything according to his will, he heareth us' (1 John 5:14).*

2. *"I have never pleaded for their salvation in my own name, but in the blessed name of my precious Lord Jesus, and on his merits alone (John 1:14).*

3. *"I always firmly believed in the willingness of God to hear my prayers (Mark 11:24).*

4. *"I am not conscious of having yielded to any sin, for 'if I regard iniquity in my heart, the Lord will not hear me' when I call (Psalm 66:18).*

5. *"I have persevered in believing prayer for more than fifty-two years for some, and shall continue till the answer comes: 'Shall not God avenge his own elect, which cry day and night unto him?' (Luke 18:7)."*

a healing forgiveness

Her husband had abandoned her and the children. As if all that responsibility wasn't enough, now she was crippled with arthritis. She asked Rev. Cho for healing. "Have you forgiven your husband?" he asked.

"No! I can't! I hate him!" she sobbed.

"You must forgive him. This will cleanse your spirit of bitterness which may be preventing your healing. It will also release the hand of the Holy Spirit in his life."

She agreed and left to spend much time in prayer and fasting. The next week, she was back.

"Pastor, this is my husband whom we have been praying for." As she looked at her husband, she said, "Please tell the pastor what happened."

"A week ago," said the delinquent husband, "I started feeling very guilty as I was at home with the other woman. I could not stand the pain that I felt inside. Suddenly, I started to think of my wife and children whom I had abandoned. Not being able to relieve myself from the guilt that I felt, I thought of committing suicide. As Sunday approached, I decided to come to church, hoping to get forgiven and feel better. I then noticed my wife sitting across the auditorium. That is when I decided to ask her and God for forgiveness. Can God forgive me?"

"Yes, he can forgive you." Pastor Cho watched the man become a believer in Christ that day. Later, with more fasting and praying, the woman was able to leave her wheelchair and be healed. "I do not mean that everyone who is crippled or handicapped is suffering because of unforgiveness. Yet, many would be healed if they would only learn how to forgive."

—Paul Yonggi Cho, *Prayer: Key to Revival* (Word Books, 1984)

do thou likewise

John Wesley met some old acquaintances on the street one day. "I heard that you and Mr. So-and-So had become enemies. Have you come to terms with him?"

"No, I haven't. Why should I? He's the one who should be blamed. I'll never forgive him, for I am the one who was hurt."

Looking directly into the man's eyes, Wesley said, "Then you should never again commit sin. I don't think you can say you have never committed a sin. You have so far because somebody has forgiven your faults. But if you say that you don't want to forgive someone who has wronged you, from now on don't expect to be forgiven by anybody else either." At

this, the man lowered his head and repented bitterly of his faults.

—Paul Yonggi Cho, *Praying with Jesus* (Creation House, 1987)

CONFESSION IN PRAYER

confession of sin

Many people are beginning to find out what David knew so long ago when he wrote, "Would not God search this out? For he knows the secrets of the heart" (Psalm 44:21). Since God knows us inside and out anyway, wouldn't it pay to confess our sins to him and get them over with? One man found this true after feeling jealousy over an opportunity offered his friend but not him. The next day, he brought the whole situation to the Lord and confessed. "The longer I lingered in the confession portion of my prayers that day, the more I realized that I had drifted into a lack of appreciation for the tremendous opportunities the Lord had lavished on me." By confessing, God was able to get at the root cause of the sin, weed it out, and help that man move on to new levels of obedience in his Christian life. When God gets busy transforming lives, he wants nothing in the way.

—Lloyd John Ogilvie, *You Can Pray with Power*

get rid of it

When large, World War II-era bombers were hit, a few pounds could mean the difference between life and death for the crew. Discarding extra poundage wasn't so hard to do if it meant impersonal items like guns, seats, and so on. But if things got so crucial that staying aloft was questionable, the order would come to throw over cameras, souvenirs, and parachutes; that's when the grumbling would begin. It's the same in our prayer lives. It's easy to throw off habits, customs, and so on that don't affect us to the core. But when it comes to deeply entrenched habits and intensely personal parts of life, the going gets hard. Yet to maintain that spiritual vitality with the Creator, it all has to go. Never fear discarding trinkets in exchange for life.

forgiveness as a choice

"When God promises us that he will forgive us, we insult his integrity when we refuse to accept it. To forgive ourselves after God has forgiven us is a duty as well as a privilege."

R. C. Sproul tells about a man who hadn't learned that lesson.

"I've asked God to forgive me of this sin over and over, but I still feel guilty. What can I do?"

"You must pray again and ask God to forgive you," replied Sproul.

"But, I've done that! I've asked God over and over again to forgive me. What good will it do to ask him again?"

"I'm not suggesting that you ask God to forgive you for that sin. I'm asking you to seek forgiveness for your arrogance," was Sproul's reply.

"Arrogance?" the man responded. "What arrogance?"

Sproul explained that the man's repeated efforts to receive pardon were the man's attempts to prove his own humility; that he was so contrite over his sin that he felt he had to repent over and over again. His sin was too great for just one shot of repentance. He would suffer for his sin, no matter how gracious God was. "To forgive ourselves after God has forgiven us is a duty as well as a privilege."
—R. C. Sproul, *Effective Prayer* (Tyndale, 1987)

this thing is wrong!

R. A. Torrey found out the hard way what a debilitating effect sin can have on one's health, prayer life, emotions, and mental peace all at once. At one point in his career, Torrey decided to give up the generous financial support of his Christian backers and go it alone. In the course of one day, every penny of support that he, his wife, and four children were receiving came to an end. Henceforth, faith was the watchword in the Torrey family.

The money came in. Day after day, week after week, month after month. Bills were paid, halls were rented, food was purchased, the ministry continued. Then one day, money needed for a special project was nowhere in sight. Torrey went home that night and prayed. "But I went to bed, I am afraid, without much clear faith that the money would come. I was all alone in the house. In the middle of the night I was awakened by a great pain and physical distress; I was very sick. I looked up to God and cried to him that he would touch my body and heal me, and that he would send that money; but there was no answer. Again I cried to God to touch my body and send that money. Still no answer." To Torrey, the heavens seemed like brass. Satan's bitter, scornful words "Where is thy God?" seemed to reverberate in his head till the distress of soul became overwhelming. "Touch my body, heal me, and send that money," he cried, but still, no answer.

After more prayer, Torrey looked up and said, "Heavenly Father, if there is anything wrong in my life anywhere, show me what it is, and I will give it up." Immediately, he was face to face with a problem he knew existed in his life, but was always able to brush off with a "that's all right. I know it's all right. There is nothing wrong about that," but all along knew way down deep that indeed it was wrong. Again Torrey prayed, "Oh, God if this thing is wrong in Thy sight, I will give it up now." No answer. The key word in his prayer was "if." He cried, "God, this thing is wrong; it is sin. I give it up now." Instantly, according to Torrey, God touched his body and healed him completely. Soon after, the money arrived too. "Oh, how many things there are that we greatly need and that we might have at once if we would only judge and put away our sin!"
—R. A. Torrey, *The Power of Prayer* (Zondervan, 1975)

honesty—it is a virtue

A sixty-year-old woman exclaimed, "I haven't prayed in over a year!" When asked why, it was learned that she was a widow, and as far as she was concerned, it was all God's fault that her husband was dead. "I'm mad at God," she said.

A caring Christian expressed appreciation for her honesty. He told her to go home and tell God exactly how she felt; express her anger and rage—get it out. Four months later, that Christian discovered a remarkable change in the woman. After doing what was suggested, she understood a loving God's message: "I understand. You're forgiven. Be healed!"
—William J. Krutza, *Prayer: The Vital Link* (Judson Press, 1983)

be specific

Confession is not saying, "Please pray for me. I need to love people more." Everyone needs to love people more. The following is confession: "Please pray for me. My tongue has caused a lot of trouble in this church." (There must have been truth to that because her pastor leaned over and whispered, "Now she's talking.")

Charles G. Finney, a nineteenth-century evangelist, noted that a revival can be expected when Christians begin to confess their sins to one another. "At other times," he stated, "they confess in a general manner, as if they are only half in earnest." Levitical law points out the necessity for specific confession: "When anyone is guilty in any of these ways, he must confess in what way he [or she] has sinned" (Leviticus 5:5). "To sin" is a general term for a variety of actions. "To confess" is to name those sins as individual acts and seek forgiveness for them.
—Vonette Bright and Ben A. Jennings, *Unleashing the Power of Prayer* (Moody Press, 1989)

unconditional surrender

Corrie ten Boom, Dutch survivor of a Nazi concentration camp, was filled with bitterness toward the Germans. "I'll go anywhere in the world you want me to go," she told the Lord. But when God told her he wanted her back in Germany, her response was, "No, I can't go back there. They killed my sister; they ill-treated my father, and he died. Anywhere but Germany."

Because of her decision, her prayer life was diminished. The phrase "Forgive us our trespasses as we forgive those who trespass against us" frightened her. She prayed for God's grace and was finally able to return to Germany, where she turned an empty concentration camp into a home for refugees. "If we claim to have fellowship with him yet walk in darkness, we lie and do not live by the truth" (1 John 1:6).
—Vonette Bright and Ben A. Jennings, *Unleashing the Power of Prayer* (Moody Press, 1989)

key ingredient

The Great Awakening, the East African Revival, the Welsh and Korean Revivals, the movement at Asbury College and the one in the Solomons in the '70s, as well as the revivals of individual people the world over all the time—what do they all have in common? Repentance. "If we confess ours sins, he is faithful and just and will forgive us our sins and purify us from all unrighteousness" (1 John 1:9).

CONFIDENCE IN PRAYER

"glorify thy name"

Near the beginning of the twentieth century, Samuel Zeller ran a retreat center on Lake Zurich in Switzerland. It was a place for those tired of body, tired of mind, and tired of soul. Zeller was an unusually gifted man: preaching, healing, wisdom, administration. But perhaps his greatest gift was his ability to pray.

His prayers were not emotional escapades or fervent displays of religiosity. They were calm, quiet, and confident. Zeller knew God, and that gave him confidence in prayer. When he prayed, he said what had to be said. No wasted words, no long appeals, just natural conversations with God in which he asked for what was needed.

Yet Zeller did not try to dictate to God. The recurring theme in every prayer was that the name of God be glorified. If he asked for miracles, he prefaced it with "If it will glorify Thy name." If he asked for an instantaneous healing: "If it will glorify Thy name." Zeller understood that prayer. He himself was stricken with a deadly ailment that could kill him at anytime. But he kept working, for he knew that it too was to glorify God's name.

CONSTANT PRAYER

pray continuously

Pray always? Without ceasing? God delights in unceasing prayer, but it doesn't mean we have to drop to our knees and drop out of life. Consider the brilliantly gifted surgeon who was also a committed Christian. When the surgical procedures got complicated and a life was on the line, he invariably set down his instruments, stretched, asked the Great Physician for help, and resumed his work. He recognized where his gifts came from and knew his ability to perform was dependent on God's guidance.

Another man, when feeling the pressure in the boardroom to make very important decisions, leans back in his chair and says a quick prayer. His associates have come to realize that some of his most ingenious suggestions come after just such a "stretching" time.

—Lloyd John Ogilvie, *You Can Pray with Power*

prayer habit

General Stonewall Jackson said, "I have so fixed the habit (of prayer) in my mind that I never raise a glass of water to my lips without asking God's blessing, never seal a letter without putting a word of prayer under the seal, never take a letter from the post without a brief sending of my thoughts heavenward, never change my classes in the lecture room without a minute's petition for the cadets who go out and for those who come in."

just do it

Charlie Shedd recounts several methods of prayer he's run across over the years:

— One man has converted his car into a chapel. On his sun visor is a list fastened with a rubber band. It contains the names of those whom he is remembering in prayer.

— A football coach said he does his praying during his morning shower.

— An executive of a fence company says that if he doesn't remember his flock by five o'clock, he goes out in the fence yard and does his praying before he goes home to his family.

— A clerk said, "All day long I meet people. They take lots of time trying on hats. In the interims I pray. Sometimes people remind me of those whom I have promised to remember. They tell me this is 'javelin' praying, and I find it a wonderful way to keep in tune."

— One man prays early in the morning before breakfast.

— Another man starts his day in the attic in a favorite chair in prayer.

— Here's a lady that prays before bed each night. "It's a great way to go to sleep," she says.

— Another man spends his lunch hour in prayer. With the door shut and all phone calls deferred, he has a nice quiet time with the Lord.

— Here's an interesting idea. "My best praying is hooked up with my emotions. When I am blue, I pray for my people and ask God to bless them when they're blue. If I'm worried, I pray for their worries. Most folks have fears, money problems, temper flashes. Do you think this is good? I feel sure it is, and it does me good too."

The point is, all these people are praying. Find what works for you, and join the ranks of those who are in the thick of the spiritual battle.

—Charlie Shedd, *How to Develop a Praying Church* (Abingdon Press, 1964)

infrequent muff

Since Jesus is with us everywhere we go anyway, why not talk to him? One man, who travels a lot, says he no longer dreads the times alone because he knows Jesus is in the car or plane with him. "I see him in the car, on the plane. I see him in the hospitals. I would never enter a hospital room without pausing outside the door to say, 'Please precede me, Lord Jesus, let this person see You and not me!' In meetings, the Holy Spirit can calm hard feelings, at play he can make things even better. At home, the family can be brought under the influence of the Holy Spirit through continual intercession.

"I have been practicing his presence in this manner for about fourteen years now, but I want to insert a word of honesty here, and level with you. There are some days I am more successful at it than others. Some days I hit the ball out of the park. Some days I do just fair, and some days I strike out completely! But I have hope because I am noticing lately that as I grow a bit along the way, the times when I muff the entire day are growing further and further apart!"

—Arnold Prater, *You Can Pray as You Ought* (Thomas Nelson, 1977)

DEATHLESS (PRAYERS ARE)

do not stop

"When you know you are praying the will of God, do not stop. The answer will come. You may not see it, but it will come." B. J. Willhite saw that in his aunt. She prayed for her two sons until her death, but neither of them accepted Jesus Christ. Not long after she left this world, however, her younger son gave his life to Jesus and walked with him for many years. The older son held out a long time, but then, just months before his death, he too surrendered his life to Jesus and joined his praying mother in glory.

—B. J. Willhite, *Why Pray?*
(Creation House, 1988)

DEMONS CAST OUT THROUGH PRAYER

the faith of a child

Ma-Na-Si was a twelve-year-old Chinese boy at the mission school in Chefoo. He went home for the holidays, and while standing on the steps of his father's home, spied a horseman approaching at full speed. The son of a pastor, Ma-Na-Si was used to guests, but this man was an avowed unbeliever from a village full of unbelievers. He looked very distraught.

"Is the 'Jesus-man' home?" he asked. Ma-Na-Si told him he was gone. The man hurriedly explained the reason for his visit. He was sent from a village some miles away to seek help for a girl who was possessed by a demon. Ranting, raving, screaming, kicking, the girl endured the tormenting, scratching, hair pulling, clawing, smashing, and tearing of the demons. The messenger told of her sacrilege, her outrageous impiety, and brazen blasphemy. He told how all these outbursts were followed by foaming at the mouth and extreme exhaustion, both physical and mental, for the hapless girl. In seeming desperation, the messenger said, "You, too, are a 'Jesus-man'; will you come?"

Only twelve years old. But Ma-Na-Si was a believer, fully yielded to the Savior. He put himself in the Master's care and agreed to go. He swung into the saddle behind the unbeliever and set off for the village.

As they galloped along, Ma-Na-Si began to probe his own heart and life. He confessed any sin he could think of; he asked God for his help; he asked God for purification and guidance on what to say and how to act, and he tried to remember Bible stories of others who had demon possession. The girl was inside a house and was being held down by several people. Before he set foot in the door, she screamed, "All of you get out of my way quickly, so that I can escape. I must flee! A 'Jesus-man' is coming. I cannot endure him. His name is Ma-Na-Si."

The boy entered, knelt, prayed, sang a hymn of praise to Jesus Christ, then, in the name of the Risen Lord, commanded the demon to leave the girl. At once she was calm. From that day on she was whole. For the village, it was the beginning of a spiritual awakening.

—*The Kneeling Christian*
(Zondervan, 1971)

DISCIPLINE AND PRAYER

wake up on your knees

I ought to pray before seeing anyone. Often when I sleep long, or meet with others early, it is eleven or twelve o'clock before I begin secret prayer. This is a wretched system. It is unscriptural. Christ arose before day and went into a solitary place. David says: "Early will I seek thee; Thou shalt early hear my voice." Family prayer loses much of its power and sweetness, and I can do no good to those who come to seek from me. The conscience feels guilty, the soul unfed, the lamp not trimmed. Then when in secret prayer the soul is often out of tune. I feel it is far better to begin with God—to see his face first, to get my soul near him before it is near another.

—Robert Murray McCheyne

You know the value of prayer: it is precious beyond all price. Never, never neglect it.

—Sir Thomas Buxton

Prayer is the first thing, the second thing, the third thing necessary to a minister. Pray, then, my dear brother; pray, pray, pray.

—Edward Payson

EFFECTIVE PRAYER

wrong direction

At the last minute, Bill Hybels was told by an Indian Christian that he would be the main speaker at that night's meeting. Doubts immediately flooded his mind. During the few hours before the meeting, he thought about the seemingly insurmountable barriers he faced: language, culture, lack of self-confidence, fear. When they arrived at the stadium and saw the sea of faces waiting for the program, his fear quadrupled. "This is going to be a disaster," he thought. "What am I doing here?"

When the first speaker ended, Hybels had about ten minutes left. Sherry, a vocalist from his church, got up to sing. "I probably should support her in prayer, but my turn is next, and when the chips are down it's every man for himself," he thought. To him, the barriers loomed so large, the mountain seemed so immovable. While these thoughts continued, he vaguely heard the words to Sherry's song:

Great is thy faithfulness,
O God my Father.
There is no shadow of turning with
*   thee;*
Thou changest not,
Thy compassions they fail not;
As thou hast been thou forever wilt be.
Great is thy faithfulness!

Great is thy faithfulness!
Morning by morning new mercies
*   I see;*
All I have needed thy hand hath pro-
*   vided—*
Great is thy faithfulness, Lord, unto
*   me!*

As the words tumbled through Hybels's mind, he suddenly became aware that his entire attention was focused on himself—his cultural barriers, his language barriers, his inadequacies, his fears. His prayers were pitiful because he was looking at his inadequacy instead of God's adequacy. "I'm praying to the Creator of the world," thought Hybels. "The King of the universe, the all-powerful, all-knowing, all-faithful God. I'm praying to the God who made the mountains and who can move them if necessary.

"I'm praying to the God who has always been faithful to me, who has never let me down no matter how frightened I was or how difficult the situation looked. I'm praying to a God who wants to bear fruit through me, and I am going to trust that he is going to use me tonight. Not because of who I am, but because of who he is. He is faithful."

—Bill Hybels, *Too Busy Not to Pray*
(InterVarsity Press, 1988)

in great detail

"God is my witness . . . that without ceasing I make mention of you always in my prayers" (Romans 1:9).

Dr. McAlister demonstrated what Paul spoke of when he and Dick Eastman made a visit to China. During their prayer times, McAlister prayed for every person on the World Literature Crusade headquarters' staff by name. He prayed for each overseas leader associated with the ministry, as well as their wives. He prayed for every major Christian leader. He prayed for every king, president, and political leader of the almost fifty Islamic and Communist nations. He did not pray for these people in a lump-sum fashion with a quick "bless" so-and-so, but prayed that each, by name, would have wisdom, strength, and so on for the tasks at hand.

—Dick Eastman, *The Hour That Changes the World* (Baker Book House, 1978)

asking for peanuts

George Washington Carver of Tuskeegee Institute is remembered as a famous scientist, but few realize he was also a Christian and a man of prayer. According to Carver's own testimony, he would enter the laboratory each morning and pray, "Dear Mr. Creator, what do you want to show me today?"

Carver confessed that initially his prayers were not very specific. At first he prayed, "Dear Mr. Creator, what was the universe made for?" and the Lord told him to be more specific. So he prayed, "Then Mr. Creator, what was man created for?" and God said he was still asking too much. Finally, Carver prayed, "Dear Mr. Creator, what was the peanut created for?" God began to answer that prayer, and over the next few years, over two hundred different commercial uses for the peanut emerged from his laboratory, including peanut butter.

EVANGELISM AND PRAYER

the worst and the best

An English cleric made the suggestion that his people pray for the worst person they knew, then go and witness to that person. Only six agreed. When he got home, he felt compelled to join the six in the exercise, thinking, "I must take it up myself. I don't know the bad people. I'll have to go out and enquire."

Approaching a rough neighborhood, he asked a surly-looking character if he was the worst man in the neighborhood. "No, I'm not. You'll find him at No. 7, down the street." He knocked at No. 7. "I'm looking for the worst man in my parish. They tell me it might be you." "No, there are lots worse than me," responded the man. "The worst man lives at the end house in that court. He's the worst man." So off went the preacher to the end of the lane. "Come in!" bellowed the man after the knock. And in went the pastor.

There he sat with his wife. "I hope you'll excuse me, but I'm the minister of the chapel along the round. I'm looking for the worst man in my district, because I have something to tell him. Are you the worst man?" The man turned to his wife and said, "Lass, tell him what I said to you five minutes ago." "No, tell him yourself," she replied. "Well," said the worst man in the neighborhood, "I've been drinking for twelve weeks. I've had the D.T.'s and have pawned all in the house worth pawning. And I said to my wife a few minutes ago, 'Lass, this thing has to stop, and if it doesn't, I'll stop it myself—I'll go and drown myself.' Then you knocked at the door! Yes, sir, I'm the very worst man. What have you got to say to me?" "I'm here to tell you that Jesus Christ is the greatest Savior, and that he can make out of the worst man one of the best. He did it for me, and he will do it for you." "D'you think he can do it even for me?" "I'm sure he can. Kneel down and ask him."

The man was not only saved, but became a radiant testimony of what Jesus can do, and was used mightily to bring other drunken people to Jesus Christ.

—*The Kneeling Christian*
(Zondervan, 1971)

Christ in Kashmir

An Indian soldier who had recently become a Christian was transferred to Kashmir, a place in northwest India where Christian work had been slow.

When he arrived, he found a Muslim lady who had been demon-possessed for several years. Relatives had taken her from one holy spot to another without results. Moved by compassion, he asked to pray for her. After praying in Jesus' name, she was instantly freed. The Muslims were overwhelmed.

A Muslim with a severe heart problem came and asked him to pray. He prayed, and the man was healed. A woman with a large goiter came; he prayed and the goiter was gone within two weeks. The Muslims, who placed great importance on places dedicated to God, gave the soldier three acres in a prominent location for him to worship God. There he built a small church and was soon inundated with people who wanted to become Christians. Today there is a small congregation there because of a soldier who wanted to display Christ's compassion.

—Wesley L. Duewel, *Touch the World Through Prayer* (Zondervan, 1986)

Sunday school prayers

R. A. Torrey was preaching to five thousand people at an evangelistic meeting in Sydney, Australia. Among those who stood up at his invitation to accept Christ was a whole row of young women—eighteen in all. "Someone's Bible class," thought Torrey. When the meeting was over, a young lady came up to him, positively beaming with smiles. "That is my Bible class," she said. "I have been praying for their conversion and every one of them has accepted Jesus Christ today."

At a similar meeting in Bristol, England, a prominent manufacturer had invited the twenty-two men of his Bible class to attend the meetings. All agreed except one. At the meeting, twenty accepted Christ. The twenty-first accepted Christ in the train on the way home, and the twenty-second (the one that didn't go) accepted after the others told him the wonderful news of salvation. The

teacher later told Torrey that he was praying for their conversion and was willing to make the sacrifices necessary to get his prayers answered. "What revival we would have if every Sunday school teacher would go to praying the way he or she ought for the conversion of every scholar in his or her class!" stated Torrey.

—R. A. Torrey, *The Power of Prayer* (Zondervan, 1975)

from 73 to 86

The church was seventy-seven years old and meeting in a converted schoolhouse. They had been challenged to pray big—to set some large goals. The seventy-three members talked and strategized, analyzed their evangelistic outreach and talked some more. One man suggested that by year's end they have one hundred members. A total of twenty-seven converts! That had never happened before in the history of the church. After more talking, the people decided on a challenging, yet in their opinion, more realistic goal—ten converts in one year. At first they prayed for the entire community. Then, under the pastor's suggestion, began praying for specific people. Within four months seven people had been baptized. By year's end, thirteen. The faith of those seventy-three people in the seventy-seven-year-old church grew.

—William J. Krutza, *Prayer: The Vital Link* (Judson Press, 1983)

all that prayer

Billy Graham's extremely successful 1984 "Mission: England" was successful because of prayer. In 1983 a team had gone to England to prepare the way. Vonette Bright recalls: "I found an expectancy and a desire for God to move in England like I have never seen before in my life. The women there were determined that their praying was going to save their country from disaster. We had prayer seminars and prayer groups formed all over England, and they started to pray. . . . A year later I heard from Billy Graham's manager in England that Billy Graham was having the greatest results he's ever had in his whole ministry."

In the first meetings in Bristol, 8 percent of those huge audiences accepted Jesus Christ for the first time. In Sunderland, 15 percent of those audiences—huge audiences—accepted Jesus Christ. Half of those people had never gone to church. The manager asked Bright if she knew the reason for the spiritual response in England. "It is because of all that prayer," she said.

—Vonette Bright and Ben A. Jennings,
Unleashing the Power of Prayer
(Moody Press, 1989)

salvation's sweeping tide

The Prayer Fellowship of All India Believer's Association in India wrote the following letter in testimony to God's ability and willingness to work through the prayers of people:

As a result of the International Prayer Assembly for World Evangelization held in Korea in 1984, and as a result of continued prayer, the following results have been seen. In the places where the gospel has not reached so far, such as Vypen Island, as a result of the work being done by AIBA, thousands from the fishermen caste have come to the Lord. Bamboo and clay workers who have been ignored before have been contacted, and now thousands of them have come to saving grace of Jesus Christ. The name of Jesus

Christ was not even heard amongst the Scheduled caste and tribes, and now thousands of them have come to Christ.

In Gujarat State, there were hundreds of villages where the name of Jesus had never reached, but today the situation has completely changed, and thousands of tribals have come to Christ.

In the district of Trichur, there is a place called Muringpoor which was ignored by all, as it was a leper colony. As a result of continuous prayers, our ministry reached Muringpoor—preached the Word of God to the lepers—and now we have a leper congregation over there. Praise the Lord. It has proved that nothing is impossible to our heavenly Father.

—Vonette Bright and Ben A. Jennings, *Unleashing the Power of Prayer* (Moody Press, 1989)

mere children

Pandita Ramabai ran a boarding-school in India that catered to fifteen hundred Hindu girls. One day some of the Christian girls approached a missionary woman and asked what Luke 12:49 meant—"I have come to bring fire on the earth, and how I wish it were already kindled!" She tried to put them off, not being entirely sure herself what it meant, but they were determined to find the meaning of that "fire." To get it, they resorted to prayer. Those prayers resulted in the infusion of the Holy Spirit in their lives. "A very Pentecost from above was granted them."

Filled with divine vigor, they went to a mission house where the author of *The Kneeling Christian* was staying, and said, "May we stay here in your town and pray for your work?" The missionary let them pray in his barn, and as he sat down to supper, a national pastor came over. Before long the pastor was weeping, confessing sins of which the Holy Spirit had recently convicted him. Soon after, another Christian came, and another, and another, confessing wrongs and repenting of sins. What followed was a remarkable time when backsliders were restored, "believers were sanctified, and heathen brought into the fold—all because a few mere children were praying."

—*The Kneeling Christian*
(Zondervan, 1971)

prayer = evangelism

Evangelism is prayer. S. D. Gordon said, "The real victory in all service is won beforehand in prayer. Service is merely gathering up the results." W. Stanley Mooneyham added, "Let us stop complaining that we don't have enough people, enough money, enough tools. That simply is not true. There is no shortage of anything we need—except of vision and prayer and will. Prayer is the one resource immediately available to us all. If more Christians were on their knees praying, more Christians would be on their feet evangelizing."

Robert Speer wrote, "The evangelization of the world depends first upon a revival of prayer. Deeper than the need for workers; deeper, far, than the need for money; deep down at the bottom of our spiritual lives, is the need for the forgotten secret of prevailing, worldwide prayer. Missions have progressed slowly abroad because piety and prayer have been shallow at home."

—Dick Eastman, *Love on Its Knees*
(Fleming H. Revell Co., 1989)

evangelism incognito

"Think on God. The way to think on God, of course, is to think on him as revealed by Jesus—loving, loving the people whether they have been good or not, forgiving and full of compassion, always meeting penitence with pardon. See him responsive to the cry of help at all times—moving out in healing to the sick."

Forbes Robinson took that approach to prayer to heart. This man, who used every opportunity he had to present Christ to people, confided in a friend later on in his life:

"As I grow older I become more diffident, and now often, when I desire the Truth to come home to any man, I say to myself: 'If I have him here he will spend half an hour with me. Instead I will spend half an hour in prayer for him.'"

This man thought, breathed, slept, and ate evangelism. Quite naturally, it led him to prayer. The two cannot be separated. Do you have a spare half hour? Go to the prayer room and evangelize in secret. God desires and hears prayer!

—W. E. Sangster and Leslie Davison, *The Pattern of Prayer*
(The Epworth Press, 1962)

EXTENDED PRAYER TIMES

I can echo the testimony of thousands who can testify that their spiritual lives would be far less effective had they not repeatedly set apart [extended prayer] times. God has revealed his will to me in ways and concerning matters that I had not even thought about prior to extended time alone with him. I would not want to have missed those experiences for anything in the world, for they had a tremendous effect upon all my later service for the Lord.

—Wesley L. Duewel

set apart for a day

Charles G. Finney, an evangelist used by God in the 1850s, is considered by some to be the greatest evangelist since the apostle Paul. More than half a million people discovered Christ during the revival that began in his meetings. In the two-year span of 1857-58 alone, more than a hundred thousand people were saved as a result of his ministry. Of those, 85 percent went on to join a church and continue growing in their spiritual life.

What made Finney's impact so powerful? He wrote about the Holy Spirit filling him, a filling "that went through me, as it seemed, body and soul. I immediately found myself endued with such power from on high that a few words dropped here and there to individuals were the means of their immediate conversion. My words seemed to fasten like barbed arrows in the souls of men. They cut like a sword. They broke the heart like a hammer. Multitudes can attest to this. . . . Sometimes I would find myself in a great measure empty of this power. I would go and visit, and find that I made no saving impression. I would exhort and pray with the same results. I would then set apart a day for private fasting and prayer . . . after humbling myself and crying out for help, the power would return upon me with all its freshness. This has been the experience of my life."

—Wesley L. Duewel, *Touch the World Through Prayer* (Zondervan, 1986)

prayer: worth the effort?

The Sialkot Convention was founded in India in 1904. To this day it continues to have a positive effect on the church. And that perseverance, that ability to bless through the decades, is a result of extended prayer. John N. Hyde, Presbyterian missionary to India, was one of the founders of the convention along with R. M'Cheyne Paterson. Before one of the first conventions, they together waited before God for thirty days. A little later George Turner joined them, and for twenty-one days these three men prayed and praised God for a mighty outpouring of his power. As a result, literally thousands over the years came into the kingdom through their prayers. Was it worth the effort? You decide.

—Wesley L. Duewel, *Touch the World Through Prayer* (Zondervan, 1986)

an ancient habit

Extended times of prayer are nothing new. It's quite possible that Enoch involved himself in a prayer retreat before "he was no more, because God took him away" (Genesis 5:22-24). Moses, the man to whom God was revealed more fully than any other person, spent two periods of forty days each on Mount Sinai alone with the Lord. And Elijah (1 Kings 17:2-6) spent much time in prayer to God when he was by the Kerith Ravine. For more examples, look to Jesus. And what was Paul doing when he disappeared into Arabia for three years (Galatians 1:17-18)? Examples abound; they're just waiting to be found.

FAILURE IN PRAYER

the trap of rhetoric

Praying in cliches? One missionary thought so. She visited a midweek "Prayer Meeting" in a little town one evening. The people mentioned the sick, the pastor, the worship services, the church school, the community. One person asked God to bless the missionaries around the world, and another prayed God's blessing on the president of the country.

Five years later, that same missionary visited that same church's midweek prayer meeting. It was like entering a time warp except the names of the sick had changed. She thought:

Haven't any of these people expanded their vision of the operation of God in the world and the significance of prayer in the life of the church? Haven't any of them become involved in community life so that they would have fresh, up-to-date concerns about which to pray? Hasn't anything happened in their lives to promote dynamically fresh approaches to God, especially items about which they are thankful? Are they so locked into their little church's world that they haven't been able to tap into God's concerns for the entire world? Haven't any of them encountered spiritual changes that would inspire new concepts of God and new desires to relate better to God? Haven't they learned some new ways to express themselves in conversation with God? Haven't any of them had contacts with unchurched people who need the Savior? Apparently not!

Rhethoric. Cliches. Banalities. It doesn't have to be that way. Why can't prayer constantly vibrate with reality, with depth, with a living, moving pulse that comes from a relationship with the object of our prayers?

—William J. Krutza, *Prayer: The Vital Link* (Judson Press, 1983)

"bless": overused

The Central African missionary told of the regional missionaries' prayer habits. Given a list with five other missionaries on it, they would pray each day with an impersonal "bless" because they knew so little about each other. One day he was praying, "Bless Marge, bless John, bless Bill. . . ." When he was done, he flipped the page for the following day's list, and there was his name right on top. He was pained right to his soul, for he realized that the next day people all over would be "blessing" him as he had them. He vowed then and there that in the

future he would learn as much as possible about the subjects of his prayers so he could talk to God sincerely about them.
—William J. Krutza, *Prayer: The Vital Link* (Judson Press, 1983)

FAITH AND PRAYER

no celestial bellhop

God is not a celestial bellhop nor a mild-mannered Oz of sorts. He is a God of order, a God who has given certain guidelines regarding prayer in his book to us, the Bible.

For instance, Jesus' statements regarding prayer often get us in all sorts of trouble. "Ask and it shall be given to you"; "If any two of you agree on anything, ask and it shall be given"; and "Everything you ask in prayer, believing, you shall receive." It wouldn't be too hard to find two Christians who would like to rid the world of cancer, AIDS, and war. But their prayers in this area, no matter how intense, will come to naught because they took those passages and isolated them from the rest of the Word, from other statements of God. God said that wars, disease, and poverty will be present at the time of Christ's return. To ask for their demise now would be a premature attempt to grasp future promises of God. When we entreat God to act in our behalf, we must consider his whole Word. To pray in faith is to pray knowledgeably—with an understanding of God's whole council.

R.C. Sproul tells of a young man with cerebral palsy who asked if he was demon-possessed. When asked why he would think such a thing, this very Christian young man explained that some well-meaning friends "claimed" the promise of Scripture and "agreed" among themselves that their friend be healed of his disease. When it didn't work, they chastised him for his lack of faith. Then they claimed he must be guilty of some awful, secret sin. Finally, they decided he must be demon-possessed, leaving him with a seared conscience and confusion about his own spiritual state. His "friends" prayed to accomplish their own desires— they were exercising a Santa Claus-God mentality. That is not the prayer of faith.

—R. C. Sproul, *Effective Prayer* (Tyndale, 1987)

unshakable confidence

At certain times, God's intentions steal in and make themselves known in quiet, absolutely certain ways. R.A. Torrey tells of his first experience with that unshakable confidence:

There was a young dentist in my congregation whose father was a member of our church. This dentist was taken very ill with typhoid fever; he went down to the very gates of death. I went to see him and found him unconscious. The doctor and his father were by the bedside, and the doctor said to me, "He cannot live. The crisis is past, and it has turned the wrong way. There is no possibility of his recovery." I knelt down to pray, and as I prayed a great confidence came into my heart, an absolutely unshakable confidence that God had heard my prayer and that that man was to be raised up. As I got up from my knees, I said to the father and the doctor, "Ebbie will get well. He will not die at this time."

The doctor smiled and said, "That is all right, Mr. Torrey, from your standpoint, but he cannot live. He will die."

I replied, "Doctor, that is all right from your standpoint, but he cannot die; he will live." I went to my home. Not long after, word was brought to me that the young man was dying. They told me what he was doing, and said that no one ever did that except just when they were dying. I calmly replied, "He is not dying. He will not die. He will get well." I knew he would; he did. The last I knew he was living yet, and his healing took place between forty and forty-five years ago.

—R. A. Torrey, *The Power of Prayer* (Zondervan, 1975)

he has everything

A devoted Christian woman had been teaching Sunday school for years, actively witnessing, and living a life worthy of the name "Christian." Yet, she told her pastor, the joy, the zest of the Christian life had been missing for some years. He asked her what she was doing

about it. "I have done everything that I can think of, but all in vain."

Next, the pastor asked her what her conversion experience was like, and what she did immediately following that time in her life. "At first I spared no pains in my attempt to become better, and to free myself from sin, but it was all useless. At last I began to understand that I must lay aside all my efforts, and simply trust the Lord Jesus to bestow on me his life and peace, and he did it." The minister then asked her to try that again, to simply bow before the throne of God, trust him, and wait in childlike faith before him. "You have nothing—he has everything." She did, and some months later reported a renewed relationship with her Lord.

—Andrew Murray, *The Prayer Life* (Whitaker House, 1981)

burning bridges

"I tell you, whatever you ask for in prayer, believe that you have received it, and it will be yours."—Mark 11:24

A piece of property adjacent to the [congregation's] present facilities came up for sale for $2,850,000 cash. Charles Stanley and his congregation looked into a loan, but interest was 21 percent. Believing God wanted them to make the move in faith, they opted for making the purchase without the bank's help.

Over the course of the previous year, the congregation had given more than $1,200,000 for property and renovation. Two weeks before the deadline they had collected only $125,000 more. It looked impossible. At the close of the next service, a young man and his wife offered his wedding band for the fund. It was all they had left because of a robbery that had just taken place. At the second service, Stanley shared the sacrificial spirit of the couple, and people began lining up and down the aisles to give their diamond rings, bracelets, pendants, watches, and necklaces. Others promised cars, campers, stocks, bonds, and so on. By Friday, they had another $1,350,000.

A lot more money was still needed. Stanley's faith often took major nosedives. "I soon saw a pattern. When I would try to figure out just how we could come up with the money, my faith would waver. But as long as I accepted my utter helplessness, my faith soared like an eagle."

On Sunday, the deadline was only twenty-four hours away and $1,500,000 was still needed. Stanley had made a tough decision the night before, and now he presented it to the congregation. "We must burn every bridge and cut off every avenue of escape. Our faith must be in him and him alone." He held up a strand of hair and cut it with a scissors, signifying their cutting off all routes of escape. "When I did that, something happened to the congregation. They were released. By that Sunday evening they gave an additional $1 million. "Thirty minutes before the deadline we had our $2,850,000."

—Charles F. Stanley, *Handle with Prayer* (Victor Books, 1982)

FAITHFULNESS IN PRAYER

never give up praying

Never give up praying. Never give up praying for a need. Think what would have happened had Daniel quit after five or ten days. God is faithful, and he will hear your prayers. Pray, pray, pray. Let the balance sheet of prayer weigh heavily in your favor.

A Korean woman was distressed at her daughter's moral wanderings. It seemed that the more she prayed, the farther her daughter wandered. Then she heard a message on the need for faithful, constant prayer. She prayed and did not get discouraged. One day, as she prayed, she suddenly knew that God was able to handle the situation. In her heart, she knew her daughter was being worked on by the Holy Spirit. Within a few days, her daughter attended church, gave her life to the Lord, and is now actively serving him with her mother.

—Paul Yonggi Cho, *Prayer: Key to Revival* (Word, 1984)

Luther's lines

A letter written to Philipp Melanchthon about the prayers of Martin Luther:

"I cannot enough admire the extraordinary cheerfulness, constancy, faith and hope of the man in these trying and vexatious times. He constantly feeds these gracious affections by a very diligent study of the Word of God. Then not a day passes in which he does not employ in prayer at least three of his very best hours. Once I happened to hear him at prayer. Gracious God! What spirit and what faith is there in his expressions! He petitions God with as much reverence as if he was in the divine presence, and yet with as firm a hope and confidence as he would address a father or a friend. 'I know,' said he, 'You are our Father and our God; and therefore I am sure You will bring to naught the persecutors of Your children. For should You fail to do this, Your own cause, being connected with ours, would be endangered. It is entirely Your own concern. We, by Your providence, have been compelled to take a part. You therefore will be our defense.' While I was listening to Luther praying in this manner, at a distance, my soul seemed on fire within me, to hear the man address God so like a friend, yet with so much gravity and reverence; and also to hear him, in the course of his prayer, insisting on the promises contained in the Psalms, as if he were sure his petitions would be granted."

Luther, like Wesley, Müller, and so many others, learned to pray with purpose. For them, God was not a distant deity to grovel before or perform for, but a personal friend, a Father always near at hand, always ready to listen to his children. There were no barriers. Theirs were relationships built on intimacy. When they looked up to see their loving God, the clouds of obscurity and distance fled, and the face of the Father became clear. So it is with those who yield entirely to the heavenly plan. God will not fail to hear their prayers, will not fail to bend his ear to the heartfelt pleadings of the servant who confidently expects God to listen.

—E. M. Bounds, *Purpose in Prayer* (Moody Press)

pray expectantly

On a return journey to England, as Adam Clarke records in his autobiography, the winds became fierce, and navigation proved difficult. John Wesley, reading below deck, noticed the confusion of the crew and the anxiety of the travelers. "What is wrong?" he inquired. He was told of the adverse weather conditions and said, "Then let us go to prayer."

"Almighty and everlasting God, You have sway everywhere, and all things serve the purpose of Your will; You hold the winds in Your hands and sit upon the water floods, and reign a King forever. Command these winds and these waves that they obey You, and take us speedily and safely to the haven where we would go."

The prayer seemed more an offering of faith than of desire. The potency of the simple petition was felt by all. After opening his eyes, Wesley rose, made no comment, and resumed reading. Clarke went on deck and found the vessel on course, under sail. She stayed that way till they reached the harbor. Wesley said nothing about the sudden change in weather. He expected to be heard and took for granted that he was heard. Praying with purpose—Wesley lived and prayed in a way that assured him he had the ear of God.

—E. M. Bounds, *Purpose in Prayer* (Moody Press)

wait upon the Lord

George Müller of Bristol, England, was at the harbor that morning, waiting to set sail from Quebec to Liverpool. About a half hour before departure, he asked the agent if a deck chair had arrived for him from New York. "No," replied the agent, and assured Müller that it could not possibly come in time for the trip.

Major D. W. Whittle, who was traveling with Müller, had recently purchased a chair at a nearby place and suggested he go buy one. "No, my brother," said Müller. "Our heavenly Father will send the chair from New York. It is one used by Mrs. Müller. I wrote ten days ago to a brother, who promised to see it forwarded here last week. He has not been prompt, as I would have desired, but I am sure our heavenly Father will send the chair. Mrs. Müller is very sick on the sea, and has particularly desired to have this same chair, and not finding it here yesterday, we have made special prayer that our heavenly Father would be pleased to provide it for us, and we will trust him to do so."

Müller went on board in total peace, confidently expecting the chair. Whittle was left to wonder if perhaps his friend had carried his faith principles a bit far, when for a few dollars he could have bought a chair for his wife. "I was kept at the express office ten minutes after Mr. Müller left. Just as I started to hurry to the wharf, a team drove up the street, and on top of a load just arrived from New York was Mr. Müller's chair. It was sent at once to the tender and placed in my hands to take to Mr. Müller, just as the boat was leaving the dock (the Lord having a lesson for me). Mr. Müller took it with the happy, pleased expression of a child who just received a kindness deeply appreciated, and reverently removing his hat and folding his hands over it, he thanked the heavenly Father for sending the chair."

—E. M. Bounds, *Purpose in Prayer* (Moody Press)

I've been praying

In the late 1960s, Sammy Tippit, founder and president of God's Love in Action, was asked by Pastor L. L. Morris to preach a series of evangelistic messages at his small Baptist church in Monroe, Louisiana.

Tippit agreed but found himself in deep discouragement and despair in the weeks preceding the meetings. The Vietnam War, the drug culture, rebellion, Eastern mysticism, and racism were occupying the thoughts of youth. There seemed to be no interest in things spiritual.

"I believe we ought to cancel the evangelistic meetings," said Tippit to Morris. "There is no interest. We will be wasting my time, your time, and the church's time." Nonplussed, Morris replied, "I've been praying. God has given me assurance that he is going to do something special during these meetings."

Tippit preached as scheduled, but the first service was a dismal experience. When it became clear that there would be no response from the few gathered, he looked over at Morris with an "I told you so" expression on his face. After, Morris responded, "I've been praying. It will be OK."

On Thursday night Tippit preached again. Only fifty people came. At the end of the evening, however, a church leader came forward and prayed with Pastor Morris. With tears in his eyes, he confessed alcoholism and being a poor role model for the church youth. Then he pleaded for the church's forgiveness.

Something happened. A powerful wave of brokenness and prayer washed over the church. People crowded to the front, weeping, asking forgiveness, praying.

The next night the church was full. By Sunday night, there wasn't enough room. Pastor Morris said, "I've been praying, and I believe we ought to extend these meetings another week." Tippit knew better than to argue. The group moved from the church to the local university.

Pastor Morris said, "I've been praying. I think we ought to talk to the former Louisiana governor. He owns the local television station, and we should ask him for time on television to tell what God is doing in our city."

Tippit's response: "I don't think he will help us." Morris: "I've been praying, and God will prepare his heart."

They got what they wanted—two fifteen-minute television spots to show the world what was happening in Monroe. Then the governor said, "You're having problems with lack of space. Do you think that the civic center would be big enough?" After a few strategic phone calls, the civic center was theirs, free of charge.

Tippit was stunned. Morris just smiled. Forever after, Tippit's ears rang with the words, "I've been praying." That humble pastor proved that victory does not come from magnificent schemes, expert publicity, or financial holdings, but victory comes from the Lord.

—Sammy Tippit, *The Prayer Factor* (Moody Press, 1988)

it's habit forming

What is it to be habitually in prayer? To live in constant communion with the Creator of the universe? One Scotsman summed it up nicely in his answer to the question, "Do you expect to go to heaven?" "Why, man, I live there!" was his reply. Those steeped in prayer, those who walk close to God all ways and always, live in the courtyard of heaven. For them, heaven has already begun because they are so often in the presence of the supreme resident of that place.

Horace Bushnell was one of those who lived near heaven's gate. He discovered he had an incurable disease and soon after met with his friend, Rev. Joseph Twichell. As they sat outside looking at the stars, Bushnell said, "One of us ought to pray." Bushnell began, and as his prayers ascended, he buried his face in the earth and poured out his heart to God. Recalls Twichell, "I was afraid to stretch out my hand in the darkness lest I should touch God."

Samuel Rutherford found that even a prison cell cannot break the bind between God and his praying servants. When confined to a cell because of conscience' sake, he turned to his God in prayer. For him it was one of the sweetest conversations ever, for Jesus himself entered the enclosure and "every stone flashed like a ruby."

David Livingstone, credited with opening Africa to the gospel, was a man of prayer. "O Divine One, I have not loved Thee earnestly, deeply, sincerely enough. Grant, I pray Thee, that before this year is ended I may have finished my task." Livingstone died that same year. His men found his cold body kneeled in prayer beside his bed. What a smooth transition for him from the courtyard to heaven itself.

—E. M. Bounds, *Purpose in Prayer* (Moody Press)

in sickness and in health—pray!

In a small farming community lived a man named Jorn. From day one, Jorn experienced more than his share of troubles. Poor eyesight and a weak body made it difficult for him to earn a living.

Jorn humbled himself before God and learned to live with his pain and sorrow. Little by little, the difficulties of life drove him deeper and deeper into a life of prayer. His burden was for the community. He never ceased intercessing for those who lived there. God blessed Jorn and exalted him. He became the spiritual counselor to the whole parish. People would come to his little hut for advice and help, and if he could offer nothing else, he would at least give to them from the ample supply of the love he had. And he would pray. Those that entered with heavy hearts often left without their loads of sorrow.

Later in life, Jorn's health deteriorated. He began spending more and more time in prayer for community members. He didn't lump them in categories like we are so apt to do because of the time it saves, but gave concentrated, individual prayers for people he knew well and people he never met before.

Jorn's eventual death was mourned by all. His funeral was the largest ever held in the community. Even nonbelievers came and wept at the grave, so great was the loss of this man of prayer. Jorn's life was a fulfillment of the words, "Ask, and you shall receive."

—O. Hallesby, *Prayer* (Augsburg)

growing prayer list

Cuthbert Bardsley, Bishop of Coventry, had a man on his prayer list for ten years who was constantly alternating between states of drunkenness and repentance. "May I take that man off my list?" the Bishop finally asked the Lord. God clearly indicated to him that the man was to remain in the Bishop's prayers. It seemed that the selfhood of that weak man was still precious to the Lord. At the end of that tenth year, the man finally made a commitment to the Lord, turned his life around, became a key member of the church, and devoted himself to intercessory prayer. God was faithful.

—Donald M. Hulstrand, *The Praying Church* (The Seabury Press, 1977)

runaway faith

Delores had befriended a high school girl named Becky. Becky listened, but didn't seem interested in the message of salvation. One morning, Becky's mother called Delores, crying and explaining that Becky ran away. That was in the 1970s, and dope rings in the Fort Worth area took in runaways so that parents couldn't find their children. The people feared for her life, but Delores's prayer group feared for her soul.

They started fervent prayer. As they prayed, they felt led to ask the Holy Spirit to prompt Becky to return to her mother. They asked that Delores would have another opportunity to share the gospel. That very afternoon, Becky called her mother and asked her to pick her up. That night, Delores shared Christ, and Becky became a Christian.

—T. W. Hunt and Catherine Walker, *Prayer Life: Walking in Fellowship with God* (The Sunday School Board of the Southern Baptist Convention, 1987)

FAMILY PRAYER

a mother's prayer

"God's best men and women have been reared by a mother's prayers and views, and a father's solemn consecration. Blessed, indeed, is the life of a man or woman, boy or girl, who has been heralded into the world not only by pain but also by prayer—their advent prefaced by the hand of a father or mother laying hold upon God."

The Scudder family served as missionaries in India. The father of nine remarked, "Our children were literally prayed into the kingdom by their mother." She customarily spent each child's birthday in prayer.

John Newton, author of "Amazing Grace," learned prayer at his mother's knee. Though she died when he was eight years old, he never forgot that testimony.

As a child, Dick Eastman often awoke to the sound of his mother's prayers in the morning, not an alarm clock. "Her prayers were never voiced in swift and careless fashion. Many hours drifted away in tear-filled rivers while mother prayed. The result is a family of ministers. Every child grew to serve God. Each has his special ministry."

—Dick Eastman, *No Easy Road* (Baker Book House)

I urge upon you communion with Christ, a growing communion. There are curtains to be drawn aside in Christ that we never saw, and new foldings of love in him. I despair that I shall ever win to the far end of that love, there are so many plies in it. Therefore dig deep, and sweat and labor and take pains for him, and set by as much time in the day for him as you can. He will be won in the labor.

—Samuel Rutherford

no reason for living, no hope for dying

His son used his newfound freedom at college to the extreme. Alcohol, pills, the whole package. His grades went down, he lost interest in life, he became a filthy pig due to lack of washing, and his health deteriorated. He would sit for long periods of time just staring off into space.

Then, when all seemed lost, he found Jesus Christ. Not a mellow transformation like many of us experience, but a head-on confrontation with the Creator of the universe. All his stupid rationales, his puffed-up ego, his intellectual approach, and his "free" will were beat down by the Christ of Calvary. He went home for a joyful reunion with his parents, and when the tears were dried, they asked, "Son, what happened? Your mother and I talked, we wrote and phoned, we did everything we could to reach you but nothing worked. So it couldn't have been us. Tell us, what happened?"

"Yes, it was you, Dad, but you didn't know it. It wasn't anything you said; you never could have reached me that way. I was sitting in my room one night—heartsick, defeated, and desperate—and I thought of something. You didn't know it, Dad, but when I was in high school I used to come home late, and I'd slip down the hall and you wouldn't hear me. But I had to pass your bedroom, Dad, and more than once I saw you in your pajamas, kneeling at your bedside praying for me.

"As I sat there in my room that night, with no reason for living and no hope for dying, suddenly in my mind I saw a picture of you kneeling there praying for me. I looked at my watch; it was eleven and I knew you were doing that just then. And Dad, that thought broke my last resistance, and I fell to my knees and cried out for God—and he came!"

—Arnold Prater, *You Can Pray as You Ought* (Thomas Nelson, 1977)

FASTING AND PRAYER

the gift of wednesdays

Several years ago, Dick Eastman asked God what he could give his daughters as a gift "that will touch them for the rest of their lives." Though it seemed like a strange request—a sort of eternal gift—it seemed to have been prompted by God. Soon after, Eastman heard a faint question whispered to him: "Are you willing to give your daughters a year of Wednesdays?" Eastman was baffled. It would be impractical to give up work, ministry, and other events every Wednesday to be with his daughters, and even if he could, it was doubtful that two teenage girls could. "Could you set aside every Wednesday on your calendar as a fast," the Lord suggested. "During the day when you'd normally be having a meal, you could pray."

"I could never do that," was Eastman's reply. "Why?" came the gentle voice. "For one thing, I'd forget!" "Not if you mark every Wednesday on your calendar as a fast." Eastman said yes to Christ on that day, and continued the practice for years. "I am convinced that our daughters have had a spiritual hedge about them as they encountered the personal problems of youth. And I am convinced that the greatest single help in building that hedge was the Lord's suggestion that I give our children the gift of Wednesdays."

—Dick Eastman, *Love on Its Knees*
(Fleming H. Revell Co., 1989)

fasting through the centuries

"You will be the poorer spiritually and your prayer life will never be what God wants it to be until you practice the privilege of fasting." A strong statement; does it hold any truth? Read on and decide for yourself.

In the fourth century, Epiphanius, Bishop of Salamis, wrote: "Who does not know that the fast of the fourth and sixth days of the week are observed by the Christians throughout the world?" Nine centuries later, Francis of Assisi danced, preached, sang, testified, and fasted through the streets of Italy until thousands of the youth were saved. Martin Luther was criticized for too much fasting. John Calvin fasted until Geneva was converted and there was not a house without at least one praying person. The reason Queen Mary feared the prayers of John Knox "more than all the armies of Scotland" was because of his constant prayer and fasting. John Wesley fasted twice weekly. He said he would as soon curse and swear as not fast, for "the man that never fasts is no more in the way to heaven than the man who never prays." Jonathan Edwards fasted so much that he was often weak in the pulpit, but he was instrumental in moving New England for God. Charles G. Finney, the revivalist of the 1800s, fasted each week. In fact, whenever he felt the power of the Spirit fading from his meetings, he would fast and pray for three days and nights. He reported that after such times, the Spirit's power invariably returned and moved at his meetings. In times of need D. L. Moody would send word to Moody Bible Institute to call faculty and students to a time of prayer and fasting. They would often continue on until two, three, four, or five o'clock in the morning. "If you say I will fast when God lays it on me," stated Moody, "you never will. You are too cold and indifferent. Take the yoke upon you."

The movers and shakers of the world for God were convinced that fasting is God's chosen way to deepen and strengthen prayer. Important? You decide.
   —Wesley L. Duewel, *Touch the World Through Prayer* (Zondervan, 1986)

freedom from lust

A young man came into the pastor's study and confessed a struggle with lust. The pastor gave him this challenge:

First, fast for three days. He was to seclude himself and spend his time praying positive prayers. Not, "Lord, please help me" prayers, but prayers that thanked God for victory. Second, he was to fill his mind with Scripture. He was to read passages that spoke to his need and dealt specifically with his problem. He was to meditate on those passages and be assured of God's presence and power. Third, he was to fast one day each week for the following three weeks.

A month later, the man returned. "I was tempted to give up [fasting] every hour, but by the evening of the second day, I knew victory was possible." He said he experienced a total freedom from lust, even though the temptations would never cease to exist.
   —Charles F. Stanley, *Handle with Prayer* (Victor Books, 1982)

GOD KNOWS BEST IN PRAYER

a parent's desire

Monica, the mother of Augustine, prayed that he would not go to Rome as planned, but that he would become a Christian and that she would be able to influence his life with her presence. On the night before his departure, she went to a chapel by the sea and prayed earnestly. Yet when she emerged from the sanctuary in the early hours of the morning, she discovered that his ship had already left. Though she didn't realize it, her petition was refused but her real request and desire was granted. For it was in Rome that her rebellious son met the godly Ambrose, who led him to Jesus Christ. How comforting to know that God knows best.

attitude check

Judy had a wonderful singing voice and used it to glorify God. Yet she didn't do it willingly. It usually took a little coaxing and prodding to get her to sing. Then she was diagnosed with growths in her larynx. Surgery was recommended.

Suddenly, the thought of not being able to talk with friends, to laugh and sing, all seemed like a tragic loss to Judy. She struggled and prayed again and again, "Please, just help me learn to be happy about conforming to Your will. I don't know how I can face not being able to talk, with my family responsibilities and the fact that I love to be around people."

It was during that time that her attitude about singing began to change. No longer a chore, it became an intensely joyful experience. She wanted to perform because it was a precious way to glorify the God she served. She prayed for future opportunities to sing his praises.

She went in for a presurgery checkup. The doctor looked in her throat, looked at her files, then looked puzzled. "There is nothing there any more!" he said in amazement. Judy went home as fast as she could to tell her husband. His reply surprised her. Unknown to her, he had prayed every day that the Lord would heal her, while she never thought of such a prayer. Now, God had not only healed her, but changed her attitude as well.

—Douglas F. Kelly, *Why Pray?*
(Wolgemuth & Hyatt, 1989)

GOD WORKS THROUGH PRAYER

manageable labor

In February 1985, about four hundred people gathered at St. Patrick's Church in Canonsburg, Pennsylvania, to pray. The McGraw-Edison company had told its employees that without a considerable "giveback" in wages, the plant would close. Union leadership said no. If the plant closed, the town would be devastated. On that day, Rev. David Kinsey, along with the ministers of the town and labor and management personnel from McGraw-Edison, their families, and praying people, met to ask God to change hearts and history.

At the climax of the meeting, a leading Christian spokesperson, the senior management representative for McGraw-Edison, and the president of the local United Steel Workers Union, stood together in front of the church. Labor prayed for management, and management prayed for labor. Two days later, management changed its offer (though there would still be a reduction in salary), and labor changed its vote.

—John Guest, *Only a Prayer Away* (Servant Publications, 1985)

powerful prayer

At times, God waits for his people to pray. Consider the following: At the end of a prayer meeting, a godly woman begged those present to pray for her unsaved husband. "He won't set foot in a place of worship," she said. The leader suggested they continue praying, and many earnest prayers were offered on the husband's behalf.

A very devoted husband, he often met his wife at the church after her meetings. On that particular night he was early, and he decided to wait just inside the door, something he had never done before. He entered, moved a little closer, then took a chair near the door. He overheard earnest petition while waiting for his wife. During the walk home, he asked, "Who was the man they were praying for tonight?" "Oh," she replied, "it is the husband of one of our workers." "Well, I am quite sure he will be saved," said the husband. "God must answer prayers like that." Later that evening, he asked again, "Who was the man they were praying for?" She answered with a similar answer. While in bed later that night, he could not sleep. He was under deep conviction of sin. He woke his wife and asked her to pray for him.

That man could have entered the church any night of the year to wait for

his wife. All it would have taken was a little prompting from God. Yet he did not
enter until praying Christians begged the
Father to move the man's heart. Had they
not prayed, it's questionable what his
actions would have been. But they did,
and he did. Praise God!

—*The Kneeling Christian*
(Zondervan, 1971)

marriage made in heaven

In 1970 Douglas Kelly was studying
at the University of Edinburgh. He fell in
love—from a distance—with an English
girl who was also studying there. Instead
of asking her out for dates, the shy
Douglas began to pray that God would
prepare her heart for marriage to him. He
prayed for two years and during that time
the girl showed very little (if any) interest
in him. Yet he prayed on and one day
popped the question. She said "yes."

Did Douglas force the Lord's hand?
"As the years passed and children were
born and the parents engaged in
Christian ministry, there was more and
more evidence—in small as well as in
large ways—that they were truly meant
for each other; that they made a team
intellectually, spiritually, culturally, as
well as physically and family-wise. Only
God could have brought them together."

—Douglas F. Kelly, *Why Pray?*
(Wolgemuth & Hyatt, 1989)

GUIDANCE THROUGH PRAYER

prayin' Abe

Abraham Lincoln often received clarity in decision making after falling to his knees in prayer. Lincoln once said, "I have been driven many times to my knees by the overwhelming conviction that I had nowhere else to go; my own wisdom and that of all around me seemed insufficient for the day." He went on to explain the Lord's answers to prayer. "I have had so many evidences of his direction, so many instances of times when I have been controlled by some other power than my own will, that I cannot doubt that this power comes from God. I frequently see my way clear to a decision when I am conscious that I have not sufficient facts on which to found it. I am satisfied that, when the Almighty wants me to do, or not to do a particular thing, he finds a way of letting me know. I talk to God, and when I do, my mind seems relieved and a way is suggested."

Taylor's legacy

Hudson Taylor was based in the city of Swatow, China, but was on his way to Shanghai to get the medical instruments and medicines that he had left there earlier. When he arrived, he discovered that the building housing his supplies had burned to the ground. Everything had been destroyed. With very little money, he sat down to think. He decided to hike to Ningpo where he could purchase supplies from another missionary, then take a boat back to Swatow. It was hot. The oppressing heat beat down on Taylor as he trudged along the canals, preaching as he went. At one point he was so weary he had to hire coolies to carry his baggage. He set off, then had to wait through a long, hot afternoon for them to catch up. When they arrived, he learned they were opium addicts and were unable to finish the journey. He dismissed them and, leaving the chief coolie to hire more, set off once again. This time, however, his baggage never caught up. The coolies had taken the baggage and headed for the hills. Completely discouraged, he stayed in an inn and found it full of bugs and rats. It was not a good night.

The next morning he set off for the coast. He arrived after a long, hot, discouraging march, but was unable to find a place to stay. Inns didn't want him because he was a foreigner. Police harassed him. Then a young man tried helping him find lodging but abandoned Taylor at one o'clock in the morning. Taylor ended up on the steps of a temple, but forced himself to stay awake to keep the robbers off that were lurking nearby.

The next morning his "guide" from the previous night returned and demanded an extraordinary amount of money for his "services." Losing his temper, Taylor grabbed the fellow by the arm, shook him, and told him to go away. Weary, broken, and discouraged, he set off for the long journey back to Shanghai. For eight miles he limped along, wondering why God had abandoned him.

Suddenly, he understood it all. He had, in effect, been denying the Lord. He never asked God's guidance and protection along the way—it had been his own journey and plan from the very start. All his anger and weariness was released in a flood of tears of repentance. As he confessed, his journal tells us, there came flooding into his heart a "glorious sense of the presence and forgiveness of Christ." At that moment the initiative and control for the journey passed from the shoulders of Hudson Taylor to the Lord, where they belonged.

When he got back to Shanghai, he found a letter and a check waiting for him with the exact amount of money needed to resupply. He also learned that had he gone back to Swatow immediately as planned, he would have been arrested and probably executed.

Taylor recounts that all his worrying and fear were unnecessary. Events may have happened the same way, but all the emotional pain and trauma could have been eliminated had he just trusted God to guide him right from the start.

—Ray C. Stedman, *Jesus Teaches on Prayer* (Word Books, 1975)

weighed down

In the far north of Scotland lived Willie Black, pastor of a small country church. Week after week for almost a decade, Black preached the Word of God.

He grew to love his people and grew to love the Word.

Black was keen on having his people interested in missions, so he had missionaries stop in whenever they could. One time he had one in from Korea.

As he listened to the missionary speak, he felt a heavy weight; he could hardly get out of his seat later to give the closing remarks. The feeling gradually left, and he thought he'd seen the end of it.

The next day, however, the feeling returned—with a vengeance. He prayed, "Lord, if someone mentions the word Korea today, then I will respond to the sense of burden being laid on me yesterday and know it was from Your hand." The family was leaving for vacation, so he wasn't too worried about running into anybody who knew what was going on.

They spent that night with a former classmate, and Willie shared his experience, careful not to mention any specific country or geographic region. The friend laughed and said, "Willie, maybe the Lord is sending you to Korea!"

A month after arriving in Korea, Willie learned the rest of the story. A Korean knocked on his door and asked if this new missionary would please teach him and some of his friends how to do expository preaching. "We have been praying for a long time for someone with these skills. Surely you could teach us! We started praying especially in . . ." and he named the precise month when the burden had come down on Willie.

—Douglas F. Kelly, *Why Pray?* (Wolgemuth & Hyatt, 1989)

HEALING AND PRAYER

20/20 faith

Loren, a member of St. Stephen's Episcopal Church (pastored by John Guest) near Pittsburgh, relates the following story:

I was in the Eye and Ear Hospital three days before John visited me. I had been operated on for a detached retina. At that time, I was 99 percent blind in my left eye. I had been told that with the operation, I would probably regain 25 percent of my vision. Three days after the operation, the surgeon decided that the operation was a failure and I would have to have more surgery. With the second operation, if successful, I would have less than 25 percent vision. That was not a happy thought, but I had no alternative. I had to submit to the operation. I was certainly in great distress the night before surgery. The lights were out in the room, the door opened, and there was John Guest.

I was very happy to see him. John sat by my bed, held my hand and prayed a healing prayer. He left, and I was at peace for the first time that day. For some reason my thoughts turned to a passage in the Bible that I had read long ago, the tenth chapter of the Gospel of Saint Mark, beginning at the forty-sixth verse. Jesus was leaving Jericho and along the road were many people gathered to see him. Among them was a blind man named Bartimaeus, and he called out as Jesus passed, "Jesus, Son of David, have mercy on me!" Jesus said, "What do you want me to do for you?" And the blind man said, "Master, let me receive my sight." His sight was restored and Jesus said, "Go your way; your faith has made you well."

I was relaxed and went to sleep. The next day I was rolled into the operating room, hooked up to the intravenous tubing and knew that within a very short time, the Pentothal would be turned on. Within a second or so I would be asleep. I knew something had to be done quickly, because I knew I had been healed.

I asked that the doctor be brought in. They told me he could not be disturbed because he was scrubbing up, preparing for the operation. And I said, "Well, get him, and don't let me go to sleep!" The doctor came in and asked what I wanted. I said, "Doctor, I think a change has taken place in my eye. I think I have been healed. Will you look at it?" He did and said, "You're right!"

The people in the operating room were in turmoil. They said, "How did it happen?" I told John about this later, and he said, "I didn't do it, it was done by the Lord." Regardless of who did it, I feel that the Holy Spirit was truly at work that night. The next day I walked out of the hospital, and I had my sight. As of a checkup a month ago, I have 20/20 vision in my left eye.

—John Guest, *Only a Prayer Away* (Servant Publications, 1985)

songs of victory

The power of praise was introduced to Dick Eastman during his daughter's illness. She was in bed with a temperature of 104, and it was rising rapidly. "Recalling the victory of Judah in 2 Chronicles 20:22, I began to sing a song of praise over Ginger. Instantly the fever broke, and sweat actually began to pour down her forehead into my hands."

Eastman shared the experience at a later date on television. A young woman saw it and recalled it at a crucial point in her own life. She was in the hospital about to be operated on for a potentially life-threatening situation. Her fever started to rise and her vital signs were rising sharply. She asked the nurse for permission to have her family come in and sing songs of victory. It was quickly granted, and as the family began to sing, blending their voices in a song of victory, her vital signs began to drop, as did her fever. As the song ended, her temperature was 98.6. God had met them in their song.

—Dick Eastman, *Love on Its Knees* (Fleming H. Revell Co., 1989)

not so unusual

An industry executive went to the plant clinic for a routine checkup and was horrified to learn he had a dark mass on one lung. He and his wife entered the hospital for a biopsy, feeling like anyone would feel in their situation. While at the hospital, his wife called members of the church, and within five hours an all-night prayer chain had gone into action. That night, as the man lay awake trying to pray, he suddenly felt an unmistakable presence in the room. Peace invaded his soul, and he slept. When X rays were taken the next day, the spot was gone. The two X rays were compared; the first had a dark mass, the second was clear. "Have you ever known this to happen, doctor?" asked the man. After a long, thoughtful look, the doctor replied, "More often than anyone has any idea of."

—Helen Smith Shoemaker, *Power Through Prayer Groups* (Fleming H. Revell Co., 1958)

prayer and healing

Healing is often dismissed by many as hocus-pocus, emotionalism, and impossible. Yet consider this testimony from a very intelligent, cautious, practical, and rational man.

He was sitting in church one Sunday evening, agonizing inwardly about some physical pain he was going through. At one point in the service, he prayed to the Lord, telling him how much he needed the Lord. "I felt completely devoid of power. Then . . . I felt a hand on my shoulder. I looked around to see if someone in the pew behind me was touching me or was trying to get my attention. The people behind me smiled but clearly indicated that they had not touched my shoulder. Then it happened again. After that I felt a warmth surge through my body. I felt the hand that had touched my shoulder was now connected to an arm that was joined by another arm to embrace me. I felt loved, accepted, cared about deeply. The Lord was answering the prayer I had prayed about my needs. I felt his Spirit surging through me. The tensions in my mind relaxed, my body felt calm, and my emotions were filled with joy. It was as if an electric current passed through every fibre of my being. Could it be that I received a touch from the Lord?"

—Lloyd John Ogilvie, *You Can Pray with Power*

evidence

C. Peter Wagner, author and teacher on church growth, wondered if he had the gift of healing. "I was open to the possibility that it might be a gift," he writes, "but I needed more experimentation to find out for sure." After much prayer and advice from other believers, he asked God to give him some evidence of the gift—if he truly possessed it—within the next four months.

Of the substantial evidence he received, two items in particular stood out. The first happened when he was addressing about a thousand pastors and their spouses at a conference in a hotel. "During the worship session I felt an overpowering presence of the Holy Spirit, and God spoke to me directly in my spirit telling me to conduct a mass healing. I had never even thought about such a thing previously, but I knew I must obey God. As a result, at least fifty people who had short legs, back pains and other skeletal problems were healed that night."

The second event took place when Paul Yonggi Cho, pastor of Yoido Full Gospel Church of Seoul, Korea, heard about Wagner's gift and wanted to witness it for himself. "The next day God sent in an Egyptian Coptic pastor who as a teenager had been run over by a train, and whose leg had been stiff, weak, deformed, and short ever since. God moved powerfully, and in Cho's presence the pastor's leg lengthened, and he was able to place his full weight on it for the first time since the accident."

Cho took that story with him to Korea and told his congregation. A woman whose hip sockets had been disintegrating listened carefully. After the service, she and Cho talked about it and decided it would be good if she went to Pasadena to have Wagner look at it. When she arrived, she entered Wagner's office on crutches. When she left, the crutches were left behind. Subsequent X rays showed that where the deterioration had previously been, there was now growing bone tissue.

"I do not believe that the gift of healing is a prerequisite to pray for the sick," writes Wagner. "But rather all Christians have the role of laying hands on the sick and being open to see God use them as channels for healing."

—C. Peter Wagner, *How to Have a Healing Ministry Without Making Your Church Sick* (Regal Books, 1988)

will you pray for me?

Johannes Verkuyl, Reformed missiologist in Indonesia, writes,

"One evening I was working on a manuscript in Kwitang, Jakarta, when someone knocked at the door. It was a medical doctor with a daughter who had serious neurological disorders on her face. He said that he was a medical doctor and that he had consulted many colleagues for his daughter without results. He added that he was a Confucian, but his daughter had read at a Christian school in a children's Bible that faith healing took place by Jesus of Nazareth. . . . Now she asked me to pray for her recovery. I explained to her that I was not a 'prayer healer' and that I was always wary of unconditional prayers for healing, for then too much emphasis is placed on whether or not the healing took place, and there is often too little interest in the deeper significance of Jesus for the totality of human life. She seemed to understand this, and then she asked with disarming sincerity, 'But you will pray for me?' I did pray and she was healed."

That incident led Verkuyl to a large network of people whom he later reached with the gospel.

—*International Bulletin of Missionary Research*, October 1986

HEROES OF PRAYER

Those who have eternally shaken the world, those who have demonstrated the power of the risen Savior in their very beings—they are the men and women who have known God, who have spent so much time with him that it shows in their very features. Throughout history there have been men and women who have demonstrated that it takes not a spiritual "superstar" to accomplish great acts for the kingdom of God but humble, believing people—like you—who are willing to take God at his word, sacrifice their own personal desires, discipline themselves to "watch and pray," and leave the rest up to God. The following people share a common thread called prayer: a thread that weaves together a tapestry of spiritual success experienced in their very lives.

Brainerd: prayer personified

David Brainerd was a man of incredible spiritual dimensions. No ninety-eight-pound spiritual weakling with satanic sand kicked in his face, he was the Christian equivalent to Atlas. His strength came not from programs, committees, groups, or memberships, but from the hardest of spiritual disciplines: prayer.

Because of his commitment to prayer, Brainerd's life was exceedingly fruitful. The testimony of others shows what impact he had on the world of his day. He valued nothing more than sweet communion with his God, whether at home or in the wilds of early America, where he went to proclaim the message of hope to the native peoples.

Jonathan Edwards said of Brainerd, "His life shows the right way to success in the works of the ministry. He sought it as the soldier seeks victory in a siege or battle; or as a man that runs a race for a great prize. Animated with love to Christ and souls, how did he labor? Always fervently. Not only in word and doctrine, in public and in private, but in prayers by day and night, wrestling with God in secret and travailing in birth with unutterable groans and agonies, until Christ was formed in the hearts of the people to whom he was sent. Like a true son of Jacob, he persevered in wrestling through all the darkness of the night, until the breaking of the day!"

To wander through the pages of Brainerd's personal journals is to wander through experiences few people have. Prayer, fasting, and meditation filled the days when he lived with Native Americans in the wild. "When I return home," he wrote, "and give myself to meditation, prayer, and fasting, my soul longs for mortification, self-denial, humility, and divorcement from all things of the world." He goes on to say, "I have nothing to do with earth but only to labor in it honestly for God. I do not desire to live one minute for anything which earth can afford."

Here, Brainerd tells of an especially excruciating day of intercession.

Feeling somewhat of the sweetness of communion with God and the constraining force of his love, and how admirably it captivates the soul and makes all the desire and affections to center in God, I set apart this day for secret fasting and prayer, to entreat God to direct and bless me with regard to the great work which I have in view of preaching the gospel, and that the Lord would return to me and show me the light of his countenance. I had little life and power in the forenoon. Near the middle of the afternoon God enabled me to wrestle ardently in intercession for my absent friends, but just at night the Lord visited me marvelously in prayer.

I think my soul was never in such agony before. I felt no restraint, for the treasures of divine grace were opened to me. I wrestled for absent friends, for the ingathering of souls, for multitudes of poor souls, and for many that I thought were the children of God, personally, in many distant places. I was in such agony from sun half an hour high till near dark that I was all over wet with sweat, but yet it seemed to me I had done nothing. O, my dear Saviour did sweat blood for poor souls! I longed for more compassion toward them. I felt still in a sweet frame, under a sense of divine love and grace, and went to bed in such a frame, with my heart set on God.

The person of prayer is the person God flows through unhindered. Brainerd was such a man, but it's important to remember that he, too, was a sinner like everyone else. What made him God's extraordinary tool is that he heard Jesus say, "Call upon me, and I will answer," and he believed him.

time well spent

John Welch, a Scottish preacher, thought the day a waste if he did not spend eight or ten hours in prayer. His wife would often complain when she woke up in the middle of the night to find her husband on the floor—weeping. He would reply, "O woman, I have the souls of three thousand to answer for, and I know not how it is with many of them!" Another Scottish preacher said, "I ought to spend the best hours in communion with God. It is my noblest and most fruitful employment, and is not to be thrust into a corner. The morning hours, from six to eight, are the most uninterrupted and should be thus employed. After tea is my best hour, and that should be solemnly dedicated to God."

Bishop Asbury said, "I propose to rise at four o'clock as often as I can and spend two hours in prayer and meditation." Samuel Rutherford rose at three in the morning to meet God in prayer. Joseph Alleine was up at four o'clock and prayed until eight. If he heard other tradesmen up and working before he was up and praying, his reaction was, "O how this shames me! Doth not my Master deserve more than theirs?"

a thousand suns shining at noonday

William Carvosso was a Methodist class-leader of humble origins. He was a preacher first-class but never aspired to be one. He was a writer first-class but never aspired to be one. He was a soul-winner first-class but never aspired to be one. He just wanted to be faithful to his Lord and know him better. Here's a sample of Carvosso's spiritual life:

I have sometimes had seasons of remarkable visitation from the presence of the Lord. I well remember one night when in bed being so filled, so overpowered with the glory of God, that had there been a thousand suns shining at noonday, the brightness of that divine glory would have eclipsed the whole. I was constrained to shout aloud for joy. It was the overwhelming power of saving grace. Now it was that I again received the impress of the seal and the earnest of the Spirit in my heart. Beholding as in a glass the glory of the Lord, I was changed into the same image from glory to glory by the Spirit of the Lord. Language fails in giving but a faint description of what I there experienced. I can never forget it in time nor to all eternity.

Many years before, I was sealed by the Spirit in a somewhat similar manner. While walking out one day, I was drawn to turn aside on the public road, and under the canopy of the skies, I was moved to kneel down to pray. I had not long been praying with God before I was so visited from him that I was overpowered by the divine glory, and I shouted till I could be heard at a distance. It was a weight of glory that I seemed incapable of bearing in the body, and therefore I cried out, perhaps unwisely, "Lord, stay Thy hand." In this glorious baptism these words came to my heart with indescribable power: "I have sealed thee unto the day of redemption." Oh, I long to be filled more with God! Lord, stir me up more in earnest. I want to be more like Jesus. I see that nothing will do but being continually filled with the divine presence and glory. I know all that Thou hast is mine, but I want to feel a close union. Lord, increase my faith."
—E. M. Bounds, *The Weapon of Prayer* (Reprinted by Baker Book House)

HINDRANCES IN PRAYER

stories

304

HINDRANCES IN PRAYER

pure heart

The couple came for marital counseling. As they described their situation, the pastor realized the problem: she was suffering from demonic oppression. He told them what it was, and they quickly agreed to pray for her deliverance. The pastor prayed, and they went home.

The husband called three days later. The situation was even worse. "Why didn't God answer my prayer?" wondered the pastor. He began to meditate on Scripture, and God brought to mind an area of disobedience in his life. That sin had negated his power and authority to bind Satan from that woman's life. He confessed and made things right with the Lord, then invited the couple back. This time, a miraculous change swept over her. The erratic behavior stopped; her oppression lifted; she became happy, and the marital relationship was restored.

"There can be no known sin in our lives. Sin means a divided loyalty. God will not trust his authority and power to anyone who is not completely yielded to his purpose. But when we do sin, we must confess and repent. Not just so we can get God's power back, but out of a genuine spirit of sorrow and grief over our sin."

—Charles F. Stanley, *Handle with Prayer* (Victor Books, 1982)

HOLINESS AND PRAYER

reduced to ashes

A man in Eastern Europe spent years in prison for his faith. Even after his release, there was the possibility of incarceration at any moment. Yet through it all, he lived a life of devotion to Jesus.

While in prison, one of his major concerns was his sons. Though top in their classes, they would have no opportunity to go on to university because of their faith. After graduation, the oldest son went to work in a factory.

From his cell, the man prayed and prayed some more. One day, the head of the communist party in the factory approached the boy and said he would recommend that he be allowed to study at the university. He did, the son studied, and became a leading scholar of that nation. Over the years, the father prayed every one of his sons into university.

When asked about the explosive power of his prayers, the man replied: "Many people come to my country and want to make a big fire for God. I do not want to make a big fire for God. I want to be consumed by God's fire until I am ashes. When I am ashes, then I will see the glory of God. When I am consumed totally by God's fire, then I will see his glory. Holiness and prayer are inextricably intertwined. There is no power in prayer without complete allegiance to the will of God."

—Sammy Tippit, *The Prayer Factor* (Moody Press, 1988)

When Moses was before the burning bush, God said, "Take off your sandals, for the place where you are standing is holy ground" (Exodus 3:5). The only thing separating Moses from holy ground was his sandals. Often, what keeps us from reaching holy ground in our prayer life is the little things, those little sins we refuse to take off. Shed them! Discard them! And walk on holy ground.

IMPORTANCE OF PRAYER

pray the work

For Mother Teresa of Calcutta, prayer is a "given." "We are not social workers," she said. "We are contemplatives right in the heart of the world. For we are trying to pray the work—to do it with Jesus, to do it for Jesus, and to do it to Jesus."

Commenting on her life, *Time* magazine reported, "Most living saints, activists or no, of course get down on their knees and pray, some for hours a day. In the traditional concept of sainthood, in fact, prayer is an essential condition of sanctity, the key to the deeds that surround it. Most of today's saintly people would agree that the concept has not changed." Mother Teresa told the correspondent, "To keep a lamp burning, we have to keep putting oil in it." She said to keep building her own faith, "I had to struggle, I had to pray, I had to make sacrifices before I could say 'yes' to God."

—Donald M. Hulstrand, *The Praying Church* (The Seabury Press, 1977)

IN JESUS' NAME

for Charlie's sake

At a Christian convention a man got up and spoke on the subject of "For Christ's Sake." "He threw new light upon that passage. I had never seen it in that way before," said evangelist Dwight L. Moody.

When the war broke out, the man's only son enlisted. Even though he wasn't familiar with soldiers or the military, the man's heart went out to soldiers immediately. A Soldiers' Home was started in the city where the man lived, and he was asked to be president. Sometime later, he said to his wife, "I have given so much time to these soldiers that I have neglected my business." So he went to his office the next day determined to get work done. Later on, however, a soldier opened the door to his office and entered. The man ignored him, kept on writing. At last the soldier put down a soiled piece of paper which contained his son's writing. "Dear father, this young man belongs to my company. He has lost his health in defense of his country, and he is on his way home to his mother to die. Treat him kindly for Charlie's sake." The man put down his work at once and took the soldier to his home. There he kindly cared for him until he was able to be sent home to his mother. The man took the soldier to the station and sent him home with a "God bless you, for Charlie's sake!"

"Let our prayers, then, be for Christ's sake," cried Moody. "If we want our sons and daughters converted, let us pray that it be done for Christ's sake. If that is the motive, our prayers will be answered."

power of attorney

The pastor, along with all his other duties, was now supervising the building of a new church. The men in the congregation were doing all the labor. One Sunday after church he was approached by an old friend who was also an influential building contractor. "Pastor, are you getting builders' discounts from the wholesale outlets in the area?"

"No," said the pastor. "None of the wholesale outlets will sell to me because I don't have a license."

"I was afraid of that. Tomorrow, I'll pick you up at about ten o'clock."

The next day the contractor took the pastor around to all the wholesale outlets in the area. Because of the volume of work he did, he was treated with preference in every single place. Not only was it good treatment, it was good treatment by the manager. Speaking to each manager by name, Don, the contractor, said,

"From now on this man is to be considered as Don Speer. He represents me. Anything he chooses to purchase is to be put on my account, and he will sign my name for me."

For the next few years, the pastor was treated with respect whenever he walked into one of those places. Even if he only wanted a few nails, he got preference over other customers because of the one he represented.

Isn't that what Jesus offers us when he says, "ask the Father in my name"? When we approach the heavenly Father, we come representing Jesus. We are commissioned to do business for him as though he himself were here transacting that business!

—Judson Cornwall, *The Secret of Personal Prayer* (Creation House, 1988)

INTENSITY IN PRAYER

persistence pays

Prayer must be intense and persistent. Prayers said with depth and intensity are prayers said in complete dependence on God. The following shows the effects of intense prayer.

Years ago, the captain of a whaling ship was fighting high seas off Cape Horn. His destination lay south, but to get there meant fighting powerful, gale-force winds. The ship was going nowhere. Near midnight, the captain thought, "Why batter the ship against these waves? There are probably as many whales north as south. Suppose we run with the wind instead of against it?" With that, he changed course and headed due north.

"Boats ahead!" The cry rang out from the masthead an hour after changing course. Four lifeboats containing fourteen sailors bobbed around the vessel. After several days of drifting, the men's frantic, intense prayers for rescue were answered, and just in time; they would not have lasted another day.

Intense, fervent prayer—the kind that storms the gates of heaven. That is the prayer that gets results, that holds Satan at bay.

—Dick Eastman, *No Easy Road* (Baker Book House)

an emotional plea

Balancing emotions and intellect in prayer is a necessity. Too much intellect gives rise to cold, precise prayers that are often reduced to formula and procedure. Too much emotion gives rise to emotionalism and blubbering, unreasonable outbursts of feelings.

Romanian Christians have learned the balance through their years of persecution and suffering. One of their "secrets" to knowing the mind of God is their great knowledge of Scripture. To ask a young Romanian Christian which verse he or she is memorizing would lead one to find which book he or she is memorizing. When they pray, they quote. But mixed with the intellectual ability to memorize is a freedom to pray with the emotions. They weep when praying for non-Christians. They rejoice when they thank God for his abundant blessings. And, through it all, they pray with hearts set on doing the will of God. One lesson to be learned from them is that if we desire to find God, we must pray with our intellect and our emotions.

A Romanian served as Sammy Tippit's interpreter for a series of evangelistic meetings in Bucharest. After one such meeting, the two men met for prayer and wept for the lost of that city. Later, they walked to the edge of the Danube

River and prayed some more. Writes Tippit, "I will never forget my friend lying prostrate on the ground, crying out to the Lord for his country, 'Oh, God, if it takes the blood of the martyrs to bring our country under the rule of Christ, then I gladly offer my blood, but, please, let your kingdom come and your will be done in the hearts of the Romanian people'"—a powerful example of prayer laden with emotion and undergirded with intellect.

—Sammy Tippit, *The Prayer Factor*
(Moody Press, 1988)

relentless

Physically, David Brainerd was about as weak as they come. But spiritually he was a dynamo of energy, a relentless man-of-arms in the battle of prayer. He died from consumption at an early age, but not early enough to stop him from going to the pre-settled forests of Northern Pennsylvania to work among the native peoples there. At times, when the snow was deep and the wind cold, Brainerd would go out into the forest, kneel in the snow, and labor with God in prayer. So intense was his praying that he would be wringing wet with sweat, despite the cold. God heard Brainerd; he sent a mighty revival among the Indians.

But Brainerd was also praying for his father-in-law—Jonathan Edwards—and God heard that prayer too. Edwards, one of the mightiest thinkers our nation has produced and the only metaphysician to be inducted into the American Hall of Fame, was so used by God that those who heard him preach ("Sinners in the Hands of an Angry God," for example) would literally cry to God for mercy. R. A. Torrey concludes, "Ah, that we had more men who could pray like Brainerd; then we would have more men who could preach like Edwards."

—R. A. Torrey, *The Power of Prayer* (Zondervan, 1975)

INTERCESSORY PRAYER (POWER OF)

just ask and believe

The Viet Cong (VC) were in no position to take wounded prisoners. Anyone who couldn't walk would probably be tortured to death—or just shot. Lying on the ground with useless legs, the major knew he had reached the end of the line.

Only a few minutes earlier he had been a passenger on a helicopter. Ground fire knocked them out of the sky, sending them careening into the trees below. When the major came to his senses, he realized he couldn't move because of his wounds. All around him were the cries of his comrades, also immobilized. The VC were moving in, the sound of rifle fire was clear. The major wanted to pray, but didn't know how. He had gone to church all his life, but realized for the first time that he had never really talked to God before. Suddenly, he "felt" someone say to him, "Just ask and believe!"

In anguish, he cried out, "Oh, God, please help me!" It was the first time he had talked to God, but even as the realization dawned, the VC moved closer.

Miles away, another army helicopter was flying back to base. The pilot of the chopper had a sudden, overwhelming urge to turn and go east. "But why?" he wondered. He was on his way north, and all the military rules he knew seemed to scream that a turn east was totally illogical. Nevertheless, he made the ninety-degree turn and headed east. Then he sensed an urge to fly low and slow. Again, military rules demanded either high and slow, or low and fast. He was a sitting duck for ground fire if he did that. Listening to the urging, he dropped to treetop level and began looking. He didn't know what he was looking for, but something was out there. There it was! He spotted the remains of a helicopter scattered over the jungle floor.

It could have been there for weeks for all he knew, but he wanted to check it out. The density of the jungle made it impossible to land, so a crewman was lowered via winch. When he got to the ground, he found the wounded men. One by one they lifted them up to safety, then the crewman hooked himself up and was pulled to safety. Just as he left the ground, the VC came into view and started firing. The pilot took off, and within minutes the wounded men were in the hospital.

The major, from his hospital bed, told that story to the army chaplain. When he finished he said, "Chaplain, I just wanted you to come and help me thank God for his goodness to me. I'm going to serve him the rest of my life."

—Chaplain (LTC) Merlin R.
Carothers, *Prison to Praise*
(Logos International, 1970)

from Russia with prayer

In April 1986, glasnost had its beginning. *Glasnost,* a Russian word denoting the new openness in the Soviet Union, was, in a sense, forced on the Kremlin by an incident at Chernobyl—a toxic leak at a nuclear power plant just outside the city of Kiev. Here's one example of how God was moving in that incident.

In May of that year, Dick Eastman was preparing to take a School of Prayer to Poland at the invitation of Mark Geppert, a Pittsburgh pastor. Six weeks before his departure, Mark announced a schedule change. "I'll meet you in Warsaw as planned, but first I'll be going to the Soviet Union for a month." When asked what he planned to do in the USSR, he replied, "God spoke to me a few days ago and told me I was to go to Russia to pray. He told me exactly where to go and what to pray about. I'm to pray that God will shake all of Russia. I'll ask him to use current events—whatever they are—to shake what can be shaken, so doors will open to the gospel and believers will have a new freedom to worship."

Geppert went, and Eastman continued his preparations. He didn't think too much more about Mark's itinerary until the shocking news of the Chernobyl nuclear accident began entering the West. He dug out Mark's schedule and began figuring. Mark's schedule called for a train ride that weekend that would take him right through the disaster area. He would leave Kiev on the evening of April 25, and pass close to Chernobyl in the early hours of April 26—the exact time of the nuclear plant's explosion.

When the two were finally reunited in Poland, Geppert told his story. He had spent four days of prayer in Kiev, ending on Friday, April 25. "I went to the square in the center of Kiev and sat down under a huge statue of Lenin. Every fifteen minutes I changed the focus of my intercession for believers in Russia. I could tell when a fifteen-minute period passed because there was a gigantic clock in the square that let out a bong each quarter hour. On the last day, the day I made my final prayer visit to the city square . . . I was suddenly convinced God had heard and that even then something was happening. Something that would shake the Soviet Union. Something God would use to bring more freedom. I began to lift my voice in praise, sitting there underneath the statue of the founder of communism in Russia. But at the same time I needed a confirmation that God had heard me, so I cried out to him: 'O God, give me a sign, even a little sign.' I waited, wondering what might happen next. And just then in the distance the hands of the huge clock moved into the twelve o'clock position." Geppert explained that every day at that time, the clock would issue twelve loud gongs. "I waited for twelve chimes, but they never came. It was as if God was saying an old pattern was over. The very next day I began hearing about Chernobyl."

Later, according to Eastman, closer study was made of the plant's meltdown. Scientists determined that the first major mistake happened twelve hours before the actual meltdown, putting it within minutes of Geppert's declaration of praise.

—Dick Eastman, *Love on Its Knees*
(Fleming H. Revell Co., 1989)

the old stump

The almost four hundred men in the military's air wing in post-war Germany seemed to have no desire for things religious. The young chaplain assigned to the wing felt discouraged, a sense of failure. One morning, after a low turnout to chapel, he took his despair with him into the forest and fell on his knees in prayer by an old stump. He poured out his heart to God and asked what he might do. "Go to the PX where the men are, and I will show you what to do," God seemed to say. So he went.

The PX was filled with men, smoke, and the smell of stale beer. Across the milling crowd, the chaplain spied a young pilot in a corner. In his hand was a letter. On his face was a look of despair. "Go and sit down by that man," he heard God say. He obeyed.

He said nothing. Eventually, the letter was handed over. His wife wanted a divorce. She had met another man; she was tired of waiting for her pilot-husband.

The chaplain began telling of his own grief. He told about the small attendance, his own despair, how he went to the old stump to pray, and how God told him to come to the PX and look for someone who might need him.

When he finished, there were tears in the pilot's eyes. "I guess that is the way I feel, too, only I feel like a failure as a man and as a husband. Why don't we go out to the old stump together? Possibly if we pray together we will both find out what to do." Together they went and kneeled in the forest. The pilot got direction on how to treat his wife and the man who stole her love. When they were finished, the chaplain asked the pilot to come by his office the next morning.

He showed up with two friends, both looking for answers to their own personal pain. Two mornings later there were eight. By week's end, so many tried to crowd into the tiny office that they had to find a larger room. Three weeks later, three hundred men attended his service of holy communion. Before long, the air wing became famous all over Europe for the dynamic Christian quality and commitment of its men. From one man praying to three hundred men in service to the Lord. That's the power of intercession.

—Helen Smith Shoemaker,
Power Through Prayer Groups
(Fleming H. Revell Co., 1958)

the secret

One man carried a secret with him for years. He was a missionary in a land known for its diseases. When he returned, he met with an old friend, and the two of them spent an evening in discussion. The friend, knowing of the difficulties the missionaries faced in that land, asked him how he had fared with the fever.

The missionary hemmed and hawed, not wanting to divulge his secret, but the friend persisted. He gave in. "When I was about to sail for the mission field, I naturally went around to my friends in my home community to say good-bye. In this connection I called on an elderly believing woman in a tenant household. As I bid her good-bye, she clung to my hand and, looking me calmly in the eye, said quietly, 'I am going to pray to God for you and ask him to save you from the fever in order that you may devote all your strength to your work out there.'"

With tears of joy in his eyes, the missionary concluded, "And I have not felt the fever once during all these years." Though that elderly woman could not go, she was able to do an incredible work for God's kingdom, even though she was thousands of miles away.

—O. Hallesby, *Prayer*

advice not allowed

The phrase "I've been praying for you" often signals the onslaught of unasked-for advice and the raining down of solutions (unsolicited) with the fury and intensity of an April shower. One man discovered an alternative when he overheard a conversation between friends. "I've been praying for you," said the one. The other replied tersely, "Thanks, but tell me—what did you pray for? Hope you're not like some of my friends who tell me they have a pipeline to heaven and tell God exactly what I ought to do. The problem is that they all have conflicting guidance. If I followed them I'd go off in all directions." The other, sensing the obvious hostility, said, "The conviction I get as I pray for you is that God loves you very much, knows the bind you're in, and will not leave you or forsake you."

Later, when the hostile one was ready to talk and deal with his problem, whom did he call? The one who showed him sensitivity. After talking for a long time and finally spelling out what he thought the solution might be, his friend gently responded, "I think you're on target. That fits with what I've sensed the Lord is trying to say in your need."

—Lloyd John Ogilvie,
You Can Pray with Power

set free

The man's alcohol addiction made him abusive to wife and family. When he brought his friends over to drink one evening, it was the final straw. "Dear, I love you, but I cannot take your drinking," said his wife. "Now you are bringing these drunks home with you. I will not stand for it. I am going to pack my bags and leave. Tomorrow when you wake up, I shall not be here. Good-bye!"

It was a rather sobering speech. Knowing she was a devoted Christian, the man knelt before her and cried, "Lord, please deliver me from the terrible spirit of alcohol!" As if drunkenness wasn't enough, now she thought he was mocking her religion. She had heard his promises to quit drinking so often it had no effect on her anymore. As she prepared to leave, he became even more desperate. As he wept, he seemed to hear a voice deep inside him say, "You will be set free by morning."

"I know for sure that by tomorrow I will be totally delivered," he told his wife. It was obvious by the look in her face that she didn't believe this latest con-job, but because of her love, she gave him one more chance. Imagine her surprise when the next morning all his cigarettes and alcohol were gone. In the factory that day, he told all the employees he had been freed from his affliction. They dared not laugh openly but assumed this was just another snow job. As time went on, however, it seemed to be true: the man was changed. According to the author, the family is now serving Jesus and attends church regularly.

—Paul Yonggi Cho, *Prayer: Key to Revival* (Word Books, 1984)

message received

At the height of the Welsh revival, a Welsh missionary wrote home begging the people to pray that India might experience a similar revival. So the coal miners met for a half hour each day at the mouth of the coal pit to pray for their friend overseas. In a few weeks' time, the message came through, "The blessing has come."

missionary tactic

In Korea, a few missionaries met daily to pray. At the end of a month, nothing had happened, so one man proposed disbanding. "We should pray more, not less," was the response of the others. So they prayed another four months. Suddenly, the blessing began to pour forth. Church services were broken up by confession and weeping over sins. Multitudes flocked to the churches—some out of curiosity, some to mock, some in search of peace. But all were touched by the hand of God. One notorious rogue, the leader of a robber band, attended and was converted. He immediately went to the police chief and turned himself in. Since there was no law in Korea to deal with those who had no accuser, he was dismissed! One missionary remarked: "It paid well to have spent several months in prayer, for when God gave the Holy Spirit, he accomplished more in half a day than all the missionaries together could have accomplished in half a year."

—*The Kneeling Christian*
(Zondervan, 1971)

physically frail, spiritually strong

Marianne Adlard was a young, bedridden girl in London. After reading some of the accomplishments of Dwight L. Moody, she began to pray that he would be sent to her church. In 1872 Moody took his second trip to London but did not intend to do any work. He met Marianne's pastor, however, and he asked him to come and preach. After the service Moody asked if anyone wanted to decide for Christ. Hundreds stood up. Shocked at the response, Moody asked again. They all stood up a second time. Four hundred people were received into that church over the next ten days. A burning desire to know who was behind all this caused Moody to search. That's when he found Marianne Adlard. "I began making inquiries and never rested until I found a bedridden girl praying that God would bring me to that church. He had heard her, and brought me over four thousand miles of land and sea at her request."

—Frank C. Laubach, *Prayer:
The Mightiest Force in the World*
(Spire Books, 1959)

intercessor-watchmen

Hundreds of thousands of people received salvation as a result of the work of Charles G. Finney. But there were two lesser-known men who also played a part in his work; they were Father Clery and Father Nash.

When Finney went to Britain for several weeks for meetings, these two elderly men accompanied him. They did not delve into public relations, did not sit on the podium behind Finney, did not head up crowd control, and did not offer public prayers. What they did was far more important. The found a dark, damp basement room for twenty-five cents a week and stayed there on their knees, prevailing in prayer. With tears and groans, they interceded for Finney's work; they were his intercessor-watchmen.

—Wesley L. Duewel, *Touch the World
Through Prayer* (Zondervan, 1986)

In New Zealand, a man excitedly showed his guest his prayer room. "You see, I am now retired and can spend my whole day in prayer. I wash and shave, have my breakfast, and then spend my hours in this room." He kept a large loose-leaf notebook filled with pictures of missionaries, national coworkers, maps of various nations, and other items. "You see, every day I go around the world in prayer." What eternal dividends he will collect in heaven on his investment in prayer!

don't roast the pastor

In a Cornish parish of the Church of England was a vicar lacking salvation. His interest was not in the real things of God, but in restoring old churches and the beauty of the rituals. Some of the people in the church began to pray for his salvation. Each Sunday morning they would go to church and see if their prayers had been answered yet. One Lord's Day, as he rose to speak, those who had been praying realized he was a changed man. "The parson's converted!" they shouted. He was converted and endued with a power from on high. God used that pastor for many years in England to bring people to himself.

In Hartford, Connecticut, was a brilliant pastor. But his doctrine was far from sound. Three godly men recognized the problem, and, instead of spreading stories or talking about him in his absence, they covenanted together to pray each Saturday night for their pastor. Long into the night, Saturday after Saturday, they would pray. One Sunday morning as the pastor got up to preach, they knew their prayers had been answered. He was still the brilliant pastor, but his heart and doctrine were sound. Prayer for ministers will accomplish far more than a verbal "roasting" ever could.

—R. A. Torrey, *The Power of Prayer* (Zondervan, 1975)

there's a cost

Intercessory prayer is serious business. It often means putting your life on the line for others. With the prayer comes action, action that may cost in time, money, and pain.

Steve has been battling multiple sclerosis for almost thirty years. At times the pain is so bad that he cannot sleep. Specialists are unable to locate or determine the reason for the pain, yet the pain throbs on. Yet Steve is not a bitter man, not a twisted shell of a man who dwells on his own bad fortune. Steve is an intercessor, one who considers it his special privilege to come before the throne of mercy on behalf of others. His friends recognize that. They have a brain-injured son who demands much time and energy. Rarely a day—or night—goes by without Steve's

intercession. But along with those prayers is a genuine display of concern. When the parents of that child are at their wits' end, Steve and his wife gladly take the child home with them for a time. When that child needed large amounts of money to go to a special school, Steve and his wife organized a fund drive and contributed greatly of their own without telling a soul. Steve knows what intercession means— and costs.

—William C. Brownson, *Courage to Pray* (Baker Book House, 1989)

it's all in the attitude

God does have the best interests of his children in mind. Carl's twenty-two-year-old son left home and was living with a bunch of guys just outside of town. Carl knew his son had been doing drugs before he left, and now Carl heard that he was a drug dealer. His two main concerns were that his son would come home and not get arrested, so that's what he prayed for.

While praying one morning, Carl realized how selfish his requests were. He was quite well known in town and was afraid an arrest would tarnish his reputation. So he prayed, "Lord, if the only way to deliver my son from this sin is to allow him to be arrested, then I'm willing for that to happen—even at the expense of my reputation." A few days later the police called. His son had been arrested for the possession of illegal drugs. As Carl drove to the station to pick up his son, he realized God had been waiting for him to have the right attitude before allowing his son to go home. God honored that obedience. Together they rebuilt their fractured home. The next time the son left, it was to study for the ministry.

—Charles F. Stanley, *Handle with Prayer* (Victor Books, 1982)

unplugged

One day my husband walked out of the sanctuary of our church and encountered our custodian fairly dripping with perspiration. He was a giant of a Christian, but was gradually losing his ability to think and work effectively because of hardening of the arteries. As my husband saw him struggling with the vacuum cleaner he looked down, and there lying on the floor was the plug. The dear man had vacuumed the whole auditorium and didn't have the plug in the outlet!

Isn't that what happens to many of us? We work, we pull, we struggle, and we plan until we're utterly exhausted, but we have forgotten to plug into the source of power. And that source of power is prayer—the "effectual, fervent prayer" of a righteous person that avails much.

—Evelyn Christenson, *What Happens When Women Pray* (Victor Books, 1989)

John of Cronstadt, a nineteenth-century Russian priest, said, "Why has our sincere prayer for each other such great power over others? Because of the fact that by cleaving to God during prayer I become one spirit with him, and unite with myself by faith, and love, those for whom I pray; for the Holy Ghost acting in me also acts at the same time in them, for he accomplishes all things."

across the seas

For an entire two-week span, Wesley Duewel felt compelled to pray for his son in America. "I was alone in the house, so lost in prayer for him that for a while I did not notice the passing of time or the existence of space. As I prayed on and on it suddenly seemed that I was kneeling beside John with my hand on his shoulder, praying for him. I know not how long I prayed, or what I said, but I know my arm of prayer had spanned the land and oceans for thousands of miles, and my hand was on John's shoulder. It was as real as if I were by his side. Then assurance came, and I rose from my knees and later gave my Sunday evening message."

Other duties kept Duewel from writing his son till the following day. In his letter he began explaining the peculiar events of the previous day, when suddenly, in the middle of paragraph number two, a telegram arrived. "God is my captain," it began. His son had given his heart to Jesus Christ during the exact time that Duewel had been in prayer for his soul.

—Wesley L. Duewel, *Touch the World Through Prayer* (Zondervan, 1986)

molders of destiny

Rees Howells showed that God is vitally concerned for the way history flows and that he responds to prayer on the global scale. During World War II, Howells and those in the college where he taught spent a Saturday afternoon in prayer regarding the war in North Africa. After a long struggle with prayer, they came through to victory. "I thought Hitler might be allowed to take Egypt," said Howells, "but I know now he will never take Egypt—neither Alexandria nor Cairo will fall." At the end of the meeting he said, "I have been stirred to my depths today. I have been like a man plowing his way through sand. But now I am on top of it, now I am gripping it; I am handling it. I can shake it."

At the same time, miraculous events were transpiring in Egypt. The city of Alexandria was the prize—held by the British, wanted by the Germans. Involved in the battle was Major Rainer, whose responsibility it was to supply the Eighth Army with water and who gave the account of what happened. Rommel, the Desert Fox, was moving his troops ever closer to Alexandria. What lay between him and the city were exhausted British troops, fifty tanks, and a few field guns. The Germans had far superior firepower. Both sides were exhausted from the heat and dehydration.

"The sun was almost overhead," wrote Rainer in *Pipe Line to Battle*, "and our men were fast reaching the end of their endurance, when the Nazis broke. Ten minutes more and it might have been us. Suddenly the Mark IV tanks lumbered back from the battle smoke. And then an incredible thing happened: eleven hundred men of the 90th Light Panzer Division, the elite of the German Africa Korps, came stumbling across the barren sand with their hands in the air. Cracked and black with coagulated blood, their swollen tongues were protruding from their mouths. Crazily they tore water bottles from the necks of our men and poured life-giving swallows between their parched lips."

Rainer goes on to explain the unexpected surrender. The Germans had gone about twenty-four hours without water. While they continued to fight and run over British positions, they were overjoyed to find a six-inch water line. Desperate for water, they shot holes in it and drank the liquid as it gushed out. Their thirst was such that no one realized they were drinking seawater.

Rainer was the one in charge of the pipeline. Wanting to test it one more time, he used seawater rather than precious fresh water. "The day before it would have been empty. Two days later," added Rainer, "it would have been fresh water." Because of the Nazi's extreme thirst, their familiarity with brackish water, and the heat, they didn't detect the salt. Had Howells not responded to God's urgent call for prayer, things could have been very different. Prayers uttered by intercessors often shape destiny.

—Dick Eastman, *No Easy Road* (Baker Book House)

x-rated

They were all members of the local Right to Life chapter, and they all shared a common desire to see their community remain morally clean. So it's no wonder that their ire was raised when a local bar announced plans to introduce a striptease as part of its entertainment.

First, they besieged city hall with phone calls; then they began calling all the churches in their small, northern California town. Then, following a plan laid forth by a group called Christian Family Renewal, they would contact city, state, and federal government officials. Finally, they would seek to influence the legislative processes. But none of that was necessary. Even though no one spoke to the owner of the bar, he suddenly decided to get out of town, and the new owner wasn't interested in that type of entertainment. A quiet but significant victory had been won by prayer alone.

—Douglas F. Kelly, *Why Pray?* (Wolgemuth & Hyatt, 1989)

LISTENING TO GOD IN PRAYER

a lesson on rewards

An old missionary couple had been working in Africa for years and were returning to New York City to retire. They had no pension; their health was broken; they were defeated, discouraged, and afraid. They discovered they were booked on the same ship as President Teddy Roosevelt, who was returning from one of his big-game hunting expeditions.

No one paid any attention to them. They watched the fanfare that accompanied the president's entourage, with passengers trying to catch a glimpse of the great man.

As the ship moved across the ocean, the old missionary said to his wife, "Something is wrong. Why should we have given our lives in faithful service for God in Africa all these many years and have no one care a thing about us? Here this man comes back from a hunting trip and everybody makes much over him, but nobody gives two hoots about us."

"Dear, you shouldn't feel that way," his wife said.

"I can't help it; it doesn't seem right."

When the ship docked in New York, a band was waiting to greet the president. The mayor and other dignitaries were there. The papers were full of stories about the president's arrival, but no one noticed this missionary couple. They slipped off the ship and found a cheap flat on the East Side, hoping the next day to see what they could do to make a living in the city.

That night the man's spirit broke. He said to his wife, "I can't take this; God is not treating us fairly."

His wife replied, "Why don't you go in the bedroom and tell that to the Lord?"

A short time later he came out from the bedroom, but now his face was completely different. His wife asked, "Dear, what happened?"

"The Lord settled it with me," he said. "I told him how bitter I was that the president should receive this tremendous homecoming, when no one met us as we returned home. And when I finished, it seemed as though the Lord put his hand on my shoulder and simply said, 'But you're not home yet!'"

Yes, there are rewards for faithfulness, but not necessarily here.

—Ray Stedman, *Talking to My Father*

reconciled!

In his book *You Can Pray with Power*, Lloyd John Ogilvie tells of a misunderstanding with a friend that deteriorated their relationship to nothing.

Ogilvie, feeling no desire to forgive or reconcile the relationship, decided to just forget the whole mess. "Some weeks later, an uneasiness began to grow in me. I couldn't shake the man out of my mind. That was followed by a mysterious desire to pray about him." Following his urges, Ogilvie turned to prayer. Almost immediately, his attitude took a turn for the better; new empathy for the causes behind the man's behavior and the man's unspoken needs became clear. As he continued to pray, asking for guidance on how best to patch up the relationship, a strategy began to form. It became obvious to Ogilvie that the plan was from the Lord, thus enabling him to ask for help with great boldness. He implemented the plan and it worked. Of course it worked. "The Lord was initiator and inspiration from start to finish."

Ogilvie goes on to tell how prayer has helped him with decisions in life. Confronted with two options, he chose one that left him feeling hollow, lost, on the wrong path. "There was a jangling static in my spirit. It lasted for days. When sleep was interrupted by the disturbance, I knew something was very wrong." This time, Ogilvie decided to pray before making his decision. He asked the Lord to be very clear about what he should do. If the disturbance was from on high, he asked "that it continue and grow." But if his previous decision was right, he asked that "the disturbance be taken away." The trauma became almost unbearable, leading him to pray, "Lord, now I know I'm on the wrong track. Show me what you want me to do." After a few more hours in prayer, Ogilvie reversed his prior decision and was almost immediately flooded with inner calm and confidence.

the vision

While praying in her simple, country home, Bolette Hinderli experienced an inner vision of a man in prison. She saw his face as clearly as the reader sees the type on this page. "This man will share the same fate as other criminals if no one takes up the work of praying for him," she heard the accompanying inner voice say. "Pray for him, and I will send him out to proclaim my praises among the heathen."

For months Bolette prayed. And each day she would scan newspapers and listen to testimonies of converted Christians. She hoped to someday hear of someone who was converted in prison.

Much later, during a trip to a city in Norway, Bolette heard that a former prisoner, now a Christian, would be speaking that night in a local church. She sat in the pew waiting for the message. Then Lars Olsen Skrefsrud, the guest speaker, walked to the small pulpit. Immediately she recognized him—the face was the face of the man she had seen in her vision. Without question, it was he for whom she had been praying.

—Dick Eastman, *The Hour that Changes the World* (Baker Book House, 1978)

listening and loving

It is impossible to distinguish between listening and loving. Consider the parents of a newborn. It's the middle of the night, and the baby starts crying. Previous experience has told the parent that it's probably nothing serious. Maybe a little dampness, maybe a dream, a little cold; nothing that desperately needs the parent's immediate attention. The parent has also learned that if he or she does not go immediately, the crying will eventually subside and everyone can sleep again. Yet why is it that when the baby starts crying in the middle of the night, the parent swiftly climbs out of bed to comfort that baby? The answer is love.

If human parents respond in such a way, think how our Father in heaven must feel when we, his children, cry out. It is impossible to distinguish between listening and loving.

Philippians 4:19 in vivid color

The author of *The Christian's Secret of a Happy Life* had a friend who would visit her for two to three days at a time. She found her visits a time of terrible testing. Prayer was necessary before she came. At one point, this "friend" announced her plans to come for an entire week. The woman felt that nothing but an entire evening in prayer would do to fortify her for this great testing. So with a plate of bread, she entered her bedroom and knelt in prayer. No sooner had she knelt when the verse "God shall supply all your needs according to his riches in glory by Christ Jesus" popped into her head. "When I realized that, I gave him thanks and praised him for his goodness. Then I jumped into bed and slept the night through. My guest arrived the next day, and I quite enjoyed her visit."

—*The Kneeling Christian* (Zondervan, 1971)

an audible voice

Tony Guest was a nominal Christian at best. His brother, a devout Christian, gave him a J. B. Phillips translation of the Bible to take home and read, but it was shelved for weeks. Then one day Tony got the urge to read. He skimmed through chapter 1 of Matthew, then dug into the narrative telling of Jesus' birth and early ministry. When he

was halfway through the Sermon on the Mount, he heard a voice say, "Jesus is my Son, you know."

He looked around. The kids were playing quietly in the other room, his wife was in the kitchen. It was obvious that they hadn't heard the voice. Tony went upstairs and knelt by his bed to pray. As he prayed, his life passed before his eyes, and he wept at all the wasted years. Suddenly he knew that Jesus was God's Son and that everything apart from Jesus was meaningless.

—John Guest, *Only a Prayer Away* (Servant Publications, 1985)

right on time

In 1969, while preaching at a revival in Virginia, Charles Stanley felt compelled to pray. He returned to his room early after each night's meetings and prayed on his knees. One night he took out some paper and drew a circle with five lines leading from it. At the end of each line, he wrote a word that he thought the Lord may have been impressing on him. On the fifth line he put a question mark, expecting another word later. The next night the word came. He felt the Spirit telling him that God was going to move him. He asked when, and the Lord made it clear that it would be in September. That September, Stanley began pastoring the First Baptist Church of Atlanta.

"Sometimes he shows me something for today and sometimes he shows me something that will happen the next week or the next month. But I've never been to God about anything he did not willingly answer. He does not always answer my prayers according to my time schedule, but he is always on time."

—Charles F. Stanley, *Handle with Prayer* (Victor Books, 1982)

MIRACLES THROUGH PRAYER

the miracle girl

The voice on the other end of the line was anxious. "My wife just had a paralyzing stroke!" Ned's wife, Laura, not yet forty, was unable to move. Ned called the ambulance. Then he called the pastor to activate the prayer chain. The pastor got the prayer chain going—more than fifty people in all—then drove to the hospital. They prayed and laid hands on Laura. The pastor left to preach, but returned as soon as he could. When he walked into the hospital, he was met by Ned, who quickly led him into his wife's room. She was sitting up in bed, dressed, wearing a smile, and able to greet people with her once paralyzed voice. Not only that but she could walk. The paralysis had left her! For the previous few hours, hospital administration, heads of staff, and doctors all rushed in to see the unbelievable sight. After a few days of careful observation, she was home perfectly well.

—Donald M. Hulstrand, *The Praying Church* (The Seabury Press, 1977)

heaven's royal engineers

Dan Crawford had just returned to the mission field after a furlough and was in a hurry to get to his station. But a deep stream, flooded by heavy rains, made crossing impossible. No boats were available, and there was no other way. So they camped there by the banks of the river and prayed. As they prayed, a tall tree that had been waging war against deteriorating banks for years suddenly began to totter and fall. It fell right across the stream, providing a perfect, natural bridge. "The royal engineers of heaven had laid a pontoon bridge for God's servants," stated Crawford.

—*The Kneeling Christian* (Zondervan, 1971)

money matters

R. A. Torrey relates the following story:

"One day in Northfield, Mass., I received word from Chicago from Mr. Fitt, Mr. Moody's son-in-law, saying that we needed five thousand dollars at once for the work in Chicago, and asking me to pray for it. Another member of the faculty of the Bible Institute was in Northfield at that time, and that night we went out into a summer-house on my place and knelt down and prayed to God to send that money. God gave my friend great confidence that he had heard the prayer, and my friend said to me, 'God has heard the prayer and the five thousand dollars will come.' A telegram came the next day from Indianapolis saying five thousand dollars had been deposited in a bank in Indianapolis to our account and was waiting our order. Though we had prayed and expected, Mr. Fitt could hardly believe it when he heard it. He sent down to our bank in Chicago and they made inquiry to the bank in Indianapolis to see if it were true. They found out that it was."

—R. A. Torrey, *The Power of Prayer* (Zondervan, 1975)

incredible sight

The couple's oldest son was legally blind in one eye. With glasses and concentration, though, he was able to read and get along fairly normally. Then, in the seventh grade, his good eye was seriously damaged by a racquetball. Now his parents faced the prospect of having a son with permanently impaired vision.

The boy was out of school for a few days and could hardly watch television. His parents alerted many friends, relatives, and prayer chains, and all began praying. There was even a group of inmates in the local jail who prayed for their son. Then they took him to the optometrist, who took X rays and so on. When he came out to give his analysis, the doctor said, "There seems to be nothing wrong! There was a little scarring, but that was all!"

"What were the results of the exam?" she asked.

"They were fine!"

"But yesterday he could hardly see. How could it happen so fast? People have been praying, but . . ."

"Sometimes," said the doctor, "that is what will do the trick."

—Douglas F. Kelly, *Why Pray?* (Wolgemuth & Hyatt, 1989)

MISSIONS AND PRAYER

the "secret" to his success

Yohann Lee, overseas director of World Literature Crusade, is a Korean Christian who was born in China to missionary parents. As director of an overseas ministry, Lee has seen more than eight million written decisions for Christ. When asked what he attributes these extraordinary results to, Lee says, "The prayers of the saints directly affect the proportion and degree of the Holy Spirit's power over a newborn babe in Christ. Prayer is where it all begins and where it all ends." A. T. Pierson adds, "Every step in the progress of missions is directly traceable to prayer. It has been the preparation for every new triumph and the secret of all success."

—Dick Eastman, *The Hour that Changes the World* (Baker Book House, 1978)

coincidence?

In 1886, the few members of the fledgling China Inland Mission gathered at a conference. It was agreed that no fewer than one hundred new missionaries were needed. As they discussed this almost impossible challenge, someone said, "Is anything too hard for God?" The company turned to passionate, earnest intercession. As they prayed, they were seized with the conviction that their prayers would be answered. That very year saw a marked increase in the number of people who stepped forward or expressed interest in the China Inland Mission. Before the year ended, one hundred new missionaries had been sent out. Other mission agencies also testify to such "coincidences."

—Donald G. Bloesch, *The Struggle of Prayer* (Harper & Row Publishers, 1980)

MISUSE OF PRAYER

misplaced dependence

The elderly woman's reputation was that of a prayer warrior. Her path to becoming one, however, was painful indeed. Early in her adult life, she was widowed and left with a son. She decided that he was going to be one of the finest Christian young men ever, so she began reading books on how to raise children, she sent him to the best schools, and spent great chunks of time with him. "But," she said in a voice laced with tears, "I hardly ever prayed for him." Her son committed suicide at age twenty-five.

"Only then did I see that I had depended too much on myself and not enough on God." That lesson has taught her the supreme importance of including God in everything. It taught her not to focus on her own feeble strength, but on God's might and omnipotence! She recognized that we are mortal and God is Sovereign; our destinies lie in his hands.

—Richard L. Pratt, Jr., *Pray with Your Eyes Open* (Baker Book House, 1987)

PRAYER PARTNERS

the Lewis Awakening

The Lewis Awakening, also known as the Hebrides Revival, had humble beginnings in these Scottish isles. Two elderly women (one was eighty-four years old and blind, the other eighty-two years old and afflicted with arthritis), in the village of Barvas on the island of Lewis, agreed to pray nightly for a revival in their community. Night after night they prayed and interceded. After some time, unknown to them, a group of young men began praying on the other end of town. As the ladies prayed, God revealed to them that the Rev. Duncan Campbell, minister of the Church of Scotland and one-time principal of the Faith Mission Training Home and Bible College in Edinburgh, would come to Barvas to lead them. They wrote him, but he cordially declined, saying his schedule was too busy. They responded, "You may say you will not come, but God says you are coming!"

Some time later, at a British convention, the local pastor suggested that Campbell come for special meetings. Thus, in December of 1949, Duncan Campbell finally reached the Hebrides to lead a series of meetings. It was then that God's awesome power fell on the village, bringing conviction of sin and revival. The power spread from village to village from 1949 to 1953, transforming the very life of the community. It was not unusual for people to be sitting in their homes and suddenly be overwhelmed by the Holy Spirit. They would fall on their faces in disgust over their sins and weep in repentance. There were times when the revival spirit was so powerful that shops would be closed and church services would last several hours or even days. Prayer meetings became the norm in many of the communities. From everything known about the revival—in human terms—the whole thing began with two elderly women on their knees before God.

—Wesley L. Duewel, *Touch the World Through Prayer* (Zondervan, 1986)

the missing ingredient

In 1941 OMS International began its work in India. The first twenty-five years of hard work showed little fruit; perhaps one new church started each year. When Wesley Duewel left India in 1964 for furlough, he was praying on the plane and felt compelled by God to recruit a thousand prayer partners to pray for fifteen minutes each day for the work in India.

Some years later, Duewel was back in Allahabad, India, with a senior leader during a day of prayer. "All of us are seeing results beyond anything we have known," he said. "Are you surprised?"

"Yes. Praise the Lord," responded Duewel.

"You ought not to be! Did you not go to America and get a thousand people to pray fifteen minutes a day for us?"

"More than that."

"Then why are you surprised?"

"Thank you, George," said Duewel. "I needed that reminder. Why should we be surprised when God answers prayer!"

Duewel said their churches now number about three hundred with some twenty-five thousand believers and twenty-five or more new churches established each year. "One thousand prayer warriors united in praying for harvest was the secret!"

—Wesley L. Duewel, *Touch the World Through Prayer* (Zondervan, 1986)

unplanned reunion

Wesley Duewel recounts the joy he received from a prayer partner in this incident:

"While traveling on a bus in Northern Ireland years ago, I was praying for my meeting to be held that night in a rural town. As I hungered to enlist more prayer support for India, I was inspired to write a poem. I became so absorbed with my writing that I was unaware of the passing scenery or my traveling companions. Suddenly I was startled to hear my name called. Looking up, I found a woman standing in the aisle. 'I just happened to notice you sitting here,' she said. 'I recognized you from a picture in your missionary paper, and just wanted to tell you that, for the past eighteen years, I have been praying for you every day, and especially for your wife, Betty.' Tears sprang to my eyes as I realized that God had graciously allowed me to meet one who had invested in prayer for me and my family."

—Wesley L. Duewel, *Touch the World Through Prayer* (Zondervan, 1986)

PERSEVERANCE IN PRAYER

divine appointment

Father John Bertolucci sensed the Lord telling him to pick up the hitchhiker. While they were driving along the New York freeway, the young man told Father John about his life, his wanderings, and his need to return to the Lord. He also said that his mother had been praying for him for years. "She even sent me some tapes by an Italian priest. . . ."

"An Italian priest?" asked Father John. "Do you know his name?"

"Oh—I don't know—Bar—Buto—something or other."

"Bertolucci?" said the priest.

"Yeah, that's it," replied the young man.

By the time the young man was dropped off at his exit, he had given his life to Jesus Christ. Father John deserves some of the credit, but the real credit lay with the man's mother. Her prayers were powerful, and God answered them.

—Ann Shields, *God Answers Prayer* (Servant Publications, 1984)

an example

Years ago, a man in New Jersey was condemned to hang. No influence or pressure could convince the governor to issue the condemned man a reprieve. Finally, the man's wife and their ten children went to see the governor. They fell on their faces before him and pleaded for him to have mercy on the husband. His heart was moved, and he immediately granted reprieve.

—D. L. Moody, *Prevailing Prayer* (Moody Press)

a ferocious pounding

"Ask and it will be given to you; seek and you will find; knock and the door will be opened to you."—Luke 11:9

No feeble scratch or gentle tap on the door for this woman. Hers was a ferocious, calculated, persistent pounding. And she was heard. Her husband was an unbeliever and forbade any talk of things religious in the house. But she could talk to God. She covenanted to plead her husband's case for twelve months.

When it was over and he showed no sign of yielding, she decided to give it another six months. Every day she went alone and prayed for his conversion. The six months passed and still no sign of repentance. "Should I give up on him?" she thought. "No," she said. "I will pray for him as long as God gives me breath." On that very day, her husband came home from work and instead of sitting down for supper, went up to the bedroom. She waited, and waited, and waited. Finally, she climbed the stairs and peeked inside. There he was on the floor, weeping. God convicted him of sin. Not only was he convicted, he was changed; and he went on to be used of God in a mighty way in that corner of England.

—D. L. Moody, *Prevailing Prayer* (Moody Press)

persistence pays

The father felt a tremendous burden to pray for his backslidden son. His son used to be a missionary, but of late had drifted far from the Lord, was unrepentant, and showed no signs of remorse. The father, at meetings in a distant state, became so burdened one day for his son that he asked to be excused from the meetings so that he could pray. Hour after hour he prayed. In the afternoon came a knock. "Sorry to disturb you," said the hostess, "but there's a long-distance call for you." The father went to the phone, and the first words he heard were: "Dad! I've come back to the Lord!"

—Wesley L. Duewel, *Touch the World Through Prayer* (Zondervan, 1986)

knocking on heaven's door

Dwight L. Moody was sensing a lack of power at some meetings in a city, so he called together all the mothers and asked them to meet to pray for their children. About fifteen hundred mothers came to pray for their kids. A widowed mother said, "I wish you would pray for my two boys. They have gone off on a drunken spree; and it seems as if my heart would break." A few of the other ladies gathered around and said, "Let's have a prayer meeting for these boys." They cried to God for the souls of her sons, then waited to see what God would do.

The boys' itinerary for that evening wasn't exactly wholesome. They were going to meet at the corner where the Christian meetings were being held, then head off for a wild evening of drinking and sin. The one brother got there early, and seeing all the people go into the meeting, decided to go in for a short time to warm up. The Word of God cut through him while standing in the doorway, and he gave his heart to the Savior.

Meanwhile, the second brother was waiting outside. A youth meeting was being held in a church nearby, and he decided to see what it was all about. The Word of God cut through him, like it did his brother, and he too gave his heart to the Savior.

While that was happening, the first son went home to tell his mother the good news. He found her on her knees, knocking at the mercy seat. In the middle of her intercession, he walked in and declared her prayers answered. A short time later, the second son did too.

—D. L. Moody, *Prevailing Prayer* (Moody Press)

two crowns

Two Christian women with unbelieving husbands agreed to spend one hour together each day in prayer for their salvation. They kept that up for seven years, then asked, "Is this really worth it? Our prayers seem useless." They decided to continue praying till the day they died. Three years later, one of the ladies was awakened in the middle of the night by her husband who was in great distress because of sin. In the morning, she couldn't get to her friend's house fast enough to tell her what had happened, but met her halfway on the same errand! "Ten years of united, persevering prayer was crowned with the conversion of both husbands on the same day."

—D. L. Moody, *Prevailing Prayer* (Moody Press)

just a matter of time

In 1844, George Müller told how he felt a conviction to pray for five individuals. Eighteen months passed before a single conversion. He prayed five more years before the second was converted. At the end of twelve-and-a-half years, the third obtained salvation. Forty years later, the other two were still holding out, but Müller said he was happy to continue praying. He believed it was just a matter of time.

memories of a saint

Charles Finney's memories of Able Clary:

"He had been licensed to preach; but . . . he was so burdened with the souls of men that he was not able to preach much, his whole time and strength being given to prayer. The burden of his soul would frequently be so great that he was unable to stand, and he would writhe and groan in agony. I was well acquainted with him, and knew something of the wonderful spirit of prayer that was upon him. He was a very silent man, as almost all are who have that powerful spirit of prayer."

Finney's comments on Clary's work in Rochester, N.Y.:

"The first I knew of his being in Rochester, a gentleman who lived about a mile west of the city called on me one day and asked me if I knew Mr. Able Clary, a minister. I told him that I knew him well. 'Well,' he said, 'he is at my house, and has been there for some time, and I don't know what to think of him. I have not seen him at any of our meetings. He prays nearly all the time, day and night, and in such agony of mind that I do not even know what to make of it. Sometimes he cannot even stand on his knees, but will lie prostrate on the floor, and groan and pray in a manner that quite astonishes me.'" Finney told him it was all right. "It will all come out right; he will surely prevail."

—R. A. Torrey, *The Power of Prayer* (Zondervan, 1975)

a rare work ethic

He wasn't a cleric; he was a layman. But that didn't stop him from taking a short sabbatical in the Abbey of San Georgio Maggiore, which is located on an island in the bay outside of Venice, Italy.

He found himself wandering the dark halls and corridors one evening. As he rounded a bend in the ever-twisting passageways, he came upon a solitary figure, kneeling in prayer on the hard floor. The man watched the "pray-er" as if watching from a secret room. The man's mouth moved, but no words came out. And his body shook like he was on drugs, or hallucinating, or some other equally dreadful thing. At last, the man ceased praying, crossed himself, and sat next to the layman. It was then the layman noticed the tears on the praying man's cheeks. "You were crying," he observed. "It was not grief," the monk replied. "What then?" asked the man. "It was the hard work of praying," he responded.

So few, too few, take prayer seriously enough that it becomes hard work. This prayer is the kind that goes down into the deep abyss of the human soul to strive with God. In such prayers an abbey is no longer an abbey, a church is no longer a church, a hospital room is no longer a hospital room, a dinner table is no longer a dinner table—but each becomes a corner of heaven.

—Errol G. Smith,
Praying with Confidence
(Discipleship Resources, 1989)

the wedding gift

At that time she was a young, attractive woman. She was the bridesmaid in her friend's wedding. And that was the day she started praying for the salvation of her friend, the bride. Fifty-three years later, when the one-time bridesmaid was in her eighties, she received word that her prayers were answered. The friend finally accepted Jesus as Lord and Savior.

PERSONAL DEVOTIONS

the prayer plunge challenge

The United States space shuttle is an incredible, complex piece of machinery—a tribute to the capabilities and genius of some of our best scientists and engineers. Yet even with all its sophistication, the shuttle cannot function properly without direct communication with earth. It has immense potential if it communicates with people who understand it best.

Humans, too, are incredible, complex pieces of God's work. And like the shuttle, human beings have immense potential if they communicate with the one who knows them best. How to do that—to communicate with the creator—has stumped people since time eternal. Sin has dulled our senses, weakened our discipline, and zapped our zeal. Yet communing with God can be done by anyone.

In *Teach Me to Pray*, W. E. Sangster gives easy, accomplishable steps to get believers on the path of prayer. What his small book amounts to is a challenge: Try these steps for one week, and see what happens.

A.M. Begin by spending just fifteen minutes in the morning with God. First, be still. "I'm here to meet God" is a good reminder. Then, adore. Think of God's incredible greatness. Third, give thanks for friends, family, food, and everything else. Fourth, dedicate things to God: relationships, job, your life. Fifth, ask for guidance for each aspect of life. Sixth, intercede for others. Bring their needs before the throne of grace. Then bring your own needs before God, and finally, wait. Wait to hear what God wishes to say to you.

P.M. End your day with just five minutes of prayer. Review the day. Confess sins that come to mind, then commit the day to the Lord and yourself to his keeping for the night ahead.

Ben Johnson tried the challenge. Though skeptical at first, he later noticed profound changes. In *An Adventure in Prayer*, Johnson writes,

"After a week, I noted several changes in my attitude. For one thing, I had begun to value the prayer time in the morning and evenings as moments to become conscious of God in my life. Enough change had occurred in one week to encourage my continuation of the journey. As the days went by, I actually began looking forward to those appointments with God. At the end of the first month, I could detect several observable changes in my feelings, attitudes, and behavior.

"For one thing, my awareness of God's presence during prayer became more and more frequent. God was manifesting himself to me. Second, my God-awareness in prayer carried over into daily life. The presence of God refused to be confined to stated times and places. Third, my attitude toward other people changed. I began to listen more effectively and became sensitive to persons' hunger for God. Fourth, strange providences of God began occurring in which he made me aware of persons he sent my way, persons for whom he wanted me to pray and to share a word of hope. Finally, there were those 'synchronistic events' which Carl Jung described: the type of events labeled 'coincidence' by the uninitiated, but are seen as answers to prayer by the eyes of faith."

make it a point

A look at any given day in Martin Luther's calendar would reveal the following:

"On a typical day I am charged with the pastorate of three congregations. I teach regularly at the seminary. I have students living in my house. I am writing three books. Countless people write to me. When I start each day, therefore, I make it a point to spend an hour in prayer with God. But if I have a particularly busy day and am more rushed than usual, I make it a point to spend two hours with God before I start the day."

can we not tarry?

"The greatest benefactor this age could have is the man who will bring the preachers and the church back to prayer."

But how? How can men and women again learn to wrestle in prayer as Jacob wrestled till he got the blessing; as Elijah prayed till the rains came; as Jesus prayed in all-night vigils? Saints there are who will extol prayer, who will preach on the need for prayer, who will read books about prayer, but few are those who will give of themselves—pride, time, sweat, tears, their very selves—for the oft-neglected but oh, so necessary art of prayer.

Effective prayer demands time alone. Henry Martyn lamented that "want of private devotional reading and shortness of prayer through incessant sermon-making had produced much strangeness between God and my soul." He recognized that short, quick, "McPrayers" caused malnutrition of the soul and dehydration of the spirit. The decayed spiritual life, a passionless Christian, a joyless child of the King—all could be revitalized with longer and longer stays in the inner room.

"We live shabbily because we pray meanly," says E. M. Bounds. "A Christly temper in its sweet and passionless fragrance would not be so alien and hopeless a heritage if our closet stay were lengthened and intensified." It is there, in the closet, that we become calm, quiet, and utterly still before our Maker. It is there that we become winners, victors, conquerors. "Our ability to stay with God in our closet measures our ability to stay with God out of the closet. Hasty closet visits are deceptive and defaulting." We can never do enough real praying, and real praying takes place in an unhurried place; alone with God. "To pray is the greatest thing we can do: and to do it well there must be calmness, time, and deliberation; otherwise it is degraded into the littlest and meanest of things. True praying has the largest results for good; and poor praying, the least."

—quotes taken from *Power Through Prayer* by E. M. Bounds. Reprinted by Baker Book House.

PERSONAL EVANGELISM THROUGH PRAYER

what goes around . . .

A young convert asked the vicar for some Christian work. "Have you a chum?" asked the vicar. "Yes," replied the boy. "Is he a Christian?" "No, he is as careless as I was." "Then go and ask him to accept Christ as his Savior." "Oh, no!" said the lad, "I could never do that. Give me anything but that." The vicar thought and said, "Promise me two things: that you will not speak to him about his soul, and that you will pray to God twice daily for his conversion." The boy answered that he would be delighted to do that. Before the end of two weeks, however, he was back. "Will you let me off my promise? I must speak to my chum!"

When a Christian begins praying for the lost, that person often becomes the answer to those very prayers.

—*The Kneeling Christian*
(Zondervan, 1971)

conversational prayers

Jack and Mary were new in the neighborhood and desired to meet the neighbors. "Lord, we'd like to get acquainted with our neighbors, and if they don't know you personally as their Savior, we'd like to introduce them to you."

A good request, but it was a description of a goal, not a clear step to take. "Lord," prayed Jack, "I'd like to meet the fellow living next door in some casual way and begin to get acquainted with him. I'd like to begin today, and I believe you can arrange it for me. Thank you, Lord." Scarcely had the day begun when their children got into a quarrel over a tricycle with the neighbor kids. Both fathers rushed out and Jack took all the blame. Then he stuck out his hand and said, "Hi, I'm Jack, just moved in, glad to meet you." The first request had been granted. The first step had been taken.

Second step: "Lord, I'd like to know what that man is interested in, so we could become friends." Within two days the answer came: football.

Third step: "Lord, I need two complimentary football tickets, and could I have them by this weekend, please?" The tickets came. The friendship grew.

Fourth step: "Lord, I'd like to invite this new friend to the Bible class I teach a few miles from here. Would you put it into his heart to accept when I ask him to go with me tonight?" He accepted.

Fifth step: "Lord, Mary and I would like to invite my friend and his wife to our home some evening this week and have a little talk and Bible reading together." They came and enjoyed a nice evening together.

Sixth step: "Lord, next week when I ask them over again, will you prepare their hearts, so that they will be ready to accept you as their Savior? I believe this is the time to ask for this, and I thank you for all you'll be doing in the meantime to draw them to yourself." The next week the neighbors came willingly and gladly accepted Jesus Christ.

This method of conversational prayer is excellent for evangelism, but it's also good for guidance in getting a job, taking a trip, buying or selling a house, doing a special project, or any number of things. Nothing is too small or insignificant for our heavenly Father.

—Rosalind Rinker, *Prayer: Conversing with God* (Zondervan, 1959)

simple math

Matthew 28:18-20 became an intensely personal burden to five high school students. Each made a list of three friends whom he wanted to claim for Christ. The first week they met daily to pray that the friends would sense their need for a Savior. The second week they prayed that they would be instruments of God. The third week they prayed for opportunities to speak to their friends about Christ. Fifteen students received Christ that week.

—Bill Bright, *How to Pray* (Campus Crusade for Christ, 1981)

PETITION

relevant, challenging, powerful

Newport Beach, California, had a large number of modern-day pagans. Wealth, indifference, unconcern, and apathetic attitudes wrapped in lavish surroundings describes how Ray Stedman felt when he was asked to bring a message at a local breakfast meeting. Along with feeling challenged by the situation, Stedman felt much inability. So before the meeting, he asked God for three things: that his message be relevant, challenging, and powerful.

"What I said that morning was neither clever nor profound. . . . I merely tried to call attention to the moral revolt that is widespread in the United States today and the fact that it is eating away at our national life and destroying the very foundation of our government—things that you read and are hearing today on every side. I tried to point out something of the moral emptiness of such a way of life, how futile and meaningless and purposeless this kind of life seems to be, and what the Christian answer is."

After the meeting, two police, visibly shaken, approached Stedman. "We know what you are talking about. This is the first time we have ever heard anything that seems to suggest an answer. This is what we desperately need down in this area." The mayor was so moved that he wanted it to become an annual event. He also welcomed the team to hold breakfast meetings throughout the area.

"Whatever you need, ask, and it shall be given you. If you ask anything in my name, I will do it."

—Ray C. Stedman, *Jesus Teaches on Prayer* (Word Books, 1975)

the bank of heaven

Charles H. Spurgeon once said, "There is no need for us to go beating about the bush, and not telling the Lord distinctly what it is that we have at his hands. Nor will it be seemly for us to make any attempt to use fine language; but let us ask God in the simplest and most direct manner for just the things we want. . . . I believe in business prayers. I mean prayers in which you take to God one of the many promises which he has given us in his Word, and expect it to be fulfilled as certainly as we look for the money to be given us when we go to the bank to cash a check. We should not think of going there, lolling over the counter chattering with the clerks on every conceivable subject except the one thing for which we had gone to the bank, and then coming away without the coin we needed; but we should lay before the clerk the promise to pay the bearer a certain sum, tell him in what form we wish to take the amount, count the cash after him, and then go on our way to attend to other business. That is an illustration of the method in which we should request supplies from the Bank of Heaven."

PRAISE IN PRAYER

help from the kitchen

Brother Lawrence, who was a cook in a monastery just outside of seventeenth-century Paris, had one of the most menial jobs the monastery could offer. Yet despite his humble surroundings, Brother Lawrence wrote a book called *The Practice of the Presence of God*, which has influenced people for generations.

His days were filled with baking, cooking, dishes, mopping, and scrubbing. Yet despite all the hubbub and noise, he managed to cultivate a permanent attitude of praise. He used to take mental "time-outs" and briefly direct his attention and praise to God. His life became such a channel of the peace and joy that comes from intimacy with the Father that people, including bishops and leaders of states, would travel from all over Europe to meet him. He never left the kitchen to learn that. He simply began praising God where he was. Praise made his prayers powerful and transformed his life.

—Douglas F. Kelly, *Why Pray?*
(Wolgemuth & Hyatt, 1989)

grief buster

His was a private grief. Unconsciously, his grief caused him to cease praising God in his prayers. For five days he begged God for relief from his own private pain, and continued on in praiselessness.

On the fifth day it hit him. "If I praise God on the 'mountain-top' but refuse to praise him in the 'valley,' I am not praising God at all—I'm praising my feelings." So he went to his prayer closet, knelt, and resolved to praise. Without too much effort, it became obvious that there were many things to praise God about. He had salvation; his family was godly; his job was secure. He'd been focusing on the dark, gloomy aspects of life while ignoring all the beautiful things God had done. Soon the heavy weight of sorrow left him, replaced by joy in the presence of the Lord.

Habakkuk had a similar experience. In chapter 3, he begins by listing six really terrible things, then concludes with the following:

Yet I will exult in the Lord, I will rejoice in the God of my salvation. The LORD God is my strength, and he has made my feet like hinds' feet, and makes me walk on my high places.

—T. W. Hunt and Catherine Walker, *Prayer Life: Walking in Fellowship with God* (The Sunday School Board of the Southern Baptist Convention, 1987)

REVIVAL IN PRAYER

revival: pure and simple

On September 23, 1857, Mr. Lanphier, a humble, city missionary, began a prayer meeting in the Dutch Reformed North Church in New York City. At first, hardly anyone showed up. One time there were only two, another time, one. But after some time, interest began to develop and large crowds began attending the meetings. Soon it was necessary to find a bigger room, then to split into groups. Before long, not only were churches holding praying people, but several public buildings, including theaters.

From New York to Philadelphia and on west did the fire spread. At one point, it was thought necessary to begin preaching too, but few showed up, opting instead for prayer, so the preaching idea was scrapped and all energies were devoted to prayer. "The whole emphasis was on prayer, and our whole nation was shaken by the power of God as it had never been shaken before, and perhaps has never been shaken since," stated R. A. Torrey. "That is the kind of revival I am longing to see more in our city; yes, throughout our whole land; yes, throughout the world. Not a revival where there is great preaching and marvelous singing and all kinds of bewildering antics by preachers or singers, or skillful managers or manipulators; but a revival where there is mighty praying and wonderful displays of the convicting and converting and regenerating power of the Holy Spirit in answer to prayer."

—R. A. Torrey, *The Power of Prayer* (Zondervan, 1975)

no longer hidden

Decades ago, God had a hidden intercessor in Great Britain. After this man's death, it was discovered in his diary that he had been praying for a mission agency in China for years. A list containing more than twenty mission stations in China was recorded in those books, along with notes indicating that God had enabled him to pray the prayer of faith for revival in those places. When it was researched, it was learned that God had sent spiritual awakening to each of those places over a period of years, in the exact order in which his hidden intercessor had prayed. "What rewards and holy surprises heaven will disclose when God's children who travailed in prayer receive their special rewards!"

—Wesley L. Duewel, *Touch the World Through Prayer* (Zondervan, 1986)

SCRIPTURE PRAYING

Müller's method

George Müller of Bristol, England, obtained the English equivalent of almost ten million dollars in his lifetime through prayer. Müller didn't pray for a thing just because he wanted it or even if it was (in his opinion) greatly needed for the Lord's work. When Müller was burdened to pray for something, he first checked Scripture. Sometimes he would search the Word for days before he would pray about his burden.

Commenting on his method of prayer, Müller said he would search Scripture "not for the sake of the public ministry of the Word, nor for the sake of preaching on what I meditated upon, but for the sake of obtaining food for my own soul. The result I have found to be almost invariably this, that after a very few minutes my soul has been led to confession, or to thanksgiving, or to intercession, or to supplication; so that, though I did not, as it were, give myself to prayer, but to meditation, yet it turned almost immediately more or less into prayer." Then, with finger on the promise and heart tuned to God, he would plead that promise and so receive what he asked for. He always prayed with an open Bible before him.

—R. A. Torrey, *The Power of Prayer* (Zondervan, 1975)

housing crunch

The family was scheduled to move to Scotland in December for an eight-month sabbatical, but by mid-November still had no place to stay. So they joined friends in prayer and claimed the promise in Jeremiah 33:3: "Call to me, and I will answer you, and show you great and mighty things, which you do not know."

Soon after, they were given a place to stay at a cramped residential center. They moved in, and a month later the miracle happened. A beautiful old house, which was once a children's home, was being converted into something else, and the owners wanted someone to live there, do some upkeep, and identify areas that needed work. Not only was it in a beautiful spot, but there were thirteen bedrooms and six bathrooms for the nine-member family. Great and mighty things indeed!

—Douglas F. Kelly, *Why Pray?* (Wolgemuth & Hyatt, 1989)

SMALL GROUP PRAYER

no axe to grind

Tuesday mornings at 6:30 was when this group got together. They had but one thing in common: their desire to pray. Plumbers, doctors, lawyers, assembly-line workers, teachers, an artist, an engineer, and others, all came despite the weather because of an intense desire to pray. The fruits of their time together were obvious in their relationships at work, at home, in churches throughout the state, and in their own personal spheres of influence. They had no training in speaking, but it was the very simplicity of their testimonies that made them so powerful. They had no axe to grind, only a story to tell.

After the pastor left that parish and moved to Kansas City, he asked his original group if they would come to Missouri and help him start a similar group. "Have faith, will travel" seemed to be their slogan as they piled into cars and, at their own expense, traveled more than a thousand miles so they could share what prayer was doing in their lives.

There was a small group of "prayers" in the church, the result of six months of intercessory prayer. But the retreat with the first group really brought the people out. Simple stories of how prayer had affected lives so lit a fire in the hearts of the Kansas City group that with-in a year more than seventy men were involved in a number of prayer groups in the church.

When the pastor moved to Minnesota, he again asked the original group to come and help him start another one. And once again the effect was the same. When he moved to Ohio . . .

—Donald M. Hulstrand, *The Praying Church* (The Seabury Press, 1977)

creative groups

William Brownson has had years of experience with small groups. Here's just a sampling of some of the creative ideas he's put into practice:

— a group that prays for inactive members

— a group that studies ancient Christian creeds and prays over what they learn

— a group that prays for evangelism teams and ministry

— a group that prays for each other's needs and burdens

— a group that prays for the world around us and especially for warring nations

— a "book club" that discusses all sorts of good books and then spends time in prayer

The number of reasons for getting together for prayer is limited only by the imagination. Finding someone else with a similar heart's desire is often the first step needed to form a group that prays regularly. Put the word out!

Who knows? There may be several people just waiting for such an opportunity.

—William C. Brownson, *Courage to Pray* (Baker Book House, 1989)

STRENGTH THROUGH PRAYER

no other place to go

Abraham Lincoln himself said that when he entered the presidency, he was not a Christian. But as the overwhelming burdens of that office and the tremendous responsibilities of the Civil War era weighed down upon him, he began to think. Then, while walking among the graves of the soldiers at Gettysburg, there burst upon him an awareness of his need of the Savior. He later testified that it was there he became a Christian.

Lincoln learned to pray, not to get, get, get from God, but to receive strength. "I have been driven many times to my knees by the overwhelming conviction that I had absolutely no other place to go." That continual reliance on God through prayer did much to form one of the United States' greatest presidents.

—Ray C. Stedman, *Jesus Teaches on Prayer* (Word Books, 1975)

motivation from beyond

Earlier this year I sat in the front room of a fifth-floor walk-up apartment in Berlin. My host was a former psychiatrist who had given himself to the work of the Lord after his conversion. He pastors a congregation of two thousand people who worship in a rented warehouse in West Berlin. Having just told me about the staff of workers he heads, the Bible school he leads, and the daily radio broadcast he airs, he shared with me his plans to begin a weekly television program, which is a real pioneer action for Europe.

"Dear brother," I said, "please accept a word of caution from an older minister. You have only so much energy. If you spread yourself too thin, you will not have sufficient strength to continue. In addition to your expanding ministry, you have a wife and five children who need you."

"I understand what you are saying," he responded. "I now pray three hours daily. If I do, indeed, go on TV, I have promised God that I will increase that to four hours of daily prayer."

"Please ignore what I just said," I replied. "With that prayer schedule, you'll make it." He had obviously learned the secret of unloading his tensions upon God in prayer and receiving divine strength in return. Prayer had become a cathartic and a motivating strength for him, and so it must be for us.

—Judson Cornwall, *The Secret of Personal Prayer* (Creation House, 1988)

THANKSGIVING IN PRAYER

dog days of gratitude

H. A. Ironside was eating in a cafeteria. The place was full, and the only seat available was right across from a man already seated and eating. Asking if he could join him, the man merely grunted at Ironside. So, after setting down his tray, he followed his usual custom of thanking God for the food. With bowed head and closed eyes, Ironside said a silent prayer. When he looked up, the surly man was staring at him. "What's the matter, something wrong with your food?" he asked. "No, I don't think so, it seems all right to me," replied Ironside. "Have you got a headache, or something?" "No, I haven't," said Ironside. "Why do you ask?"

"Well, I noticed you bowing down and putting your hand up to your head and closing your eyes. I thought maybe there was something wrong with your head." "No," said Ironside. "I was simply returning thanks to God for my food."

The man snorted in disgust. "Oh, you believe in that bosh, do you?" Ironside responded with a question, "Don't you ever give thanks?" The stranger responded, "No, I don't believe in giving thanks for anything. I just start right in." Ironside ended the conversation with, "Oh, you're just like my dog. He never gives thanks, either; he just starts right in."

It is we who need to give thanks to God; it is we who must always be ready to show gratitude to the one who created us, who gives so freely to us, who loves us so much. Only through gratitude, constant and generous, can we avoid the sin of ingratitude.

—Ray C. Stedman, *Jesus Teaches on Prayer* (Word Books, 1975)

thanksgiving opens doors

I was once ministering in a congregation that seemed bound in spirit. The limited praise was anemic, and God's presence seemed far away. I stopped teaching and suggested that we pick a bouquet of thanksgiving to present to the Lord. I asked for individuals to express their thanks to the Lord for something very specific and to confine it to a sentence. One said, "I thank God for my wife." Another thanked God for salvation.

As each sentence was spoken, I reached out my hand as though I were picking a flower, and then I placed that flower into the bouquet I was collecting in my left hand. After many persons had offered thanks to God, I asked everyone to stand while I presented the bouquet to the Lord. It seemed that I had hardly begun to offer their thanks to God when we became very conscious of the presence of God. Thanksgiving moved into praise, and our praise lifted us into worship. A session that had been dull became lively, and from that point on the teaching of the Word produced almost immediate response from the people. We had found our way into God's presence through thanksgiving.

—Judson Cornwall, *The Secret of Personal Prayer* (Creation House, 1988)

thanks a lot

What's there to be thankful for? Here's a small sampling of things to show gratitude for:

— an inquisitive mind that seeks to know God
— the working of the Holy Spirit
— goals the Lord helps us set, causing us to be our best
— the Word of God that challenges us to be more like his Son
— God's ability to hear the unspoken struggles of the soul
— all those around who show what it means to be Christlike
— all those who are abrasive, giving us an opportunity to practice patience
— for who you are and what you believe
— for those that support you in times of trouble
— for those who share in your happiness
— for trials and tribulations, which teach perseverance
— for everything

"I have learned to be satisfied with what I have. I know what it is to be in need and what it is to have more than enough. I have learned this secret, so that anywhere, at any time, I am content, whether I am full or hungry, whether I have too much or too little" (Philippians 4:11-12).

joy in sorrow

While ministering in France, Judson Cornwall received word that his mother-in-law was dying. His thoughts while flying home were thoughts of dread; he was the last surviving male member of that family, and so would be responsible for much of the funeral as well as trying to comfort all the sisters and aunts.

In the funeral parlor, Cornwall challenged the family to be thankful that their mother's years of suffering and pain were over and that she was with Jesus and reunited with her husband. "In the mercy of God, a real spirit of thanksgiving gripped our hearts. Replacing the deep sorrow, it became the prevailing attitude during that week. After the funeral, the director told me, 'I wish that more Christians could display their joy in God during times of grief and sorrow. This has been a dynamic demonstration of faith in God.'"

During that funeral, many unsaved relatives came to understand God in a way they had never understood before. "Rejoice always, pray without ceasing, in everything give thanks; for this is the will of God in Christ Jesus for you" (1 Thessalonians 5:16-18).

—Judson Cornwall, *The Secret of Personal Prayer* (Creation House, 1988)

what if . . .

What if, starting tomorrow morning, the only things that continued to exist were the things which you thanked God for. Did you thank him for the toothpaste? Then no more toothpaste. Did you/do you thank him for air to breathe?

And what about the lungs that make breathing possible? Oops! No more lungs and no more air. Did you/do you thank him for your abilities, your finances, all the bills you have to pay and the ability to pay them, your talents, gifts, hobbies, and interests? Sorry, they'll all disappear.

If you think about that little scenario, it gets across the idea that everything we have and do is dependent upon God. Try to make thanksgiving and acknowledgment part of the very air you breathe. It may just keep that air around a little longer!

UNANSWERED PRAYER

so much for unanswered prayer

I've had the feeling that God neither heard nor responded to my prayers. I have gone from feelings of guilt that something must be wrong with me, to doubt about whether God cares.—Lloyd John Ogilvie

Ever feel that way? Has the old description of frustrated attempts in prayer, "I feel like my prayers don't go beyond the ceiling" ever tumbled across your lips? Almost everyone gets discouraged about seemingly unanswered prayer from time to time. Understanding some reasons behind "unanswered" prayer will help us see that getting everything we ever ask for will just reduce the Creator to a blessing machine, and we as his children to spiritually spoiled misfits.

Lloyd John Ogilvie's introduction to television ministry was for him a poignant lesson that God's plans and timetables are always better than ours and that sometimes we're just not ready for an answer. At the start of his television career, Ogilvie knew exactly what had to be done. He had the program's format drawn up, the guests lined up, interviews scheduled, and closing meditations written. Three pilot programs were shot, all complete successes. Everything, humanly speaking, was ready to launch.

But money suddenly became scarce. Every effort to raise enough for syndication fell through. Some potential sponsors had reasons, others couldn't explain their decisions.

Ogilvie was confused. He prayed, asking "What's wrong, Lord? What have I missed in what I thought was your plan for me?" For weeks, everything was silent as he contemplated failed dreams and unanswered prayer. Then the phone rang. Not just once, but several times throughout the day. All the callers—who were trusted friends—had basically the same idea as this man's message: "Lloyd, you've spent all your life allowing the Lord to teach you how to preach the Bible for people's deepest needs. Don't spend time on television interviewing and featuring famous names. Just do what you do best—talk to people about their hopes and hurts and introduce them to the abundant and eternal life in Christ. I was praying about you this morning and aching over your period of unanswered prayer, and suddenly I felt a rush of inspiration about your need. It was so strong, I wrote it down. What came to me is what I've just shared with you. I may be off base, but pray about it and see if the Lord confirms it in your own heart and mind."

Ogilvie gave up his television plans completely. Within days, a member of the church donated a large sum of money to be used for a television show—if Ogilvie would make preaching the main focus of the show (the same advice his friend gave on the telephone). Other events happened that allowed a program to go on the air that has since expanded to reach over three hundred American cities. When Ogilvie gave up his own plans and turned them over to the Lord, God answered. His timing, planning, financing, and strategizing is always better than ours. So much for unanswered prayer.

—Lloyd John Ogilvie, *You Can Pray with Power*

nothing mysterious

The following is a conversation R. A. Torrey had with a young woman in Chicago:

"Miss W. thinks that I ought to have a talk with you."

"Why, Jennie, does Miss W. think you should have a talk with me?"

"Because I am in great perplexity. I am perplexed because God does not answer my prayers."

"Oh," said Torrey. "There is nothing to be surprised about in that. Does God anywhere promise to answer your prayers? God does tell us very plainly in his Word whose prayers he will answer." Torrey then quoted 1 John 3:22, ". . . and receive from him anything we ask, because we obey his commands and do what pleases him."

"Now, Jennie, does that describe you? Are you studying the Word of God every day of your life to find out what God wishes you to do, and do you do it every time you find it?"

"No, I do not," she responded.

"Then there is nothing mysterious about God's not answering your prayers."

—R. A. Torrey, *The Power of Prayer* (Zondervan, 1975)

UNITED PRAYER

prayer: more than skin deep

The young woman was beautiful, energetic, a happy wife and mother—and recently diagnosed with a form of incurable dermatitis. It would slowly destroy her beauty and youth.

She became rebellious and very apprehensive. Her husband and mother wondered how long she would be able to stay on her feet. It was a demoralizing sight. Being people of prayer, they formed a prayer chain for this woman they both loved and prayed for a week straight. They also agreed to attend a healing service for the girl.

The miracle began with diminishing rebellion and apprehension. She began to enjoy life again. Then her skin condition improved. Then money was given, enabling the family to spend the summer in a cottage on the seashore. Eight months later the skin condition was almost completely gone. And best of all, the young woman found Jesus Christ.

—Helen Smith Shoemaker,
Power Through Prayer Groups
(Fleming H. Revell Co., 1958)

prayer meeting *a la* Fulton Street

One hundred years ago a group of businessmen became concerned for America's spiritual and moral welfare. They instituted the "Fulton Street Prayer Meeting." Daily they met at noon to pray for revival. At first only a few shared in the prayer meetings. Soon an estimated ten thousand people were praying. The result—which no serious student of evangelistic history can deny stemmed almost directly from the Fulton Street prayer meetings—was a literal revival of religious concern across America. Within two years a million converts were added to the churches of this country. In one month New York City churches reported fifty thousand new members. The flood tide of spiritual awakening burst its Manhattan bounds and engulfed New England, leaped mountains to the Midwest, and spanned the prairies to sweep across the Rockies and the deep South. Even Canada felt the impact.

This was Fulton Street, one hundred years ago.

Now in this year of our Lord, 1957, people are praying once again. The miracles of modern communication have linked continents instead of counties.

Not ten thousand, but literally hundreds of thousands are praying.

But while the quantitative aspect may differ from the prayers of 1857, the goal is precisely the same. Once again people are concerned for the need of a spiritual and moral awakening in America.

—Jerry Beaven, "100 Years from Fulton Street" in *American Mercury*

pentecost at Herrnhut

Count Ludwig von Zinzendorf founded the community of Herrnhut in the 1720s as a refuge for anyone fleeing religious persecution. Moravian Hussites, Lutherans, Calvinists, and Roman Catholics were all together at one site. As may be imagined, there was plenty of bickering and infighting, for the Calvinists were still praying for the destruction of Rome, while the Lutherans prayed for the end of Calvinism!

For three years, this religious bickering and doctrinal mud-slinging continued. Zinzendorf's response was to break the community into small groups for sharing and prayer. He kept escalating the prayer watch until it was continuing around the clock. Then, on August 13, 1727, Herrnhut had its own "Pentecost" at a sunrise service; all present were filled with a powerful measure of the Holy Spirit. This was evidenced by an outpouring of love between those who shared hate only hours before.

At this point only did Herrnhut begin to be an effective missionary community. Its explosion of outreach far surpassed the outreach efforts of other Protestant efforts up to that time. And Zinzendorf, seeing the results of unity, went on to promote renewal, seeking to draw all denominations—including Rome—together in a loose network of communication, or, as Richard Baxter put it, "unity without uniformity."

—Vonette Bright and Ben A. Jennings, *Unleashing the Power of Prayer* (Moody Press, 1989)

WARFARE PRAYER

little-read book

On my first trip to China in 1978 I often saw tables stacked high with Mao Tse-tung's *Little Red Book*, a collection of political sayings bathed in atheism. The devastating Cultural Revolution of the 1960s resulted largely from a strict allegiance to the tenets set forth in this *Little Red Book*.

I decided to bring a copy home for use in my intercessory prayer time. I placed the small book in my backyard prayer chapel, and whenever I started my intercession, I was reminded to pray for China's spiritual deliverance. Day after day for more than two years I would clutch the small, vinyl-covered red book in my hand, commanding it to be removed as a factor in Chinese society. My prayers were almost violent. I shouted against the influence of this book, often remembering how I had seen youth in the fields of China reading it as if they were sharing in a small group Bible study setting.

Imagine my amazement when next I visited Hong Kong to see a front page news story of Mao Tse-tung's picture being taken down throughout China. I read every word of the English language article. One paragraph leaped out with special excitement: "And as far as Mao Tse-tung's *Little Red Book* is concerned, it is as if it has disappeared from the face of the earth."

—Dick Eastman, *Love on Its Knees*
(Fleming H. Revell Co., 1989)

preparation

The Alaskan bull moose is a powerful beast with monstrous antlers. During the fall, males of the species literally go head-to-head in a battle for dominance. The one with the biggest horns, most weight, and greatest stamina generally wins. If, during one of the collisions, one of the horns snaps off, victory is ensured for the other moose.

Though fought in the fall, the real battle takes place in the spring. In quiet meadows and on shaded hillsides, the selection of nutrients and food will determine the strength of the budding antlers, the distribution of weight, and the degree of stamina. To fail in the quiet moments of selection is to fail in the heat of battle.

The eternal battle rages. Satan picks his battlefields. Christians fight not with weapons of this earth, but with the sword of the Spirit. The real battle takes place in the quiet of the prayer chambers. Those who commune with God during lulls in the battle will be the ones who fight victoriously when the battle rages. That's the lesson from the moose: spiritual strength, endurance, and wisdom are best developed before they're needed.

a call to arms

The World Prayer Missionary concept involves prayer warriors from around the world who pledge to pray for a certain geographic location in the world. Soon after it was introduced, commitment cards from intercessors indicating a wish to enlist began to pour into headquarters.

As more and more cards poured in, Dick Eastman felt it necessary to have a special time of prayer to commit these first intercessors to the glory of God. At the monthly day of prayer, several people gathered for prayer, including Armando, an older gentleman who was born near the Albanian border.

In the prayer chapel, all lights were out except one, a lighted globe in the center of the room. As each person took a handful of cards, they began to pray. They prayed that these intercessors would grow into an army of warriors committed to binding Satan's influence on earth in every corner of the world. Then it was Armando's time to pray.

It was a simple prayer asking for God's blessing on all the intercessors. Then he paused. His head nodded and tears rolled down his face. "God . . . He just talk to my heart. He tell me I must tell you that as soon as you raise up an army that binds every demon on earth, his kingdom shall come."

—Dick Eastman, *Love on Its Knees*
(Fleming H. Revell Co., 1989)

will the real enemy please stand up?

No matter how hard she tried, she just couldn't get along with her unsaved father. She found herself becoming bitter.

As she prayed, the Lord showed her a strategy to combat her negative feelings.

It was important for her to understand that the conflict was not between her and her father. It was between Satan and the Spirit of Christ that dwelt within her. When seen in that light, she was able to see clearly that her father really did love her. She no longer saw him as the enemy, but as a tool in the hands of the enemy.

Instead of reacting in anger, she would go to her knees in prayer.

Satan often uses that tactic in our churches, causing God's children to fight and bicker. The reason these skirmishes are rarely settled is because we're not dealing with the real enemy—Satan.

—Charles F. Stanley, *Handle with Prayer* (Victor Books, 1982)

chew on this

A young woman really struggled with her eating habits. She knew it was a weakness in her life and was determined to overcome it. So the first thing she did was to pinpoint the lies she had convinced herself to believe: she thought she studied better if she snacked; she thought she had to eat every time she felt hungry; she told herself that eating helped her handle her emotions.

She accepted the truth that God loved her and that she was a new creation in Jesus Christ. Then she took portions of Scripture, like Colossians 3:3 and Galatians 5:24, and memorized them. Every time she was tempted to eat, she would "chew" on the truths of those verses. She was victorious from that point on.

—Charles F. Stanley, *Handle with Prayer* (Victor Books, 1982)

WORSHIP AND PRAYER

usher in inspiration

There are times when the worship in a church is dry and listless. People are there out of tradition, the pastor hasn't prepared a very good sermon, and there's a noticeable lack of the Holy Spirit. One couple did their best to combat that whenever they could. When traveling, they would often slip into the back row of a church and pray for the service. "It is a hard fight to pray against such a frozen current, but the harder it is, the more it is needed. So we literally fight for God. We pray for everybody, as well as for the pastor. While we are praying with intense concentration, we feel the Holy Spirit moving the speaker; his voice takes on a new timbre, his face a new radiance. He leaves the written sermon, which becomes too cold for him, and utters inspired words which come to him."

—Frank C. Laubach, *Prayer: The Mightiest Force in the World* (Spire Books, 1959)

RESOURCES *for* PRAYING CHURCHES

INTRODUCTION

357

INTRODUCTION

Hundreds of Christian ministries dedicated to evangelism, discipleship, and prayer dot the evangelical landscape. They exist for the purpose of channeling the prayers of God's people toward God's work in the world. The prayer ministries you find here were selected with two criteria in mind: all have a broad prayer focus, and all merit your investigation. Use the information here to learn more about these ministries, the resources they offer, and ways in which you can support their prayer activities. This section also includes classic and contemporary books on prayer, as well as available newsletters and magazines to inform and motivate your prayer life.

PRAYER MINISTRIES

A.D. 2000/United Prayer Track
Global Harvest Ministries
P.O. Box 63060
Colorado Springs, CO 80962-3060
719-262-9922
FAX: 719-262-9920
E-mail: 74114.570@compuserve.com

Purpose: To mobilize as many of the existing national and international prayer networks as possible to synchronize their prayer activities toward the goal of a church for every people by A.D. 2000
Focus: Worldwide with emphasis on the 10/40 Window

Bibleless Peoples Prayer Project
Wycliffe Bible Translators
P.O. Box 628200
Orlando, FL 32862-8200
1-800-992-5433
E-mail: prayer_ministries@wycliffe.org
Website: www.wycliffe.org

Purpose: To assign persons to pray daily for a specific language group, by name, until that group has a translation of the Bible in their language
Focus: Praying for every known language group in the world still without Scripture in their own language

Canadian Prayer Alert
P.O. Box 300
Vancouver, BC V6C 2X3
Canada
604-514-2000
FAX: 604-514-2002
E-mail: prayer@ccc-van.crusade.org

Purpose: To mobilize Canadians to pray for leaders in Canada and for revival and spiritual awakening through a nation-wide network of prayer partners
Focus: Canada and beyond

Canadian Revival Fellowship
P.O. Box 584
Regina, SK S4P 3A3
Canada
306-522-3685
FAX: 306-522-3686
E-mail: crf@dlcwest.com

Purpose: To help God's people fulfill his conditions in 2 Chronicles 7:14, believing that he will then send spiritual awakening on the unsaved
Focus: Worldwide with emphasis on North America

Canadian Prayer Track
2146 Robinson St., Suite 1B
Regina, SK S4T 2P7
Canada
306-569-8999
FAX: 306-569-1536
E-mail: tvtehc@msn.com

Purpose: To be a catalyst to inform, motivate, network, mobilize, and provide resources for Canadian Christians to pray for the work of spreading the gospel across Canada and the world. Publishes the quarterly prayer newsletter *Global Prayer Advance* in an effort to mobilize Christians and churches to intercessory prayer that will enable the unreached to be reached and churches to be multiplied throughout the world
Focus: Canada and beyond

Concerts of Prayer International
P.O. Box 770
New Providence, NJ 07974
908-771-0146
Toll-free: 877-NOW-HOPE
FAX: 908-665-4199
E-mail: copi@aol.com
Website: www.nationalprayer.org

Purpose: To mobilize and equip a movement of united prayer worldwide, to pray for spiritual awakening and world evangelization
Focus: National and international prayer movements, especially citywide interdenominational prayer gatherings

Every Home for Christ
P.O. Box 35930
Colorado Springs, CO 80935-3593
719-260-8888
1-800-423-5054
FAX: 719-260-7505
E-mail: lstein@ehc.org
Website: www.sni.net/ehc

Purpose: To serve, mobilize, and train the church to pray and participate in a systematic personal presentation of the gospel to every home in the world
Focus: Supported by more than 400 denominations, serving in more than 100 countries worldwide

Houses of Prayer Everywhere (HOPE)
P.O. Box 141312
Grand Rapids, MI 49514
616-453-9311
1-800-217-5200
FAX: 616-791-9926
E-mail: info@hopeministries.org

Purpose: To help churches saturate their communities and cities with *Houses of Prayer* that will pray for, care about, and share the blessings of Christ with those who live or work near them
Focus: To provide equipping, resources, and ongoing support for individuals, churches, city-reaching coalitions, and denominations that are committed to prayer-evangelism

Intercessors for America
6 West Market
P.O. Box 4477
Leesburg, VA 20177
703-777-0003
1-800-872-7729
FAX: 703-777-2324
E-mail: usapray@aol.com

Purpose: To serve the church by encouraging effective prayer and fasting for the United States, the church, and their leaders
Focus: Christians in the United States

International Renewal Ministries
8435 N.E. Glisan St.
Portland, OR 97220
503-251-6455
FAX: 503-254-1268
E-mail: irm@multnomah.edu
Website: www.multnomah.edu

Purpose: To facilitate renewal and revival through renewing and strengthening individuals, families, and ministries resulting in widespread evangelization of the lost and a change in society (includes Pastors' Prayer Summits)
Focus: Church leaders worldwide

March for Jesus USA
P.O. Box 3216
Austin, TX 78764
512-416-0066
FAX: 512-445-5393
E-mail: mfjusa@compuserve.com
Website: www.mfj.org

Purpose: To call Christians of all denominations to unite and take the joy of knowing Jesus to the streets with praise, prayer, and proclamation
Focus: United States and beyond

Mission America
5666 Lincoln Drive, Suite 100
Edina, MN 55436
612-912-0001
FAX: 612-912-0002
E-mail: missionamerica@compuserve.com
Website: www.missionamerica.org

Purpose: To mobilize the church to pray for and lovingly and appropriately share the gospel with every person in America by year-end 2000
Focus: Local churches, denominations, and parachurch ministries

Moms in Touch International
P.O. Box 1120
Poway, CA 92074-1120
619-486-4065
FAX: 619-486-5132
E-mail: mitihqtrs@compuserve.com

Purpose: To encourage mothers and others to meet together on a regular basis to pray for their children and the schools they attend
Focus: International, with emphasis on the United States

Mothers Who Care
P.O. Box 300
Vancouver, BC V6C 2X3
Canada
604-514-2000; 604-514-2099
1-800-563-1106
FAX: 604-514-2124
E-mail: mothers@ccc-van.crusade.org

Purpose: Network of mothers across Canada praying for schools their children attend, as well as teachers and school administration staff
Focus: Canada

National Day of Prayer Task Force
P.O. Box 15616
Colorado Springs, CO 80935-5616
719-531-3379
FAX: 719-548-4520
E-mail: ndptf@aol.com
Website: www.nationaldayofprayer.org

Purpose: To provide resources for anyone wishing to participate in the National Day of Prayer (first Thursday of May)
Focus: Americans worldwide

National Prayer Committee (U.S.)
P.O. Box 770
New Providence, NJ 07974
908-771-0146
Toll-free: 877-NOW-HOPE
FAX: 908-665-4199
E-mail: natlpray@aol.com
Website: www.nationalprayer.org

Purpose: To provide servant leadership to the national prayer movement through projects such as the National Day of Prayer, the Nationally Broadcast Concert of Prayer, *Pray!* magazine, and Forums for National Revival
Focus: United States

Promise Keepers
P.O. Box 103001
Denver, CO 80250-3001
303-964-7600
1-800-888-7595
FAX: 303-433-1036
Website: www.promisekeepers.org

Purpose: A Christ-centered ministry dedicated to uniting men through vital relationships
Focus: North America and beyond

Reachout Ministries
3961 Holcomb Bridge Road, Suite 201
Norcross, GA 30092
770-441-2247
FAX: 770-449-7544
E-mail: 72002.1704@compuserve.com

Purpose: To assist and equip youth leaders in local churches for strategic ministry through the church, including "See You at the Pole" and "Pole 2 Locker" (youth devotional)
Focus: International

RENOVARÉ
8 Inverness Drive East, Suite 102
Englewood, CO 80112-5624
303-792-0152
FAX: 303-792-0146
E-mail: 103165.327@compuserve.com

Purpose: Working for the renewal of the church of Jesus Christ through the use of small group meetings, conferences, one-day seminars, personal and group retreats, devotional readings, and long-term commitment to renewal
Focus: International

U.S. Prayer Track
7710-T Cherry Park Drive, Suite 224
Houston, TX 77095
713-466-4009
FAX: 713-466-5633
E-mail: eddiesmith@xc.org

Purpose: To mobilize and equip millions to pray for revival and spiritual awakening in the United States
Focus: United States

Waymakers
P.O. Box 203131
Austin, TX 78720-3131
512-419-7729
FAX: 512-219-1999

Purpose: Equipping sustained movements of united, on-site prayer such as prayerwalking and houses of prayer, that open ways for Christ to be seen, followed, and celebrated in every people and place
Focus: United States and international

RECOMMENDED READING

Blackaby, Henry T., and Claude V. King. *Experiencing God* (Broadman and Holman, 1994)

Bonhoeffer, Dietrich. *Psalms: The Prayer Book of the Bible* (Augsburg, 1970)

Bounds, E. M. *Power Through Prayer* (Baker)

Brother Lawrence. *The Practice of the Presence of God* (Revell, 1958)

Bryant, David. *Stand in the Gap* (Regal, 1997)

Christenson, Evelyn. *A Time to Pray* (leader guide and study guide) (Harvest House, 1996)

Duewel, Wesley L. *Touch the World Through Prayer* (Zondervan, 1986)

Dunn, Ron. *Don't Just Stand There, Pray Something* (Here's Life Publishers, 1991)

Eastman, Dick. *Love on Its Knees* (Chosen Books, 1989)

Foster, Richard. *Prayer: Finding the Heart's True Home* (Harper Collins, 1992)

Hallesby, O. *Prayer* (Augsburg, 1975)

Hawthorne, Steve, and Graham Kendrick. *Prayerwalking* (Creation House, 1993)

Houston, James. *The Transforming Power of Prayer* (NavPress, 1996)

Hunt, T.W., and Catherine Walker. *Prayer Life* (Southern Baptist Convention Sunday School Board, 1987)

Hybels, Bill. *Too Busy Not to Pray* (InterVarsity Press, 1988)

Johnstone, Patrick. *Operation World* (Zondervan)

Murray, Andrew. *The Ministry of Intercession* (Springdale, PA: Whitaker House, 1982)

_____. *With Christ in the School of Prayer* (Revell, 1953)

Packer, J. I. *Keep in Step with the Spirit* (Revell, 1984)

Pedersen, Bjorn. *Face to Face with God in Your Church: Establishing a Prayer Ministry* (Augsburg, 1995)

Postema, Donald. *Space for God* (CRC Publications, 1983, 1997)

Rinker, Rosalyn. *Prayer: Conversing with God* (Zondervan, 1959)

Sheets, Dutch. *Intercessory Prayer* (Regal, 1996)

Sproul, R. C. *Effective Prayer* (Tyndale, 1989)

Spurgeon, Charles H. *Twelve Sermons on Prayer* (Baker, 1971)

Storms, C. Samuel. *Reaching God's Ear* (Tyndale, 1988)

Thielicke, Helmut. *Our Heavenly Father* (Baker, 1974)

Tryon, Jr., Howard A. *Praying for You* (Kregel, 1996)

Wagner, C. Peter. *Prayer Shield* (Regal, 1992)

_____. *Warfare Prayer* (Regal, 1992)

_____. *Churches That Pray* (Regal, 1993)

PRAYER BULLETIN INSERT

The *Prayer* bulletin insert published by Church Development Resources is a 5½" x 8½" prayer resource published bimonthly. The insert includes stories of answered prayer, ideas for prayer ministries, brief teaching articles on prayer, and helpful prayer resources.

What will it do for my church? *Prayer* bulletin insert is intended to give your congregation fresh, new ideas on prayer. It will stimulate and encourage people to pray. Its brief, pointed articles explore different approaches to prayer, explain how prayer is linked to spiritual health, and present the Bible's teaching on prayer. True stories of how God answers prayer will encourage your members' faith in God—a God who hears and answers requests.

Prayer bulletin insert can also help your church become aware of the broader prayer movement spreading across North America. You'll gain new ideas for observing the National Day of Prayer, information on the national prayer symposium, and updates on international prayer concerns. You'll also learn about excellent resources and newsletters from organizations dedicated to prayer.

Using *Prayer* bulletin insert. Order sufficient copies to include in each church bulletin. Make a special note of its availability in the bulletin itself and from the pulpit, encouraging members to read it for use in their family and personal devotions.

Distribute extra copies to prayer groups in your church. Encourage people to put it in their Bibles and use it as part of their daily devotions. Place extra copies on your church literature table. If your church offers an adult class on prayer or spirituality, you may want to use some of the articles and quotes to spark discussion and to suggest practical ways to put the principles of prayer to use.

Prayer bulletin insert is available by annual subscription in multiples of fifty copies or by single issues (fifty-copy minimum). Order from CRC Publications, 2850 Kalamazoo Ave. SE, Grand Rapids, MI 49560, or call toll-free 1-800-777-7200.

OTHER PRAYER RESOURCES

The Arsenal
*A list of prayer and spiritual warfare
resources*
Wagner Institute
P.O. Box 62958
Colorado Springs, CO 80962
719-277-6741
FAX: 719-262-9108
E-mail: arsenal@pcwagner.net

The Capitol Hill Prayer Alert
Update on national issues
Sound the Trumpet Ministries
325 Pennsylvania Ave. S.E.
Washington, DC 20003
703-754-3629
FAX: 703-754-3838
E-mail: chpagt@aol.com

Global Prayer Digest
*A monthly guide for use by groups or individ-
uals in praying for unreached people groups
worldwide*
1605 Elizabeth St.
Pasadena, CA 91104
626-398-2249
FAX: 626-398-2263

Intercessors for America Newsletter
Monthly prayer information
On Watch in Washington
Weekly D.C. information update
Intercessors for America
P.O. Box 4477
Leesburg, VA 20177
703-777-0003
1-800-872-7729
FAX: 703-777-2324
E-mail: usapray@aol.com

Pray! Magazine
A magazine dedicated to prayer
P.O. Box 35004
Colorado Springs, CO 80935
719-548-9222
FAX: 719-598-7128
E-mail: pray.mag@navpress.com

U.S. Prayer Directory
*A directory of U.S. prayer ministries and
ministers*
U.S. Prayer Track
7710-T Cherry Park Drive, Suite 224
Houston, TX 77095
713-466-4009
FAX: 713-466-5633
E-mail: 75711.2501@compuserve.com